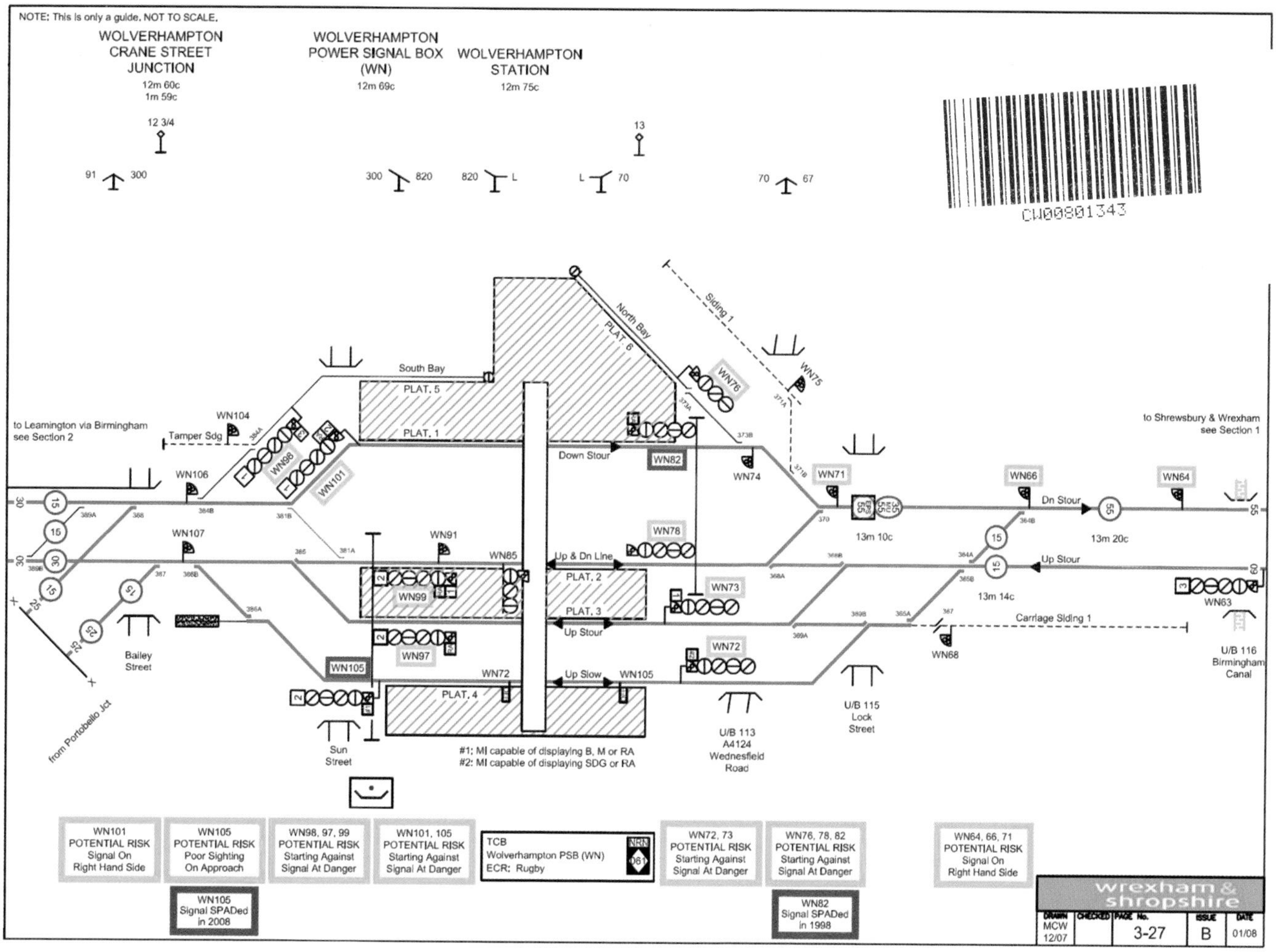

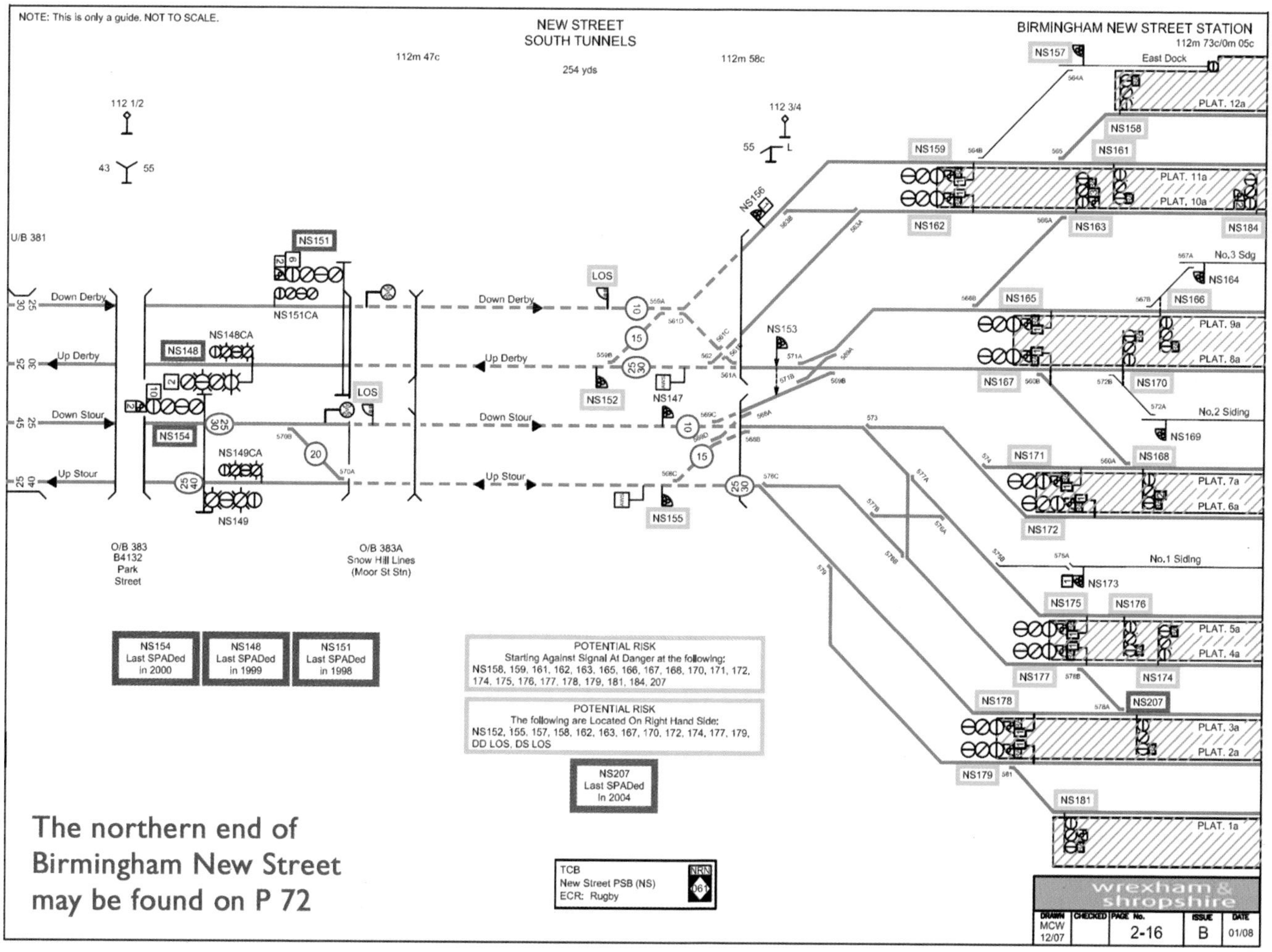

NOTE: This is only a guide. NOT TO SCALE.

WOLVERHAMPTON CRANE STREET JUNCTION
12m 60c
1m 59c

WOLVERHAMPTON POWER SIGNAL BOX (WN)
12m 69c

WOLVERHAMPTON STATION
12m 75c

CW00801343

to Leamington via Birmingham see Section 2

to Shrewsbury & Wrexham see Section 1

South Bay
PLAT. 5
PLAT. 1
North Bay PLAT. 6
Siding 1
Tamper Sdg
Down Stour
Up & Dn Line
PLAT. 2
PLAT. 3
Up Stour
Up Slow
PLAT. 4
Dn Stour
Up Stour
Carriage Siding 1
13m 10c
13m 14c
13m 20c

Bailey Street
from Portobello Jct
Sun Street
U/B 113 A4124 Wednesfield Road
U/B 115 Lock Street
U/B 116 Birmingham Canal

#1: MI capable of displaying B, M or RA
#2: MI capable of displaying SDG or RA

WN101 POTENTIAL RISK Signal On Right Hand Side	WN105 POTENTIAL RISK Poor Sighting On Approach	WN98, 97, 99 POTENTIAL RISK Starting Against Signal At Danger	WN101, 105 POTENTIAL RISK Starting Against Signal At Danger	WN72, 73 POTENTIAL RISK Starting Against Signal At Danger	WN76, 78, 82 POTENTIAL RISK Starting Against Signal At Danger	WN64, 66, 71 POTENTIAL RISK Signal On Right Hand Side

WN105 Signal SPADed in 2008

TCB
Wolverhampton PSB (WN)
ECR: Rugby

WN82 Signal SPADed in 1998

wrexham & shropshire

DRAWN	CHECKED	PAGE No.	ISSUE	DATE
MCW 12/07		3-27	B	01/08

NOTE: This is only a guide. NOT TO SCALE.

NEW STREET SOUTH TUNNELS
112m 47c
254 yds
112m 58c

BIRMINGHAM NEW STREET STATION
112m 73c/0m 05c

U/B 381
Down Derby
Up Derby
Down Stour
Up Stour
East Dock
PLAT. 12a
PLAT. 11a
PLAT. 10a
No.3 Sdg
PLAT. 9a
PLAT. 8a
No.2 Siding
PLAT. 7a
PLAT. 6a
No.1 Siding
PLAT. 5a
PLAT. 4a
PLAT. 3a
PLAT. 2a
PLAT. 1a

O/B 383 B4132 Park Street
O/B 383A Snow Hill Lines (Moor St Stn)

NS154 Last SPADed in 2000	NS148 Last SPADed in 1999	NS151 Last SPADed in 1998

POTENTIAL RISK
Starting Against Signal At Danger at the following:
NS158, 159, 161, 162, 163, 165, 166, 167, 168, 170, 171, 172, 174, 175, 176, 177, 178, 179, 181, 184, 207

POTENTIAL RISK
The following are Located On Right Hand Side:
NS152, 155, 157, 158, 162, 163, 167, 170, 172, 174, 177, 179, DD LOS, DS LOS

NS207 Last SPADed In 2004

The northern end of Birmingham New Street may be found on P 72

TCB
New Street PSB (NS)
ECR: Rugby

wrexham & shropshire

DRAWN	CHECKED	PAGE No.	ISSUE	DATE
MCW 12/07		2-16	B	01/08

wrexham & shropshire

Open Access - the one that got away

Geoff Plumb

The Inside Story of the

Wrexham, Shropshire & Marylebone Railway Company

2006-2011

Disclaimer:

This book is the sole work of the authors and contributors. It should not be taken as necessarily expressing the views of any of the companies involved in Wrexham & Shropshire throughout its existence. Specifically, the book does not seek to state the views of WSMR (Holdings) Ltd., The Wrexham, Shropshire & Marylebone Railway Co. Ltd., Renaissance Trains, The Chiltern Railway Co. Ltd., DB Regio UK Ltd. or Arriva UK Trains Ltd. and its subsidiaries.

ISBN - 978-0-9571456-1-0 (hardback)

Published by:

www.adlestroppress.co.uk

Design & Graphics, photographs, and maps by:

Gordon Rushton
unless otherwise attributed

Printed by:

Amadeus Press, Ezra House, Littlewood Drive, Cleckheaton
West Yorkshire, BD19 4TQ

Contents

wrexham & shropshire

Open Access - the one that got away

Richard Harper

&

Gordon Rushton

The Inside Story of the

Wrexham, Shropshire & Marylebone Railway Company

2006-2011

The Wrexham and Shropshire train in all its glory hums towards Haddenham and Thame Parkway with the 11.27 train from Wrexham to London Marylebone on Tuesday 22nd December 2009. The locomotive is 67013 Dyfrbont Pontcysllte. **Photo: Geoff Plumb**

If Wrexham and Shropshire is remembered for anything it will be the superb service. Steward Pat Burke from Wrexham does his stuff for the camera on a photoshoot in early ex-Virgin Mk3 spelndour. **Photo: Graham Whistler**

Introduction

Beeching presided over a radical pruning of the UK railway system fifty years ago. The atmosphere of decline and despair for railway people of those times is largely forgotten; railways were out of fashion, to be gelded and relegated to a minor role. The events of those times spawned attitudes within government that shaped the landscape for the policy of Railway Privatisation. In case it may be thought that the idea of Privatisation, and more narrowly Open Access, was arrived at by a calm and logical set of careful interlocking strategies, the first two chapters lay out, for those who didn't live through it, some of the effects of the earlier jumbled policies for the railways that followed the disastrous failure of the 1955 Modernisation Plan. For those that did live through it, this account has been informed by Richard Faulkner and Chris Austins' excellent book 'Holding the Line'.

The Wrexham and Shropshire story plays out with a seemingly prescribed legislative backdrop, but there are disturbances underneath. The 'return of the railways', manhood restored, was not assured. It still suffered from a lack of coherent, long-term transport strategy. The unexpected, sustained levels of growth in rail transport demand altered everything. History repeats itself, but not quite; the errant twists are fascinating. Here is the story within them of a railway company that tried and failed - or did it? You decide.

Wrexham & Shropshire will be remembered for the fact that each three-carriage train had at least three people to tend the paying customers, which meant that the standard of on-board service was really good. One of the features of travelling with Wrexham & Shropshire was the long journey time. It took four hours and six minutes to reach Wrexham from London. One can expect to get from London to Shrewsbury by car in just under three hours on a clear road. This meant that the people who would use Wrexham & Shropshire were those with time on their hands, or to whom a direct service was a major advantage, and that was a restricted market.

There were originally five WSMR services each day. For those wanting a day in London or the provinces, the two return services in each direction were either too early or too late. Yet there were unrealised hopes of improving matters quickly, once the service started. At the time of its inception the demand for transport to the places it proposed to serve was considered to be high, and so was the price for getting there. The prospects of a cheaper but marginally slower alternative, with truly improved service, looked good, better perhaps than sister service Hull Trains.

The 'privatised' railway regime preserved only a fig leaf of the competition originally promised in the spirit of the 1993 Railways Act. Open Access should have encouraged entrepreneurs to 'pitch in' to promote services to disadvantaged towns and cities. This sounded plausible in Tory-speak, but to a Department for Transport ,beset with the inter-dependent concerns of trying to meld a series of franchises according to the ill-expressed and often impractical desires of their political masters, it was an unlooked for and potentially dangerous complication.

Mr Branson's skilful and daring initiatives with the Virgin West Coast franchise led to a fleet of sleek, hi-tech, rapid, new-age trains, that depended on extreme utilisation to get the best from it. The West Coast railway had been rebuilt at colossal expense. The investment cost to the franchisee led to hard bargaining, and the insertion of a protective agreement, moderating competition during the length of the franchise (until 2012). Without investment and electrification, it is easy to see why places like Shrewsbury and Wrexham did not, and could not, enjoy regular, fast, direct services to London as in days gone by.

Despite the growth of the popularity of rail travel, despite the boon that the Wrexham area and Shropshire may gain from through service, calls in Wolverhampton and Birmingham were prohibited, as being primarily abstractive, except for passengers to and from the north. Thus the new service was forced to call unsuccessfully at Tame Bridge Parkway. With long journey times remaining, and traffic restricted, the WSMR future became bleak: service patterns elsewhere doubled; fares tumbled; the recession bit, and the case for Wrexham & Shropshire assets to be used profitably elsewhere became compelling.

However, the key factors weren't just the events themselves, but the order in which they happened. As a general comment the Establishment cannot escape the whiff of sulphur over their flaccid 'approval' of Open Access. It seems that the delicate mechanisms of the DfT 'plan' thwarted any strategy for proper rail competition. Subsequent franchising events in 2012 seemed to point to the lack of a bravura performance in managing risk.

This story does not have a happy ending, despite expertise, passion, effort, much expenditure, and no risk to the taxpayer. Read on for a sombre warning that the good guy does not always win.

This is very much what the trains from Birkenhead (Woodside) to London Paddington would have looked like, south from Wolverhampton (Low Level), hauled by a King Class locomotive. On 28th May 2005 locomotive 6024 King Edward 1 *passes Dawlish Warren with the Torbay Express.*

Chapter 1 A Little History

One could be forgiven for thinking that the rail network in Britain was carefully planned and executed - it was not. A chink of opportunity was all it took for rail connection to be won or lost. Britain's second city, Birmingham, was in the centre of a gigantic battle between two of Britain's most active and entrepreneurial railway companies, the Great Western Railway and the London and North Western Railway. The L&NWR was first on the Birmingham city scene, with a fine service from Liverpool (Grand Junction Railway - 1837) and London (London and Birmingham Railway - 1838). They consolidated and expanded, being joined by the Birmingham and Gloucester (1841) and the Birmingham & Derby Junction (1842) to build Birmingham New Street by 1854. The city was expanding at a massive rate and the railways were at the heart of the matter. The Great Western Railway arrived in 1852 to build Birmingham Snow Hill by 1858, and this was joined from Worcester and Stourbridge in 1867, when by that time the railway tentacles had spread right across the city. The big players were the L&NWR and Midland at New Street, and the Great Western at Snow Hill. Both stations became large transport hubs, but New Street, with its Midland connections and the northern arm of the L&NWR had a wider range of connections, and tapped more large cities as destinations than Snow Hill ever did. There the matter rested for a century. The LMS group of services from Euston were running via Rugby and Coventry to Birmingham New Street with eight or nine through services each weekday, not at regular intervals, with the

By 1966 through service from Birkenhead to Paddington's days were numbered; upon start of the electric service from Liverpool Lime Street service would cease. In late 1966 there was a brief flowering of interest, when one of the last two Hughes-Fowler 'Crab' 2-6-0 locomotives No. 42942 was bulled up and unmercifully thrashed to Chester, on the six-cars that would go on via Shrewsbury and Wolverhampton to London. The locomotive is seen here on a darkling October afternoon at Port Sunlight on the 1445 from Birkenhead (Woodside) to London (Paddington) a journey of 5½ hours.

Earl of Mount Edgecumbe *stands at Birmingham (Moor Street) Station with eight cars on 29th October 2011, at the front of the Inter-City Express, though this time to London (Marylebone). The scene recreates the era of fast steam trains, and this train was non-stop to London.*

fastest, *The Midlander*, taking 2hrs 40 minutes for the journey: but for the most part it was three hours or so. The BR(LM) trains called at Wolverhampton High Level. The LM services at Shrewsbury were those from Crewe, with through services from Manchester and Liverpool towards Hereford. Any service from Crewe to Birmingham went via Stafford and Wolverhampton High Level.

The GWR group of services ran through from Chester and Wrexham to use the line via Wolverhampton Low Level to Birmingham Snow Hill. The quality of service from Paddington to Wolverhampton was a cut above the

BR 5000hp Class 87 electric locomotive 87004 Britannia, waits to leave Birmingham New Street for Wolverhampton with a train from London Euston on a freezing cold morning in 1978. These locomotives had been introduced for the extension of electrification from Weaver Junction to Glasgow in 1974. The name of the game was now fast, interval services on main routes, and the old GWR main line to Chester was now a 'minor line', not deserving of an interval service of through trains from Chester to London via Wrexham and Wolverhampton.

GWR route - Fortunes fall and rise

1966	Connection reinstated between Smethwick West and Galton Junction on the Stour Valley Line to allow services to transfer to Birmingham New Street	1980s	Snow Hill site is redeveloped, but room is left underneath for a station
03.03.67	The last day of full main line operation from Birmingham Snow Hill, services were about to be reduced from 181 to 74 departures.	1985	Snow Hill is re-opened and Moor Street is closed, with tracks being laid back through the Snow Hill tunnel under a scheme promoted by the West Midlands PTE.
06.03.67	The new electric service to Euston opens from Birmingham New Street. Birmingham Snow Hill loses its through main line services.	17.05.93	Re-establishment of through services from Birmingham Snow Hill to London by Chiltern Trains (though to Marylebone, not to Paddington).
March 1968	Closure of Snow Hill Tunnel, thus rationalising many commuter services. Except for the Wolverhampton Low Level shuttle, trains either departed from Moor Street or New Street. Now only 10 services used Snow Hill.	25.09.95	Restoration of through services from Birmingham Snow Hill to Stourbridge Junction.
May 1972	Withdrawal of the shuttle trains led to the closure of Snow Hill and all stations to (and including) Wolverhampton Low Level.	31.05.99	Midland Metro takes over the former GWR line to Wolverhampton with trams ascending into the streets at Wolverhampton, rather than following the rail route to the Low Level Station. Any prospects of through service reinstatement from Snow Hill to the north are now removed.
1976-77	The Snow Hill station structure was demolished. Everything now went to New Street.		

LMS. Some ten trains a day ran, not always hourly but at standard times. The *Inter-City* made it from Paddington to Wolverhampton Low Level in 2hrs 22minutes, a far superior service than anything from Euston. Plus many of the GWR and later BR(W) trains ran on, via Shrewsbury and Wrexham to Chester and Birkenhead. When proceeding from Birkenhead Woodside to London, the six-carriage train grew, and became grander and grander. The rather common (though sprightly) tank engine was changed for a larger locomotive at Chester. That backed on with extra carriages and drew the train on via Wrexham. At Shrewsbury or Wolverhampton the most splendid locomotive, a GWR Castle or a King would place a restaurant car on the train and head for London. This was the sort of elegant and distinguished service that people remembered for generations. In the post-Nationalisation decline of the railways, the rationalisation of the system included the proviso that investment would be made in the remainder. The Beeching years were aimed at removing duplication, and creating a fast and efficient, modern core railway that would pay its way. Fate dictated in almost whimsical ways what would and would not remain. The investment in electrification went to the more populous former LMS group. Thus in the rationalisation, the electrified and thus passenger-hungry, electric line to Euston displaced the former Great Western routes, and the removal of 'spare' capacity led to the closure of Birmingham Snow Hill, and the line

Trains like these served the route from Wolverhampton to Shrewsbury and Wrexham in the 1980s. They could be rattly, smelly, noisy and rather unpleasant to travel in. In this period rail had to 'make do' until new investment came with Sprinter trains in 1984. Wem station in 1973. **Mike Mensing**

Wrexham, Shrewsbury, Birmingham and Banbury to London (Weekdays) Comparisons

Operator	**W&S**	BR(W)	BR	**W&S**	BR(W)	BR(W)	BR(W)	**W&S**	BR(W)	BR(W)	**W&S**	BR(W)
Timetable	***2008***	*1961 S*	*1975 S*	***2008***	*1961 S*	*1961 S*	*1961 S*	***2008***	*1961 S*	*1961 S*	***2008***	*1961 S*
Wrexham	**05.12**			**07.25**	07.32	08.40	09.52	**11.23**		12.44	**15.23**	15.35
Shrewsbury	**05.52**	07.30	0740	**08.07**	08.34	09.35	10.42	**12.07**	12.50	13.40	**16.07**	16.34
Wolverhampton		08.33	08a21		09.35	10.30	11.36	**12s47**	13.24	14.35	**16s47**	17.33
Birmingham (Snow Hill)		09.00	08.48 NS		10.00	11.00	12.00		14.00	15.00		18.00
Tame Bridge Parkway	**06.44**			**09.02**				**13.02**			**17.02**	
Leamington Spa		09.28			10.28	11.28	12.28		14.26	15.28		18.31
Banbury	**07s46**			**10s06**	10.55	11.55	12.54	**14s06**		15.56	**18s03**	19.00
London (Paddington)		11.10			12.15	13.15	14.20		16.00	17.15		20.35
London (Marylebone)	**08.57**			**11.23**				**15.22**			**19.22**	
London (Euston)			10.19									
					B	B	B		C	B		B
Journey time from Shrewsbury to London h/m	**3.05**	3.40	2.39	**3.18**	3.41	3.40	3.38	**3.15**	3.10	3.35	**3.15**	4.01

Notes:

1961 S	1961 BR(W) 1975 summer timetable	**s**	stops to set down only
a	arrive	B	from Birkenhead (Woodside)
NS	Birmingham New Street	C	Cambrian Coast Express

Shrewsbury, Birmingham and Banbury to London (Weekdays) - time comparison

	W&S	BR	BR(W)	Virgin
Timetable	***2008***	*1975 S*	*1961 S*	*2011*
Shrewsbury	**05.52**	0740	12.50	07.47
Wolverhampton		08a21	13.24	08c45
Birmingham (Snow Hill)		08.48 NS	14.00	09.10 NS
Tame Bridge Parkway	**06.44**			
Banbury	**07s46**			
London (Paddington)			16.00	
London (Marylebone)	**08.57**			
London (Euston)		10.19		10.34
			C	
Journey time from Shrewsbury to London h/m	**3.05**	2.39	3.10	2.47

Notes: as above, plus
c change from Arriva to Virgin

Above: *Not all the day's trains are shown from 1961, but enough to show how the railways then tried to be 'all things to all men'. Running the train from Birkenhead (Woodside), with attachments at Chester and Wolverhampton hardly offered much in the way of rapidity, but it was a wonderful through service with a wide range of calls. To get an early arrival in London in 2008 W&S had to leave extremely early. The 1961 spread of timings was as much about serving the 'other' places as Shrewsbury, but it was a good service. Although the 1975 electric service from Wolverhampton was an improvement, the evident logic was to make people from 'beyond' change trains. This hated requirement was entrenched after Virgin took over. The Shrewsbury market was significant to planning of WSMR and the town had a long memory of its fall from grace by those who destroyed the GWR, and then removed through trains to London. The question was how quickly could Wrexham & Shropshire trains get to Marylebone; fast enough to attract enough traffic to live off? Wrexham was a hope for traffic, but driving to Chester was always a customer option.*

Left: *The fastest that Wrexham & Shropshire could do with its circuitous route was 3h05m Shrewsbury-London, and that was 'at the crack of dawn'. Most transits were 3h15m. The change of trains via Arriva and Virgin can reduce the transit time to 2h47m, and the 1975 early through service with its loco change at Wolverhampton did well with a transit time of 2h59m. Of course today the West Coast train from Stafford takes 1h20m to get to London, so this is a better option for those living on the east side of the town. In 2013 the fastest rail journey to London was to change at Wolverhampton AND Stafford, where a 2h25m transit is regularly possible. On Birmingham to London, the Wrexham & Shropshire offer was from Tame Bridge Parkway. The question was wether a five train service from this location would attract traffic from the West Midlands. Telford was important too, but with no historical comparison.*

Left: *These services seen passing each other near Worcester Shrub Hill, are formed of Centro Class 150 unit Sprinter trains of 1984, built by BREL York, incorporating Mk3 bodyshells. These two-engined, 572hp, 75mph trains have air-bag suspension that gives an incomparably superior, quiet ride to previous trains. They replaced the rattly DMUs shown on Page 12, and served the non-electric lines left around Birmingham, as frequent visitors to the reopened Snow Hill Station. The picture was taken on 5th March 2004. There was of course no longer any ex-GWR line - see below.*

Right: *The Metro proves that the planner's grip on traffic prediction is as tenuous in the upwards direction as it is in the downward direction. It now carries about 5m people per year, and follows the route of the old GWR line, climbing out into Bilston Road, and (in 2013) terminating just outside of Wolverhampton town centre, without yet doing a loop round the town. It stops at Snow Hill too, and will soon penetrate the city streets to make a connection with New Street Station. Only a portion of the 'tram plan' was ever implemented and if it is not to be built, then arguably reinstatement of the old GWR route to 'heavy rail' could be for the greater good. Tram 14 is at Wolverhampton St Georges, 29th March 2012.*

through to Wolverhampton Low Level, that carried the through services to Shrewsbury, Wrexham and Chester. The low point of this contraction was 1968, when Snow Hill Tunnel closed, cutting the route back to Moor Street, and severing all connection with the south. Snow Hill Station site closed in 1972, and was cleared in the 1980s.

There was an electrification 'frontier' for services at Wolverhampton High Level. Wolverhampton Low Level Station was closed. Such through services as there were to Shrewsbury were run from Euston, but expensive engine changes from electric to diesel were required to run north of Wolverhampton on the old GWR route. This was a practice that came under severe pressure as the years went by, from the need to reduce costs and increase the utilisation of rolling stock. By May 1975 there was only one weekday (two Sunday) through service from Shrewsbury to Euston: the 07.40, arriving in Euston at 10.19; a 2 hours

***Left:** When Virgin Trains won the franchises for West Coast and Cross Country trains, their inheritance from Inter-City for West Coast services was a mixed bag of Mk2 and Mk3 carriages, headed by DVT trailers and a fleet of Class 86, 87 and 90 electric locomotives. Trains offered speeds of up to 110mph. The charismatic Richard Branson and his team won the franchise with a promise, later fulfilled, to introduce technically advanced, high-speed tilting trains in exchange for route modernisation and protection from competition. Virgin got this; WSMR got DVTs. The picture is at Birmingham International in 2003.*

***Right:** In 2002 Virgin Trains began to introduce tilting Pendlino Class 390 trains on their electrified services. The nine-car units were capable of running at 140mph, but the West Coast Route Modernisation scheme did not deliver in-cab signalling, limiting speeds to 125mph. Services from London to Liverpool, Wolverhampton, Birmingham, Preston, Glasgow, and Manchester were transformed. Steady reductions of journey time culminated in a radical increase in service frequency on Birmingham and Manchester routes in 2009 . In 2012 units were increased in capacity by the addition of two extra carriages. The picture shows Rugby in 2005.*

39 minute journey, with a restaurant car included.

There were trains through Shrewsbury to other destinations, like Aberystwyth, Wrexham and Chester, but the objective was that Wolverhampton would be the changing point. A bay platform was built for the purpose; it was out in the rain in the northern corner of Wolverhampton High level station. Salopians were not pleased! The service had become miserable and slow. Wrexham people just drove to Chester or Crewe. Salopians either drove to Stafford or to Wolverhampton on the new M54. The route patronage declined markedly, with old diesel multiple units, and the line from Wrexham to Chester was made single track.

The 1960s policy of relying on roads for transport crashed and burned. It wasn't possible to keep up with demand, either politically or financially, by building new

***Right:** Freight is cyclical, and this is expressed in the number of trains run. The disparity between 120kph and 300kph meant that as the high speed services were introduced, it became more difficult to path freight trains, especially when flights of several high speed passenger services had to be accommodated. This had a singular effect on the story to follow in this book; as traffic demand rose, paths could be difficult to find for any new service. Here a container train hauled by GBRf Class 66 714, coasts to a stop at Rugby Station, facing south, on 11th August 2005. As round Birmingham, there is a diversionary route, via Northampton.*

***Left:** The Cross-City Line from Lichfield to Redditch was given a massive boost in 1993 by electrification, and the introduction of 323 EMUs built by Hunslet TPL. This train is seen standing at the northeastward end of the service, Lichfield Trent Valley. At Aston the route crosses the main diversionary route round Birmingham, the Grand Junction lines, on its way into Birmingham New Street station, also joining there with the Walsall line services. All these lines figure later in the story of trying to find suitable paths and routing for the Wrexham & Shropshire service.*
The picture was taken on 21st June.2001 of a lunchtime train awaiting departure to Longbridge and Redditch at 13.50.

motorways, and reshaping city centres to give priority to cars - traffic congestion throttled access. The roads continued to become more and more congested. The fabulous inter-connecting M6, M5, and M40, once proud arterial routes with the A38M, Aston Expressway offering access direct to the heart of Birmingham resembled car parks over embarrassingly long sections of the day. Much later an avoiding route, the Midlands Expressway, the M6 Toll demonstrated the point that tollways crush demand, thus the congestion was hardly relieved until the peak of the peak made it intolerable. No government wished to suppress road demand and promote other modes of transport like rail by a general introduction of motorway tolls. However, fuel prices started to rise steeply and by 2008 they were high. Warnings of the effect of fuel prices on demand appeared during the oil crisis of 1973, to tweak the minds of the planners against a totally road-based national programme for transport. Electrification

Railways Round Birmingham

of the West Coast Main Line muted the rapidly growing 'local' air shuttle services, and they diminished. The train began to look like a better option, and forward looking local authorities began investing in rail. New trains came on the scene in the 1980s, and the West Midlands PTE reopened Birmingham Snow Hill, for local services to the south in 1987, though the Inter-City route was still intended to be from New Street to London Euston. The new Sprinter, Class 150, Class 158, and other trains, plus reorganisation of British Rail into business sectors, started to make helpful changes that set passenger figures on the rise. Through services from Snow Hill to London (now Marylebone) started again in 1993. Trains at the tunnel-connected Moor Street Station ceased to use the terminal platforms there, and terminated in Snow Hill instead. In 1995, services resumed from Snow Hill to Smethwick and Worcester, operated by the Central Divison of Regional Railways (later Central Trains). The increase in patronage led to the establishment of the Midland Metro tram route in 1999, where once the GWR ran. The tram was not introduced without controversy, and of course it meant that the restoration of former through rail services was no

Left: *The new town of Telford was built on industrial and agricultural land in the 1960s and 1970s to reach a population of 162k in 2009. The town is on the M54 motorway, connecting it with Shrewsbury, Wolverhampton and Birmingham. Driving time from the centre of Telford into Wolverhampton is 25 minutes. A new station opened in 1986, yet in 2014 (post WSMR) Shropshire remains the only county in England with no through rail services to London. The services it has run south to Wolverhampton and Birmingham and north to Shrewsbury and into North Wales.*

Right: *The town of Shrewsbury, with over 600 historic buildings, is chock full of history. Although the county town of Shropshire, with excellent road connections, it cannot muster a through service by rail to the capital. This is a matter of resentment. In days gone by, 8 trains a day and a sleeper went to London (Paddington). To be ignored thereafter is an affront. When Wrexham & Shropshire came along there was an undisguised welcome, though as the story will outline, the lure of high-speed services from Stafford also had significance.*

longer possible later, to cater for the increasing traffic. The fate of the old GWR through route via Birmingham and Wolverhampton to Shrewsbury, Wrexham and Chester was sealed. The planned greater expansion of the Metro tramway that justified this policy hasn't happened yet.

South of Birmingham New Street, traffic on the Euston to Birmingham and Wolverhampton line, electrified in 1967, grew rapidly. The line from Coventry to Leamington Spa had closed to passengers in 1965, but it was reopened as a passenger line again in 1977 as the traffic grew to connect the new Birmingham International Station, built in 1976 to serve Birmingham Airport and National Exhibition Centre. The West Midlands Passenger Transport Executive (WMPTE, later Centro) local passenger train initiatives added extra trains, and growth continued as the cross-country services via New Street ran via International and Coventry. After the West Coast Main Line rebuilding, with a fleet of new trains, the Virgin franchise offered a radical increase in service frequency. Birmingham International Station doubled its traffic between 2004 and 2010 to reach over 4m passengers.

Procurement of the comfortable 168 Clubman diesel units by Chiltern Railways managed to transform their operation from a purely commuter service into a long distance, time-competitive business. West Coast Route Modernisation gave them a boost; their own expertise and enterprise did the rest.

Chiltern Railways

The old GWR Wolverhampton to Chester line lacks investment. Of course it doesn't serve London, though there are services from Chester to South Wales operated by Arriva Trains Wales. This service, on 10th May 2008, is being operated by Class 150/2 Sprinter multiple units that have by now penetrated back to Birmingham (New Street) as a destination; the Wolverhampton change has gone. At Gobowen the Oswestry branch is not used, so enterprise has its limits, plus the signalling is still the old semaphore style. Unlike the electrified lines south of here, little has changed.

A nine-car northbound Pendolino tilts into the curve at Milepost 65 on the West Coast Main Line on Tuesday 28th September 2006. *It was unclear then just how excellent the frequency and speed of the service from Stafford to London would become and how the market would respond.*

London Midland began from small beginnings to serve the Trent Valley, eventually offering a magnificent service from Crewe, hourly, culminating in 110mph runs excluding Northampton, direct to London. No Moderation of Competition rules applied to this excellent initiative (at the taxpayers' expense). Who's going to bother to go to Tame Bridge when they can go via Birmingham, or direct to London from Lichfield or Tamworth?

The Birmingham Cross-City line between Redditch and Lichfield City was electrified, and local and semi-fast services were introduced that boosted service frequency. The North East, South West Line service frequency began to rise, with trains entering New Street and using the Birmingham West Suburban Line to rejoin the route. The Grand Junction lines avoiding Birmingham centre were ever busy with freight traffic diverted from the main lines.

After privatisation, with fuel prices leading inflation, there was an accelerated surge in rail passenger traffic as the market discovered the reliable and frequent Centro local train services. This became marked, and sustained. In fact the tenets of privatisation set out by the Major government, post-Thatcher were eroded. Railways were not to be left entirely to the 'market', and the government became more and more enmeshed as traffic rose, adjusting franchises, specifying new service provision and quality, setting fares, and even defining train types and lease/purchases. Much tactical control was exerted by the government and its agencies, partly in answer to the inexorable growth in demand. Investment was put into quadrupling major sections of the Trent Valley Line to increase capacity, and to allow freight to avoid the Birmingham area. It was a remarkable reversal of fortune from the days of Ernest Marples and Dr Beeching. Massive increase of patronage was driving the privatised railway carryings upward. Including the post privatisation period, between 1992 and 2005, the annual passenger kilometres in UK rose from 32.5bn to 42.4bn. Passenger journeys were boosted from 737m to 1083m during the same period. This growth didn't stop. By 2010 the kilometres had reached 51bn and the journeys 1258m.

Although Birmingham Snow Hill Station had increased from 2m passengers in 2006 to 3.5m in 2010, the tram plateaued at 5m journeys, overall. Putting the railway back may well have been a better option - now this was no longer a choice. However, the Chiltern Railways franchise, built on the reinstatement of trains between London Marylebone and Birmingham, with new rolling stock in 1998, grew traffic rapidly. Route upgrades that reduced the journey time, complemented the process, encouraging further traffic growth. Chiltern was serving a useful chunk of the old Great Western route: offering Snow Hill, Moor St, Solihull, Warwick, Leamington, and Banbury, through trains to London. It is relevant to the story later to note how Chiltern made successful efforts to improve its services and grow the market. It was assisted by the West Coast Route Modernisation engineering works, but also

In 2004 the old order at London Euston was changing rapidly, as more Pendolino sets were delivered. Later, service frequency would be enhanced to unheard of levels, but there still seemed to be a viable niche for traffic from the Shropshire towns. It was a major area not catered for by the 'big boys'.

managed to grow its own market and to keep hold of it.

Northwest of Birmingham and Wolverhampton, the line to Shrewsbury, Wrexham and Chester had no investment, and still did not have direct services to London. Arriva Trains Wales were one of the franchisees serving the line, but their remit concerned services to and from the Province. Central Trains (later London Midland) concentrated on local and regional services. Virgin had electric trains to the 'wire end' at Wolverhampton, where diesel trains began. Thus the limit of the London train remained at Wolverhampton. However, regular services from Chester via Wrexham and Shrewsbury, and from Aberystwyth to Wolverhampton did run through to Birmingham New Street, making the Stour Valley line one of the busiest UK two-track main lines. Eventually Arriva services were extended to Birmingham International. This did not seem portentous at the time, and the number of through trains was not great, but those that did run through made a much more comfortable connection into the Virgin London service, and of course, later, not every Virgin train went though to Wolverhampton - partly because of the traffic density on the Stour Valley Line.

So in 2006, though there seemed to be no interest from the major players in through services to Shropshire and to Wrexham from London, there was considered to be traffic on offer. In the 1970s, a new town, Telford, had been built on the M54, 17 miles northwest of Wolverhampton. The most rapidly growing town in Shropshire, it was high league table of UK towns: the Telford population reached 162k in 2009 - well over twice that of Shrewsbury!

So to the north of Wolverhampton now lay Telford and the populations at Shrewsbury (pop. 60k), 30 miles away and Wrexham (pop. 63k), 60 miles away. Such large centres of population with no through London service offered an opportunity, as it appeared that none of the franchise holders currently serving these towns was likely to offer this facility. Yet Wolverhampton, with 250k population, did have the London rail connection. Thus was the germ of the idea of the Wrexham & Shropshire service conceived: a through service to London from Wrexham and the Shropshire towns, and a useful service from Wolverhampton to destinations not served, like Leamington and Banbury. Indeed it may be able to link those towns with stops at Birmingham International and Coventry. The prospects for traffic - even if the journey time was rather slower than a direct Euston service - were thought to be good.

The first down run of the first through working from Wrexham to Marylebone on Monday 14th April 2008. 67013 is at the head of the train while 67015 is on the rear, here north of the site of the old junction at Ashendon. **Geoff Plumb**

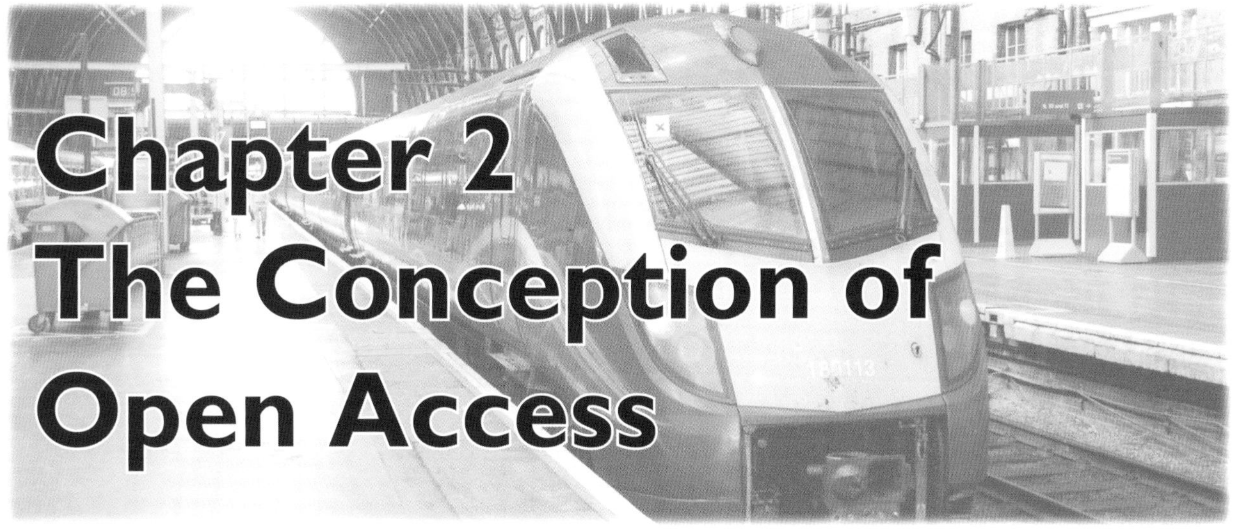

Chapter 2 The Conception of Open Access

Rail Privatisation - a short history

How did we get here - lest we forget?

The most important influence upon the railways in the 1950s was the failure of the politically based 1955 Modernisation Plan, which was meant to offer radical improvements in the nationalised British Railways's performance, and to eliminate the deficit by 1962, at a cost of £1.2bn (£26bn today)[1]. No such results were delivered; industrial problems, and the rapid rise of road competition, drove increasing losses to over £3bn[2] in today's values!

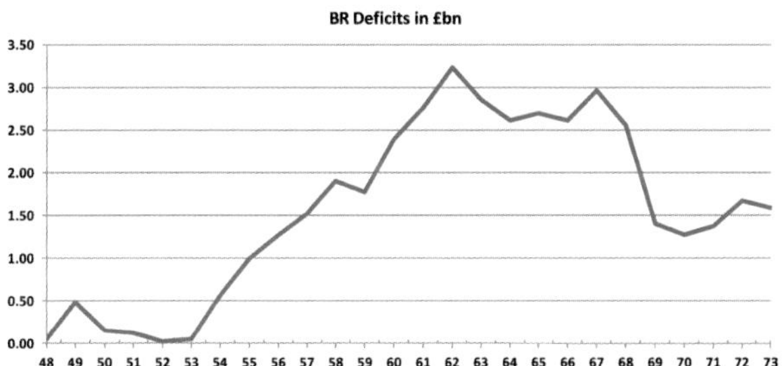

Some 50 years after, there is much 'tut-tutting' about Beeching and his actions. Here are the reasons in 2013 monetary values why there was a 1963 Reshaping Report. In 10 years the railway deficit went from almost zero to £3.23bn - doesn't that mean action was justified?

The dissatisfaction with a failure to stem the losses despite investment spawned the Stedeford Committee, the report of which was never made public - presumably the news was so bad. The outcomes were draconian measures.

The 1962 Transport Act followed the report, and Dr Richard Beeching was appointed as the Chairman of the British Railways Board with two vulnerable tenets. The first was that railways were old fashioned and inappropriate as the principal means of transportation in Britain. Investing large sums in them had not brought back the expected returns. The second was that reducing the railways to a profitable core was a sensible policy. Beeching's report *The Reshaping of British Railways* justified and set out this strategy, and an additional document, *The Development of the Major Trunk Routes* was produced in 1965 to outline where investment could be made to support those railway activities worthy of development. Both sets of recommendations were carried out. Fifty years on, it is still clear that there were major flaws in these policies.

It was pointed out as justification for closure that one third of the network was contributing 1% of the total traffic, and that this was unsustainable. The logic ran that therefore the one third should be closed, and this was carried out without mercy in the 1960s. It was considered rational that motorways be built to facilitate the passage of freight and car traffic by road, and as part of a co-ordinated plan, encourage a home car industry (and win votes). The lesson to be learned from those times is to note how the potential for co-ordinated transport was overlooked. When rail closed, the replacement provision was to be bus (which normally did not last long), and, until the 1968 Transport Act, there was no provision made for social need.

The real economic damage that was done to some communities from the precipitate removal of their train

1 Note that the 2012 railway improvement package, extended the original £5bn Bristol etc. electrification investment by £9.4bn. This shows just how vast the 1955 Modernisation Plan spending actually was. Today's plan envisages funding some of the work by fares increases, and a steady +5% traffic growth may offer some hope for this intention. In 1953-1962 the BR deficit rocketed - not at all what was intended! Perhaps then the investment was on declining figures and intended to stem them, whereas today investment is on a rising market and is intended to sustain this.

2 These figures - sourced from Gourvish - BR 1948-73 - are adjusted to 2013 prices, and include the passenger grant from 1969.

Liverpool (Exchange) Station in 1964, with a stopping train to Wigan (Wallgate) in the platform. The 1947 built, Fairburn, 2-6-4 tank locomotive belongs to Lostock Hall locomotive shed, near Preston. The three carriages are of the non-corridor (no loo!), suburban variety, and this short formation can accommodate 240 people, probably enough for the demand that day if the customers strolling along the platform are representative. These services were neither pleasant nor profitable. Needless to say, the line, the train and the station were all swept away.

services, and replacement by an often short-lived bus service, was largely ignored within government. People protested, but in many cases they were brushed aside, as the protests remained local and unco-ordinated. When matters became 'political' there was less 'brushing', but in those days, protests were less well organised. Worse still, the savings claimed by the Beeching cuts were not audited and checked upon - as many were never achieved, and in some cases the financial case for closure was narrow, short-term, and uncertain. Thus a wider examination could well have retained rail service, by finding innovative solutions - as Gerard Fiennes and others were later able to - by championing Pay Trains and the 'basic railway'. The government's tactical determination was not to answer transport needs, it was to close the uneconomic parts of the railway system. The strategic determination seems to have been strangely absent.

The graph on the previous page shows that the British Rail deficit was halved in ten years after the cull began. Yet, in accepting wholesale line closures, the massive infrastructure investment that belonged to the 'people' in each case was largely wasted. Lines were removed with indecent haste, and the land was often sold piecemeal to adjoining landowners, which seemed to prevent any possibility of reopening. It was foolish not to consider current alternatives and future possibilities. There was little consideration given to mitigating transport problems by alternative means, like offering lines to local authorities (as in the 1968 Transport Act) or to private enterprise. Closure was what had been embarked upon - closure was what was going to happen. Closure was evidently the only answer to be considered; except of course when politics entered the fray.

Closures of the railway caused a great deal of public reaction, even if protests were largely ineffective. Yet it would hardly not cause reaction as things were being taken away from people. Yet with losses like the ones on the graph overleaf, the Conservative, Macmillan administration was quite clear that it had a duty to act. Transport Minister Ernest Marples was up for the fight (and it happened that

Barmouth Bridge, the longest wooden bridge in Britain, carrying the Cambrian Coast Line across the Mawddach Estuary. This is the Line of the Seven Marginals, still with us today, nearly fifty years after post-Beeching attempts at closure. Yet privatisation has so far brought us marginal advantages, when there are unexploited summer visitors that could use the railway for leisure transport and appreciate its remarkable scenic beauty. Open Access doesn't reach here, and although volume is climbing, there is little intermodal thinking, yet much defensive action aimed at 'reducing the loss'. Interesting that the 'profitable' Ffestiniog/Welsh Highland carries many more passengers than the Cambrian Coast Line.

Marples Ridgeway - no connection of course - gained a number of motorway construction contracts).[3] The effects of railway closures were far from short-lived; the row entered the public consciousness, and this has hampered further erosion of the rail network ever since.

It is interesting to note that 'railway experts' were much listened to for proposals for the 1955 Modernisation Plan. The general assumption seems to have been that restoring the train set to pre-War glory would make it run much better. Wider thinking was absent, as much of the investment did not anticipate the rising trends of change, like the flight from wagonload freight traffic to road. After the 1955 Modernisation Plan failed to yield other than increases in the BR deficit, railwaymen do not seems to have been listened to ever again - at least they got the blame for its failure. They were not heeded for the Beeching closures; they were not much heeded for Privatisation. And this is the point of offering this history, as the coming Open Access story here develops.

Some closures proposed in *The Reshaping of British Railways* never took place, and some lines not highlighted did. The Central Wales Line (Heart of Wales Line) did not, on the pretext of being necessary for freight. Yet it ran through six marginal constituencies. The Cambrian Coast Line was not chosen by Beeching to close. The Cambrian Lines ran through seven marginal seats. There were some zealous railway servants, and ardent adherents of Beeching's closure culture, who sought disposal of this railway in 1968. Reg Dawson rather blighted the 'closurists' with a leak of the intention via the Railway Gazette to the Times. Matters became most unpleasant, but a strong public reaction saw an end to the closure ambitions.

Steam finished in 1968, electrification of the West Coast Line was completed between Euston, Birmingham, Manchester and Liverpool, but although this was successful,

3 Ernest Marples, MP for Wallasey, resigned as Managing Director of Marples Ridgway in 1951, but held 80% of the shares, that he sold to his wife (later Lady Marples) to avoid a conflict of interest. He championed motorways as the Minister of Transport whilst closing the railways, and owned a company that got contracts to build them. No wonder the accusations flowed, and who says such scandals are a 21st century phenomenon?

This Class 114 diesel multiple unit was built in Derby in 1956. Seen here at Sheffield (Midland) in 1979, after 23 years it has now been refurbished by South Yorkshire PTE. It is waiting to set off on a fifty-mile trip from Sheffield to Lincoln. Class 114s were fitted with two 150hp engines which hardly gave it better performance than the steam trains it replaced, though it was arguably more comfortable, being fitted with a toilet. Yet such an old, slow train that had to be refurbished rather than replaced was a clear indication that Britain was not putting very much investment into its railways.

passenger volumes were in decline until the early-1980s. Freightliner trains as described in *The Development of the Major Trunk Routes* began to run from August 1968. As wagonload freight disappeared from the system, the container trains increased and the business expanded.

Although the case for rationalisation, for improvement of the way the railways worked, was sensible and arguably should have been attempted continuously, and not left until deficits rose to high levels, the closure programme underwent some strange aberrations. Labour won the 1964 General Election, and had made promises to halt the Beeching closures. Yet they did not, and another look at the graph tells us why. They won an increased majority in 1966, and so Harold Wilson ruled until displaced by Edward Heath in 1970. It was Barbara Castle who was Transport Minister from 1965-1968. She reneged on the promises to halt the cuts, but introduced legislation to support socially necessary services.

The 1968 Transport Act set up the Passenger Transport Authorities as well as the arrangements for funding socially necessary services. The basic suggestion that the railway system should be trimmed was correct; the way that it was done was wasteful and inefficient - by a blunt instrument. The legacy was not good: the public became suspicious of further alterations to the system, and in the 1960s governments starved the declining railways of investment which created problems that were then complained about. British Rail was seen as a large and expensive monopoly, and this view dogged its existence, making it less effective, although by any sensible measure it was offering rather better value for money than its continental cousins. To make matters worse, the better performing British Rail was assaulted by the media for failing to be like the French, Swiss and German systems that were said to be superior.[4]

Railway management was no less skilled than management in other industries. Successive BRB Chairmen fought strenuous rearguard actions against policies that they saw as counter to the railway interests. At the time the steady attrition of long-term renewals and maintenance was repeatedly warned against. It was what

4 Ironic then after years of this that HS2 receives such a critical reception?

The Class 123 diesel trains, designed at Swindon in 1963 and based on the standard Mk1 Inter-City coach of the time, lasted until 1984. In comparison with the IC 125 they were antediluvian. This train waiting to depart Sheffield (Midland) at 1745, was on a Manchester to Hull via Sheffield working in 1976, and is an example of why BR was considered to be backward. To some these trains were the acme of the 1st generation of BR diesel trains - perhaps they had not enjoyed the oily smell of their interior when their heaters were malfunctioning, that left them grubby and smelly throughout.

Sir Peter Parker, Chairman of British Rail from 1976-1983, was alluding to when he talked of 'the crumbling edge of quality'. Remarkably obedient, the railways made do with 'less', shouldering the blame for problems inflicted upon them. The 'Marples Doctrine' cast a long shadow.

British Rail became a media joke for expensive, crowded, unpunctual and dirty trains; in the 1970s the 'curly sandwich' jokes were legion. The system was suffering from underinvestment, railway pay was below the national average, commuter services were indeed overcrowded and unpunctual, but BR performance was considerably better than the shower of criticism that fell upon its head justified. Alas there were constraints placed upon what 'spokesmen' were permitted to say. It was forbidden to talk to the press except via 'official mouthpieces', and sometimes even they were constrained to offer platitudes. It was not considered acceptable to go on the attack, or to defend vigorously, using the lack of investment as evidence, and certainly not to blame the government. There were casualties, as some of those who stepped out of line were dismissed: perhaps the most notable was Eastern Region General Manager , Gerard Fiennes in 1967.[5]

In the 1970s British Rail's investment went into new Inter-City trains, with the air conditioned Mk2 carriage, and further electrification: Weaver Junction (West Coast) through to Glasgow, talked about since 1968, was completed in May 1974. The improvement was palpable. Yet there was more in the pipeline. Groups of people had been looking at high-speed trains. One was going really high-tech, with a tilting, 140mph, Advanced Passenger Train. The others were extending the bounds of existing technology, with a 2,500hp diesel at both ends of a train, designed to achieve 125mph. In the event Britain's disfunctional sense of self worth 'sank' the APT - as BR Chairman Richard Marsh (1971-1976) said in response to cost complaints, the equivalent was 'the development cost of Concorde's ashtrays'. The diesel train was deployed with a comfortable passenger vehicle, the Mk3 carriage, to be a 125mph success in speed and comfort that immediately boosted the market for rail wherever it went.

5 I Tried To Run A Railway ISBN 0-7153-8926-2

When it came in 1976, Inter-City 125 took the main lines by storm. It revolutionised timetables and encouraged growth on a major scale. Yet, curiously enough, there was a flatlining of investment from 1974 - 1980, and then investment dropped to a lower level for seven years, and there was the Serpell Report. It seemed that railways were still seen by many as having a limited future. The picture is taken in York in 1978.

Inter-City 125 changed the game for the railways. Journey times tumbled, reputation grew, and the train has remained in service for over forty years. Introduction of it took place first on the London to Bristol and South Wales services, then between London York, Newcastle and Edinburgh, eventually replacing Deltic hauled services from 1979-1982. The modern look of the trains, a vigorous advertising campaign, and many 'familiarisation' trips caught the public's imagination. The result was an immediate surge of patronage on the routes where Inter-City 125 was introduced. The effect became hard to ignore, as it showed that given the right investment, rail could easily take premium traffic from the roads.

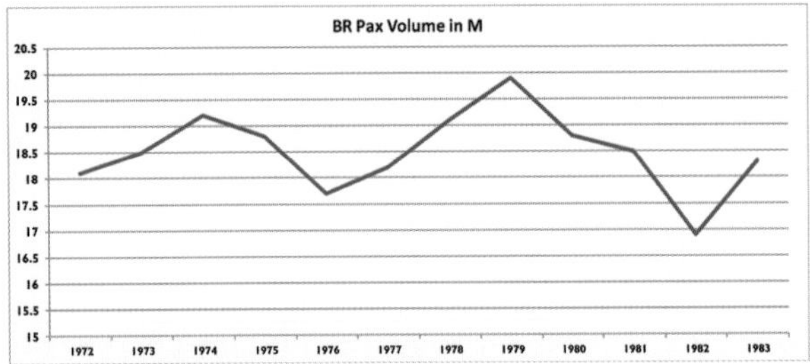

1972 passenger carryings (from Gourvish) indicate the more general 'health' of British Railways after Beeching, yet it was an unclear picture. The dips in GDP are marked in 1976 and 1982. There was a successful effort to attract patronage to InterCity trains by increasing their speed. This grew in success with InterCity 125, but on rural and 'industrial' lines rail had become a 'distress purchase'. Commuting fluctuated in line with the state of the economy.

In general the mid to late 1970s saw investment with figures between £175m - £226m[6], and it was no longer quite so simple to point clearly to the size and remedy for the BR deficit. The waters were muddied by so many conflicting factors: the politics of the varying need for railways; public resistance to closures; the effect of losses on the PSBR[7]; the requirements of the PSO[8]; the constant jostling of the railway unions; the BRB methods of cross-subsidy[9]. It was all rather like nailing a jelly to the wall. Yet soon to appear was someone moulding jellies of her own. The the Callaghan administration was in deep trouble,

6 Gourvish British Rail 1974-1979, at constant 1979 prices

7 Public Service Borrowing Requirement

8 Public Service Obligation - support for branch lines considered socially necessary

9 Of course the BRB never cheated on its figures - but who was to say without an impossibly complex audit that costs were all allocated honestly. If Crewe to Shrewsbury (loss making) was within the PSO, and Crewe to Euston (profitable) was not how creative can accounting be for cross-subsidy before discovery?

This Class 321 looks unkempt as it runs out of Bletchley on the Down Slow Line, with an afternoon service from Euston to Northampton, showing the dying embers of British Rail . There wasn't any appetite for privatisation, it was change again - and there had been lots of that. Many thought it change for change's sake, as Sectorisation was a recent doctrine that had brought with it excellent results, and there were breakthroughs in train design.

with a minority government, which culminated in the 1978-9 Winter of Discontent and a Parliamentary vote of no confidence, despite their tendency to throw subsidies around. The unions were not co-operating with Labour to govern the country. It appears that either the union leadership was working to an external agenda, a theory always considered a 'cop out', or they were deluded enough to think that the 'trick' with Edward Heath could be played again. They would soon find otherwise. The Conservative Manifesto was clear on what was to follow.

Margaret Thatcher: dawn of privatisation

Margaret Thatcher was Prime Minister from 1979 to 1990. At the time of her election there was a bad run on the Pound, and Britain's manufacturing sector was in headlong decline. This was not a good time for the railways; they were unionised, beset by demarcation and restrictive practices. The new Prime Minister disliked them, considering British Rail an unwieldy state-owned monolith. Thankfully Inter-City 125 was there to demonstrate that even limited investment when placed in a 'winning' product allowed railways to win traffic from road.

Thatcher policies included the privatisation of state owned industries. She believed that the doctrine of socialism, as practiced by the Attlee administration of 1945, was still manifest in the detached public organisations like the railways, that in her view needed the bright lights of the free market to illuminate them. Successive Conservative governments had felt uneasy but impotent against the core of the large nationalised industries, notably the railways, taken into the State by the mould-breaking legislation of the Attlee administration. Though elected with a majority of 43 in 1979, the Thatcher, radical, right-wing policies were hardly populist, and unemployment reached 3m. Margaret Thatcher might have lasted for one term, were it not for the victory in the Falklands War. Timed beautifully, the successful outcome of the war offered a majority of 144 seats in the 1983 General Election. After this, she turned her attention to the 'enemy within', and sought a clash with a major union that she intended to win. It happened to be the miners' union, but for a while it looked as though the rail unions would be included. During the miner's strike, as coal wasn't being mined, and stocks at power stations were vast, the railwaymen were not placed

Scotland enjoyed a narrow vote in favour of devolution in 1978, and an overwhelming majority in 1997. Chris Green demonstrated that a simple market focus on an integrated railway was possible. ScotRail is now controlled by the Scottish Executive with devolved powers for the railway designed to complement the economic potential of the area. Performance and progress has so far shown to be rather better than for the English approach run by the DfT, although Network Rail controls the infrastructure in both cases. 170 411 stands at Dundee in 2012

in the spotlight, or a similar fate might have befallen the rail industry as it did the mines.

Although the actual privatisation of the railways was devoutly wished, Margaret Thatcher thought it too complicated to achieve in her second term. However, steel, water, British Telecom and others went to the private sector. In the 1980s, sectorisation proceeded within British Rail, separating its disciplines into discrete units, like Regional Railways, Inter-City, Network South East, Scotrail, and Railfreight, but all the subsidiaries were sold off. Hotels, ships, engineering and workshops were all sundered, sometimes splitting business interests and reducing intermodal links. Even station trading and refreshments, and on-board services headed into the private sector in 1982, depriving us forever of the curly sandwich. Full railway privatisation remained in the 'too difficult' bag until the Major administration came to power (from 1990 -1997). When her unpopular policies eventually did for Margaret Thatcher, as she was thought to be an electoral liability for the 1992 General election, she handed on to successor John Major a determination to privatise the railways, to get rid of British Rail, and to introduce free-market competition into the industry. The intention was placed in the 1992 Conservative Manifesto, and unexpectedly the Conservatives were returned to power, so John Major decided to do it.

The Chairmen

Whilst the privatisation threat was present, the BR Chairmanship progressed through some wise counsels. Sir Peter Parker (1976-1983), cultured, articulate and careful, led BR through the difficult industrial relations problems of the 1970s, and into the Thatcher Premiership. He was replaced by career railwayman Robert Reid, formerly BRB Vice-Chairman. He created the BR sectors. Interested in the railways, Reid was appointed in 1983 as a mature 62-year old, to be Chairman of BR for seven years. A passionate railway supporter, he sought no glory, just performance; he was diplomatic, able and determined. He dealt with difficult trades unions through the miners' strike, and tickled investment money from a difficult Conservative administration. It was he who managed to win the electrification of the East Coast Main Line, and

The East Coast Line was electrified between 1985 and 1990. This picture is of Adwick, just outside Doncaster, in summer 2013, with a Leeds to London express headed towards Doncaster. The picture shows the lighter nature of the overhead line equipment than on the West Coast Line, as shown in the picture of Bletchley (P29). The DoT pressed for wire headspans and wider spacing between masts (apparently against engineering advice) and this has led to a larger incident of de-wirements in high winds, and consequently lower reliability, for which the Railways are blamed - how little the public know!

he was clear on the need to follow the wishes of the elected government - but to get the best out of this for the railways. Sir Bob Reid followed from 1990 to 1995, when his predecessor's contract expired. He came to the Railways Board from being the CEO of Shell UK Ltd. Sir Bob, from Cupar in Fife, became Chairman at 56, and after he left assumed a number of prestigious chairmanships. He argued strongly and firmly against splitting the railways away from control of the infrastructure, fearing the return of inefficiencies long wrestled with and overcome during sectorisation. He warned against the creation of a legal minefield with separate franchises, as it would distract the organisations from the business of running cost effective and efficient rail services. Sir Bob was an advocate of 'vertical franchises'; his advice went unheeded. The chairmen were obliged to follow the policies and instructions of the Secretary of State for Transport - it didn't mean that they agreed with their instructions. Senior railway managers took their instructions from the Chairman, and a similar direction applied, with the same qualification.

It is interesting to note that under these chairmen and the governments concerned, no one argued for any form of private enterprise open access of devolved railway services, despite large numbers of heritage railways operating at a profit in Britain, and examples of local railways running successfully in Germany, Austria and Switzerland.

The 1993 Railway Act

Having won the election on 9th April 1992, the victorious Major administration were pleased to develop a plan to carry out the privatisation before the Railways Bill was published the following year. Although the management of British Rail strongly advocated privatisation as one entity, a British Rail plc in effect, Prime Minister, John Major favoured setting up a vertically integrated set of large companies, not far in concept from the LMS/GWR/SR & LNER that had existed from 1923-1948. Both of these proposals might have been more effective than the system introduced. The Treasury advocated the creation of seven, later 25, passenger railway franchises, as a way of maximising revenue. The Treasury were listened to and not the railwaymen. Perhaps the immense intellects at the Adam Smith Institute, who had advised the Treasury, had overlooked some fundamental truths governing resilience

One of the Heathrow Express Class 332 units built by CAF/Seimens stands at London Paddington. The service opened on 23rd June 1998 with the line from the airport to the junction owned by BAA, and the remainder by Railtrack (Network Rail). The service is operated under a 'command agreement' between BAA and BR (now Network Rail) is therefore open access. This agreement was very favourable to BAA.

when recommending fragmentation, or perhaps they didn't know what the railwaymen knew.

The passage of the Railways Bill was controversial. There wasn't a public call for rail privatisation, and there was much lobbying against the Bill. The Labour Party was opposed to it, and promised to renationalise the railways when they got back into office, as and when resources allowed. Although they talked a lot they didn't do it after their election to power in 1997, with a majority of 179, but there was good reason for this.

The Railways Bill became the Railways Act 1993 on 5th November 1993 and the organisational structure dictated by it came into effect on 1st April 1994. The Act broke up British Rail into over 100 private companies: train owners (leasing companies), infrastructure, maintenance and renewal companies, freight train operators, passenger train operators, an infrastructure owner, and many others. The Office of the Rail Regulator (ORR) approved the contracts for the use of railway facilities. Franchise Agreements with the passenger train operators specify minimum service levels, controlled fares, and the amount of subsidy or premium to be paid over the course of the franchise. Franchises were first the responsibility of the Office of Passenger Rail Franchising (OPRAF), then its successor the Strategic Rail Authority (SRA) and now with the Secretary of State for Transport.

Section 17 of the Railways Act 1993 deals with Open Access, though in reading the Section, this provision for competition does not stand out as it did in John MacGregor's White Paper of July 1992. In 1993 the Regulator quietly dropped the requirement for competition by open access, although the provision 'remained'.[10]

The Railways Act 1993 created Railtrack to own and control the network infrastructure, British Rail passenger services were split into Train Operating Companies (TOCs), with fixed term franchises on offer to competitive bidders. The network infrastructure maintenance and technical functions were privatised as 'going concerns' by being sold off to the highest bidder, but remained under

10 HoC Library SN/BT/1157 - 18.03.10

The £2bn, 2005 rebuilding scheme for the West Coast Main Line to take 140mph trains was part of the ambitious plan to bring together the combination of tilting trains, a modern railway, and entrepreneurial management. Not everything came to fruition; there was major disruption, it was over time and over budget, but the resulting speed and frequency of the trains raised the standard. Moderation of competition was needed to protect the investment but of course this had unforseen circumstances on competition. No 140mph trains run on this route.

the control of Railtrack by contracts, which of course were overseen by the Office of the Rail Regulator (ORR). Existing rolling stock ownership was transferred to rolling stock companies (ROSCOs) and contracts were made with the TOCs to hire, operate, and maintain the stock. This did not preclude TOCs making arrangements to obtain new rolling stock outside the ROSCO system.

Existing passenger services were taken over by the franchised TOCs, generally (but not always[11]) on a seven year term, subject to the control of the government's agency, the Office of Passenger Rail Regulation and Franchising (OPRAF). Routes and service levels (the timetable) were specified by a Passenger Service Requirement (PSR). This protected services on unprofitable routes (that continued to be subsidised as specified within the TOC contract). Minimum levels of service were specified, with the timetables for early and late trains, and expected journey time standards. In general, the PSR was designed to protect around 80% of the rail services then operating.

11 Virgin Trains negotiated a 15 year contract including protection from competition - but it was by no means straighforward subsequently, as the investment was duly made by Virgin, but the railway was not rebuilt to time.

Rail privatisation was designed to work by means of a flexible set of plans, held together by contractual relationships; all was deemed to offer the successful franchisee an acceptable financial return to their shareholders. The 'free market' essence was that if the TOC management was able to improve on the key indicators set by OPRAF, and observe the PSR, within the fares set, then they were welcome to reap the benefits of improvements in traffic volume increase, and/or cost savings from their good work. On the other hand, should quality levels fall by poor management, then this failure would visit the bottom line. Should service standard consistently fall below nominated levels, then the TOC would have the franchise 'repossessed' and relet at the next bid-point., The danger for the failing TOC would be 'reputational' in trying to win a further term, or a franchise elsewhere.

This was an ingenious concept of interlocking plans for the railways that by driving out inefficiency would allow innovation, good service, and commercial competition to offer the public a market-led train service that included

There were certain parts of the network where the old system of cross-subsidy continued unsung. At Glasgow Central on 9th March 2009, East Coast and Virgin trains stand together, about to launch for the same destination, London. Both services have doubtful profitability 400 miles out from the Capital. It wouldn't need much cherry picking by an open access operator seriously to harm carefully laid arrangements. Matters have changed since.

safeguards for socially necessary services. The rather innocent view was that the whole was thought to offer a better value for money operation, with much higher quality of service levels than that previously provided by the 'ponderous and ineffective' unresponsive monolith that was British Rail. Perhaps when proposing the fragmented solution for privatisation the Adam Smith Institute did not have access to the value and weight of some of the inner workings of the 'unresponsive monolith'? However lawyers had many reasons for creamy satisfaction - what business.

Railwaymen (apparently discounted) said that British Rail managed better than other railway administrations to achieve the performance of the business sectors and exampling the advances made, adding that at the very moment when so many of the blocks to progress had been removed, the disruption of privatisation was being imposed. It was pointed out that such a complex web of contractual relationships would replace the 'bureaucracy of British Rail' with another, run by lawyers. Aside from the expected franchise bedding-in process, the degree of cross-subsidy that British Rail was a master at managing incognito suddenly became apparent. There were railway routes that were financial liabilities in need of investment such that a seven-year franchise was deemed by prospective bidders as unsustainable; for the investment needed there was little time to generate a return. Franchises were bought by bus companies, unpractised in managing enterprises dependent on a massive infrastructure base, and thus they faced a steep learning curve within a limited timescale. On the other hand, there were franchises that could become most profitable if the franchisee could attract new custom. The signs that an explosion of demand was on the way were not clear enough to be reflected in early franchise agreements. When it came it was rapid and unexpected, and needed time for a reaction. Politically uncomfortable profits and uncomfortable subsidies arose in the 'supported' sectors, as well as big bills for arrears of maintenance and renewal. There were worse consequences to follow, outlined in Chapter 12, and the bone-headed media never caught on to allocate blame. From here the Open Access story is now followed.

In 2002 the Voyagers revolutionised service. They were concentrated on providing a regular clock-face timetable on the key cross-country routes, answering a demand that BR had not, by offering significantly better quality at better frequency. Extra growth brought big problems of capacity; a clock-face timetable did not mean clock-face demand. Independent TOCs meant service co-ordination nightmares for Cross Country operations.

Open Access - the procedures

In the terms of the 1993 Railways Act, the definition enshrined in the industry's regulatory framework describes Open Access passenger train operators as "those who operate services purely on a commercial basis. These are companies who identify an opportunity to run a service which is not currently being provided."

The ethos of open access was that although permission was needed, and the timescale and services were defined, the risk was all the operators not the taxpayers', in exchange for a little extra commercial freedom. The freight business, from Cornwall to the Highlands of Scotland, is run through the Open Access provisions of the 1993 Railways Act. However, the same principles applied to passenger services have been a lot more difficult in their realisation. This may be because the problem of 'that little extra commercial freedom' - it smacks of spoiling 'best laid plans'.

Most opportunities in the passenger railway are franchises let by DfT, and these are time-limited, and can only be secured through success in a bidding competition. Bidding is expensive, and there are no guarantees, with most of the big transport groups achieving a success rate no higher than 25%. Open Access represents a rather different 'non-compliant' choice, driven by the promoting shareholders. It was gradually made clear that such an operation would be the exception rather than the rule. OPRAF specified routes and service levels, thus unless they were derelict in their duty, surely any opportunity for open access would be rare. However, certain things 'happened'. For example the innovative Virgin Voyager certainly made an impact on cross-country services in terms of service frequency, if not seats available, across the core of the services. Yet originally, the range and complexity of such services was wider than was prudent. First of all they could not serve everywhere, and it was not long before rationalisation, and sensible consolidation, left large gaps. Secondly there were destinations like Hull, Blackpool, Barrow, Sunderland, Shrewsbury that had no 'wires', and so through services from London did not run, or were exceedingly thin. And there were places like Nottingham and Liverpool that had no service to Scotland,

The Silverlink (via Northampton) service from London to Birmingham was the slower, cheaper way to Birmingham than Virgin. Suddenly the service had 20 minute stops placed in it at Northampton, making it less competitive from Milton Keynes than Virgin, who ran a (very full) hourly service. Silverlink seemed stifled; was this the ORR doing his abstraction duty, pathing problems, or was it the preparation for the London Midland franchise that emerged? As LM now run a competing service with Virgin, perhaps the second answer is more likely - but doubts (like the 20 mins) remain.

yet there was a demand, or potential demand, for through services that was no longer being answered. There were other quite important potential flows, either in isolation or in conjunction, that OPRAF were not specifying service to, nor had indicated any intention of doing so. The question was, if someone wished to have a 'punt' at running a train service to places 'off the beaten track', would open access applications to serve such destinations be countenanced?

It was assumed that Open Access was a method where a potentially high risk operation could be trialed without the full franchise machinery. The risk taker would determine the timetable, and all aspects of the service specification, including the type of trains, staffing levels, on board service, and fares – although fare levels would have to take note of rates charged by competing operators, when constrained by the fares regulation system defined by government. Open Access contracts are approved by ORR for agreed terms of usually no greater than five years (though this varies), open access operators are required to continue to demonstrate the benefits their services deliver, and a commitment to the future of the business. Securing the right to operate an open access service in the first place depends on demonstrating the case for the proposed service, not on competition. Approval to run a new open access service is granted by the Office of Rail Regulation (ORR) and will be refused if primarily abstractive to another franchise operator by means of the Moderation of Competition rules to be described next.

Open Access passenger service supporters point to its role serving new markets, providing choice for consumers, implementing innovative approaches, contribution of additional income by paying access charges to Network Rail, and to other train operators for the use of their stations, and an absence of risk to the taxpayer. Detractors draw attention to the financial impact of the open access competitor on established businesses. There is no doubt that some of the passenger revenue the open access operator will earn will be abstracted from an existing franchised operator. The ORR has a duty to guard against 'unfair' abstraction. Detractors also draw attention to the fact that franchised operators pay track access charges to Network Rail for access to the network, some of which

There was nervousness within government about the likelihood of franchises being let unless terms were reasonable. GNER earned the best reputation of any of the franchised TOCs for quality of service, grew volume and earned profit. Later franchises had more stringent financial commitments. GNER (train shown here on the Up line at Offord) objected greatly to Open Access operator Hull Trains. GNER replacement NEx withdrew and East Coast was 're-nationalised', yet the ORR permitted two Open Access operators, Hull Trains and Grand Central because they satisfied the MoC requirements.

are fixed and some of which are variable, on the basis of the volume of traffic operated. Open Access operators only pay the variable element of track access charges, and therefore it was felt they do not pay the true costs of network access, and so are cross-subsidised by the franchises. Protection for franchisees in certain areas to the exclusion of open access, and any other proposals, was enshrined within the Railways Act 1993. Moderation of Competition (MoC) legislation was applied to protect against the abstraction of traffic rather than public benefit, and this special condition applied to Virgin[12].

To be successful, an application to ORR needs to show that a wide variety of issues have been considered and dealt with, to demonstrate a genuine service proposition rather than abstracting the best traffic from an existing service. There needs to be capacity on the network to accommodate the proposed timetable and the management must show the necessary experience. The cherry-picking criteria are governed by ORR's 'primarily abstractive' test. The ORR undertakes an economic evaluation of the proposal, assessing in particular the passenger revenue forecast, and the sources of that revenue:

> *"Where an operator is seeking to introduce a new service that competes with the existing services of one or more other operators, we will wish to consider the extent to which such additional services would benefit passengers and not be primarily abstractive of the incumbents' revenues. The operator's application should therefore specify what benefits passengers are likely to gain and the extent to which service volume growth is expected to lead to passenger volume growth."*
>
> ORR 'Criteria and procedures for the approval of passenger track access contracts' – fourth edition, May 2006

The issue of network capacity and performance is factual. Timetables are drawn up, which account for all other services on the network. The timetables make use of known running times for the proposed rolling stock, and account for all other trains which have contractual rights.

12 Virgin's special protection affected Wrexham & Shropshire rather seriously. Details are given later, how and why.

Mike Jones (left) Open Access railway entrepreneur, talks with one of the Bombardier engineers about the forthcoming order of 170 Class DMUs for the Hull Trains service, at the Derby factory. The backdrop is a similar Scotrail Class 170. Hull trains was a carefully thought out innovation that did well. It was therefore used as a model for the Wrexham and Shropshire service - indeed WSMR traffic forecasts were more favourable.

Account must be taken of the margin between trains along each route section and through every junction. Trains may be permitted by the signalling system to operate 3 minutes apart on heavily trafficked sections. Elsewhere the timetable may be fatally confined by Victorian infrastructure or mechanically operated signals, and single lines rationalised to be sans passing loops. Producing a timetable that complies with all the rules of the route – whilst at the same time maintaining a commercially attractive journey time, is a complex and frustrating task, given that the rail network operates at high utilisation levels across many parts of the UK., and that those 'experienced' managers know full well how much the rules may be stretched for established operators to fit each other in on *a quid pro quo* basis. One bears in mind here that regulation rests with the signallers, and they are now employed by Network Rail. The ORR scrutinises the proposed timetables, and the assessment of their performance impact, as part of its evaluation of any application. ORR needs to be sure that the applicant has the skills, finance, and experience to run a railway company

Open Access - existing services

The first UK domestic passenger open access service was **Heathrow Express**, introduced in 1998 and run by the British Airports Authority, it operates every 15 minutes throughout the day between 05.25 and 23.25 from Heathrow Airport to London Paddington, and is the primary public transport link to the airport. The introduction was discrete, and did not affect any other TOC, and there was pathing for the trains (just) to run in and out of Paddington. A later addition was the service, joint with First Great Western, Heathrow Connect, that operates an 'all stations' electric service to the airport at 'Great Western' prices. This was introduced in 2005.

Grand Central was originally promoted by a team of former British Rail managers, backed by private shareholders. The company's application for access to run services from Sunderland to London King's Cross was considered at the same time as the franchise operator GNER was seeking to secure a new ten year term from DfT[13]. Assurances were given that Grand Central would

13 MoT 1979-81, DoT 1981-97/2001-2, DfET&R 1997-2001, DfT 2002-13

be unlikely to secure approval, and if they did, financial protection would be offered. In due course however, ORR approved Grand Central's application for three return services each day, and GNER received no protection. The July 2005 bombings in Central London had seen GNER suffer against challenging targets. GNER pursued its case to the High Court, where Mr Justice Sullivan ruled that the granting to Grand Central of Open Access rights was not illegal. It was a lesson of the GNER/Grand Central case that whilst ORR took account of the views of stakeholders, including DfT and Network Rail, in granting approval, they had sole responsibility for the decision, and operate under a mandate to promote competition.

Service to Sunderland began in 2007, with three services per day, growing to five. In May 2010 a service of three trains a day began between London Kings Cross and Bradford. In November 2011, Grand Central was taken over by Arriva UK Trains, which itself had been taken over by DB in 2010. (See page 185)

Hull lost the majority of its daily through services to and from London, though the city had retained a single train for the business executives, to London in the morning, and home in the afternoon. Two former British Rail executives, John Nelson and Mike Jones, through their Renaissance Trains business founded Hull Trains with GB Railways in 2000. **Hull Trains** first ran three return services a day using Class 170 *Turbostars*. With the introduction of the Class 222 *Pioneers*, six return services a day were run by 2006. By 2008 this number had increased to seven return services a day. In 2008, 80% shareholder GB Railways sold out to First Group. In 2009 First Hull Trains gained Class 180s units as a 'saving' and passed on the 222s to East Midlands Trains. The reliability record sagged. The service, although now well established, then went through some difficult times, with the depressed state of the local Hull economy limiting growth. In March 2009, ORR extended access rights to 2016, and in 2011 reliability levels had been restored, with four 'Adelante' units in service, operating seven return services each weekday, five on Saturday and Sunday, and profitability has returned.

How Wrexham & Shropshire started

The original idea for Wrexham & Shropshire was developed by Renaissance Trains, a collective of railway professionals who had long experience in the industry. John Nelson was Managing Director of Network SouthEast in BR days, and Mike Jones was the Senior Business Manager for RACAL Telecoms. Both had been instrumental in setting up Hull Trains in the late 1990s. In forming Renaissance Trains they were joined by Pete Wilkinson, managing director

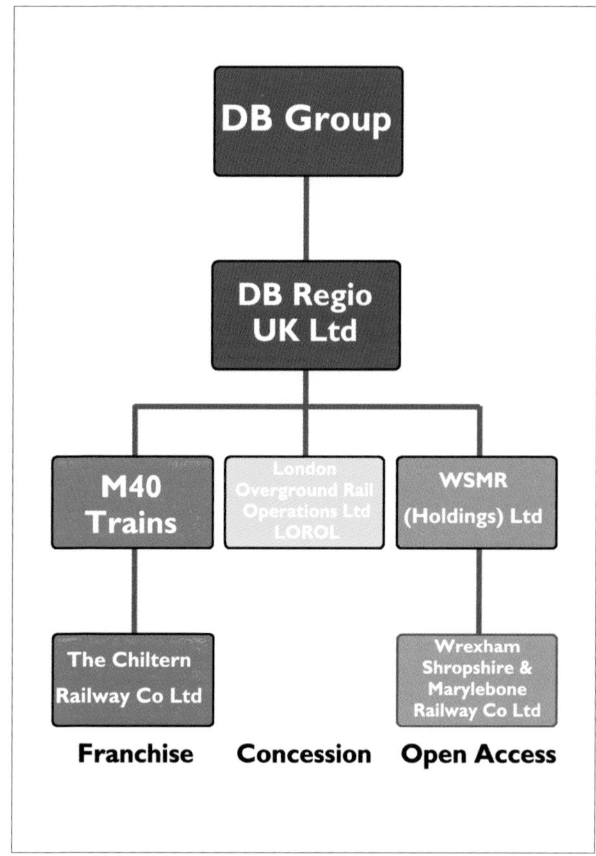

The organisation structure after DB acquired Laing Rail in 2009.

of consultancy First Class Partnerships, and Mary Bonar, a lawyer with a wealth of experience in railways through the privatisation process. The Renaissance team had begun promoting the idea for a new service between Shropshire and London, and first approached Laing Rail – the parent company of Chiltern Railways – in 2005. Laing had been a major shareholder of Chiltern since it was privatised in 1996, and was in the process of adding a 50% share of London Overground operator LOROL to the portfolio. Wrexham & Shropshire started life as a 50/50 Joint Venture between Renaissance Trains and Laing Rail, the umbrella organisation for rail interests of John Laing.

By 2008, John Laing had sold its rail interests to Germany's national railway DeutscheBahn. At this point the shareholder of Wrexham & Shropshire became DB Regio UK, with the same subsidiary structure as Laing Rail, as shown in the diagram. In the 21st Century, DB had embarked on a strategy of growth through acquisition and also purchased UK freight operator EWS, which became part of the DB Schenker logistics organisation. In 2010 DB acquired Arriva, considerably expanding its Europe-wide passenger operations, and with it, subsequently, came Open Access operator Grand Central.

67013 **Dyfrbont Pontcysyllte** *on Saturday 24th January 2009, running from Aylesbury to Wembley Depot, seen just past the foot-crossing south of Little Kimble station at 14:38, in glorious sunshine.*
Geoff Plumb

Chapter 3
Finding the trains

Finding the trains

It is something of an understatement to say that getting hold of the right fleet is fundamental to the successful promotion of a new railway business. The post-privatisation railway in the UK is fortunate in that a number of different companies lease trains to the industry. In theory this offers a number of alternatives and competition in the market to keep prices down. In reality of course, trains are often bound into long term leases with operators – long term deals of course offer discounts for the operator over short term alternatives. Therefore trains are often only available for a short window of time, although as circumstances change operators sometimes sub-lease their trains.

The initial internal business plan for Wrexham & Shropshire, prepared in late 2005, made a working assumption that 3-coach, Class 170 trains would be operated. These trains were used to launch Hull Trains, and were almost identical to the sizeable fleet of Class 168s that had been operated successfully by Chiltern Railways since 1998. With 100mph capability, good acceleration, large windows, and flexible options for internal configuration, they offered considerable advantages over alternatives. In particular, the Class 158 'Express' units built for British Rail's Regional Railways sector in the early 1990s are a large fleet, but it was always felt their 90mph capability, relatively poor acceleration and interior layout meant they weren't quite

An Anglia Class 170, three-car multiple unit train waits in Platform 9 at Kings Cross, ready to work a Hull Trains service on 4th June 2001. Hull Trains were able to borrow units from Anglia to start their service, until they had a short build for themselves, divining that these could be 'handed on' when growth called for even better trains. Like Hull, the Class 170s were the 'ideal' vehicles to start the Wrexham & Shropshire service, as they were flexible and economic to run. It was a great shame that they were 'not available'. It was always wondered whether this was somehow a rather doubtful decision.

Central Trains were willing to swap 4 of these Class 170, 3-car units for 158s. It was all ready to happen, and Wrexham & Shropshire would have been rather different! However, the Central Trains franchise was ending, and DoT had 'plans' that did not include Wrexham & Shropshire, thus the deal was declared not possible - was this 'doubtful' as a decision? Here Central Trains 170 639 waits in Derby with a service to Cardiff on 8th March 2001.

good enough for Wrexham & Shropshire. So in parallel with other work being carried out on the timetable, and regulatory approvals for the service, discussions were held with the train leasing companies to explore availability of Class 170s and any other similar alternatives.

There was of course the choice of a brand new fleet. The structure of the rolling stock industry in the UK means the costs of operating new trains are not dissimilar to those incurred operating 10-year old trains, since the rolling stock leasing companies make the capital funding available, and recoup this over the lifetime of the train at long term rates – a bit like a mortgage. When Hull Trains started operating in 2000, the company sub-leased a number of 3-car Class 170s from associate company Anglia Railways. This arrangement was quickly followed by an order of brand new trains from the manufacturer for similar trains to Hull's own specification, allowing the initial fleet to be returned to Anglia. This interim arrangement also meant Hull could get started without having to wait for new trains to come off the production line which would have delayed things – a typical timeframe is a year from placing an order to having trains in service.

The timing of Wrexham & Shropshire's development meant that neither approach employed launching Hull Trains were possible. Chiltern Railways had no spare Class 168s it could make available, even on a short term basis, and Bombardier was closing down the long running Class 168/Class 170 Turbostar production line due to changes in European legislation concerning engine emissions with which the train no longer complied. The replacement design, Class 172, would not be available in time for Wrexham & Shropshire, and in the event the first vehicles of this new type did not enter traffic with London Overground until 2010. New build was not seriously considered for the start up of Wrexham & Shropshire. Alternative manufacturers, such as Siemens, may have been able to supply within a reasonable time period, but the financial commitment of any order for new trains could not be risked until regulatory approval had been gained. Once the Regulator had said yes, it was important to start running trains as quickly as possible, and it was calculated that this could be done in six months. Waiting a year for new trains to be built before running could start was not something desired.

The old Virgin! Stoke Hammond, WCML, at 14.00 on 5th April 2003. An Up Virgin express consisting of DVT and eight Mk3 cars, with a Class 87 locomotive at the rear, passes at a steady 110mph. As Pendolino electric multiple units came on stream, the locomotive hauled equipment was cascaded. In essence, for most of it, rustication to a field in Warwickshire was its destination - but not for long!

Trying to lease the ideal fleet

With short term lease and brand new options limited, Andy Hamilton and Pete Wilkinson went to see what the leasing companies had available to offer. The Class 170 fleet was preferred, due to its 100mph capability, and similarity to the Chiltern fleet. Porterbrook Leasing were the main owner of this fleet. At the Project Board meeting on 9th May 2006, Andy and Pete confirmed that:

> *"there is now a firm offer of rolling stock from Porterbrook. This is proposed to be 4 x 3-car Class 170s in the number range 170101 to 170110, currently on lease to Central Trains... [who have] agreed to a swap and to receive Class 158 vehicles as replacements. The vehicles will be released... in January 07."*

Central Trains also operated a large Class 158 fleet, and would gain some cost savings through the swap; so it seemed everyone would benefit from the deal. For Wrexham & Shropshire, these 3-car, Class 170s were ideal, as they had originally been specified for use on Midland Main Line services from London St. Pancras to Nottingham and Derby, and already included a First Class section in the middle coach.

It wasn't long before this proposed deal hit trouble. The Central Trains franchise ended in spring 2007, along with three others – Midland Main Line, Silverlink and Virgin Cross Country. The DfT wanted to merge various elements of these businesses, to create three, larger franchises. Train services across all of these franchise areas had enjoyed significant growth in the decade since rail privatisation. Driven by a growing population, economic and tax 'measures', road congestion, and increasing fuel costs, rail demand nationally had grown 50% in those ten years, encouraging improved services and more capacity at peak times. The UK railway volume was booming, and one of the objectives of the new franchises, starting in spring 2007, was to continue to accommodate expected growth in the most efficient way. So the DfT and the bidders for those franchises were reluctant to allow four potentially valuable Class 170s to end up with Wrexham & Shropshire. As the discussions with Network Rail concerning the timetable and the WSMR application for access became more complex, and therefore delayed, in mid 2006, so the option of Class 170s slipped away, as the franchise competitions concluded, perhaps to the relief of DfT.

Class 67 - data sheet			
Characteristic	Description	Characteristic	Description
Power type	Diesel-electric	Traction motor type (4)	EMD D43FM
Builder	Meinfesa: Alstom, Spain	Multiple working with:	Classes 59, 66
Date	1999-2000	Top speed	200kmh
Number made	30	Power output (engine)	3200hp/2386kW @ 900rpm
UIC Wheel Classification	Bo'Bo'	Power output (at rail)	2500hp/1864kW
Gauge	1435mm	Tractive effort	32,000lb/144kN
Wheel diameter	965mm	Train heating (index)	66 (330kW)
Minimum curvature	75m	Locomotive brakeforce	780kN
Wheelbase	bogie 2.8m, pivots 11.63m	Train brakes	air
Length	19.71m	Operator (owner)	Angel Trains
Width	2.71m	Operator (TOC)	EWS/DB Schenker
Height	3.93m	Operator (sub-hire)	W&S/Chiltern Railways
Weight	88 tonnes	Axle load	22 tonnes
Fuel capacity	4927 litres	Route availability	RA 8
Motor type	EMD 12N 7103GB-EC diesel 2 stroke	Nickname	skips, buckets, cyclops
Alternator type	EMD AR9AC6HEX		

The bodyshell is a monocoque, load bearing Alstom design, the traction motors are bogie frame hung, geared for 125mph running (a maximum of 143mph was obtained on test in Spain). The 22 tonne axle load did cause a 110mph restriction until the bogies were modified, but they don't run with 125mph stock. They have buffers and screw couplings but are also fitted with buckeyes attached to a swing arm mount.

Enter loco-hauled

Alternatives were needed quickly Finding suitable trains in what was, in theory at least, a free market was proving to be difficult. Passenger demand was growing strongly, many trains were locked into long term deals, and the timeframe for new build created too great a delay, even if suitable new trains were available.

The eventual solution took advantage of another post-privatisation development. As part of its 15-year franchise for the West Coast Main Line services, won in 1997, Virgin Trains had completely replaced the fleet of Mk3 coaches inherited from British Rail with 'Pendolino' trains. State of the art, able to tilt round corners at higher speed, these 125mph trains were transforming journey times on the UK's busiest main line. Some of the Mk3 coaches displaced had found a home on the Anglia main line, but a great many coaches had no further work, and many were languishing in a field in Warwickshire. It was Mark Laney who first suggested loco-hauled Mk3 coaches. Mark is a timetable specialist and had been helping with the Wrexham & Shropshire timetable, after a spell working for the Laing group on franchise bidding. Mark's background included spells in the rail freight businesses so he had contacts that also proved useful.

English Welsh & Scottish Railway (EWS), the UK's largest freight company, had bought a fleet of 30, powerful locomotives with 125mph capability, called Class 67 in the late 1990s, to haul overnight trains for Royal Mail. Royal Mail had pulled out of rail as part of its logistics chain in 2004 leaving the almost brand new Class 67 fleet with little work. With 3200bhp/2386kW and a top speed of 125mph, it was thought they would easily match the performance of a Class 170, so Mark suggested serious consideration to employing Class 67s hauling comfortable Mk3 coaches.

Testing the theory

EWS had converted three Mk3 coaches into a 'company train', complete with meeting space and dining area. They were keen to demonstrate its capabilities, in the hope that they could find work for some Class 67s. So a test run to Wrexham with the EWS company train was organised at the start of October 2006. The test run began not from Marylebone, but from Paddington, for reasons of available paths at the time desired, and operated via Reading, Banbury, Coventry, Wolverhampton and Shrewsbury to Wrexham General The test passed off without a hitch. After the success of the first run, a second test run was organised with the aim of demonstrating operation over

Left: *Locomotive 67011 in old EWS colours heading a Royal Mail train in the station at Cardiff on 2nd July 2001. Ordered from Alstom (Spain) as a powerful, fast locomotive unit, with the same diesel engine as the Class 66, the type was expected to earn its keep on the mail contract, and on other high-speed loco hauled services. They were no sooner run in and providing reliable service than the mail contract departed to road, yet no loco hauled services ever had suitable 125 mph rolling stock; thus Class 67s were left with little to do.*

Right: *The EWS 'company train' at Wrexham on 29.09.06 topped and tailed by two Class 67 locomotives. This was a test for the Wrexham and Shropshire operation, it demonstrated the practicality of doing the job as well as permitting a number of stakeholders to accompany the train and appreciate exactly what was proposed. The scene is of technical discussions taking place on the platform at Wrexham General Station. Such an event caused quite a stir - that is what it was meant to do.*

Wrexham & Shropshire

the south end of the route. On 29th September 2006, this second test run left London Marylebone at 1017, timed just in front of a Chiltern service to Birmingham which was first stop High Wycombe. This was a precursor of the normal pattern for W&S services, and the xx.17 departure from Marylebone was to become very familiar – indeed 1017 was the departure time of one of the services in the first W&S timetable. This test run followed a route via High Wycombe, Banbury, Leamington, Coventry, Bescot and then via the Grand Junction lines to Wolverhampton, before heading via Telford and through Shropshire to Shrewsbury and then to Wrexham General. The opportunity was taken whilst having the EWS Company Train available, to invite a number of WSMR stakeholders to meet us at Wrexham. The momentum was building for Wrexham & Shropshire. By running a test like this, not only were was the viability of Class 67s and Mk3 coaches being demonstrated to the market, but the clearest signs were being made to the railway industry and to the local politicians that WSMR were serious about making Wrexham & Shropshire happen, with the opportunities that would bring.

Right: *There was quite a full order book at the time for Bombardier made Class 172 units. This was a train that would have had a long delivery time. They could have been a good unit to use on the WSMR service, economic in operation, comfortable, able to perform with all the other trains on the corridors where they were to operate, and with a respectable onward market if the trains were upgraded or in the event that the service was unsuccessful. However, it was not to be - units could not be available in time. This 2 car unit is seen on the London Overground, Gospel Oak to Barking service on 18th August 2011.*

Bringing things to a head

The concept of Class 67 operation for Wrexham & Shropshire was not universally accepted within the Laing Rail Group. Senior Chiltern Railways staff were determined that "loco-hauled trains will never operate into London Marylebone". Their concerns were not without foundation of course – there is a good deal of difference between a Class 165 diesel multiple unit and a Class 67 locomotive hauled passenger train. In operational terms, there is also a lack of compatibility, so what happens if a train fails? If it's a Class 67, how can you rescue it given it can't easily be coupled to a DMU and is also very heavy? It was necessary to be satisfied that Class 67 could deliver the timetable it was wished to operate, particularly in terms of journey times, and that financially it was viable, given the cost assumptions in the business plan were based on Class 170 operation.

Andy Hamilton and Richard Harper were becoming increasingly concerned that there was a danger Wrexham & Shropshire would secure approval but have no trains to operate the service. So a detailed paper setting out a comparison of options was presented to the Wrexham & Shropshire Board on 6th December 2006. At this stage, it was envisaged that ORR approval would be gained in spring 2007, and that operations could therefore begin in autumn 2007.

The paper set out each of the options in turn:

- Class 170s would no longer be available before December 2008 at the earliest, and therefore were not a viable short term option
- Class 158s offered no financial benefit, and would require significant refurbishment in order to deliver the ambience, First Class, and catering offer demanded by the business plan. Furthermore, any refurbishment programme also created risk if the start date depended on its completion
- New trains – principally the Class 172s option – were rapidly rejected on the basis of timescales for the first deliveries
- Finally the loco-hauled option was considered in depth. The Class 67 was considered to be the only viable locomotive option, and it was recognised that EWS were very keen to see them utilised on traffic appropriate to their capabilities.

However it was also noted that there were two main concerns from Network Rail in relation to the weight and track impact characteristics of the locomotive, with consequent effect on the track, and the performance risk associated with the single power unit on the locomotive. A detailed statistical analysis had been carried out which showed that in terms of both frequency of failure and the likely number of delays caused, the Class 67 was predicted to perform better than both Chiltern's existing Class 168s and the Class 158 option. Whilst there were still concerns relating to the impact of a locomotive failure en-route, this analysis gave a great deal of comfort that performance impacts would not be of significant concern. Of course when the train service started running, the statistical analysis was found to be correct, and locomotive failures

Left: *The Class 180 units were becoming available from First Great Western but they suffered from a reputation for unreliability (which may or may not have been manageable), plus they were 5 car sets, and that was rather outside the W&S business model. Here First Great Western 180 106 rolls through Didcot on its way from Worcester to London on the 2nd August 2003. For a time they disappeared from the FGW services, yet they did not spend too long in the rusty siding and were all taken up for work by several TOCs, Hull Trains, Grand Central and again by FGW as their reliability problems were gradually overcome.*

Right: *It is interesting to think that the displacement of the Class 442 Wessex units from the Portsmouth and Weymouth services could have led to their use on Wrexham & Shropshire. It was only an outside chance, and in the event they were all spirited away to Gatwick Express and Brighton services. However, the interest was caused from their being made up with Mk3 coaching stock, their possible availability, and their potential suitability for push-pull working.*
An unidentified Southwest Trains Class 442, trundles through Clapham Junction en route to Waterloo on 12th August 2005.

were in the most part limited to the start of journeys, with little consequential delay on other train services. At this stage, the option of both Mk2 and Mk3 coaches were considered in some detail. Both were readily available for lease or purchase, although the board paper noted that Mk2 vehicles, whilst cheaper, were older, in poorer condition, and indicated that running them for longer than five years was not advisable. Mk3 coaches on the other hand were a better proposition, carried more people, were technically superior, and more comfortable to ride in. Andy Hamilton and Richard Harper went to Long Marston in Warwickshire during November 2006, to inspect the former Virgin Trains Mk3 coaches which were stored there. A large number of coaches were available, although it was clear that standard class coaches and Driving Van Trailers (DVTs) were in short supply, and so early decisions were required to secure the necessary fleet.

The paper concluded with a discussion of other options which had emerged. It had been suggested that a small number of Class 180 units, no longer required by First Great Western, would be available. Relatively

A Virgin Cross Country service skirts the wall at Dawlish on 28th August 2005. Hull Trains managed to get the next version the Cl 222, Wrexham and Shropshire could not. They may well have been ideal for the service but there were none to be had, cost and timescale prohibited any new build.

Left: The introduction of Class 390 Pendolino units released a fleet of Mk3 cars and DVTs still capable of a great deal of life. To begin with no one wanted them, and they went into store. Reality indicated that here were economical units designed with maximum comfort and operating flexibility in mind. What was needed was to find a suitable locomotive to haul them, and an extremely versatile train was in prospect. There were issues with the control system, but those could be dealt with. Here is an up Virgin train, preparing to leave from Watford Junction, 12.10.2001

Right: There was no doubt in the customers' minds that the most comfortable carriage in operation was the Mk3 Open First. Despite their airline leanings, Virgin's Mk3 seats were the nearest to the old first and Pullmans that the public loved. Thus they were popular, and when ousted from service, they only dwelt in the sidings for a relatively short time before they found other employment. Even in standard class, the Mk3 seats are comfortable; rather a contrast to the meagre upholstery that 'fire regulations' have bullied TOCs to accept today on the latest trains.

modern, with First Class and buffet cars, and capable of 125mph, these trains initially appeared attractive but were too expensive to lease and operate, compounded by the fact that they were five coaches long, whilst the business plan indicated a three coach train was appropriate initially. Secondly, it had been suggested that a small number of Class 442 electric units, made redundant by a new fleet on South West Trains and not desired elsewhere, would be a suitable if slightly unusual alternative to Mk3 coaches. This was dismissed owing to a lack of clarity concerning availability, and in the event the entire fleet was leased by Southern. The paper concluded with a recommendation that the Class 67 and Mk3 solution should be pursued, with the next step being to secure through negotiation the best possible financial deal.

Class 67s and DVTs

Inherent in the Class 67 solution was the proposal for push-pull operation. In this mode, each train operates as a fixed set with a locomotive at one end and a driving van

Right: *Any of the technical questions about the practicality of the control system was answered by taking out the EWS Company Train on test. It is seen here on the stakeholders' run to Wrexham on 29th September 2006. On this occasion it was topped and tailed by two Class 67 locos, but it also ran with a DVT, and EWS technical people had substituted that with a direct cable into the locomotive control system. 67029 Stands on the Chester end of the train, that is standing in the loop platform that Wrexham and Shropshire trains would eventually use.*

Wrexham & Shropshire

Left: *Hull Trains initially ran with 170 units hired in from Anglia. There was a connection between Hull and Wrexham & Shropshire, and so the Hull Trains operating experience was available for consultation. Their view was that it was necessary to operate a minimum frequency of five services per day before the market could be addressed effectively.*
Here is a Hull Trains 170 unit one of five services from Kings Cross to Hull, taken just north of Arlsey, running at full speed on 31st July 2004. The first stop after Kings Cross for this service is Grantham - so it has a while to run yet.

trailer, or DVT, at the other. So the locomotive pulls the train in one direction and pushes it in the other, with a control system running down the train enabling it to be driven from the cab of the DVT. The attractions of this method of operation are obvious, with fewer locomotives required and no need to attach and detach them at each end of the journey. British Rail started using this method of operation in the 1970s between Edinburgh and Glasgow, and subsequently expanded it to many of the main Inter-City routes in the 1980s. A large number of DVTs were built for the West Coast Main Line at this time, and were made redundant at the same time as the Mk3 coaches, and so they would be available to Wrexham & Shropshire.

A vital aspect of DVT operation is the means of controlling the locomotive. British Rail had used a low frequency electrical signal using an existing circuit within the coaches to achieve this. The system is called time division multiplex or TDM, and was not reliable enough. The team were concerned that the possibility of poor communication using TDM would lead to failure or

Left: One of the acquired DVTs arrives on a low-loader at Axiom for refurbishment. The surplus loco-hauled trains, no longer required after the arrival of the new Pendolinos, lay in sidings at first - but not for long. It was gradually realised that these trains represented an excellent opportunity for those who wanted excellent vehicles for hire at a reasonable price. And there were those in Chiltern who were astute enough to get in there and obtain some as well as WSMR. Needless to say, many are back on the tracks again now - but none have yet been converted to carry passengers. **WSMR**

cancellation of trains and sought an alternative. Fortunately, the EWS company train was operating with a DVT and had already employed a different solution utilising a very robust and separate cable run the length of the train, and linking to the standard American Association of Railroads (AAR) control system used on the Class 67.

How many trains?

By this stage, the rolling stock requirement had been defined. Business case work to establish passenger numbers and revenue had been through a process of development and iteration during 2006 in order to inform the company's business plan and financial projections, and to provide the ORR with clear information. Hull Trains had started running with just three trains a day, and feedback from John Nelson and Mike Jones suggested that it was only once that service had expanded to five trains per day that there was a sufficient critical mass of train service to enable effective marketing. Wrexham & Shropshire proposed to start with five train services each weekday. Projections of passenger numbers indicated that loadings on the peak trains would be below 150 until year five of the business plan. It was calculated that a train which comprised of 20-25% first class would provide the right balance between the two classes, and so 130 standard class seats and 30 first class seats was considered optimal.

The expected timetable meant that three train sets would be required to operate in service each day, and operationally a spare train would allow for cover in the event of failures, and for heavy maintenance requirements. Four train sets each comprising three coaches means a total of 12 Mk3 coaches, four DVT vehicles and four locomotives.

Securing the trains

By April 2007, commercial negotiations with EWS had progressed well, and a deal covering the refurbishment, provision, and maintenance of both locomotives and coaches was being discussed. It was also clear that Porterbrook Leasing were prepared to sell Mk3 coaches and DVTs rather than lease them. EWS were prepared to reach a deal to refurbish the coaches through their subsidiary Axiom, to an agreed price and specification, to construct a maintenance package for the train sets to suit our needs, and were even willing to provide drivers if required during the start-up phase. The ownership of the coaches was also open to agreement – EWS would consider a purchase and lease arrangement, or were equally happy if WSMR owned them.

Discussions with Porterbrook had progressed by May 2007 to the detail of a sale agreement, and specific vehicles were being considered as part of a short list. It was decided that the coaches and DVTs would be purchased by Laing Rail, rather than progressing with a deal in which EWS purchased and leased the trains, in order that the fleet could remain in the ownership of one of the Wrexham & Shropshire shareholders. However, whilst the coaches were available at an attractive price, it was difficult to justify completing the sale without confirmed work for them – and that meant the gaining ORR approval. This was taking longer than anticipated as described elsewhere, and during the summer of 2007 continued growth in passenger numbers across the UK led several other operators to express interest in Mk3 vehicles. So in August 2007, Laing Rail made a speculative purchase of 12 coaches, and took out an on option to purchase the four necessary DVTs, which were not being sought by other operators.

Patterns of light and shade fall on WSMR DVT 82305 as it waits departure time from platform 3 at Wrexham General station. It was soon to leave as 1P13, the 11:23 for Marylebone with 67014 on the rear. 11:13, Tuesday 16th June 2009. **Geoff Plumb**

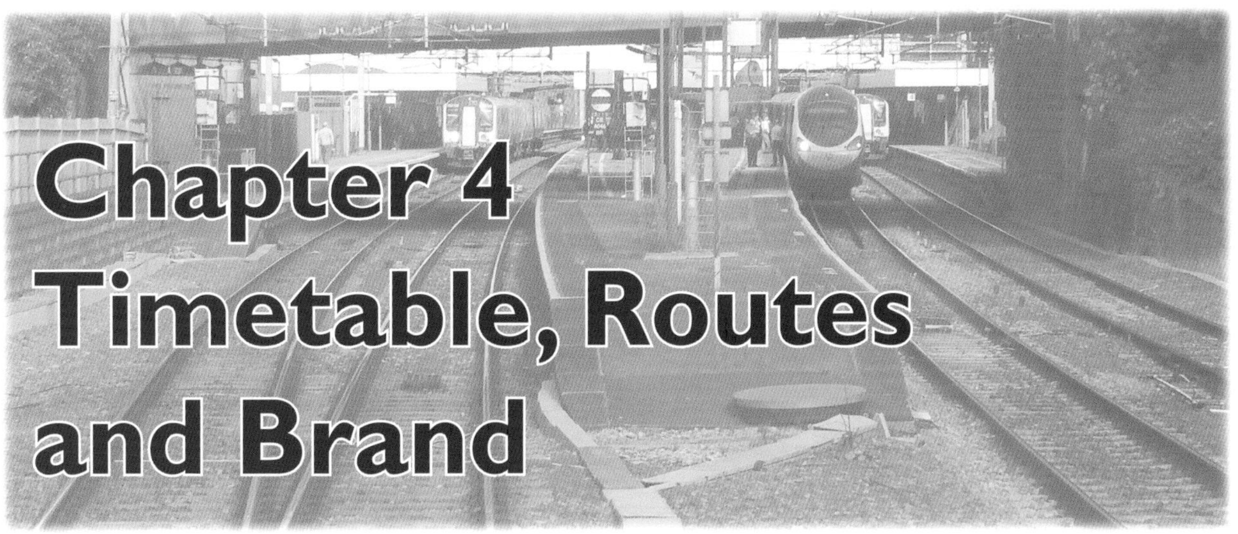

Chapter 4 Timetable, Routes and Brand

The Timetable

The initial work by the Renaissance Trains directors had identified a four trains per day option, from Wrexham via Shrewsbury, Telford and Walsall: major centres, all of which had no through train service to the Capital. After the establishment of the Joint Venture, the whole ethos of service provision was re-examined, and every element of the potential train timetable was revisited as part of an exercise to determine with as much certainty as possible where the northern terminus was best to be sited. Wrexham is 40 minutes by rail, north of Shrewsbury, with a potentially useful hinterland fed by road from the west and towns along the way, like Ruabon, Oswestry, Llangollen. However, Shrewsbury to Wrexham is a long way, if assets can be employed more efficiently on a shorter journey. Perhaps the option of running only to Shrewsbury itself would have been a more cost-effective? In favour of the longer stretch, there were opportunities to capture a larger market, and everyone felt Wrexham would be an attractive place to base the new operation, in Wales,

Weekday Timetable Specification from December 2006 ORR Application

	Set 1	Set 3	Set 2	Set 1	Set 3
Wrexham	05.50	08.00	12.00	15.00	18.00
Gobowen	06.10	08.20	12.20	15.20	18.20
Shrewsbury	0630.	08.40	12.40	15.40	18.40
Telford	06.50	09.00	13.00	16.00	19.00
Wolverhampton	0710.	09.20	13.20	17.20	19.20
Banbury	08s10	10s20	14s20	18s20	20s20
Marylebone	09.15	11.25	15.25	18.25	21.25
	Set 2	Set 1	Set 3	Set 2	Set 1
Marylebone	0735.	10.35	13.35	16.35	19.35
Banbury	08u40	11u40	14u40	17u40	20u40
Wolverhampton	09.40	12.40	15.40	18.40	21.40
Telford	10.00	13.00	16.00	19.00	22.00
Shrewsbury	10.20	13.20	16.20	19.20	22.20
Gobowen	1040.	13.40	16.40	19.40	22.40
Wrexham	11.00	14.00	17.00	20.00	23.00

s - set down only   u - pick up only

This is the WSMR 'operators' timetable. If it could have been managed, it would have offered rather better than the frequency the GWR had done in times past. However the journey times were not much better - and did not call at Birmingham. The 2001 National Timetable shows 3hrs 48 minutes, Wrexham to Euston, with change at Wolverhampton. Although in 2001 a through train taking 3hrs 25mins to Marylebone might have looked competitive, in 2006 the Pendolino age was arriving, and three things happened as a direct result:

1. There was a radical improvement to the Stafford to London frequency and timings.

2. The frequency from Birmingham by Pendolino increased, reducing the wait at Wolverhampton.

3. From Wrexham, going from Chester on a Virgin Voyager, (from 2008) the London, journey could be done in 2hrs 03 mins!

Alas, in addition, the specification adjacent was not met by Network Rail - disaster!

Weekday Timetable Specification from Spring 2008 - as published - v- ORR Application

	Set 1	ORR	Set 3	ORR	Set 2	ORR	Set 1	ORR	Set 3	ORR
Wrexham	05.42	05.50	07.25	08.00	11.10	12.00	15.10	15.00	18.10	18.00
Ruabon	05.49	-	07.32	-	11.17	-	15.17	-	18.17	-
Chirk	05.55	-	07.39	-	11.23	-	15.23	-	18.23	-
Gobowen	06.00	0610	07.44	08.20	11.28	12.20	15.28	15.20	18.28	18.20
Shrewsbury	06.25	0630	08.10	08.40	11.53	12.40	15.53	15.40	18.53	18.40
Wellington	-	-	08.23	-	12.05	-	16.06	-	-	-
Telford	06.42	0650	08.29	09.00	12.11	1300	16.12	16.00	19.12	19.00
Cosford	06.50	-	08.37	-	12.20	-	16.20	-	19.20	-
Wolverhampton	-	-	-	09.20	12s32	-	16s32	-	19s34	-
Tame Bridge	07.15	0710	09.12	-	12.43	13.20	16.43	17.20	19.48	19.20
Banbury	08s33	08s10	10s25	10s20	14s02	14s20	18s02	18s20	21s01	20s20
Marylebone	09.54	0915	11.49	11.25	15.23	15.25	19.22	18.25	22.15	21.25
Transit time	4h 12m	3h 25m	4h 24m	3h 25m	4h 13m	3h 25m	4h 12m	3h 25m	4h 05m	3h 25m
	Set 2	ORR	Set 1	ORR	Set 3	ORR	Set 2	ORR	Set 1	ORR
Marylebone	06.45	07.35	10.17	10.35	13.17	13.35	16.10	16.35	20.03	19.35
Banbury	08u00	08u40	11u29	11u40	14u30	14u40	17u30	17u40	21u14	20u40
Tame Bridge	09.06	-	12.41	-	15.37	-	18.41	-	22.23	-
Wolverhampton	09u25	09.40	12u55	12.40	15u55	15.40	-	18.40	22u36	21.40
Cosford	09.36	-	13.07	-	16.07	-	19.07	-	22.47	-
Telford	09.45	10.00	13.15	13.00	16.15	16.00	19.15	19.00	22.56	22.00
Wellington	09.52	-	13.21	-	16.21	-	19.21	-	-	-
Shrewsbury	10.08	10.20	13.41	13.20	16.38	16.20	19.41	19.20	23.15	22.20
Gobowen	-	10.40	14.07	13.40	17.04	-	20.07	19.40	23.36	22.40
Chirk	-	-	14.12	-	17.09	-	20.12	-	23.41	-
Ruabon	-	-	14.19	-	17.16	16.40	20.19	-	23.48	22.40
Wrexham	10.44	11.00	14.26	14.00	17.23	17.00	20.26	20.00	23.56	23.00
Transit time	3h 59m	3h 15m	4h 09m	3h 25m	4h 06m	3h 25m	4h 16m	3h 25m	3h 53m	3h 25m

s - set down only u - pick up only

Reality is compared here with aspiration. The comparisons were not good. Like many of the 'deals' it seems that this one (over transit times and routes) evidently did not have enough in it to create the glitter in the eye of the authorities than did say, the Virgin deal. Of course it was on a smaller scale but this disappointing result was a 'take it or leave it' offer from Network Rail that was accepted with the view that something better later, would be pressed for with vigour. Had there been a little more prescience in 'Olympia', then more may have been done to ease the path for WSMR. It was not - for reasons outlined in later chapters. Some interesting time comparisons from this timetable are:

***Shrewsbury:** The latest departure permitted from London to allow a 10.00 arrival in Shrewsbury was 06.45. Alas, from Euston the 07.43 with change at Birmingham New Street would put a customer in Shrewsbury at 10.19. Although customers with this aspiration were apparently generally quite scarce.*

***Tame Bridge**: Anyone wishing to access Tame Bridge itself, could leave Euston at 10.43 and with a change at Birmingham New Street, would be there at 12.35 - a transit time of 1hr 52 mins. By Wrexham & Shropshire, the 10.17 from Marylebone arrived at Tame Bridge at 12.41, a transit time of 2hrs 24 mins. It was hardly a surprise then that the tiny segment of the market heading for Tame Bridge was sub-divided to almost zero for WSMR.*

***Wrexham:** To Wrexham the time differences are even less favourable. By the 08.10 train from London Euston, Wrexham could be reached at 10.38 with a change at Chester, a transit time of 2hrs 28mins. WSMR took 3hrs 59 mins. Wrexham & Shropshire it seems was for* bon viveurs *only - a rare breed. The basic frequency of the WSMR timetable was five departures per day. Competitors generally managed an hourly frequency. This timetable was obliged to be accepted if WSMR wanted to run. The intention was to work on it incrementally to reduce transit time, and there was great optimism that this was possible. Part of the problem leading to the WSMR demise was the subsequent inability to reduce throughout journey times enough. Transit via the Stour Valley Line was effectively closed, if Wolverhampton and New Street calls were barred. The slow trip along the Grand Junction was 'set' by the call at Tame Bridge, and that was an unavoidable problem. (for Birmingham routes - see the map on Page 56)*

At Wrexham there was the consideration of the two unused bay platforms at the south end of the station, that were no longer used for anything. This was a potentially useful facility, if it could be used to stable trains in relative security, which would then allow services to originate from Wrexham. It would also allow trains services to be altered short-term in emergency, and provide a platform level entrance for supply and cleaning. This facility elevated Wrexham to the status of front runner as a northern terminus for the planned service.

Mark Edlington

remote from competitor's depots and direct competition for staff, with the real prospect of some funding support for start-up. Positive support from Wrexham Council and the Welsh Assembly clinched the service base at Wrexham. Thus the argument for advancing no further than Shrewsbury was lost. The crucial factor was the existence of the south-facing bay platforms at Wrexham. These bays were relics of busier times in the past, when services began from Wrexham (General) and ran to the Cambrian coast via Ruabon and Llangollen. Since the collapse of the railway mail, newspaper and parcels businesses, the two platforms had lain seldom used. The existence of these bays, still connected to the signalling system, still with track and viable platform edges, meant an economic refurbishment for them to be turned into stabling points for the relatively short trains that were expected to run on the new service. When these features were combined with the availability of office and catering storage space in the station buildings, that had all been refurbished relatively recently, Wrexham seemed ideal. The base was secured, the ORR timetable application was now a clear aspiration and the question of routing had to be settled.

The Available Routes: Wolverhampton to Leamington Spa:

The Stour Valley

Securing a route across the West Midlands had problems. The Wolverhampton to Birmingham Corridor, the Stour Valley Route, is one of the most intensively used pieces of twin-track railway in Britain. The north of Birmingham services run that way, include London services, and all cross-country trains. There are many other local train services that use the line; for example there is an half-hourly local service run to service the intermediate stations for the West Midland Passenger Transport Executive. Obtaining paths on this section with no prior claim, as an incoming 'Open Access' competitor, offered problems. The first response from Network Rail was that there were no paths available. Persistence then indicated that perhaps there may be paths, but at irregular intervals, on an overcrowded section - thus better avoided. The tactics of setting up a clamour, and then waiting in the wings with oft repeated applications, was not tried and tested at that time. It would clearly be a long business to win 'accommodation' from the privileged 'path holders', to nudge a few minutes 'here and there', and so to generate acceptable timetable margins for a rapid dash through the Wolverhampton to Birmingham New St. There was Network Rail sensitivity that 'squeezing' paths for additional trains on the Stour Valley section was taking risks that would hazard timetable reliability. Thus the warnings against campaigning to go that way were serious; path applications would meet outright refusal, and so alternative plans were necessary, at least to begin with, until reliability could be proven, and WSMR rose up the credibility bidding scale. Transit via the Stour Valley route would have been up to 20 minutes faster than the diversion via the Grand Junction.

Via Walsall

No operator offered a direct service between the large town of Walsall (borough pop. 254k) and London, though there are frequent local, electric trains to Birmingham New

Of course the choice is limited by the lines available. The routes used by WSMR trains are marked in red. The box shows the area of detail covered in the central area map (P57), where the central area junctions' influence on routing can be seen more clearly. The green line is the Metro, which of course removed the old GWR line from possible use. The TOCs had already organised their timetables and routes, and as established users, had first claim on line capacity. Timetabled train frequency made it impractical to use the Stour Valley Line from Wolverhampton to Birmingham New Street direct. The capacity on the Grand Junction Line (the original access to the old Birmingham Curzon St station - forerunner of New St) permitted WSMR trains to be routed that way. It will be seen from the story that Moderation of Competition legislation led to the use of Tame Bridge Parkway as the pick-up stop, as Wolverhampton was barred. Once Tame Bridge had been chosen as the stopping point, the diversion via the Grand Junction was inevitable. Transit would have been up to 20 minutes quicker, had the Stour Valley Line and (permitted Wolverhampton replacement) stop been chosen. The commercial arguments for and against this are in the text. There was some capacity that permitted continuation of WSMR trains on the Grand Junction as far as Stechford, to join the congested Rugby and Birmingham Line. This meant longer mileage via Coventry to reach Leamington Spa, and the intended route to Marylebone. Note that once on the Grand Junction, passage via New Street was only avoided by this route. Services routed along the Didcot and Chester Line via Dorridge were obliged to run through New Street - they were not welcome, yet unable to stop by MoC - how silly. **Map © GRushton 2012**

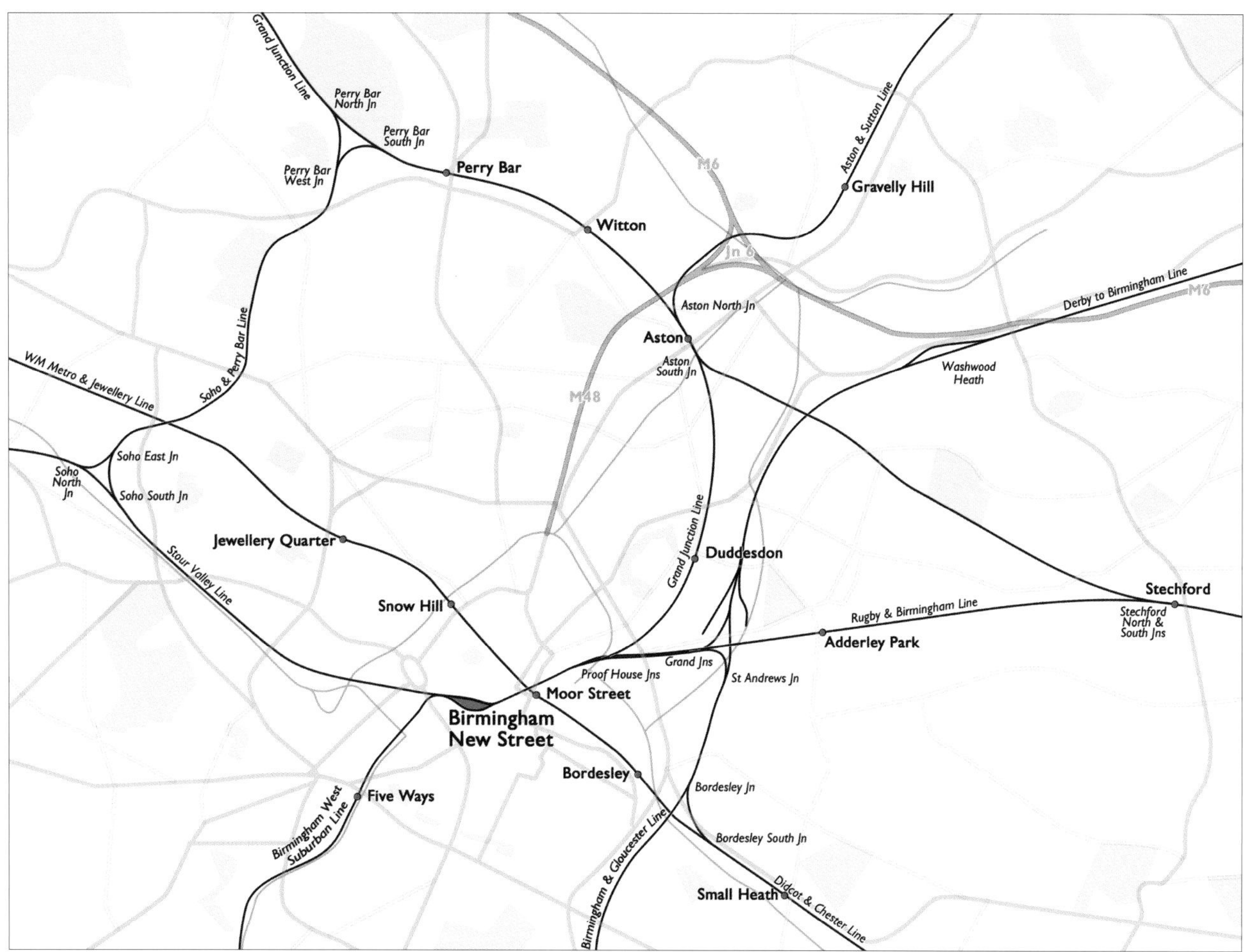

It is hardly surprising that the easiest way through is in via the Rugby to Birmingham Line, and out via the Stour Valley (or v.v.) Birmingham is a paragon of useful junctions, that are almost 'go anywhere' - except ex-GWR to Stour Valley! The problem for Wrexham and Shropshire was how to avoid going through Birmingham New Street (BNS) - this was only possible via Leamington Spa, Coventry and the Stechford-Aston Line. Any train on the Didcot and Chester Line was obliged to negotiate New Street, over complex junctions: Bordesley S, Bordesley, St Andrews, Grand and Proof House. Leaving BNS, the congested Stour Valley Line (and a call at Tame Bridge Parkway) meant diversion through more complex junctions: Soho S, Soho E, Perry Bar W, Perry Bar N, Bescot, Darlaston, Portobello, Crane St, Wolverhampton N, and Oxley. Going via the Grand Junction Line, via Stechford meant competition for paths on the busy Rugby and Birmingham Line. There was no way out of this problem; the old GWR route, via Birmingham Moor St and Snow Hill was no longer on offer, as the Metro occupied a vital part. The routing adopted - as you will see - was part Didcot and Chester Line + Grand Junction, and part Rugby and Birmingham Line + Stechford-Aston and Grand Junction. This was by no means easy. **Map © Gordon Rushton 2012**

Street. Entry to Walsall is direct from the Grand Junction Line via Darlaston and Pleck Junctions. The physical characteristics of routing via Walsall required that the train reverse. This requires little time with either a unit or push-pull train, but it is potentially inconvenient, takes longer to signal, and is more costly in time than a straight station stop. It is possible to go on from Walsall via the Sutton Park line, either to join the North East, South West Line at Castle Bromwich Jn, or even to deviate further via Water Orton and Nuneaton, returning via Coventry and then on to Leamington. Going from Walsall on a slow route used by freight trains was unattractive, and risky operationally. The difficulties of turning west at Castle Bromwich were considerable as the line is very busy; to divert further east, via Nuneaton would have added more miles, making the journey time even longer. The via Walsall option was ruled out on grounds of the extra time for no return - bear in mind that at this stage it was thought possible to make a pick-up stop at Wolverhampton.

Via the Grand Junction to Stechford

Any option that was not via the Stour Valley Line meant a slow crawl round Birmingham, as most of the railway here is slow, and it is a primary route for freight trains, with potential conflicts from the frequent service of local trains, from Walsall and from Lichfield into Birmingham New Street. Today's 'back route' round Birmingham, the Grand Junction opened in 1837. It was the original main line

Crane St Jn gives access to the Stour Valley Line on the right and the Portobello Loop on the left. It is at the south end of Wolverhampton (High Level) Station. The old GWR line entered a tunnel at a lower level on the L/H side. The lines to the left run to Portobello Jn. on the Grand Junction Line, via a much quieter line with only one passenger train a day over it. However there are restrictive speed limits over much of its length. The chances of getting paths over this line were very good. The chances of getting paths over the more rapid Stour Valley Line, were very bad.
Geoff Plumb

running in from Stafford in the north. Birmingham New Street opened in 1846 and since then the Grand Junction has been used for diversions and for freight trains, as well as having a local passenger service over parts of it. It was extended from Aston in 1880 to link with the Rugby and Birmingham Line at Stechford. This bypassed Birmingham New Street, and allowed through freight trains to run direct to the main line at Stechford. If chosen by WSMR trains, in default of the Stour Valley Line, it would take longer, as the Grand Junction Line has many junctions, and restrictions of speed to 30 and 40mph.

Via the Grand Junction Line and New Street

Another routing to avoid the Stour Valley Line was via Birmingham New Street, using the Perry Bar connection, then to and from the ex-GWR main line via Grand Junction and Bordesley. Although there is potentially good running times to be enjoyed north of Leamington Spa, the junctions through New Street are ponderous, added to the delay through the station itself (already mentioned).

The slow access to and from the south of New Street is on the western side, via (N-S) Proof House and Grand Junctions to St Andrews Jn, and then down on to the ex-GWR main line at Bordesley, to travel via Solihull and Leamington Spa, and thus to Banbury. Even so this turned out to be quicker than the option via Stechford, as what may be gained through the running speed that way was lost waiting for paths, dawdling behind local trains, and waiting in Coventry for paths to Leamington.

Transit through the busy New Street Station was hardly welcome. Although paths may exist in theory, in practice any sums of the latenesses of so many trains could conspire to make it likely that the odd train on a through journey would have to stop and wait for clearance, whether it was on time or not. Running through New Street and the Grand Junction Line on the north side requires the use of Soho & Perry Bar Jns. In either direction the amount of traffic of the opposite Stour Valley running line made it likely that a through train would have to pause. In comparison with a train entering from the south on the Rugby and Birmingham Line, and then leaving New Street to run north over the Stour Valley, the complex route that Wrexham & Shropshire was obliged to follow imposed a heavy burden on through journey time; it was unreliable and heartbreakingly slow.

Metro blocks the old GWR route

The old GWR route via Wolverhampton Low Level and Birmingham Snow Hill had been taken over by the Metro tramway. It was electrification that 'did for' the GWR route. The idea of turning the GWR route into a tramway was the first part of a planned, extensive 200km 'Light Rail Transit System', that pioneered the 'easiest ' route, Wolverhampton St Georges - Birmingham (Snow Hill), which opened in 1999. Alas by 2007 (when Wrexham & Shropshire came on to the scene) a combination of short-term thinking and a lack of vision had constrained the tramway development to that one route - without even it's much needed terminal 'balloons'. Perhaps it would have been better if it had remained a conventional railway, as by 2007, Snow Hill and Moor Street had both been rebuilt and were 'buzzing' with growing traffic; the Stour Valley

When routed via the Aston-Stechford Line, to avoid passing through Birmingham New Street, once in the stream, a rapid pace is possible. However the line is very congested, and the hourly stopping service, which by its snail-like progress grabs vast amounts of potential pathing time, occupies a disproportionate amount of line-space. To regain the ex-GWR route, progress is via the Coventry and Leamington Line. It is slow to join, with a 25mph lead-in at Coventry South Junction, and slow to transit. Trips this way were a difficult option.

Geoff Plumb

line was so short of capacity that the old conventional ex-GWR railway would have seen much use. The tramway displays that British knack, of which we shall see more later, of falling between two stools - short-term thinking.

Timetable Frequency

Network Rail was concerned about the effect of Wrexham & Shropshire's search for paths on line capacity. Efforts made to secure attractive timing for the trains did not receive enthusiastic endorsement. It seemed that there was a large wall of 'it can't be done' to climb. This lack of enthusiasm was a key debate, which would be important in the application to the ORR, and would also directly affect the attractiveness of the service.

In addition to journey time, major considerations were:

a. How many trains was it desirable to operate;

b. What was the optimum balance between costs, revenues, paths, and the availability of resources?

Renaissance Trains (promoter of the service) had initially suggested four services per day, but with a shorter route across the West Midlands. They further suggested that with an extended operating day, additional services were possible with the same number of train sets. Their familiarity with the Hull Trains operation indicated that there was a 'tipping point', achieved once the company was operating five trains per day. This was the critical mass of service, which enabled efficient staff rostering and effective marketing. Too few trains, and the business market would be deterred from using the service because there was inadequate flexibility to cater for early and late terminating meetings. This factor accounted for the success that Hull Trains had achieved but it was made more important where there were competing alternative services. By means of a series of discussions and iterations, the Wrexham & Shropshire timetable specification shown at the start of the chapter was compiled, comprising five trains each way on weekdays, spread throughout the day, aimed at business and leisure markets. It was by no means perfect, but the view was taken that once in operation, incremental improvements in journey times would result.

At this stage, Wrexham & Shropshire expected to serve Wolverhampton, offering to Marylebone a quite different service to that of Virgin Trains to Euston. The four stations in Shropshire and north-east Wales were key calling points, as was Banbury, as a connecting station for High Wycombe, Oxford, Reading and the south coast. It is important to observe the anticipated journey times, and in particular the 2¾ hours intended from London to Shrewsbury.

The promoters' aspirations were answered by offers for journey times some 40 minutes longer than those anticipated in the ORR application, and over twice as long as the transit time to Euston from Wolverhampton by the established operator Virgin Trains. In addition there were problems that arose rather suddenly over the application of an agreement with Virgin. The details of this and the problems that had to be overcome are given in the next chapter. Arising problems were met with the view that one does not turn back at the first barrier, after being told that proposals are impractical,. The decision was taken to proceed, expecting that continued presence would lead to satisfied aspirations.

GNER trains conformed with strict design and production guidelines that were co-ordinated for public consumption. The quality standards of service caught the public imagination and growth was spectacular. They were the standard to aim for until the franchise process got in the way.

Brand Values and Marketing Strategy

The base strategy determined that strong brand values be established, and the quality of service to be offered, would be so far ahead of competitors that disadvantages of slower journey time would only be temporary. Like Hull Trains, rapid growth with continuing presence would overcome inferior paths, until customer acclaim would bring both growth, and emergence into profit. This operation would be so good, and prove to be such a public boon, that a niche would be established among the established operators.

Brand

A company's brand is the 'rallying point', the point of differentiation from competitors, and the place to which the attributes of the companies products attach in the public mind - in the customers' minds. In 2006 the 'curly sandwich' image was only just beginning to be dispersed in the public mind by the rather hazy realisation that truly gigantic growth was somehow taking place on the rails, that 'car' was becoming the 'enemy of the Planet' and people were going by train. Uninformed criticism of the railways was still quite a popular sport within the media - realisation that this did not gain the laughs it once had was as slow to dawn as the understanding that the printed media is doomed to the same gradual extinction as the Beeching branch lines. Wrexham & Shropshire needed to position itself carefully, partly as a 'David' against the big operator 'Goliath', partly as a purveyor of a 'special' railway product, of exceptional quality, and as a serious operation, restoring a much-needed service that was ignored by the 'big-boys'. After determining the market positioning of the product on offer, the creation of a strong company brand, to lead and support its products was vital to success. There were already excellent examples in the privatised railway, as there were examples of dismal failure.

The promoters understood that some businesses had become strongly established with a record of continuity of growth over a long enough period to establish a strong brand – GNER, Chiltern Railways, Virgin Trains. Others had seen either a change of franchise ownership or internally driven re-branding. One or two had been consistently unable to satisfy the aspirations of their customer. The Wrexham & Shropshire promoters felt strongly that they needed to avoid the pitfalls that some had found post-privatisation. The new service must not be seen as a routine purchase; the objective was for it to feel special. As a new company in a safety-critical business, WSMR needed to come across as professional. Careful work was needed to identify a level of service that was affordable, but would be seen as outside expectation.

On hand were some excellent people, more than capable of setting up the standards that were being looked for. Neil Bates from Cre'active Design and his branding associate Peter Trickett were brought in, and carefully briefed by Peter Wilkinson who wrote a particularly professional and innovative design brief for Cre'active. He got back a beautifully crafted and carefully worked out Corporate Identity Manual for the new service. Neil and Peter had worked with Chiltern Railways on many rolling stock projects from the Class 168 'Clubman' to the refurbishment of the Class 165 fleet. In this exercise they

Wrexham & Shropshire - Brand Values

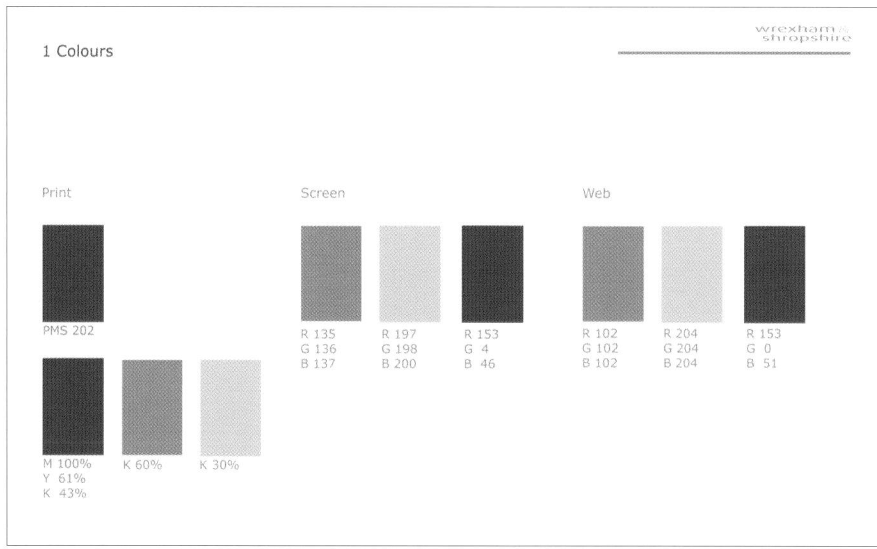

Pages from the Corporate Identity Manual*.* *There were great efforts made by Pete Wilkinson, together with Creactive, to present a restful but 'interesting' travel environment, and to make sure that all the Wrexham & Shropshire communications reflected the 'House Style'. The idea was that a well presented private company, with everything so evidently well thought out, would gain market credibility from such actions. In the early days this was adhered to strictly, and a major effort was made to sell the operation in conformation with these guidelines. Alas, the rather tawdry Cargo D, temporary, hired-in carriages (that saved the day) caused a paradox between the immaculate presentation of the advertising, and the state of the product as experienced in the train.*

excelled in offering a dignified and innovative identity that made the promoters satisfied, and when revealed to the market rapidly established the right positioning, and drew attention to the new service.

It was important to find the right name for the business. The Renaissance directors pointed to the simplicity that the name Hull Trains offered. But either 'Wrexham Trains' or 'Shropshire Trains' was only part of the story and would alienate the missing half. Communication in public with the company's full name The Wrexham, Shropshire and Marylebone Railway Company, quickly shortened to 'WSMR'. However it wasn't thought that such a group of letters would mean much to potential customers, despite the precedence of GNER. All other options which bore no relation to the geography were quickly rejected – it was considered to be of advantage to be associated with the places served. So 'Wrexham & Shropshire' was adopted as the marketing name.

The Brand Values

A lot of thought was given to how the Wrexham & Shropshire service would be differentiated from others. It was one thing setting up route, fares and timings, but it was felt strongly that to 'break the mould' the on-train experience needed to be distinctly better than with other operators. A lot of preparatory work was therefore done to define and set out the brand values, better to conform the product to them. They needed to be 'real' enough to be adhered to strictly when selling the product, to be delivered consistently, and to be noticed by the customers.. This was a vital part of effective marketing.

To clarify thinking, the core values of the business were defined as:

Wrexham & Shropshire will:

1. Always be safe and secure for customers and staff alike
2. Provide outstanding customer service
3. Always provide value for money
4. Reflect passion about what we do – in every aspect of our operation
5. Bring innovations to the market
6. Always be competitively challenging without seeking to cherry pick
7. Be a brand that stakeholders will wish to promote and for which people will want to work

In response to the design brief and the values of the business, the external branding concept was developed. and defined to a practical level. To make the interior design meet these core values, a service level specification was developed. It was determined that "...on every train operated, Wrexham & Shropshire will provide the same level of on-board service...", which would comprise:

- Standard Class and First Class accommodation
- Staff trained to deliver superior customer care
- Complimentary meal and refreshment service in First Class, delivered by a dedicated steward.
- A quality buffet refreshment service for Standard Class
- Laptop and mobile phone power sockets available at all seats
- On-board wifi, complimentary to first class passengers.

It was acknowledged that the approach to on-board service would be a key positive differentiator if the staff presence and service provided was far ahead of that provided by any other TOC on the route (or elsewhere for that matter), and that such a potentially good reputational item would strongly support the core values outlined above.

It was decided that standard class accommodation would comprise superior 2+2 seating, a table at as many seats as practical, adequate space for typically sized laptop computers, ample luggage space, an appropriate number of toilets of high quality, and a buffet service offering a range of high quality, value for money, food and drink.

First customers would be met by the Senior Steward on joining the train, with accommodation comprising:

- Comfortable 2+1 seating with significantly roomier seats than standard class
- A table at every seat with ample space for typically sized laptop computers
- Power sockets
- Adequate luggage space
- Space for wheelchair passengers
- A disabled toilet.

It was planned that the Senior Steward would provide an at-seat service to First passengers, including:

- Coffee or tea on joining the train, and throughout the journey on request.
- A complimentary newspaper
- A complimentary hot or continental breakfast (to choice) before 11.00
- A complimentary hot meal, or cold alternative (to choice), after 11.00 with vegetarian options.

Getting the best from the meals

The approach to First service levels emulated Hull

The new train in all its glory at Wellington, Shropshire on 8th September 2009. This train was almost exactly like the computer simulations that Creactive had created. The sad fact was that it had simply failed to appear, despite promises. It is said that the revenue impact for earlier appearance would have been small. But after all the 'brand value' hype, is this claim believable? A more general view is that like transit and service frequency, the late delivery of the new coaches was just another nail in the coffin. **WSMR**

Trains. The traditional restaurant car service, with a wide range of meals available and cooked to order by a chef, had declined significantly since the days of British Rail, despite highly regarded efforts to enhance and promote this approach by GNER. Other operators tried to reduce costs and wastage, and to improve consistency of service and the general results were reduced portion sizes and plated meals as a complimentary benefit in First only – with standard class customers no longer able to pay for a meal, even if spare capacity existed in the 'restaurant car.' (if there was one). There was comment that food on trains had sunk to a low ebb, except in rare cases. Here was an opportunity to differentiate Wrexham & Shropshire quite sharply from competitors. The main competitor for the service, Virgin Trains, had premium priced first class tickets and offered complimentary first class meals on its services. Experience suggested: that the level of service offered did not meet the expectations of the prices charged; that the service was intrusive, with the staff clattering around, and place settings in the way of those wanting to get on with some work. It was thought by WSMR assessors that there was little demand for the sort of 'snack-plus' catering offer that they offered in differing forms throughout the day. Wrexham & Shropshire sought to differentiate its services in first class by a big improvement on this approach by offering a full meal to those who wanted it, and drinks and snacks to those who did not. The full meals were to be of good quality, local produce, served with a personal touch. The long journey, the thinking went, would allow the staff to seem hospitable rather than intrusive on Wrexham & Shropshire.

The view was that careful calculation of the likely expenses involved to offer this 'proper' service to first class suggested that the costs could be more than recovered through even 'competitive' pricing of first class tickets, and that the favourable reputation gained by decent catering would ensure positive differentiation in favour of Wrexham & Shropshire. At the planning stage the determination to use quality on-board service as a marketing tool was strong. In service, despite the wait for the refurbished coaches, the quality of service on offer was excellent. The plan worked as it became voted as the highest quality service on the network, and all those things so carefully worked out were delivered with pleasure by helpful staff. In addition, the offer at the buffet bar also benefitted from the quality complimentary offer in First. The range of items available to standard class passengers was appreciated. There was enough flexibility on board to extend the meals to standard class as a paid-for option. This went down well, though it seems that tradition has damped down the demand for on-board full-meals.

Looking after the mobility impaired

One factor to be considered in designing train refurbishments is the need to provide wheelchair spaces and wheelchair accessible toilets. Wrexham & Shropshire's train would be relatively short in comparison to typical Inter-City trains with first and standard class accommodation, so therefore at an early stage it was concluded that to minimise the space taken for wheelchair accommodation and toilet, they would only be provided in first class. As a result, a policy was to be adopted whereby any wheelchair users and those travelling with them would be upgraded to First regardless of the ticket they had bought.

Subsequent events drive some to the view that such values were deluded, abstracting effort needed elsewhere.

67024 is topping the train while 67003 is tailing, 5Z63, the 08:33 Banbury to Marylebone WSMR training run, having just emerged from the short Brill Tunnel at 09:01 on Thursday 27th March 2008. **Geoff Plumb**

Chapter 5
Making it Happen

The Wrexham, Shropshire and Marylebone Railway Company Ltd (WSMR) made public its intention to operate an open access service on 31st January 2006, announcing its determination to apply to the Office of the Rail Regulator (ORR) for permission to run trains. It was later in 2006 that looking for something rather more direct and meaningful, the company fixed upon the brand 'Wrexham & Shropshire'. Though the company was referred to by that name, it is notable how frequently railway staff, press and public still used the initials WSMR throughout the life of the enterprise.

It took nearly a year to prepare the application to ORR. This seems a long time but in comparison with other Open Access applications was relatively quick. The length of time such an application takes is a result of the amount of work required, not just to complete the application but to demonstrate with confidence that a number of important issues had been dealt with adequately. It was on 28th April 2008 when the first train actually ran, which is remarkably quick, given the need for the regulatory items to be gone through, all the complex agreements to be reached, the finance to be put into place, the recruitment and provision phases to be achieved, the appropriate paths to be allocated for trains to run and the placement of the new service in the timetables.

Making the case to ORR

The ORR has a vital role in the development and operation of the UK's rail network. The Regulator makes the final decisions on the allocation of network capacity for train services, and agrees and monitors the funding provided for maintenance, renewal and enhancement of the network. Privatisation legislation set two types of application for the ORR to accept to run a new train service, known as Section 17 and Section 18. Whilst both applications are similar in content, a Section 18 application has the support of Network Rail whilst a Section 17 application does not. To secure the support of Network Rail and submit a joint application requires the network operator to be satisfied there is adequate line capacity on the chosen route for the services to run reliably. Support from Network Rail lends a Section 18 application greater weight of course.

During 2006, a large amount of work had been carried out jointly with Network Rail's timetable planners to develop the outline timetable into a set of schedules, taking up train timetable 'paths', that worked with all the other services running on the network. Balancing all the movements on the lines that Wrexham & Shropshire wished to use is no mean feat, and so despite a positive approach from both sides, a difference of opinion emerged. Some of the sections of railway that the trains were intended to run over were some of the most intensively used in Britain - in particular on the line between Wolverhampton and the south of Birmingham New Street. A major timetable change was being planned for the West Coast route, for implementation in December 2008. This affected all trains in the Birmingham area, including those on the route to Shrewsbury, and included a plan very much supported by DfT, to increase service frequency significantly between Birmingham New Street and London Euston. Thus Network Rail felt it could not support the proposal that line capacity would be available for Wrexham & Shropshire's trains after December 2008. The Wrexham & Shropshire team did not share this view, and felt strongly that capacity could be found with a little enterprise. However, the difference in opinion meant that Wrexham & Shropshire was obliged to submit a Section 17 application that rested on the need for convincing ORR that the capacity was

Tame Bridge Parkway is a station built near Bescot on the Grand Junction Railway and opened in 1990. It is served by four services an hour to Walsall and Birmingham New Street. Around are huge housing estates, and its free, large capacity car park is full each morning with commuters' cars. Adjacent is the busy A4031 Walsall Road. There are some 343k users of Tame Bridge annually, nearly 1/10 of Wolverhampton's passenger figure.

indeed available, and could be allocated to its proposed services.

The application to ORR consists of a form which is about 20 pages long. Applicants can improve their chances of success if they can attach supporting evidence, such as socio-economic factors, and stakeholder support. Wrexham & Shropshire's supporting evidence document was 100 pages long. The submission included details of the social and economic characteristics of the area.

> *'The day we submitted our case to the ORR was the very first time they had received a proper market-led submission serving the public interest'* claims Pete Wilkinson, Managing Director of First Class Partnerships.
>
> *'We had done a huge amount of research into the markets, and I really felt not only had there historically been markets for rail, but they had been abandoned. The area is characterised by classic market towns, all seeking to secure inward investment, in total a sizeable and important market, which at the time completely lacked a rail service to London.'*

In addition to the comprehensive supporting evidence, the Wrexham & Shropshire submission also attached a total of 59 letters of endorsement from a variety of individuals and organisations, demonstrating the considerable level of support that had been received. The application was submitted in December 2006. By this point, the company believed it had compelling answers to all the issues ORR might pose.

Moderation of Competition

During the preparation of the ORR application, it became clear there was a problem which would prevent WSMR achieving all of its desired objectives. During the first round of franchise contracts let in the mid 1990s, protection was afforded preventing competition, with protected flows defined in the track access agreement with Network Rail. This protection was called 'Moderation of Competition' (MoC), and it existed for all franchised operators. ORR's 'not primarily abstractive' test was said to require any new service to be inside a 30% limit, which Wrexham and Shropshire achieved. What became apparent in a meeting with Network Rail was that Virgin Trains had enhanced

The station is well served, neat, tidy, and the staff are helpful and polite. It has service north to Rugeley on the Trent Valley Line and to Wolverhampton that with a population surrounding it of 250k, ought perhaps to generate a higher user rate per year. In fact it appears that the populace around are not filled with wanderlust by rail as the unfolding story will reveal. That was not at all obvious in 2007, when WSMR thought they had found a real gem.

protection from competition within their track access agreement for all flows to London until their contract expired in 2012. Thus Wrexham & Shropshire would not be permitted to carry passengers between Wolverhampton and London. In addition to Euston, protection applied to all other London termini including Marylebone; there was no escape. The protection was deemed to apply to all the stations in the West Midlands served by Virgin Trains. These onerous and previously unknown restrictions[1] prevented WSMR from serving Wolverhampton, an important market that had been identified as an opportunity, given that it only received an hourly service throughout the day, and unlike many places was not going to benefit from a frequency increase in December 2008.

In the event, WSMR chose to call at Wolverhampton in order to carry local traffic to and from Shropshire, but the inability to carry traffic to and from London, coupled with the poor running times, was a blow. Similar restrictions were applied to Banbury calls – which initially were set down and pick up only from the north – but this was an active decision designed to avoid competition with Chiltern Railways which might prejudice the ORR approval on grounds of 'cherry picking'. There was no going back.

The company decided quickly to examine alternative sources of revenue that could counteract the loss of Wolverhampton, without undermining the journey time or cost base already established. This was a problem. It might have been possible to structure the timetable to make calls at Smethwick Galton Bridge, or even Sandwell and Dudley on the Stour Valley Line. The former has no car parking to speak of, and the absence of such a vital component ruled it out; though Sandwell has car parking, it was included in the protection and so could not be used. In assessing the alternatives available, Tame Bridge Parkway, near the Black Country town of Walsall and M6 junction 9, appeared to have more potential, with even more car spaces, although it is on the alternative Grand Junction Line. Original proposals that included serving Walsall,

1 The track access agreement, a document in the public domain included this information. It is not clear why this was undiscovered, though it 'was accepted practice for Network Rail to declare information of this kind'. When they did, planning for WSMR was advanced enough to be in the 'we'll deal with this later' camp, along with transit times.

The crew training runs began on Wednesday 21st February 2008, from Banbury, with Driver Steve Roast in charge. The train is topped and tailed by 67017 "Arrow" and 67016, the train itself comprising three Cargo-D Mk.3 first class coaches. Steve peeps out of the leading cab on this historic occasion. **Geoff Plumb**

continued to be ruled out from extended journey times. The well-connected Tame Bridge Parkway with over 250 free parking spaces seemed a better bet than anything else available. The massive local population in excess of 250k can access the station within 15 minutes drive time. So with this number of people in close proximity, Tame Bridge Parkway appeared to offer an attractive alternative market prospect to Wolverhampton. A second submission to ORR, including Tame Bridge Parkway, was made on 5th March 2007, to which there were objections - in particular from Virgin Trains and Arriva Trains Wales.

The ORR's decision

On 3rd September 2007 the ORR announced their decision. Wrexham & Shropshire was to be allowed to offer the services it proposed. On weekdays, five trains would be able to operate in each direction, on Saturdays four could run and on Sundays three. The management team was particularly pleased that the level of service sought had been approved, since the Regulator had the discretion to approve a reduced number of trains if it felt this was appropriate. There was precedent for this in open access applications, since Grand Central had only been granted partial fulfilment of the number of trains it was seeking to operate. Crucially, the ORR also granted approval for Wrexham & Shropshire to run for seven years until 2014. Although the ORR would not under normal circumstances approve applications for network access in excess of five years, Wrexham & Shropshire had indicated in its application a justification, based upon the investment in rolling stock refurbishment and the 'one off' business start up costs that made a longer term appropriate. Duration is a crucial factor in making the business cases viable, and Wrexham & Shropshire had wanted ten years, but seven was considered adequate by the ORR, and that is what they approved.

With approval to commence operations secured, Wrexham & Shropshire now required to put in place the necessary licences, staff and trains before the service could start. The company's six month mobilisation programme to get into service was reviewed, and it was mooted that the first passenger services would run on 28th April 2008.

Recruiting the team

Very early on the team were clear that the staff recruited

The Wrexham & Shropshire Train Manager Team. Left to right - back row: David Gee, Richard Rayworth, Chris Turner, Steve Holt, Rob Smith Front row: Steve Owen, Gaynor Matthews, Alan Riley, Michele Holbrook, Neill Kenderdine (Team Leader), Nikki Roberts, Jane Meredith, Will Flanagan **Wrexham & Shropshire**

to operate Wrexham & Shropshire would have a great influence on the way the customers viewed the company. Staff recruitment started in spring 2007 prior to the ORR decision. It was decided to advertise and interview candidates to determine a short list, even if offers of employment had to wait. It was felt vital that the team should be recruited with excellence in customer service as a priority, and existing skills in the job as a secondary consideration. For the train driver team this was not easy to achieve, because train drivers take over a year to train from scratch so there wasn't going to be time. Thus in advertising for candidates, the company sought qualified train drivers on the basis that conversion to Wrexham & Shropshire's routes and traction could be achieved within six months. Mark Edlington was one of Chiltern's driver managers, and remembers,

'One day Andy Hamilton turned up out of the blue and was asking "how would I get a train from Marylebone to Wrexham?" so we got some Quail maps out. He scurried off with them and I remember saying to myself "I'll never see him again". Andy kept coming back though, much to my surprise. I don't know whether he had the idea he wanted me on the team for a long time or whether it slowly evolved, because I had worked with loco-hauled passenger trains with West Coast and Cross Country.'

Mark's first serious involvement was when he was released one day a week to assist with recruitment of the drivers.

'I interviewed the candidates with Chiltern colleague Jim McCullie in Wrexham. I remember Neil Farm and Paul Belton – both Chiltern drivers – were very surprised when it was me and Jim! Because it was a new company I think they thought they wouldn't know anyone. One of the questions was "did you pass your rules at the first attempt" and they both said "you should know, you took it!"

Things were different for the train manager team. With an expected three month training period, Wrexham & Shropshire could take candidates with no previous railway experience and train them from scratch. So the company set out to find the right kind of people for the business from day one. It was felt that it would be beneficial if a

In 1960, BR(WR) built single units for augmenting multiple unit train formations and branch line use. They have survived the years to become Class 121, and some were acquired by Chiltern for the Aylesbury - Princes Risborough Branch. They have proved to be useful for driver training/road-learning duties, and have been hired by Chiltern Railways to other TOCs. On Thursday 4th February 2010, 960014 was held at signal AW151, protecting Acton Wells Junction, for a considerable time, as it was now running ahead of schedule, so gave the opportunity to alight to get a shot from the trackside.

Wrexham & Shropshire

small number of the team had done a similar job before, as either a train manager, conductor or guard, but that this wasn't necessary for the majority. Advertisements were placed in the Wrexham local press, and the company was astonished with the positive response. Over 200 applied for a total of 13 train manager jobs, so the team then had to work through each of them to decide how many could be directed to the assessment centre, which became the stuff of legend. Three contrasting elements were put together – an interview, a group exercise, and some tests. The group exercise put several candidates together in a room to discuss and debating relevant issues, such as how a new train company might implement marketing. Successful candidate Rob Smith recalls,

'We had no idea what it meant to be a train manager until Andy and Richard explained the role and what was expected of us.'

At this time, three applications emerged from people with valuable experience which could be put to greater use. Neill Kenderdine was a time-served railwayman with the right credentials to take a leading part in the training of the train managers, and ultimately to lead the team. Diane Davidson had a wealth of experience in on-train catering, and Charlotte Price was leading safety management at Hull Trains. All three were asked if they would help with the company's mobilisation, and all three subsequently became part of the management team. The successful candidates joined the management team in waiting over the summer of 2007 for the ORR decision, so when the announcement came it was fantastic news not just for the company but for the 25 prospective employees who were hoping to work for the company. Suddenly everything was happening. The driver and train manager teams received their job offers, and the process of recruiting the steward teams was able to start.

Training the team

Once ORR approval had been received, Andy set the date for services to start operating – the 28th April 2008.

'It was a big ask to get ready for 28th April' recalls Mark Edlington *'but all the drivers and train managers were great. There was no contingency and they really got stuck in.'*

Training support company RPD were brought in to assist with training plans, timescales and supporting materials. Nearly all the drivers were moving on to loco work for the first time and RPD came up with the idea of training trains. Two trains were operated, one based at Crewe and covering Wrexham, Shrewsbury and Wolverhampton, and the other at Banbury covering the south end of the route. Chiltern's route learning bubble car was also used around Birmingham.

Chiltern driver Steve Roast was asked to get involved with Wrexham & Shropshire, initially to support the training.

'I said yes immediately because I thought it was an opportunity to work in a brand new company and start fresh. The only others who had done that at the time were Hull Trains and Grand Central – new rail companies for the first time in over 100 years – so I

The cab of 960014 offers the conventional controls of a first generation DMU, with the addition of new safety equipment. These trains had been built with glass screens behind the driver, and at the time of their introduction this was a great delight to passengers. Now in their semi-retirement it was what made this unit an excellent tool for road-learning for drivers, saving a great deal of time and expense. Steve Roast is at the controls as the unit cruises the lines to be learned with an audience of drivers watching from inside the vehicle.

Geoff Plumb

thought I'm going to go for that.'

Steve started with British Rail in 1979 and had lots of locomotive experience, including with Class 67s as a Royal Train Inspector. Steve's claim to fame is that he drove both the first and last Wrexham & Shropshire trains – neither of them passenger services.

'Andy Hamilton asked me to refresh on Class 67s, so I arranged with DBS for Wrexham & Shropshire to hire a special from Old Oak Common to Westbury and back – and that was the first train run by the company.'

DBS Special Old Oak Common to Westbury 04.02.08

5Z67 ThO 09+51 Old Oak Common C.S. (EWS)

Old Oak Common C.S. (EWS) 09+51; Old Oak Common East 09/55 ->CL2; Kensal Green C.Serv.Plt. a0959 d10+19; Old Oak Common East 10/23 ->RL1; O.O.Common Reception Line 10/24 ->; Old Oak Common West 10/25 ->RL1; Friars Jn 10/26 ->RL; Acton Main Line 10/27 (1); Acton West 10/29 (2); Southall 10/34 (3); Heathrow Airport Jn 10/39 (4); Slough 10/49 (6); Maidenhead 11/00 (2); Twyford 11/08 ->ML; Twyford West 11/09 (1); Reading [Plat 4] 11/15 -> (11); Southcote Jn 11/28; Theale Loop a1134 d11+40; Newbury 11/55; Bedwyn 12/04 (3); Woodborough 12/15; Lavington 12/21; Heywood Road Jn 12/25; Westbury [Plat DR] a1227 d13+27; Heywood Road Jn 13/29; Lavington 13/33; Woodborough 13/39; Bedwyn 13/47; Newbury 13/56 (10); Southcote Jn 14/16; Reading [Plat TL] 14j25 ->RL; Twyford 14/30 (2); Maidenhead 14/38 (8); Slough 14/51 (2); Heathrow Airport Jn 14/59 (2); Southall 15/03 (3); West Ealing 15/09 (1); Acton West 15/12 (1); Old Oak Common East 15/16 ->CL2; Kensal Green C.Serv.Plt. a1520 d15+40; Old Oak Common East 15/44 ->; Old Oak Common C.S. (EWS) a15+47

The trains won't be ready!

Refurbishment of the coaches had commenced with Axiom near Stoke on Trent in the autumn of 2007. The bad news came back that it was unlikely that all the vehicles would be complete in time for the launch of the service in April 2008. This situation became worse, and worse, so that as the launch date got closer, it became clear that none of the coaches would be ready. To avoid a major crisis, the team was faced either with finding stop-gap vehicles or delaying the launch (which was probably worse). Mk3 Coaches had been hired in from Cargo-D to make up trains to assist in staff training and timing runs, and they agreed that these could be available to start the business. However they didn't have enough standard class coaches or buffet cars. Chiltern had acquired vehicles that did not form part of the refurbishment programme, and together with those from Cargo-D, there were sufficient Mark 3 coaches of the right types to form the necessary sets of coaches to get the service running without delaying the launch. John Davidson was still working in Chiltern Railways at this time, but got involved in some of the preparations.

"One of my first Wrexham & Shropshire memories has to be helping on the timing runs between London and Banbury. One day we were joined by Adrian Shooter, and conversation quickly turned to the stock. It had become clear that the silver sets would not be ready for launch day but the company was determined to start services on time. We walked through the train judging if it was presentable enough for passenger service and concluded it would do for a few weeks."

Wrexham sidings

A major advantage to the Wrexham site, and one that endorsed its suitability the availability of a pair of sidings

(continued on page 77)

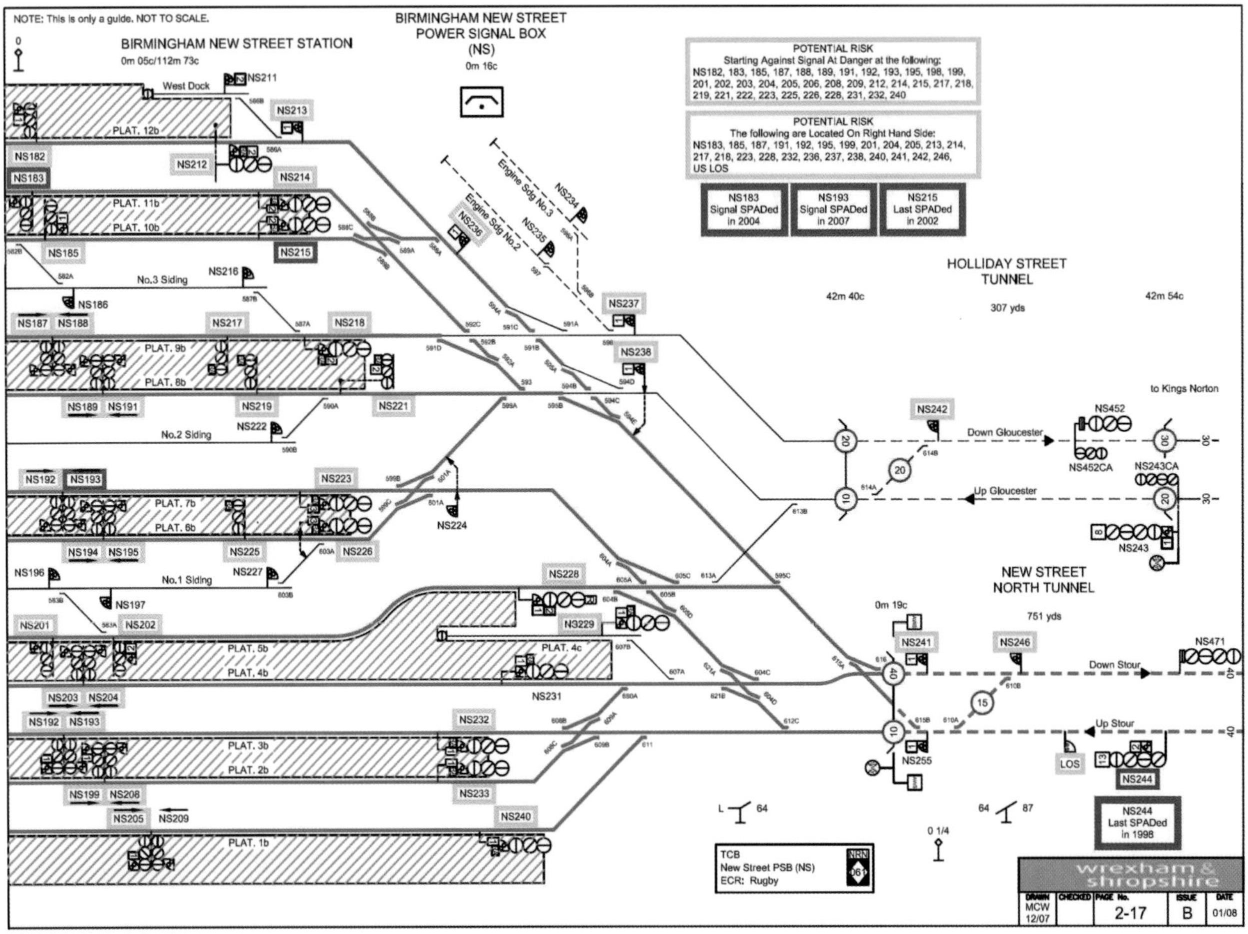

NOTE: This is only a guide. NOT TO SCALE.

BIRMINGHAM NEW STREET STATION
0m 05c/112m 73c

BIRMINGHAM NEW STREET POWER SIGNAL BOX (NS)
0m 16c

POTENTIAL RISK
Starting Against Signal At Danger at the following:
NS182, 183, 185, 187, 188, 189, 191, 192, 193, 195, 198, 199, 201, 202, 203, 204, 205, 206, 208, 209, 212, 214, 215, 217, 218, 219, 221, 222, 223, 225, 226, 228, 231, 232, 240

POTENTIAL RISK
The following are Located On Right Hand Side:
NS183, 185, 187, 191, 192, 195, 199, 201, 204, 205, 213, 214, 217, 218, 223, 228, 232, 236, 237, 238, 240, 241, 242, 246, US LOS

NS183 Signal SPADed in 2004

NS193 Signal SPADed in 2007

NS215 Last SPADed in 2002

HOLLIDAY STREET TUNNEL
307 yds
42m 40c
42m 54c

NEW STREET NORTH TUNNEL
751 yds
0m 19c

NS244 Last SPADed in 1998

TCB
New Street PSB (NS)
ECR: Rugby

wrexham & shropshire

DRAWN	CHECKED	PAGE No.	ISSUE	DATE
MCW 12/07		2-17	B	01/08

This Page - Above: *It was essential to have route knowledge for all the places encountered, and that meant knowing all routes through Birmingham New Street - stopping or not. This is the diagram of the north end, supplied as an aid to memory. Getting it right was mandatory.*

This Page - Left: *Operations Manager Mark Edlington (left) discusses the Birmingham New Street route diagram with Driver Peter Ward, when getting to grips with what was expected. No passengers could be picked up or set down on the services scheduled to run through the station. However, it was quite likely that the train would be stopped waiting for a path in the traffic.* **Mark Edlington**

Page Right - Above: *The paths through the junctions at Shrewsbury were complex - this is the route for the south end of the station. Shrewsbury, even in 2010, was predominantly signalled with semaphores, and there is a mixture of upper and lower quadrant, plus there are some colour lights too.*

Page Right - Below: *This was the largest remaining array of semaphore signals still left in Britain in 2010, and Severn Bridge Junction signal box was the largest mechanical signalbox on the system. Here is the driver's view on approach from the south, with the road set into platform 3 - a regular routing for Wrexham & Shropshire trains. You can see the signal SBJ 124 the grandest of them all), marked in the centre of the map at the top of page 73.*

Geoff Plumb

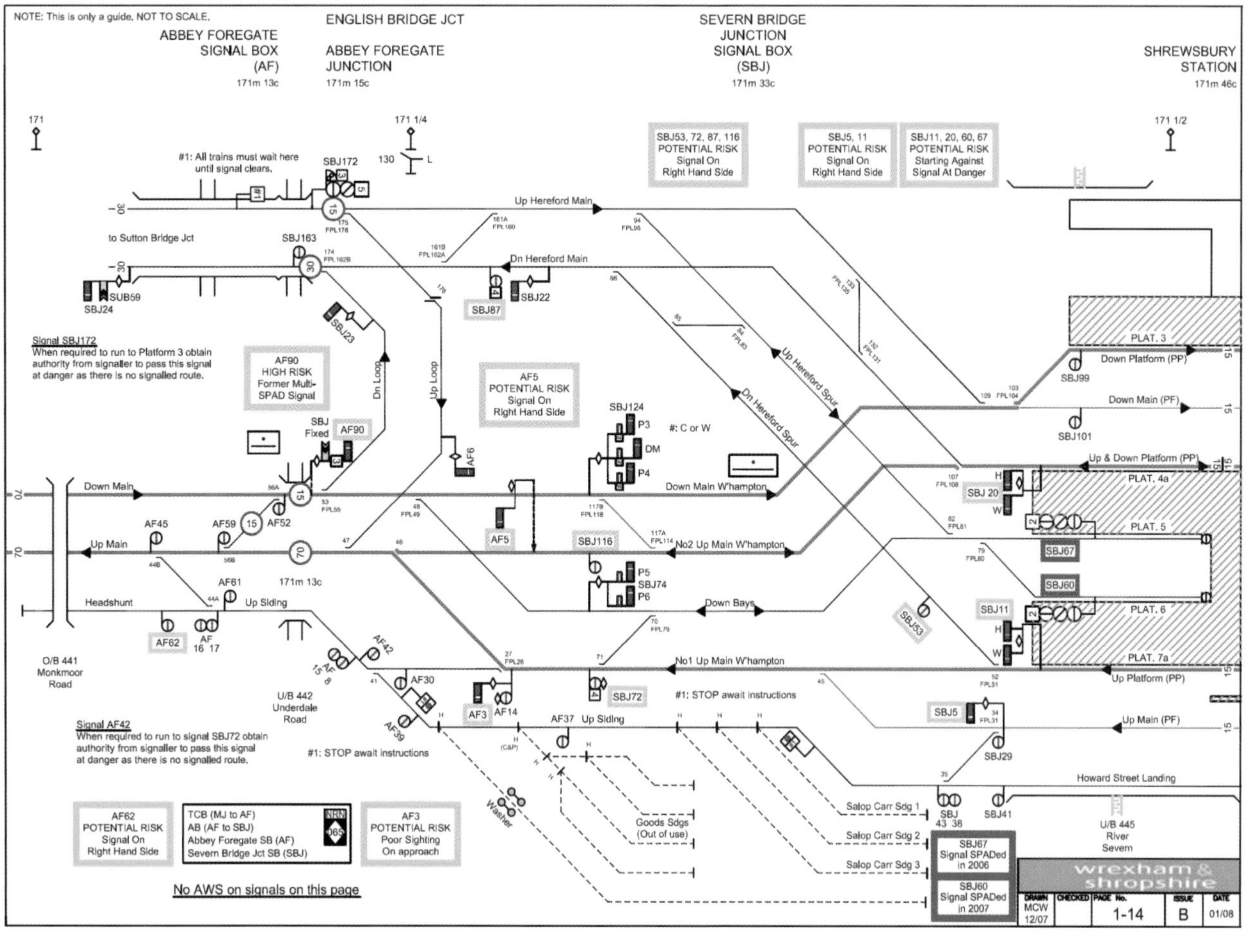

NOTE: This is only a guide, NOT TO SCALE.

ABBEY FOREGATE SIGNAL BOX (AF) 171m 13c

ENGLISH BRIDGE JCT

ABBEY FOREGATE JUNCTION 171m 15c

SEVERN BRIDGE JUNCTION SIGNAL BOX (SBJ) 171m 33c

SHREWSBURY STATION 171m 46c

#1: All trains must wait here until signal clears.

to Sutton Bridge Jct

Up Hereford Main

Dn Hereford Main

Up Hereford Spur

Dn Hereford Spur

Dn Loop

Up Loop

Down Main

Up Main

Headshunt

Up Siding

Down Main W'hampton

No2 Up Main W'hampton

No1 Up Main W'hampton

Down Bays

Down Platform (PP)

Down Main (PF)

Up & Down Platform (PP)

Up Platform (PP)

Up Main (PF)

PLAT. 3

PLAT. 4a

PLAT. 5

PLAT. 6

PLAT. 7a

Howard Street Landing

#: C or W

Signal SBJ172
When required to run to Platform 3 obtain authority from signaller to pass this signal at danger as there is no signalled route.

AF90
HIGH RISK
Former Multi-SPAD Signal

AF5
POTENTIAL RISK
Signal On
Right Hand Side

SBJ53, 72, 87, 116
POTENTIAL RISK
Signal On
Right Hand Side

SBJ5, 11
POTENTIAL RISK
Signal On
Right Hand Side

SBJ11, 20, 60, 67
POTENTIAL RISK
Starting Against
Signal At Danger

O/B 441 Monkmoor Road

U/B 442 Underdale Road

U/B 445 River Severn

Signal AF42
When required to run to signal SBJ72 obtain authority from signaller to pass this signal at danger as there is no signalled route.

#1: STOP await instructions

Goods Sdgs (Out of use)

Washer

Salop Carr Sdg 1

Salop Carr Sdg 2

Salop Carr Sdg 3

AF62
POTENTIAL RISK
Signal On
Right Hand Side

TCB (MJ to AF)
AB (AF to SBJ)
Abbey Foregate SB (AF)
Severn Bridge Jct SB (SBJ)
NRN 065

AF3
POTENTIAL RISK
Poor Sighting
On approach

SBJ67
Signal SPADed
in 2006

SBJ60
Signal SPADed
in 2007

<u>No AWS on signals on this page</u>

wrexham & shropshire

DRAWN	CHECKED	PAGE No.	ISSUE	DATE
MCW 12/07		1-14	B	01/08

Above: *67016 departs Princes Risborough with the first southbound run of Wrexham & Shropshire's training special, 5Z23, the 14:02 from Banbury to Marylebone on 22nd February 2008. Chiltern 165 017 forms the 13:54 Marylebone - Bicester North service.*

Below: *67013 and 67014 top and tail 5Z68, the 17:41 Banbury - Crewe crew training train, returning for servicing. Seen at Great Bourton just north of Banbury, running a few minutes early on Friday 11th April 2008. Note the Mk3 sleeper in the formation.* **Both Geoff Plumb**

Above: *67014 and 67013 are stabled on the upside at Banbury station on 11th April 2008. The training train had not run either of its possible trips and was waiting to return to Crewe LNWR for servicing over the weekend. The engines had been released the previous week in the new livery.*

Below: *67020 leads its train at 75mph through to the Chiltern Line at Aynho Junction. 14:06, on Wednesday 2nd April 2008. This junction was extensively remodelled in 2011, and the speed limit was raised to 90mph - too late for Wrexham & Shropshire.* **Both Geoff Plumb**

67014 and 67013 top and tail 5Z63, the up morning training run, 08:33 from Banbury to Marylebone. This was the first time the dedicated locos had worked in traffic, here approaching Ashendon Junction at 09:07 on the morning of Wednesday 9th April 2008. **Geoff Plumb**

Right: *This is a view of the two bay platforms undergoing refurbishment at Wrexham. This made the service practical, as it added a safe and easy access to the trains for cleaning machines, food, rubbish removal etc. Also added were watering facilities to allow the toilet and buffet car tanks to be filled, and power connections to allow the 250vAC sockets to be used on the trains without the need for a running locomotive to be attached to the train. The location was also secure, as well as being long enough to store WSMR trains, one on each platform.*

Mark Edlington

Left: *Wrexham (General) Station has been looked after and in consequence has a pleasant appearance. The Wrexham & Shropshire operations offices were established here, and a cafe was also opened in the station. The Welsh Assembly Government, jointly with Network Rail provided the upgrades needed to operate the service, and together with train service improvements, such as the Arriva Trains Wales, Holyhead - Cardiff and Virgin, Wrexham-London trains, the range of destinations improved greatly. The work was central to WSMR operations.*

(continued from page 71)

at the southern end of Wrexham General station, ideal for overnight stabling of the two trains required to start the service from the north each morning. Those south-facing bays had been provided years ago for the originating trains like the service to Bala, and both sidings had platform faces. This was a real bonus in this time of health and safety, as level, easy access was available to the coaches for cleaning and servicing. One could get cleaning machines on to and off the trains, and rolling rubbish containers, and trolleys with food had easy access. Of course the sidings were not in great condition, having seen little use for many years – although all the track and signalling was in place and functioning. Additional services were required to permit the servicing of today's trains and so a project developed jointly with Network Rail and funded by the Welsh Assembly was instituted to do this. A water supply was needed to refill toilet and buffet car tanks, and an electrical supply was installed to allow the lighting and power supplies in the coaches to be live so that the coaches could be cleaned without the need to keep a locomotive attached and running. The fabric of the sidings and their surrounds needed to be refurbished and this was done also.

Right: The visit of the EWS Company train to Wrexham on 29th September 2006 proved a number of things, one of which was the potential loading point for the proposed Wrexham & Shropshire service. The Wrexham (General) island platform did not have the benefit of the long canopy on the Up side, indeed stairs had to be negotiated from street to train, but it did have the advantage of not being in great demand. Thus the train could sit there during turnround almost without restriction, so when the service started, it did so from this platform.

Wrexham& Shropshire

Left: Neill Kenderdine examines one of the new Avantix ticket machines in the office at Wrexham on 27th April 2008, just before the start of service. As can be seen, the offices are not yet quite ready - but good enough to get the service started. The Avantix machine was the 'industry standard' in 2008, and allowed excellent, flexible ticketing on-board, which is always a vulnerable spot for small railway companies. With Avantix, the money went into to till straight away - they were a worthwhile expenditure.

Mark Edlington

Staff accommodation

The joint project with Network Rail and the Welsh Assembly also included accommodation for the staff who would work the trains, all of whom were to be based at Wrexham General. Back in 2007, the ticket office and waiting room at Wrexham General only occupied one quarter of the building, with the remaining three quarters vacant. This vacant space in the building was ideal for staff accommodation and so Wrexham & Shropshire eventually leased it from a reluctant Arriva Trains Wales, who initially refused. The joint project refurbished the space, installing heating and lighting as well as locker rooms, a secure cash room, a signing-on point and mess facilities, plus a small office and meeting room. There was even an opportunity to use some of the space for a café for the general public, although this was not taken up immediately given the priority of getting the train service up and running.

The programme developed with Network Rail for completion of the sidings and staff facilities at Wrexham faced a few challenges along the way, and so it was touch and go whether every single essential item would be ready in time for the launch on 28th April. In the end a number of items were not ready in time, including the heating

The Wrexham & Shropshire "Staff Special", 1Z77, is moving quickly towards the Capital with its load of staff members, complete with a complement of the next generation, looking forward to their day out in London. This was prior to the commencement of the public service on the following Monday. It was the first time the train had run at a weekend, and to make room for the demand it consisted of four coaches. The 'Managers' looked after the invited guests of staff and their families. Here, Wrexham & Shropshire Chairman Adrian Shooter supplies the demands of younger guests, and receives some tips on what goes down best.
Wrexham & Shropshire

system which took several weeks to sort out. Poor luck of course dictated that May 2008 was unseasonably cold, and Mark Edlington describes the offices as:

'a building site – they were fitting heat exchanging equipment, and dust was falling inside the building. There was no glass in the internal partition wall, and drilling was going on all day long – but we couldn't do anything else. It didn't stop the train service from commencing as planned.'

The offices at Wrexham were not large enough to accommodate the whole team, so a small office was also established at The Pump House, near Shrewsbury station. This was the headquarters with all non-operational functions based there, including finance, sales and marketing. Whilst a split location was not ideal for a small company it did mean it had an established base in both key towns on the route.

Staff special

On Saturday 26th April 2008, two days before operations commenced, a special train was arranged from Wrexham to London Marylebone to give staff and their families a day out. It was a chance to allow people to mingle, to see the size and strength of the enterprise, and to engender some team spirit. It certainly worked - everyone was highly enthusiastic, and like railway folk everywhere, the team bonded. One useful and indicative message of what was to follow was the presence of the bosses acting as hosts, with Adrian Shooter serving the staff on the journey. It could not have been a clearer message to the whole team that this new service really was intended to be inclusive - and you could just 'talk' to the Managing Director and the Chairman. This symbolic special was an excellent way to mark the end of the training period uniquely. It was, after all, the last opportunity to bring together all of the operational staff, because with shift patterns and lodge turns, there would never be another occasion when everyone could be together. It was clear from the feedback that this gesture had been highly effective. People said that they were appreciative to see who their colleagues were, and even more, to see without flowery speeches, that the people who ran the enterprise really were committed - and what's more, they were listening. It was the beginning of the process that allowed Wrexham & Shropshire to punch so far beyond its weight, despite the fact that so many factors later turned against it.

The first southbound service operated by Wrexham & Shropshire was 1P01, the 05:42 from Wrexham to Marylebone. It was made 15 minutes late after departing Wrexham, due to a power-controller problem, and was 25 minutes late arriving at Wellington when the fault recurred. The leading engine, 67025, was failed at this point. 67026 was installed at the head, and by Wolverhampton the train was 57 minutes late. Here it has reached Princes Risborough, still with the two locos on the front, but now only 38 minutes late at 09:48 en route to Marylebone. Monday 28th April 2008.

Geoff Plumb

The launch

28th April 2008, launch day, was the culmination of several years planning, and nine months of hard slog, to get the service up and running. It felt as though few in the railway industry had wanted Wrexham & Shropshire to succeed. Other operators, worried they would lose passengers and revenue, had fought a determined campaign to convince the Office of Rail Regulation to refuse the application. Network Rail, whilst not deeply opposed, had been extremely concerned at the impact on punctuality, particularly through the West Midlands where a new timetable with considerably more trains was due to launch later in the year. On the other hand, the support received from the local community was astounding. Business, politicians, local organisations and the general public had supported the application with letters and many, many positive comments. And in Wrexham, the team had been overwhelmed by the quality and quantity of people coming forward and wanting to work for the company.

A small number of stakeholders and press had been invited to a pre-launch special on 24th April, which received a very positive response and some good press coverage. Now the Great and the Good were invited to join the celebratory send-off of their restored through services to London. The launch concentrated on what was considered to be the main target markets, Wrexham, through to Telford. It must be said that some, who were expected to take an interest, did not. For example, the people of Walsall remained indifferent to Wrexham & Shropshire throughout its existence. Perhaps this is what comes of having two mighty motorways carving through your patch. In fact it was the Welsh Assembly Government, supported by Wrexham Council who were most interested in the new opportunities for Wrexham - and as had been said before, WAG put their hands in their pockets to fund the refurbished bay platforms that formed the depot. They attended the launch, and it was Ieuan Wyn Jones AM, Deputy First Minister of Wales himself who unveiled the plaque marking the investment. Shropshire folk were also enthused with the new through service to London, and three local MPs travelled to London on the first day, pronouncing it wonderful and promising continued custom.

FLEET- Brakes on Unit 67025 at Wrexham General
28/Apr/2008 0556
2/08/WAS

wrexham & shropshire

Event Summary

0556 - NR (Manchester TRC) reports 1P01 0542 Wrexham-Marylebone departed 14 mins late from Wrexham after having been unable initially to obtain brake release. WSMR On Call (ME) informed.

0612 - Andy H reports additional info regarding 1P01 brought to a stand after having departed Wrexham station, following a dragging brake indication, that Driver Belton was subsequently able to resolve.

0648 - NR (Midland Lines) report 1P01 standing on the approaches to Wellington station. Mark Edlington informed.

0700 - NR (Midland Lines) report 1P01 engine will be running round at Wellington.

0710 - Mark Edlington updated. With two locomotives on the leading end, it will present a problem at Marylebone being unable to depart back out. Mark will investigate the possibilities.

0715 - Run round move observed in place at Wellington.

0730 - Guard Rayworth reports two locos have been successfully coupled up and driver is conducting a brake test.

0732 - 1P01 departed Wellington 56 mins late.

0735 - Mark Edlington is liasing with EWS to obtain a rescue locomotive to attend Marylebone, to attach to the trailing end on arrival.

0740 - Andy Hamilton reports in the event of any doubt with the above plan, then the service is to be cancelled at Banbury.

0815 - Potential option to run ECS from Banbury to Oxford and run round again discussed and agreed and feasible.

0830 - Mark Edlington reports fresh locomotive available to attach the train at Marylebone. However, EWS have stated that the return train is unable to run with two locomotives on the trailing end of the train. With the Up Siding not being permissive, the defective locomotive is not able to be detached and then the carriages be reattached. Wembley Depot report that they are not able to accomodate the formation there to enable detaching and reattaching. Unable to run round at Banbury because the south end crossover has been out of use since June 2007.

0835 - Discussed and agreed with Andy Hamilton to cancel 1P01 at Banbury and run ECS to Oxford. Driver Johnson will conduct 5P01 from Banbury to Oxford. NR (TRC) and Oxford PSB agreed plan.

0855 - Andy Hamilton requests formation to run and divide at Marylebone, with the dead locomotive remaining in the formation. The good locomotive will then follow light. New arrangements discussed and agreed with NR (TRC) and Oxford PSB.

1030 - 0Z67 appears on TMIS ex-Wembley Mainline. 1P01 terminates 36 mins late.

1035 - 0Z67 running via Neasden [Midland] Junction from Acton, rather than prescribed route via South Ruislip.

1114 - 1J81 departs Marylebone 57 mins late.

1118 - 0J81 departs.

16:00 advised by R. McLennan that 1P33 will terminate at Banbury and 1J84 will start from Banbury.

16:46 1P33 15:10 Wrexham - Marylebone has departed 96 minutes late.

18:30 call recieved from M. Eddlington who has asked if 20:00 1K61 could depart 3 minutes late as 1J84 is starting from Banbury DCM has agreed to this. Marylebone TCS instructed to advise DSM.

Repercussions
1G26 11:20 Marylebone - Snow Hill terminated 13 minutes late.
1J81 10:17 Marylebone - Wrexham terminated 69 minutes late.
1P33 15:10 Wrexham - Marylebone part cancellation
1J84 20:03 Marylebone - Wrexham part cancellation

Report

***Right:** Looking at the very small amount of stock on the buffet car visible behind Caroline Quiney, be assured that the complete stock takes up a whole load more space. It was loading and sorting the stock for the third buffet car that was delivered late to Crewe that seemed interminable. It was an enormous effort to be made at the end of a long day. The job couldn't be done at Wrexham as the sidings were not ready!*

Gordon Rushton

***Left:** On the first day of full operations by Wrexham & Shropshire, much ran as it should. Here, 67014 tops and tails with 67012, as 1J83, the 16:10 from Marylebone to Wrexham approaches Haddenham at 17:04. All had returned to normal on the afternoon of Monday 28th April 2008, and the morning's excitement had gone away.*

Geoff Plumb

Challenges right from the start

In the week prior to launch the trains were prepared for service at Crewe. On Sunday 27th April, the day before launch, most of the on-board team were needed for the final preparation work. During the afternoon, one of the three train sets had been sent empty to London, to be in position for the first northbound working on Monday morning. However, there had been an emerging problem with the other two that required vigorous attention. Some of the hired Cargo-D coaches were being used by Hull Trains two days before, but they were still stuck in Hornsey depot in north London at 15:00 on Sunday trapped-in by engineering works. They did not arrive until 21:30, precipitating a huge effort to shunt them into the right order that took over an hour. Everyone then got stuck in, stocking up the buffet cars, putting up posters, and making sure marketing materials such as timetables were available on the train. The route from the car park to Crewe Carriage Shed saw a procession of trolleys with the stock, a task that needed multiple trips backwards and forwards, and took much longer than expected. Trips were made in search of chips and pizza to sustain 'the troops' – no easy feat on a Sunday night in Crewe, and preparations including stocking up were still going on at 02:00.

Left: *On Monday 28th April 2008 the first day of public passenger services the majority of the new services operated by Wrexham & Shropshire ran faultlessly. Here is the first northbound working from Marylebone to Wrexham, 1J80, the 06:45 departure, approaching Princes Risborough slightly early at 07:24 on the lovely Spring morning upon which the service began. The leading locomotive is 67014 and 67012 brings up the rear.*

Geoff Plumb

The first Up service, the 05.42 departure from Wrexham, ran empty from Crewe via Chester. It left on time without ceremony, as this was an uninviting hour for a civic send off. It hadn't even got out of sight of Wrexham General Station before the locomotive shut down. Paul Belton, who was the driver, got it going again but it repeated this performance at Wellington. When the controller was moved into its final position - a normal place soon after starting - the engine shut down. The controller was faulty. Mark Edlington was supervising the operations from Wrexham, and when Paul Belton reported the fault he became determined that this first train was going to get to London, come what may. So the rear locomotive was rapidly brought to the front, and the train proceeded. Alas, Network Rail control pointed out that this was not a viable solution, as when it got to Marylebone, the locomotives would be trapped. Thus, in the absence of any alternative plan, the train would have to terminate at Banbury. Wrexham & Shropshire people were finding that they were made of sterner stuff. Mark rang the locomotive's owner, DB Shenker, and arranged for a locomotive to be driven to Marylebone to bring the train back from London, thus the first train arrived 36 minutes late.

The first Down service, the 06.45 from Marylebone ran to timetable. In Wrexham, Managing Director, Andy Hamilton, having worked right through the night at Crewe, was there to welcome the invited guests and to conduct them to the extra First Class coach that had been added to the 07.25 train to London. Richard Harper had been more fortunate, he had one hour's sleep before heading off to meet and greet the guests at Shrewsbury. At 08.00, he made an impromptu welcome speech on Shrewsbury platform 4, and a few minutes later the train rolled in spot on time. Both men were running on adrenaline all morning talking to MPs, councillors, stakeholders and the press.

Of course this was only the beginning of a series of problems in unending waves that is called 'running a railway', and Andy, Richard and Mark were in the thick of it. Mark says,

'Paul Belton's problem wasn't the only one that first day, as subsequent trains had difficulties, from Class 67s being suddenly asked to behave like racehorses, when they had been doing work like ponies. It became like an open day at Wrexham General in BR times! Four extra Class 67s appeared, and there was even a Class 37 which brought a replacement loco over from Crewe, and then later towed away 67025. After the first week I remember thinking, if it's going to be like this I don't know if I can carry on. The phone rang without end – but of course things got better as everyone got used to it'.

Wrexham & Shropshire makes the news

Despite the problem with the first train, the media coverage was generally excellent..The BBC Midlands Today featured staff and passengers. BBC Radio Shropshire and Marcher Sound offered extensive coverage and there was strong local press coverage across a wide area including the front page of the Shropshire Star. Modern Railways and Rail Express covered the launch with front cover pictures in the run up to 28th April, and a number of other journals were represented, with positive coverage. It seemed that the media and the general public liked Wrexham & Shropshire. The service was now up and running.

The WSMR test train for the newly refurbished Mk.3 coaches from Wrexham to Stoke Marcroft stands on the Shrewsbury Up Main. A London Midland unit No. 170 634 stands in Platform 6 waiting to return to Birmingham. 13:34, Thursday 10th September 2009. **Geoff Plumb**

Chapter 6 Running the Railway

From the Staff's Viewpoint

The opening day on 28th April 2008, although full of excitement, was even fuller of the last minute details that displayed a wilful desire to spoil everything, and instantly dissolved any circulating optimistic thoughts. It was a shock to see exactly what was actually on offer to run the railway with. In our minds we had seen glistening silver-grey exteriors, with highlights of crimson lake; smooth interiors were imagined, with soft lighting, playing on svelte furnishings covered in tasteful fabrics. In the promoters' minds these modern trains glided smoothly along the rails, offering complete comfort, total reliability, and impressive speed, filled with happy customers.

It wasn't like that. For a start, the quality of the trains fell a long way short of what had been intended. Reality came nowhere close to the ideal! There was a 'temporary solution', 'just for a short while'. Like a flashback to the 1980s, the Mark 3 coaches were in British Rail blue and grey livery, and even had 'Inter-City' emblazoned on the side. It was clear exactly what the score was. The coaches were entirely serviceable, but very second hand. Inside the vehicles the facilities provided, and the colour schemes, reflected the previous operators. Standard class passengers were allowed to occupy the first class seats when first cars were obliged to be used. Thus, in 'cattle class' the vehicles had commendably soft cushions, and seats that all had tables that all coincided with the windows. John-James Davidson recalls:

> *"Passengers loved what were perceived as spacious, comfortable retro-coaches, a bit like a comfy*

Running Mk3 cars without refurbishment, and in blue and grey Inter-City livery was nice for the romantics, but this was not the image W&S was seeking to convey. True, when travelled in they were warm, comfortable, quiet and spacious - and a contrast to what was on offer from competitors. But there were snags. It took effort to keep all the detailed items in reliable operation. These carriages were nearing a natural refit time, and it was asking a lot to keep them running in daily service. The result was niggling snags and a continual need for trouble-shooting on a service that vitally needed reliability.

***Left:** The Mark 3 carriages were known for their comfortable and quiet ride, their roomy seating, the view out of the window, and the spacious feel of the interior. In fact WSMR had better accommodation than its competitors - but it was careworn, and this was not in the brand image of the new operation. Although the replacement Pendolinos on the Virgin services from which the Mk3 cars had come did not delight everyone, especially as the rise in patronage was leading to overcrowding, but that was put right. On WSMR these carriages were an acceptable stopgap, but not for so long.*

***Right:** The Mk3 RFM kitchen produced splendid breakfasts for years on the West Coast Main Line. Wrexham & Shropshire made even better, and Pat Burke is attending to the mushroom component. Around him is the kitchen equipment, that from time to time would display an awkward phase, that could call for the Managing Director's screwdriver. For the most part the staff did wonders with the meals, steering round the idiosyncrasies of toaster, boiler, and microwave. Everybody coped - but would have been nicer not to have had the problems.*

old pair of shoes."

To be fair, Cargo-D, the owners of the coaches, did make it clear that their usage was designed for 'excursion service', and were Wrexham & Shropshire to run them in every day service with high mileages, then it was advisable to engage in heavy maintenance, or risk niggling faults. There wasn't a choice, as the coaches of dreams were still being refitted at Axiom, and what Wrexham & Shropshire had, it must make do with; besides it was thought this was for a short time only. So at the beginning, keeping the trains running with the full range of on-board service available, presented challenges.

This railway was different, as everyone in it cared a lot, and the senior management were out and about on the trains, and not just sat in offices.

John-James Davidson observes:

"The downside was that it seemed rare to see Andy Hamilton without a screwdriver trying to fix something or other on his daily journey to and from work. Something in the galley was always broken, be it a grill, a stove, the boiler, or all of them. The on-board staff improvised tirelessly with camping stoves and kettles. In reality that is not sustainable for very long and morale was hit badly – not that passengers realised this, because the professionalism of the team

Right: *The Mk3 RFM vehicle has 6 bays of 2+1 seating, and was built in 1979, refurbished by Virgin, and taken over by Cargo-D to be hired to W&S, 'short-term', whilst vehicles were refurbished by Axiom, with all modern appurtenances. These 'stand-in' vehicles were very comfortable, and Gordon Rushton faces Richard Worrall, talking about some imponderable matter, well lubricated with tea, served in man-sized cups. It was nice, but there was a little snag. Few laptop batteries would survive the long journey, and it was not possible to charge them*
.

Graham Whistler

Left: *Train manager Michele Holbrook shares a pleasantry with a satisfied customer in first class. Travel in here was very pleasant and cosy, with the kitchen nearby. The staff atmosphere was relaxed enough for the train managers to help the stewards to the betterment of service to the customers. It was most likely that after ticket examination the train manager would check to see if the customer needed more hot water for the tea, and if the steward was busy they may well go and get it from the kitchen. This made the service level remarkably caring.*

made sure our growing reputation for service was maintained."

This 'make-do-and-mend' philosophy was made possible by the intense loyalty of the staff. Perhaps it is a peculiarly British thing to rally round and make the best of it. The customers were affected too. If there was a shortage, the staff would brightly offer an alternative, making a polite, cheery explanation of the problem. Faced with such courteous candour, the passengers almost invariably joined in the spirit of things, and potentially embarrassing minuses were turned into plusses. It may be that such a small staff, with an active and participating management, who turned up ready to help when things were wrong, was part of the reason why in such a short time, both staff and patrons were so fiercely loyal to Wrexham & Shropshire - and this showed in the service ratings. This 'cottage industry' way of running a railway was quite new to the modern age, unless you look at the better preserved lines! It will be remarked on later in context as a unique phenomenon that 'added value'

Improvising operations - 'top and tail'

The concept had included a Driving Van Trailer (DVT) at one end of the train, and a Class 67 locomotive in push-pull mode at the other. However the DVT vehicles were part of the same refurbishment programme as the Mk3

***Left:** The locomotives were the first to be painted in Wrexham & Shropshire livery. In early April 2008, 67015 stands outside Toton Traction and Maintenance Depot, now operated by DB Schenker Rail (UK). There were four locomotives painted for the service, 67012,13,14 and 15. All were eventually named, as will be seen in the text later. A fifth locomotive 67010 was later added, and painted in W&S livery, although it never received a name (which would have been* Charles Darwin*).*

G. Griffiths

***Right:** By 2008 the railway had almost universally switched to 'in-out' operation. It was not usual for locomotives to run round their trains. Marylebone did have the facilities to do this, but no staff to do it with. Furthermore, there was no shunt locomotive to release the rolling stock, nor any wish for the time-consuming palaver that would ensue. So if WSMR wished to operate, it was either in push-pull mode, or failing that, 'top-and-tail'. Locomotive 67012 (later* A Shropshire Lad*) stands at Marylebone Station Platform 4 on 9th May 2008 at 15.03.*

coaches, and as these too were also not available on start-up, the intended push-pull operation wasn't possible. Thus, at the terminals the locomotive would be obliged to run round its train, and that was now impractical. No facilities existed for this at Marylebone, and a complicated and time consuming shunting move would be needed at Wrexham. To retain operational flexibility it was decided to run with an additional locomotive. Fortunately the whole of the Class 67 fleet was bereft of meaningful employment, as the mail trains for which they had been ordered by EWS were no longer running. So there were enough of these available for EWS to supply what was needed until the DVT's were altered for their new duties. Thus Wrexham & Shropshire began operation with a locomotive at each end of the train, enclosing three Mk3 carriages, in a mode of operation known as 'top and tail'. Nominally these vehicles were supposed to be one Mk3 first/buffet, and two Mk3 standard class saloons. As has been said before, where a first saloon appeared the standard class customers could enjoy them.

For the enthusiasts locomotive hauled trains were already something of a bonanza, but the large number of different Class 67 locomotives appearing on Wrexham & Shropshire services caused a sensation. The first up run from Banbury for the Wrexham & Shropshire training train dedicated locos took place on the afternoon of Tuesday 8th April 2008. Locomotives 67014 and 67013

***Right:** On 26th May 2008, red EWS liveried 67020 leads silver EWS liveried 67029 Royal Diamond into Banbury with the 11.29 service to Wrexham, right on time. The braking with a trailing load needed to be anticipated, slow and gentle to avoid the chance of the locomotive in rear picking up its brakes and causing wheel flats. With 3,200hp available, there was no problem keeping to time whilst doing this.*

***Left:** With no DVT to ride in for driver to train manager communication, then the traditional method was obliged to be resorted to. Train manager Alan Riley stands in front of his train, waiting to give 'right away' to the driver at Shrewsbury on 2nd May 2008. At the appropriate moment, there will be the proper whistle and flag - passengers loved it.*

were outshopped from Toton only a few days earlier, resplendent in their new livery. In early May all four locomotives allocated to the service in the silver livery were working, and this delighted the devotees of locomotive haulage even more. This traditional mode of travel was becoming rare, as multiple units were everywhere, and many youths with shining faces were to be seen travelling the trains for the fun-filled experience. Indeed they were numerous enough to generate significant revenue, and the train managers (TMs) got to know them as sober and reliable citizens, each with a vast fund of knowledge.

However, for the company there were operational difficulties from 'top and tail', since without the DVT there was no proper accommodation for the TMs, and no means of communicating with the driver to confirm the train was ready to depart. So to begin with, Wrexham & Shropshire's trains were dispatched from stations using the traditional method of a green flag, waved by the train manager, and acknowledged by the driver. Passengers enjoyed this visible connection with tradition.

Without accommodation of their own, the TMs based themselves near the galley in the first class catering vehicle. This offered proximity to the public address system used by the stewards, the only one available until the DVTs arrived. The TMs used this to advantage, as circumstances brought the on-board team closer together, and inevitably led to occasions when TMs helped out with the washing up

Left: *Train manager Nikki Roberts is ready to give the 'right away' to the driver, in locomotive 67020, and has her green flag in the ready position when the camera caught her in this view at Shrewsbury on 26th May 2008. The train was running late and is the 06.45 from Marylebone to Wrexham. Nikki is working the train from the buffet vehicle, marshalled in the centre of the train. Marshalling was sometimes difficult when vehicles had to be removed for faults to be attended to. The preferred position was at the London end.*

Right: *Journey's end as Driver Instructor Steve Roast and Driver Mike York keep a close eye on things as the train approaches the bufferstops in Platform 4 at Marylebone station. This was the up run, 5Z23, 14:02 from Banbury, on board 67020 on Wednesday 2nd April 2008, dead on time at 15:23. Such training runs allowed the locomotives to be understood, the sensitivities in braking to be mastered, and thus avoid problems in service.*

Geoff Plumb

and sometimes they did more than this. Should any faults develop, the TMs were in the train, 'with' the passengers and catering staff. This promoted teamwork that included an holistic approach to passenger service, creating a good reputation that continued to develop. Being willingly homeless was not unfettered altruism, as cups of tea were continuously available; it promoted the atmosphere of a family business.

There was an unforeseen technical difficulty of having 88 tonnes of unpowered locomotive tagged on the back of the train. If the driver in the leading locomotive did not start his brake applications earlier, and more gently, it was possible for the wheels on the trailing locomotive to cease their rotation, and lock, unbeknown to any but a professional ear sat in the adjacent coach. When driving from either DVT or locomotive, the automatic wheelslide protection system guarded against this; locomotives regularly trailing trains in daily service, on short trains was not a mode of operation that had been anticipated, and so the wheelslide protection did not extend to a 'dead' locomotive on the rear of the train. In service, such skidding on the rails wore little flats on the wheel surface. The resulting irregularities caused 'bumping' of the wheels, and is undesirable, partly as the presence of an irregularity in the surface of the tyre encourages more incidents in

Left: Locomotive 67015 "David J. Lloyd" rubs shoulders with Chiltern turbo 165 020 at Chiltern's Aylesbury depot on Saturday 20th December 2008. The W&S set had worked up empty stock as 5Z67 with 67015 and 82301 the day before from Wolverhampton to Banbury, recessing there before continuing to Aylesbury. The train was there for tyre-turning, to eliminate a vehicle wheel-flat.

Geoff Plumb

Right: This is the galaxy of food from the galley, with Wrexham and Shropshire stalwarts sampling it for the camera on a photoshoot. Left, Gordon Rushton, centre, Richard Worral and right Martins Kreicis. The spare is for the photographer. It was truly excellent fare. There are examples here of the main meal choices, Cumberland sausage, chicken curry and shank of lamb. They were all good, and to please the customer, menus were rotated on a regular basis.

Graham Whistler

the same place, resulting in flats wearing on the wheels of such a size as to force the locomotive to be taken out of service merely for the simple task of having its wheels skimmed. This was expensive and it rapidly shortened tread life. The gentle and longer braking time kept the problem in check, but could adversely affect the timekeeping. There was no cheap technical remedy; the obvious solution was to get the DVTs thoroughly overhauled, and then out on the trains where they belonged.

Working together and the nice food

The close integration of the on-board team became a feature of Wrexham & Shropshire. Indeed the crewing levels were high for a three-car train. Each team consisted of four staff, the driver, train manager, senior steward and steward. Whilst the senior steward was nominally responsible for serving first class passengers, and the steward looked after the standard class buffet, in reality both stewards worked together as a team. When the DVTs were added, then normally on the journey to London, the train was driven from it. The driver was accessible, and as they were also friendly and supportive, relations were good across the whole crew (as well as the driver having access to tea and food, as required). When in the locomotive the driver could be reached by the TM's

***Left:** This was the finest full breakfast you could get on a scheduled train anywhere in Britain. The proximity of the galley, and the relatively low numbers of breakfasts being served made it sensible to spend the time with the customer ensuring that what was provided was bespoke. Then it was plated up and brought hot to the table. Served with either pots of tea or coffee this was a delicious way to progress through the countryside, and it was one of the high points of the customer experience.*

***Right:** Fiona Jones and Pat Burke man the spacious buffet in the Mk3 catering vehicle. The senior steward, was nominally responsible for looking after the first class, but in normal service this distinction was blurred and everyone worked together. The staff to customer ratio was higher than any other on all but VSOE and heritage railways, and with only three carriages, it was not a problem for anyone to access the buffet if they chose to.*

radio. There was a definite family atmosphere, one that managed to survive the tendency to exclude the passenger, and the friendly service was remarked upon by customers.

Full catering was provided on every service operated, seven days a week. In standard class, passengers could expect hot and cold snacks and drinks from the buffet counter. All first class ticket holders had included with their travel tickets a complimentary two course meal, and in practice two-course menus were offered after 1100, with a sweet course available at extra charge. The food on offer was made locally in Wrexham, chilled and then cooked on the train. The menus were changed regularly. A choice of three main courses was available and portions were generous! For those travelling before 1100, the cooked breakfast did not disappoint either, with a tasty range of locally produced breakfast items cooked on the train. You can see from the photograph above the generous nature of the breakfast, with hash-brown and black pudding as the 'extra' items. At the same time, coffee or tea was offered and after toast and marmalade, croissants and pastries. Instead of the grill it was possible to have a kipper, or scrambled egg and smoked salmon in a muffin. All first class meals were served using crockery and cutlery with no sign of plastic or cardboard; this was on train catering as it should be. If you were a foodie, then this was the trains

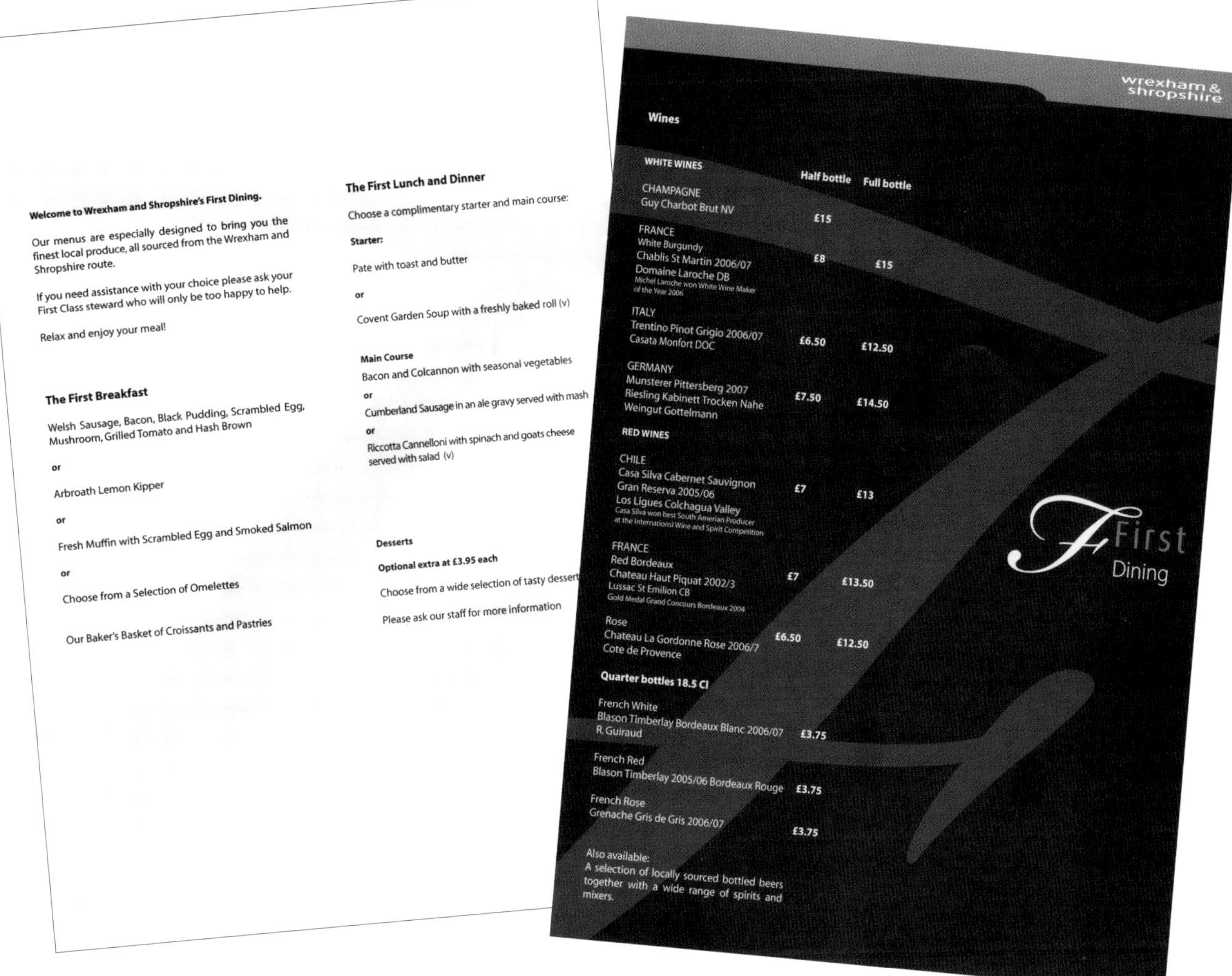

Welcome to Wrexham and Shropshire's First Dining.

Our menus are especially designed to bring you the finest local produce, all sourced from the Wrexham and Shropshire route.

If you need assistance with your choice please ask your First Class steward who will only be too happy to help.

Relax and enjoy your meal!

The First Breakfast

Welsh Sausage, Bacon, Black Pudding, Scrambled Egg, Mushroom, Grilled Tomato and Hash Brown

or

Arbroath Lemon Kipper

or

Fresh Muffin with Scrambled Egg and Smoked Salmon

or

Choose from a Selection of Omelettes

Our Baker's Basket of Croissants and Pastries

The First Lunch and Dinner

Choose a complimentary starter and main course:

Starter:

Pate with toast and butter

or

Covent Garden Soup with a freshly baked roll (v)

Main Course

Bacon and Colcannon with seasonal vegetables

or

Cumberland Sausage in an ale gravy served with mash

or

Riccotta Cannelloni with spinach and goats cheese served with salad (v)

Desserts

Optional extra at £3.95 each

Choose from a wide selection of tasty dessert

Please ask our staff for more information

wrexham & shropshire

Wines

WHITE WINES	Half bottle	Full bottle
CHAMPAGNE Guy Charbot Brut NV	£15	
FRANCE White Burgundy Chablis St Martin 2006/07 Domaine Laroche DB Michel Laroche won White Wine Maker of the Year 2006	£8	£15
ITALY Trentino Pinot Grigio 2006/07 Casata Monfort DOC	£6.50	£12.50
GERMANY Munsterer Pittersberg 2007 Riesling Kabinett Trocken Nahe Weingut Gottelmann	£7.50	£14.50
RED WINES		
CHILE Casa Silva Cabernet Sauvignon Gran Reserva 2005/06 Los Ligues Colchagua Valley Casa Silva won best South American Producer at the International Wine and Spirit Competition	£7	£13
FRANCE Red Bordeaux Chateau Haut Piquat 2002/3 Lussac St Emilion CB Gold Medal Grand Concours Bordeaux 2004	£7	£13.50
Rose Chateau La Gordonne Rose 2006/7 Cote de Provence	£6.50	£12.50
Quarter bottles 18.5 Cl		
French White Blason Timberlay Bordeaux Blanc 2006/07 R.Guiraud	£3.75	
French Red Blason Timberlay 2005/06 Bordeaux Rouge	£3.75	
French Rose Grenache Gris de Gris 2006/07	£3.75	

Also available:
A selection of locally sourced bottled beers together with a wide range of spirits and mixers.

First Dining

service for you. Yet given the unit prices of the hot meals, and the relatively low volume, such quality and quantity was not expensive. The food was believed by all to be the unique selling point of Wrexham & Shropshire. GNER had been the train service with the most accomplished service, although Virgin, Great Western and Anglia all offered restaurant service in one form or another. However the Wrexham & Shropshire service in First eclipsed everyone else. The breakfast was magnificent, and needed a long travel time to recover from. Lunch and Dinner was also very good. The menu, from pre-cooked, locally sourced suppliers, was simple but excellent. The description in the Guide to Services showed that it was:

- Fairtrade where relevant
- Free range where relevant
- Vegetarian options
- Quality and value for money
- Rotations of menus

and that the catering was available on every train, seven days a week.

The menus were varied from time to time. The First menu example above shows one choice at the time. Bacon and Colcannon was unusual, but it was delicious. Cumberland sausage in ale gravy served with mash was well beyond the normal 'bready' sausage, and was capable of defeating even the most avid trencherman. If you still had room for dessert - and there was plenty of time on the journey - then normally, there really was a wide selection. The lemon sponges were heavenly, the raspberry and almond tart with double-cream was hopelessly indulgent, and the chocolate cake was downright naughty - and there was ice cream too. One particular point was the reasonable charges for the wines. Simply because Wrexham & Shropshire customers were captives did not mean that they were overcharged. The stewards spent time with the customers, making sure that they understood what was on offer, and welcoming them into the first class with immediate offers of tea or coffee. The service was deeply appreciated. The high standard was achieved with the assistance of the Anglia Catering Manager during startup,

***Right:** The star of the show in the culinary line was most definitely the Welsh Lamb Shank. It took a few miles of line to shift this off the plate! Not only were the potatoes, sauteed in thyme and sage, delicious in their own right, the little carrot parcels seduced the consumer, the beans were soft and tasty, and the gravy was exactly the right amount, with no cloying fattiness. It may have been pub-bistro in its presentation and quality, but to get this on a train, was at a level of delightfulness unsurpassed by any other operator.*

***Left:** if you were unwise enough to apply limits to your intake, when travelling on Wrexham & Shropshire, you may have dismissed the desserts with a sense of Puritanical pride. Sad if you did, as these were on a level much nearer to heaven than the savoury courses. The star was probably the almond, raspberry and rhubarb tart. The double-cream was there to smother the tartness from the rhubarb, but the unctuous feel to it was sublime. The lemon sponge was a close, very close second.*

which was freely given. They too had Mk3 catering vehicles, and passed on their know-how. The Wrexham & Shropshire staff found deep reserves of devotion, and it certainly was not for any pursuit of a tip. Meals were fully inclusive in the price of First travel; the dessert was £3.95 extra, as were the wines and locally sourced bottled beer. Tea and coffee service continued throughout the journey, at seat to First customers; this was appreciated.

In the Standard class there were quality sandwiches, hot snacks like lasagne, quality crisps, wines, local bottled beers, and if you wanted it, you could buy from the First cooked menu. People did this - indeed there were some who bought the meal, sat in Standard, and saved themselves some money. Curiously, this didn't happen much. Those in First were mainly there because they enjoyed the service they got. That was so good, it protected the revenue from loss. Sitting in the quiet comfort of a Mk3 carriage, being waited upon for a price as low as £50 was good value, and was considered an excellent 'bet' to make sure that the traffic came. In Standard the buffet was generally busy, and people for stations north of Wolverhampton would seek out the Wrexham & Shropshire service to be able to buy from the buffet. One item that was favoured was the afternoon tea, where for a mere £5.95 a selection of ham or cheese sandwich, Bara brith, Welsh cake, scone with

***Right:** Two W&S trains pass each at Princes Risborough. On the left is the up train, 1P03, 07:25 Wrexham to Marylebone running about 4 minutes early with 67013 "Dyfrbont Pontcysyllte" on the front and DVT 82303 on the rear. On the right is the down train, 1J81, 10:17 Marylebone to Wrexham running about one minute late with DVT 82301 leading and 67015 "David J. Lloyd" on the rear. 10:56, Friday 31st October 2008.* **Geoff Plumb**

***Left:** When delivered the sliding doors were spotted as causing potential problems, as they had done for the previous operator. On occasions, as once they had opened, it was possible to have a problem with the locking mechanism, and then they could not be secured shut. To make sure that this did not happen in service on WSMR, the doors were kept shut during service until sorted in 2009. As far as the utility of the rest of the vehicle, they were excellent, comfortable to drive, accessible from the rest of the train and convenient.* **Geoff Plumb**

jam and cream and a large pot of tea for one could be indulged in. Of course such a wonderful offer across the board was noticed by the 'critics'. As a result Wrexham & Shropshire rapidly became a darling, and was rapidly approaching the status of National Treasure.

Improving operations - the DVTs arrive

The DVTs began to arrive in early October 2008, with a trial taking place on 10th October. The DVT vehicles had been built by British Rail in the late 1980s, to enable West Coast main line express trains to run as fixed push-pull formations. This eliminated time consuming terminal operations of either the locomotive running round the train to pull from the other end, or of replacing it with another. Although only 20 years old, the West Coast DVTs were made redundant along with the Mk3 coaches with the arrival of Virgin Pendolinos in 2004.

There was a snag in that DVTs were deliberately built with no passenger accommodation after an accident between Glasgow and Edinburgh, when a passenger carrying driving vehicle had run into a herd of cows and the train was derailed with fatal effect to passengers. It was determined thereafter that leading vehicles should not carry passengers. At the time this did not figure very much as DVTs were built when the railways still had a parcels

***Left:** The important thing about these two photos is that the first one shows a serious Driver Griffin at the controls of a DVT in a photograph staged for the camera at Wrexham, on turnround. This was taken for publicity use, and these photographs turned up everywhere. Not all liked the intrusion of having their photograph taken.*
Note the neatness of the cab of the DVT, complete with the timing sheet for the Down journey, that started at Marylebone at 06.45 and ended at Wrexham General at 10.44. 3hrs 59mins is a long time. when it can be done via Chester in 2hrs 28mins.

***Right:** This is the second shot taken at that time, with Peter Griffin beaming at the camera. This was taken in October 2008, when everyone was trying extremely hard to make the service work. The point of this picture is to emphasise just how obliging everyone was. Drivers are not noted for their tendency to offer beaming smiles. In this quite unusual atmosphere, the work was extremely hard, arduous in fact, but everyone was pulling the same way - and it showed. It is not an experience that everyone gets, even during a long career on the railways.*

and mails business. Thus WSMR trains were obliged to operate with a large vacant space in front. Perhaps this still did not matter for Wrexham & Shropshire, as they had few aspirations for that trade - now abandoned by the railways. However, there was another problem, and that was that the single biggest source of failures affecting the previous operator, Virgin Trains, was failure of DVT sliding doors. Thus in service they remained firmly closed and denied even the exploitation of the space for cycle traffic. Additionally the rules about DVTs carrying passengers were changed, and there was consideration given to fitting seats in them should the need arise - it never did.

Four DVTs had been selected for refurbishment by Wrexham & Shropshire from a storage facility. Refurbishment meant a mechanical overhaul, corrosion repairs, repainting in the company's livery and installation of control and communication equipment, to allow the DVT to operate with the Class 67 locomotive. DVT overhaul time was more rapid than for the coaches, as

Right: *A small organisation means that everyone became involved with even the minor affairs. To drive the service forward it was essential to appear where possible at significant venues to spread the word about the service. Here on 28th June 2008, Richard Harper stands with Chiltern Railways colleagues in the depot at Tyseley for the open day. The opportunity this gave while the service was still new had to be exploited. One can see from the cardboard box and the paucity of giveaways that this is early in the process.*

Left: *With five services per day run by three sets of second hand carriages, niggles were likely. Senior managers were out on the trains regularly. Mobile phones and laptops made that practical. Thus there were many impromptu meetings on the train, as well as contact with the customers and the working staff. Thus in such a small outfit made sure that everyone's point of view could be heard clearly. whilst building up this was extremely useful. Here, at Shrewsbury, Andy Hamilton has just alighted from the 06.45 train from Marylebone at 10.03 and is talking over a point with TM Richard Rayworth before going into the office at the Pump House.*

there was less to do, so while they had not been ready for the start of WSMR services in April, they were ready for introduction in October.

The introduction of the DVTs helped operations enormously. They brought the TMs an office from which to base themselves, from where they could announce into the train, operate the electric door locking equipment, and communicate with the driver to dispatch the train. There was the snag, that initially the unreliable doors prevented the carriage of cycles, but that was a small price to pay. The additional locomotives which had been required in top and tail mode were no longer necessary, and whilst Wrexham & Shropshire had avoided paying additional charges for these – due to the delay to the DVTs – there were also clear advantages in concentrating on the four locomotives that had been carefully selected for operation, and in helping them towards mechanical perfection.

Left: *Occasionally when items were defective, they had to go away for attention. On Wednesday 22nd April 2009, WSMR ran an empty working from Wembley Depot to Wolverton Works, one of several that were needed. Here, 67010 approaches Wolverton station with RFM M10257 in tow at 14:22, running as 5Z32, 10:17 from Wembley, but running about 48 minutes late. The train was routed via Leamington Spa and Coventry, where the loco ran round, then up the WCML to Wolverton.*

Geoff Plumb

Right: *Mucking in meant co-operation in every sense of the word. Thus it was that Gordon Rushton associate Graham Whistler was invited to record the excellence of the food, to produce photographs for general use. Diane Davidson, the food's 'author' is present, seated next to Martins Kreicis. Graham's professional photographic skills meant that an excellent record of stock photographs was obtained. It was only right therefore, that after taking the photographs we should be allowed to eat it.*

Small is beautiful

A railway running five trains a day doesn't need a giant organisation. When starting up it is wise to get out to speak to the staff at the 'sharp end', and to the customers using the service. There were not many people employed, and the urgency and all-embracing nature of the start up period meant that very quickly everybody knew everybody else. There's no room for airs and graces in a little outfit either, so it didn't matter who you were, mucking in was obligatory. On board the train, there was always something to do and so everyone would get involved if something was awry. The managing director led the way, and senior people were tolerated if they had to travel long distances to reach the Shrewsbury Office, as long as they did so on the train, so that they could join in with the myriad tasks that needed doing. It was never perfect, alas the period for overhauling the new carriages became drawn out, and the 'excursion carriages' that were being run intensively began to complain, by springing a continual list of faults. Not everyone was blessed with the managing director's skills fixing things on the move, but that didn't stop others helping to serve customers or washing up. And when he didn't have a screwdriver in his hand, the managing director would be handing out newspapers to First Class passengers. The team was effective in relation to marketing, on board service and out of hours support, but sometimes it was a strain for everyone. The customers noticed that everyone helped everyone else - it showed.

Right: The Wrexham & Shropshire maintenance was performed on a 'day-to-day' basis at the Wembley depot. For the more serious tasks like 'tyre turning' the trains went to Aylesbury Depot. of course Wrexham & Shropshire had to pay for this, but it was extremely useful having a tie-up with Chiltern to be able to get the precedent required, and the quality of service needed.

Geoff Plumb

***Left:** Just occasionally, things could go wrong and early on Wrexham & Shropshire had decided that the sensible place to manage the operation of its trains was in a Control shared with Chiltern. This was placed in Banbury and had a display showing all train running on any part of the network as a choice. Chiltern Control acted as the longstop for all operational problems. It was also able to substitute alternative resources if the need arose.*

Richard Harper

A little help from friends

Wrexham & Shropshire was lucky to be able to buy in some central functions from Chiltern Railways, taking advantage in areas where there was either an insufficient volume of workload to justify the activity in-house, or where it made sense given the quality and experience of the Chiltern team. No area epitomised this more than the control function. Chiltern has a state of the art control centre at Banbury, staffed 24 hours a day and with access to a huge amount of real time information about the railway. Adding responsibility for another 10 trains each day was a small increase in workload – although on occasions the team would refute that, given the tribulations encountered! Whilst the south end of the route was familiar to the team, it was also necessary for them to learn about the railway between the West Midlands and Wrexham prior to operations starting up too.

From the start, it was anticipated that one of Wrexham & Shropshire's trains would reside on Chiltern's Wembley depot each night. This would be the last train south each evening, which would form the first train north each morning. The train crew lodged overnight in a hotel, and Chiltern's staff cleaned and fuelled the train ready for the morning. It was not intended that maintenance work would be carried out at Wembley, but this decision was quickly reviewed and reversed. The benefits of having a spare train set at Wembley, directly accessible

***Right:** John Davidson and Tony Parkin at work promoting the service at London Marylebone. Although at one time Marylebone had a train service to 'distant parts', it had slumbered in a commuterland role for many years. Suddenly there were through trains to Shrewsbury and Wrexham, and this news needed a bit of effort to put across. These gentlemen put in that effort.*

***Left:** It is the of course the prerogative of chairmen of organisations to appear at your side with neither warning nor turbulence. Mr Shooter's arrival did not mean that there was something wrong - although it could. More often he would arrive to report, or to see what was happening. He would always take up the challenge of being asked to help, and would always be willing to talk to and take advice from his customers. This was the right sort of support that was needed, and it helped to encourage people to give of their best.*

on the route, were too great so after a few months light maintenance was transferred from Crewe where it had been carried out by EWS staff. Chiltern staff were also trained to carry out light maintenance on the Class 67 locomotives, avoiding the need for time-consuming loco swaps between Wrexham and Crewe. Advantage was also taken of financial and IT systems support.

Chiltern and Wrexham & Shropshire also shared a Chairman. Adrian Shooter led both organisations and instilled each with a strong drive for development, service and innovation. Despite a busy diary, Adrian regularly found time to check out progress at Wrexham & Shropshire personally.

'Every couple of months I spent a day up in Wrexham and Shrewsbury. I was always very impressed with the crews, who did everything they possibly could to keep the show on the road, very much encouraged by Andy. I remember one day in Wrexham there was a problem with a set – it needed an engine changing – and there was a bit of mumbling from the drivers that it wasn't their job to do it. So Andy put his smock on, and got down on to the track to uncouple the loco and couple up the new one. I don't think he had any difficulty with drivers refusing to do things after that.'

Left: *Some incidents occur and no one is aware that anything has happened. Such it was when a train managed to become divided. The incident is described below, and it was important to understand fully the reasons for it having taken place. When the professional staff got down on the track, to examine the train and to ascertain the cause, this is what they saw. The forces needed to do this were large - fortunately they were not large enough to bring any vehicle off the rails.*

Right: *The jumper cable connector between the coaches is being displayed by Wrexham & Shropshire rolling stock engineer Richard Sturgess. The damage occurred when the train became divided whilst passing through Birmingham New Street Station on 1st November 2008. The passage below describes incident. Otherwise the damage may have been a mystery.*

Adrian also spent time supporting the sales and marketing effort.

'I was really impressed with the way people like Chris Rowlands and John Davidson really got out selling the business, and I joined them at several informal lunches trying to encourage organisations like Shrewsbury School to use the service.'

How one train became two

Not everything went well, and the odd item took people by surprise. None more so than Wrexham & Shropshire's most serious operating incident, which occurred on 1st November 2008, when a train divided in the vicinity of Platform 5 at Birmingham New Street. The incident was very unusual, in that the DVT was leading with the locomotive pushing from the rear. At first it seemed that the incident was not only minor, but that perhaps nothing had occurred at all. Yet a passenger on board witnessed the train dividing, as the buckeye coupler became unfastened, and a gap appeared between two vehicles. This gap immediately disappeared when the locomotive applied power from the rear, and the couplings refastened. On examination, it was clear that in fact the incident had been a serious one, and a significant division of the train had occurred. Examination revealed that the connecting jumper cables between the coaches that

The offending new junction box, fitted to a bracket in the 'right' place.

parted had been ripped from their sockets.

The buckeye coupler between the coaches was functioning normally, since the train had recoupled. When making the modifications to allow the DVT to operate the controls of the locomotive when pushing, a new cable had been run the length of each coach, with a junction box for the new connections attached to an existing bracket on the headstock near the buckeye coupler. When a detailed examination of the damaged coaches was carried out, it was found that the pre-existing bracket on the affected coach was in a slightly different location to that laid down in the design. This means that had the bracket been where it was supposed to be, no problem would have occurred. Now, on a sharp curve, the buckeye coupler was able to swing close enough to the out-of-position junction box to lift the release lever, thereby causing adjacent coaches to uncouple. The incident was only able to occur on the sharp curves at Birmingham New Street, when it was also possible for the rear of the train including the locomotive to be held back by the gradient climbing into the station. Immediately all buckeye release levers were temporarily removed, to prevent a repeat incident. This allowed trains to continue running. A revised design for attachment of the junction box was completed and all coaches were modified by 14th November.

Too good to be true

Staff relations were extremely good, especially with the close relationship that grew up between the senior management and the drivers and train managers. One of the great things about on-train catering is that creative use of it may solve so many problems. When the train was delayed prior to departure from Wrexham, Diane Davidson's team would go out and take all passengers cake and tea – what an amazing thing that is. At Wolverhampton, Virgin's platform staff seemed to be difficult, but once the staff had started slipping them the odd bacon butty they lost their ability to be angry. Just occasionally there was a backfire. There was a late incoming train at Wrexham and Di's team had done a superb job, everyone was in the waiting room at Wrexham and had been told the train would be around an hour late. After some good work by the crews, the train got in quite a bit earlier and this effort continued with an extremely rapid turn round, and they were all left behind. Mark Edlington went over to the waiting room. 'They were quite unpleasant, and I was saying to them "how could you not have noticed the train" and they were saying that they had seen it but were told it wouldn't leave until they had joined it.'

Ticket machines and Taxis

Mark remembers one day whilst travelling with Andy

The Wrexham Cafe was instantly successful, and was the source of calming cakes and tea in moments of crisis.

Hamilton. 'At Tame Bridge Parkway Jane Meredith left her Avantix ticket machine with us and went to dispatch the train, so we hid it and said we didn't know where it was... and we'd seen someone walking through the coach and getting off, which destroyed her! We were like "Oh dear" and "what's Neill going to say?" Then she clocked us "hang on a minute... you bastards!" Jane was great because she had the ability to be very serious and deal with people. I always remember the drunk rugby players who were so out of order she put them all off late one night at Wellington, and they were saying "you should have got us a taxi" and as the train was leaving she said "its just coming now, with a blue flashing light on top!" She was tough enough to deal with people like that.'

Controlling the railway always presents challenging situations, often amplified at Wrexham & Shropshire by its small size. The company operated a weekly on-call rota system, ensuring one of six senior managers was always available 24 hours a day, 7 days a week. For the managers concerned, their on-call week could be quiet or extremely busy, down to luck more than anything else. Richard Harper recalls:

'on one occasion the phone woke me up at 2.30am and I was greeted with "Hello Richard, it's Diggory. Go, and make a cup of tea and call me back". A very bad sign, and a whole range of scenarios were flashing through my mind as I made a brew. Diggory Waite was Chiltern's duty control manager who suggested making tea as a way of giving me a chance to wake up, so I could offer a quick, clear decision'. When I phoned back, the situation was straightforward "one of the two locos at Wrexham has failed, which train shall I cancel tomorrow morning?".

The Bunny

There was one cruel and ugly incident. A little fluffy bunny from IKEA had managed to get lost. Wrexham & Shropshire, like all train companies, tended to get mobile phones, umbrellas, and occasionally a wallet left on the train, but somehow the cute bunny was never claimed. So he was adopted by Mark Edlington as a mascot. But although the bunny was safely locked away, threats were made that he would disappear - and he did, - despite being secure in a cupboard for which Mark was the only keyholder. Mark then received a blackmail letter that stated:

no more Lo d g e's
or the
Bunny
get S it!

Then a Facebook page appeared in the bunny's name, with Mark's face superimposed on the bunny, and people commented that this was exactly what the Wrexham bunny looked like. Finally, one of the bunny's ears appeared in the post.

Eventually the bunny was magically restored intact. The practical jokers had bought another bunny to play the prank. Mark saw the joke and everyone was very amused. Mark observes.

'One had to be able to take a joke as well as play one',

The Chiltern 168 reaches Wrexham. **Ian Baxter**

The first and only Chiltern train to Wrexham General

On Wednesday 21st April 2010 a service from Wrexham to Marylebone failed at Bescot. Andy Hamilton was determined to provide a corresponding northbound service and persuaded Chiltern to make a train available for Wrexham & Shropshire . Ian Baxter was the only available qualified member of staff able to conduct a Class 168 to Wrexham.

At Banbury Chiltern 168214 was waiting in Platform 1 with 1J82 1516 Banbury-Wrexham General, a train load of passengers, driver Steve Roast, Wrexham & Shropshire Train Manager Gaynor Matthews, and a mobile catering solution – flasks of tea and coffee, sandwiches and crisps. Having reached a clear understanding between the quickly-formed train crew, the 168 left Banbury at 12.32, 2 minutes late, and made its normal run to Wrexham, arriving 1 minute late at 1517, despite a 3 minute signal check at Gobowen. Rapid turnaround saw 1P33, 1525 Wrexham General – London Marylebone depart only 3 minutes late, this time with Wrexham & Shropshire Operations Manager, Mark Edlington, as the Driver, and Train Manager Steve Holt, along with another emergency catering offer.

W&S 1J61 was the first return working from Paddington, diverted from its usual route from Marylebone due to engineering works at Northolt Park. Due off Paddington at 15:06, it had been held at Greenford's signals, some of which can be seen in the background, for a Chiltern train heading the other way. It has just crossed the bridge over the canal and is now approaching Northolt, alongside the Central Line tracks. The derelict old up line can be seen to the left of the picture. 15:27, Sunday 21st September 2008. 67025 is topping the train and 67013 is on the rear. **Geoff Plumb**

Diverting with Doris

A key principle promoted by the Wrexham & Shropshire team, in pursuit of passenger happiness, and differentiation from the competition, was that when engineering works affected the normal route, wherever practicable, trains would run via an alternative route and bus replacement would be minimised. When Wolverhampton to Shrewsbury was closed, this led to diversion of trains via Crewe and Stafford. At the south end of the route any lack of availability of Marylebone led to trains diverting to and from London Paddington. The most spectacular diversions were those starting and terminating at Marylebone but running via the via the West Coast Main Line. The majority of engineering works were at weekends, and the diversions required very detailed planning ahead. James Doris was part of the Chiltern Railways performance and planning team and had responsibility for preparing the diversion plans. The weekly Special Traffic Alterations notice was naturally christened 'Diverting with Doris' as the many weird and wonderful routes expanded over time.

The most challenging section of route requiring a suitable alternative was that between Leamington Spa and London Marylebone, where there is no obvious diversion. In the last year of the company's life, the amount of engineering works on this section increased significantly as Evergreen 3, the enhancement to the Chiltern route, was beginning. The unusual decision was taken to divert trains along the West Coast Main Line as far south as Willesden, then via the North London Line, regaining the route into Marylebone at Neasden. Drivers and train managers had to learn a significant additional mileage of new railway. The diversion required the train to reverse direction at Neasden and also required signalboxes which would otherwise be closed on Sundays to open specially – but it did mean that the train could continue to serve Marylebone. James Doris recalls,

> *'Each week I would call up the signallers in the North London Line boxes to make sure they were open on Sunday, because if the box wasn't open the train wouldn't be able to run'.*

67010 heads south along the WCML at the head of the diverted 1P50, 10:47 from Wrexham to Marylebone, with 82304 on the rear of the four coach unrefurbished set. The train is seen south east of Weedon, passing the old Banbury Lane level crossing, at 13:18, running to time on Sunday 24th January 2010. All W&S trains were diverted over the weekend due to engineering works between Banbury and Leamington. **Geoff Plumb**

Here is part of the weekly Special Traffic Notice for January 2010, showing the public timetable times for Wrexham & Shropshire trains via the West Coast Main Line, including 1P50 in the photograph above. Notices such as this are part of the fabric of railway communication, ensuring staff are briefed in advance of the detail of changes to train times and routes. In this case, Wrexham & Shropshire was unable to serve Leamington Spa or Banbury due to diversion via the West Coast route so any passengers for those stations had to use alternative services. Meanwhile despite the diversion the journey time for London-bound passengers was extended only slightly.

Special Traffic Alterations wrexham & shropshire

Saturday 23 – Friday 29 January 2010

Southbound		Sunday 24 January					
Train ID		1P50	1P52	1P54	-	-	-
Wrexham General	D	**10.47**	**13.11**	**17.02**	-	-	-
Ruabon	D	10.55	13.19	17.10	-	-	-
Chirk	D	11.02	13.26	17.17	-	-	-
Gobowen	D	11.07	13.31	17.22	-	-	-
Shrewsbury	D	**11.31**	**13.57**	**17.55**	-	-	-
Wellington	D	11.44	14.10	18.09	-	-	-
Telford Central	D	**11.50**	**14.16**	**18.15**	-	-	-
Cosford	D	11.59	14.24	18.24	-	-	-
Wolverhampton	A	12s10	14s38	18s35	-	-	-
Tame Bridge Parkway	D	12.26	14.55	18.54	-	-	-
Leamington Spa	D	-	-	-	-	-	-
Banbury	D	-	-	-	-	-	-
London Marylebone	A	**14.52**	**17.53**	**21.44**	-	-	-

67012 **'A Shropshire Lad'** *leads the 05:12 Wrexham to Marylebone, across Souldern No. 1 Viaduct on Friday 25th September 2009.*
Geoff Plumb

Selling the Service

The strength of the Wrexham & Shropshire brand concept rested on its function as a through train from Wrexham, Shrewsbury and Telford to London. To do this it was to break the mould by offering exemplary service, in particular to its first class customers. It was designed to have a simple fares structure and timetables that were a good compromise to build from. The assumption was made from careful assessment that a cumulative market greater than that available for the Hull Trains service existed, and that the offer of a quality service to London would be welcome. Indeed, much questioning among the populace had shown that this was so. The concept of a core market for a through service to London from North East Wales, and the Shropshire towns was to be supplemented by Wolverhampton. The competition at starting was the Virgin Trains Wolverhampton to London, hourly operation, that was converting from Mk3 locomotive haulage to Pendolino unit trains. These rapidly gained the reputation of being cramped, full and unpunctual. It was obvious that getting out into the marketplace of the Shropshire towns quickly was key to the selling effort. It was equally obvious that the development of a range of leisure products would pay, and that constant sales effort would be required to fill seats. London was plainly the destination to begin with.

There were three major blows to this exemplary set of intentions. Firstly Moderation of Competition was applied cutting out any chance of serving the London market in either direction at Wolverhampton, or at Virgin stops anywhere south. Tame Bridge was chosen as the Midlands stopping point, with extended journey time via the Grand Junction Lines. Secondly, although Virgin in transition had discontented patronage, this rapidly melted as the service improved, and then in December 2008 timetable frequency doubled. And thirdly, the sales effort was compromised just before the start of the service by the departure of the sales manager. Gordon Rushton was asked to step in at a moment's notice to fill the role. His pedigree of a lifetime in rail passenger sales was hastily dusted off, as he joined the team at the most exciting stage in the life of a product, 'start-up'.

There wasn't time for the sales team to evaluate a strategy of how it would go about the task. Service was about to begin, and custom - lots of it - was required at once. Thus the branding concept originated by Pete Wilkinson could not be questioned, as the immediate task was to seek patronage. The branding was iterated by Peter Trickett. Peter was an independent design associate of Cre'active Design. Working with him merely meant telling him the essence of the task for which promotional material was needed, and he promptly did the rest. Alas the service was launched with almost 'nothing' - it was woefully short, and had to start from scratch. It was fortunate that half the practical selling job was seemingly 'done' by the London end, run by Chiltern Railways. They had their own priorities, but fortunately there was widespread enthusiasm displayed by the Chiltern managers at the thought of their reach extending into North East Wales. Although the staff on the ground at Marylebone were sometimes difficult, there was very soon a good working relationship, where display space, rack space, poster spots and an inquiry kiosk all became available. A problem left for attention later was the 06.45 departure from Marylebone. It was soon clear that this train would need sales attention, but the magnitude of the sales task in London meant that priorities went to the 'top' end.

In addressing the sales task it was obvious that some more bodies were needed, and part-timers Tony Parkins

Above: *Richard's boundless energy went into promoting Wrexham & Shropshire. He really delivered the goods in beating the ground where the markets lay, trying to drum up business. As a resident of Walsall it made sense for him to take the middle and top end of the area and his legions of helpers really did a good job. He is pictured here behind the promotional Routemaster London bus, complete with its WSMR advertisement.*

Below: *Tony Parkins had a long railway career in 'retail' before he left the railway to run his own business. He came back part time after he retired to work for Chiltern Railways, and of course his persuasive and persistent experience was extremely valuable in getting 'in' to outlets. Since he lives in the High Wycombe area, it made good sense for him to look after WSMR at the southern end as it was highly dependent on retail outlets - including those of Chiltern Railways.*

and Richard Worrall were recruited. Tony and Gordon had worked together on the Western Region, London Division in the 1970s. Now Tony was 'lent' by Chiltern, and asked to look after the presentation of sales material at the southern end, with particular reference to Marylebone and the Chiltern Railways' stations. In so doing he became involved in sale outlets, product development, passenger welfare and service, and all the other commercial minutiae. His wide-ranging and specialised knowledge was invaluable.

Richard Worrall had been a Labour councillor in the West Midlands. Alas a sudden change in Labour's fortunes after years in office were exhibited by his defeat and sudden ousting from office. He had been a dynamic and forward thinking Chairman of the West Midlands PTE. An election is no respecter of ability, and he was replaced by someone of a different political persuasion. Richard was the man who promoted and got the Wolverhampton tram. The irony of that was not lost on anyone, bearing in mind how useful it would have been to still have the GWR connection through Snow Hill. Richard's community connections had a serious bearing on what was to follow. When Wrexham & Shropshire came on the scene he was teaching in Wolverhampton, and had access to lots of useful people-power.

Tony and Richard were supplemented by full-time graduate John-James Davidson. He knew everyone in

***Right:** It seemed like an uphill struggle to get posters and publicity up on stations. It was by no means that people were obstructive, it was just that there was a lengthy 'process' that was hampered by our lack of knowledge of what our rights actually were. When the office and the knowledge combined, and Chris Rowlands got on the case, things began to move. At Marylebone people became more than generous. We got a poster by the kiosk and this expanded to getting more posters, having the kiosk labelled Wrexham & Shropshire and carrying all the literature.*

***Left:** The process of finding people with the right expertise was essential, in order to generate the traffic that was needed for the services. Chris Rowlands came to Wrexham & Shropshire from Arriva Trains Wales. Her post had originally been in the Travel Centre at Shrewsbury Station. So relocation to the WSMR office in the Pump House was hardly a problem. Chris spent most of her time selling and administering the successful Business Travel Service. There was ready advice available from Chiltern on start-up to do this well, and the lessons were quickly absorbed.*

Chiltern Railways and having worked 'front of house' at Marylebone, he had an extensive network of work colleagues in the operational side of the business and thus became a specialist in troubleshooting..

The sales team also connected strongly with Chris Rowlands, who had come to Wrexham & Shropshire from Arriva Trains Wales at the Shrewsbury Travel Centre. She not only knew everyone in the business at this key point, she was also the ideal person to run the Wrexham & Shropshire Business Travel Service, which like its Chiltern Railways namesake, was dedicated to persuading all the local businesses (from Wrexham, Shrewsbury and Telford) to sign up for the new service.

The Sales Task

There were three major tasks to be addressed at once:

1. The first was to make sure that suitable publicity material was produced by Peter Trickett. He was able to translate from basic idea, and to printer's proof, in a matter of days. Within a week large cardboard boxes of stuff would appear at the Pump House in Shrewsbury, or in the offices at Wrexham or Marylebone for distribution.

2. Then there was the task to insist, cajole, and plead with intermediate stations to display it. This wasn't easy, as they were not required to do so, and as all stations were managed by other TOCs, the process was like feeding coal into a steam engine - never-ending. The expensive and heavy 'standard' publicity stands were ordered, and that

Left: *Wrexham General, end of the line, and one could be forgiven for assuming that Wrexham & Shropshire was a 'best kept secret'. Wanting to put up extra information boards met excuses for prohibition by planning permission requirements, through listed building exclusion, to unreasoned refusal. In fact Wrexham & Shropshire had a right to spaces that were claimed. The booking office was helpful in taking literature and in allowing us to display a rack filled with publicity, but the twelve - foot high illuminated letters eluded us - though it's clear whose bin it is!*

Right: *The formula for Train Operating Companies allows for proportional representation of each of the operating companies at a station on the poster boards there. Thus here at Cosford, Wrexham & Shropshire was entitled to one of these spaces (Not that there were hundreds passing who would read it!). This is fine in theory, but in practice it was necessary first to produce such material, and then to mount it in connection with the agent that did the job of getting it on display. This was a palaver, and took much time and resources. You will note that this photograph is before display had been achieved.*

took ages to achieve. They were expensive, and sometimes got pushed out of the way in stations, or filled with other companies' material. Thus they had to be policed regularly, or risk a telephone call from Adrian Shooter. Posters were produced - and we had the 'right' to a certain number of spaces. The only way to redeem that 'right' was by applied charm at the locations. It was exhausting, but if it wasn't done the services would remain a well kept secret.

3. The third task was to get out to 'retail' outlets and to talk the service up, to ensure that our products were placed on sale to the public. This was diverting and full of pitfalls for the unwary. Sometimes politics got in the way, as the service introduction was unpopular, and some neighbouring TOCs were hostile, to the point of non co-operation.

The whole sales task called for a massive amount of physical effort, made even more urgent as the operation was already up and running, and demanding to be 'fed'. So this task took a huge effort from everyone, and as it was 'fire-fighting' it left little time for more mature reflection, which is what the new service seemed to lack. A Sales Manual was prepared that offered the required information that sales outlets needed to access all of Wrexham & Shropshire's services. This was a very sensible allocation of time, as without it, people were unable to

Right: *At Marylebone there was a large poster site, between the new platforms. Adrian Shooter made this available to Wrexham & Shropshire, and a large vinyl stick-on advertisement was made up to be stuck over the spot. It got a little bit crinkled in the application - this caused the staff a load of grief when mounting it, nevertheless the message was clear to all the homegoing commuters that there were through trains from their station to the West Midlands and Shropshire towns.*

Left: *Right in front of Caroline Quiney in the buffet car we placed publicity racks. These carried our own and relevant adjacent attractions' leaflets. These racks did good business - they needed to be renewed on a regular basis. The information from them was reaching the casual travellers who travelled between Wrexham and Wolverhampton Stations. Leaflets were taken by choice, so the contents were more likely read - which was the advantage of this method of spreading the word. However, one was trading up on a market that had already found the product.*

understand what the products were and how to obtain them. As an open access service, Wrexham & Shropshire had an air of the second rank about it. The sales team had by good service to outlets to disperse this impression, and instead to reassure everyone that quality train services were matched with quality sales service.

MBWA

It was essential to visit all the calling points, like for example Tame Bridge, for a chat and a 'cuppa' - the staff at these places had little to do between trains. If you were polite, presentable, carried publicity and material for the sales manual, then the people behind the glass window were invariably pleased to see you. Everyone did their time at this. For people like the Sales Manager, Gordon Rushton, with a booking office background, it was meat and drink. Apart from the more modern building surrounds, nothing had changed. To drive up from Milton Keynes and spend a day round the staffed stations, was as tedious as it gets, but it was productive, and it raised the sales profile to new heights. If people liked you they sold for you. If they got thanks and the odd 'freebie' for their pains, then they offered support - and that's what was needed. This really was MBWA (management by walking about). If you didn't do it, you didn't get. Perhaps the classic example was in Telford Bus Station. There was a travel agent in there who

***Left:** The Station at Telford, rather a featureless pile, evidently did not persuade the public to go and buy tickets. For a while, for their own reasons, they were reluctant to sell Wrexham & Shropshire. However, they were comprehensively outsold by the travel agent in the bus station. So the dullards at the station were supplanted. However, it was such an important place to seek business that persuasion had to continue until it was successful. They came round later after tempting trips to London in First. One interesting point about the station that you had to visit to experience was the massive queue of cars to get in or out of it at peak times.*

sold rail tickets. There was more than the normal whiff of railway enthusiasm in the office. You can always tell - instead of girlie calendars, there are pictures of trains. The Class 67s were exercising their magic. They were more than willing to sell Wrexham & Shropshire, but the chance of a footplate trip changed willingness into passion. That was what we were looking for. Staff at the outlets were all treated to a trip to London in First - this they found wonderful, and it raised the profile instantly.

The Internet and the Website

Wrexham & Shropshire was the first train operator to launch a new service in the maturing digital age. It was expected by potential customers that on-line bookings would be available from the start. Thus communicating with the market by web page and e-mail was an immediate method of selling. For a small company like Wrexham Shropshire however, costs associated with established railway web retailers were unaffordable. Although web marketing for small companies could be obtained very cheaply, the complexities of selling railway tickets on-line required specialist skills .

John Nelson knew a small web design outfit in Tunbridge Wells called Assertis, run by Alistair Lees who was working on cutting-edge retailing of e-tickets for Chiltern Railways, with fresh ideas and a 'can-do' approach. The work for Chiltern was acknowledged as being very good. The question was, could his organisation develop a cost-effective retailing system capable of presenting Wrexham & Shropshire brand across the Internet, with its products arrayed in an interesting and accessible manner? It was decided that they could and together with Richard Harper the yield management system was configured to allow seats at varying prices to be offered on sale to the public. The two systems were meshed to allow seating space to be released at the right price at the right time. Thus configured the system allowed WSMR to implement its own policies on pricing, and to place the emphasis on products of choice. Assertis managed to enclose the 'offer' in bright, attractive colours, keeping to Wrexham & Shropshire's designer Peter Trickett's interpretation of how things should look. This was an most excellent control mechanism for the business. It could predict income and report yield, and was a true handle on the market.

Problems with Prices

The yield management system was set up to sell space to the market at the best possible price. It regulated the number of cheaper fares available across the peak and off-peak times and used a ranking system in tiers, such that the required number of cheaper fares judged to be appropriate could be set for a service, and when these had been sold, the system offered the next fare upwards in the price scale. Progress of the sales was kept under observation, and according to demand, further cheaper tickets could be added. This way the yield for each train was maximised.

The service began with a simple, basic standard class fare of £24 single from Shrewsbury to London (Marylebone). As a £48 return fare it compared unfavourably with the

Cannot read this email, click here | Forward to a friend

Dear John Smith

Need to get to London early?

We've got 100 seats every weekday morning arriving in London at 0954. And every one of those seats is just £24.

Have a great day out in London and then return on the 16.10 from Marylebone – which also has over 100 seats every day at £24.

Our great value fares are available on every other weekday train too – book early to reserve your seat though!

Get to London before 10 am for...

...HALF the price of Virgin Trains

Over 100 tickets every weekday

Book your tickets now

Outward	Dep.	Standard Class	First Class
Wrexham General	0542	£24	£55
Ruabon	0549	£24	£55
Chirk	0555	£24	£55
Gobowen	0600	£24	£55
London Marylebone	0954		

Single fares shown only

Return	Dep.	Standard Class	First Class
London Marylebone	1610	£24	£55
Gobowen	2007	£24	£55
Chirk	2012	£24	£55
Ruabon	2019	£24	£55
Wrexham General	2028		

Single fares shown only

Fares shown must be booked in advance, are subject to availability and must be purchased by the day before travel.

First class service you can afford from £55

We offer a First Class at-seat meal service on all our trains – seven days a week. And it's complimentary – all part of the First Class service from Wrexham & Shropshire. Great value First Class fares start at no more than £55 single from all our key stations so it's affordable too.

So for extra space and quality service at your seat, First Class with Wrexham & Shropshire is a great choice for business or a special treat.

forward to a friend | buy ticket | visite website | unsubscrib to this news letter

wrexham & shropshire

You are receiving this email from Wrexham & Shropshire because you've opted in to receive communications from us. If you no longer wish to receive these messages please unsubscribe. Please note that, while we will endeavour to read all emails that we receive in reply to this email, we may be unable to respond to each one individually. The Wrexham, Shropshire and Marylebone Railway Company Ltd is registered in England (5970112). Our registered address is Great Central House, Marylebone Station, Melcombe Place, London, NW1 6JJ.

Above: *The charms of First as a product were e-mailed to the appropriate contacts that the sales team and everyone else had made. The identity of the company was not disguised in these communications, people knew what their inbox contained.*

Left: *The business segment was also sent out price and times for standard class, with a similar message, but slanted against the competition. This was effective, and generated sales for the Business Travel Service.*

Attention turned to marketing the service from the southern end, with a campaign on Banbury Station which extolled the virtues of a trip to Shrewsbury. The banners and posters were eye-catching enough to Banbury commuters, so there was some take-up of the offer. The price was extremely good. There were similar banners and posters to tempt travel from Marylebone.

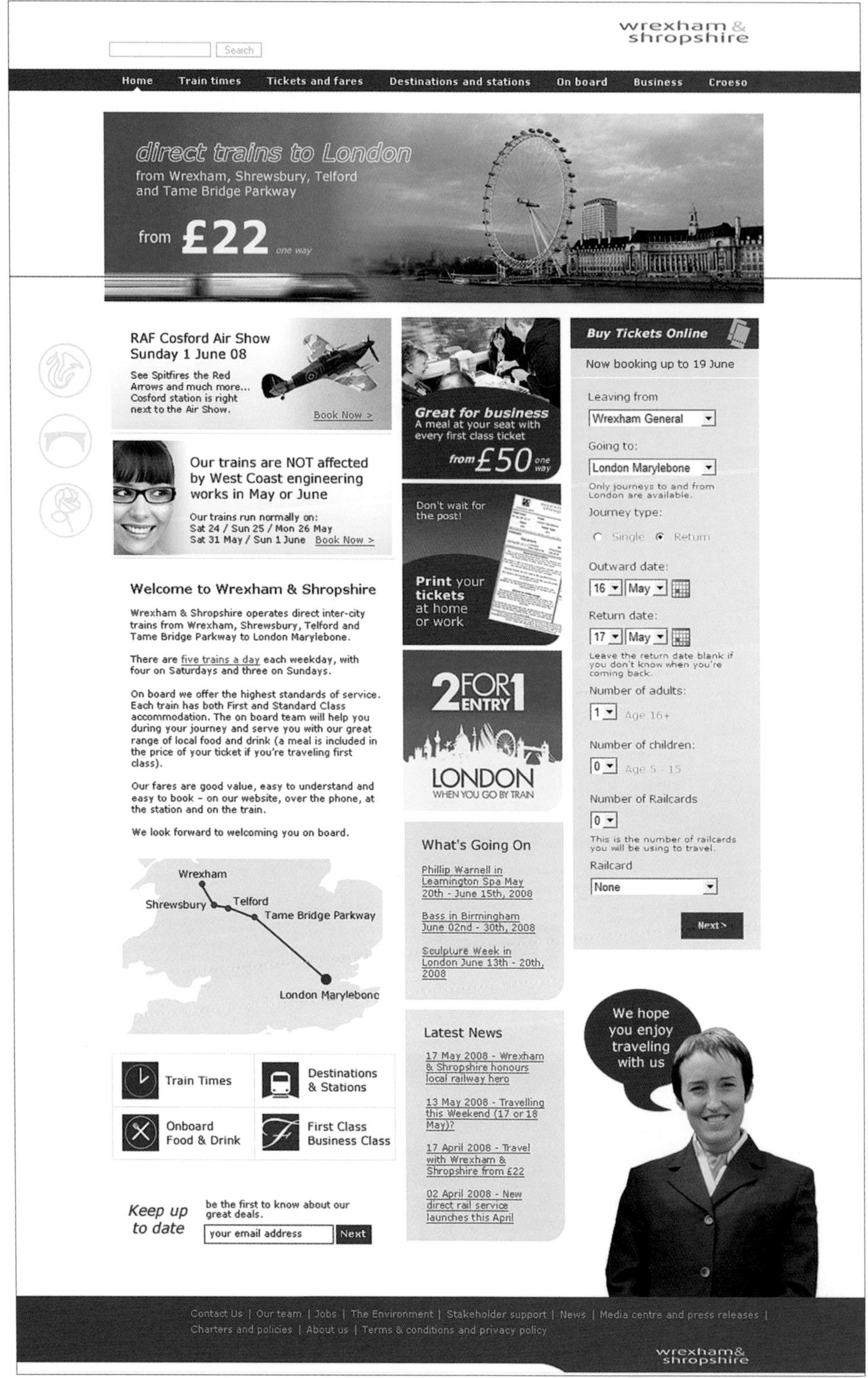

It so happened that this was one of the best sites on the Internet. The features may seem commonplace now, but in 2008 the facilities offered - like downloading tickets to the mobile phone - were at the cutting edge of technology. OK, so there were some problems in service with the mobile phone tickets, and much of that was (as usual) down to operator error. Everyone was fascinated and worked together to make it happen. There were no 'jobsworth' Train Managers; all worked to smooth any rough paths. As a result a startling amount of business came in this way; people took to it. Of course they still do, and now such systems are even stronger. The good thing was that for a little outfit, you could appeal directly to your customers, over the heads of anyone, or anything else. Sadly the mass of business was not there, as insufficient of the general population then was computer 'savvy' to take advantage of the offers. It was a bit before its time - but not very much. This was a really good attempt.

Right: *'Ruby' the big, red London Bus caused a stir wherever we took her. At Wrexham, in July 2008, outside the old library, the vehicle excited a great deal of curiosity. People did come to see what it was all about. A great deal of literature was distributed, and competition forms, timetables and special offers were all handed out, to try to generate the interest that was needed to feed traffic to the trains. This process is time consuming and a thankless task. It may appear that little progress is being made, but generating awareness took time. If there was a problem, it was that trials did not result in enough regular traffic.*

Left: *'Ruby' and the sales team went up a gear in Oswestry. This sleepy English market town (that everyone thinks is in Wales) isn't sleepy. The residents are all too aware of their isolation, and Ruby caused a considerable stir and a lot of interest. It was 23rd July 2008, right in the school holidays, so the presence of a face painter for the kids was a wise and popular addition. A great deal of literature was disbursed in Oswestry; it seemed like a location well worth a visit. Although shorn of their branch line, Gobowen, the railhead is popular, and not far away..*

Virgin, Off-Peak return. Sales were failing to come up to expectations, thus in September 2008 the WSMR advanced-single fare was reduced to £14. This was the first attempt in a common theme of reducing the fares to increase volume. The yield management system permitted the number of £14 fares sold to be limited. Numbers during the peak times were on a small scale; on off-peak trains numbers were much higher. All the reduced fare tickets had to be booked in advance, and offered a seat reservation. Yield was carefully managed.

Using an Advertising Agent

Of course the third key task was to appear in the market place, to announce Wrexham & Shropshire and then to bang the message home. Enough money was made available for regional advertising, and it was up to the sales team to supplement that in the marketplace. There was no way of the sales team alone achieving the reach needed in the target areas from Wrexham through to Tame Bridge itself. Advertising agents Brandpoint were chosen to help to get the message across. They were local to Shrewsbury and Alan Thornton had been in the business for years. He suited the regional nature of the operation. He tried to follow the twists and turns needed to tell the market what Wrexham & Shropshire was all about. The brief set by the board was calculated to appeal to a higher demographic

Here is that massive 96 sheet poster that went up right beside the M6 motorway, right by the Tame Bridge exit. It was a fiesty message, and called attention very clearly to what Wrexham & Shropshire were doing. It achieved much attention, though it did not fill the trains.

profile. It was assumed by a study of the areas served that this was most potentially effective. The first press campaign in local papers contained a frog to endorse the One Hop to London strap line. The ranine connection was not quite the association wished for. The Board was supportive in endorsing the press campaigns that the team thought they needed to drive the message home, that we were offering through trains to London. One of the big ideas was to take poster spaces to bang home the message - particularly from Tame Bridge. A massive poster on the M6, near to the exit for Tame Bridge became available to emphasise the message that there were through trains nearby to the Capital. This was made affordable by a big advertiser dropping out, so it came at a very reduced price. This was the sort of opportunity that Brandpoint were good at spotting and grabbing quickly. There was a lot of comment about the poster - it was difficult to miss. Whether it got any more business is an unmeasurable benefit , but it made Sales feel good. The star in the Wrexham & Shropshire heaven was the first class service. An opportunity arose to take another giant poster site right in Shrewsbury Station. At that time first class was becoming prohibited to managers on the grounds of economy. Since prices were so much cheaper than competitors, and the meals on Wrexham & Shropshire were so very much better, and since those using competitors also used Shrewsbury Station (and changed at Wolverhampton), the advantages of WSMR were outlined in the poster. Again, whether it was successful or not could not be proven - but it looked very good - and it was noticed and much remarked upon.

In the Marketplace

It was necessary to go out into the marketplace, to sell directly to the potential clientele and be noticed. A local supplier of rail replacement had a working fleet of London Routemasters. The owners were known to the W&S Team, and with the promise of some business, they were invited to appear, complete with bus, at the naming of 67015 *David J Lloyd* at Gobowen on 16th May 2008. The appearance certainly turned heads, and everyone

Left: *The first appearance of the London bus was at the naming of locomotive 67 015, David Lloyd at Gobowen on 16th May 2008. The unlikely combination is shown as an indulgence here because of its rarity. Both vehicles were useful to publicise Wrexham & Shropshire . Naming the locomotives, even though there were a strictly limited number, allowed civic pride to be displayed in association with the service. The bus, as 'the' icon of London, along with Big Ben, offered the clear message of the train's destination, and wherever it was placed, the large red, recognisable shape would draw curious people to see what was going on.*

Right: *In January 2009 it was time for some big messages. This huge poster site in Shrewsbury station was unused and available at the right price. It had to be done quickly but the message was conveyed in plain style. It was a bit of a double-take for Martins Kreicis, who never thought to see himself displayed thus. Although it was not mounted as neatly as could have been wished, the message was clear and strong. Did it get any business - does anyone ever know? It excited comment and it made a point.*

The Business Travel folder was produced to house various items of promotional literature, and it had to look good, or the credibility of the service suffered. The tickets were delivered in a smart looking wallet. All of this counted, but it counted by ensuring an audience and a response - it meant less if the product did not satisfy the requirements of the market. The transit time remained a disincentive to travel.

agreed that using a London Transport Routemaster in the Shropshire towns was just the thing to advertise the service. The bus therefore became a regular performer at places like Wrexham and Oswestry, but it found its most popular mark in the huge Telford shopping centre, where it was so admired that the centre forgot even to try to charge anything for it being parked there. Using this icon of London certainly provided a ready audience for the townsfolk. Indeed it encouraged custom. Good media coverage might be assumed to have penetrated the public mind - but often it has not. One has to work a lot harder than that as the media coverage normally generates the context for sales. Getting out and meeting people was the backbreaking promotional work necessary to establish a new product like this. The sell is not straightforward. Most of the people encountered had little consideration of travelling to London. They thought it was expensive by train, and that it took a very long time to get there. They were wrong about the first but right about the second. The sales activity was all about leisure transport, and so the outings had to be placed generally in the public eye in shopping areas, and was aimed at generating trial. If it was near to the school holidays, then it was wise to take a face painter to make the kids happy. It was also wise to hold a raffle for tickets to London, as well as making sure that there was appropriate publicity for the key fares and connections local to the area. Wrexham & Shropshire was very well received by the public. One is entitled to ask if this was true, then why was the service withdrawn - that answer will come later.

Encouraging Business

One of the potential sales opportunities for the Wrexham & Shropshire service was said to be Cosford station. As the venue for the 'outbase' RAF Museum, with a splendid Cold War exhibit, some 300k visitors flood to the museum each year, and it is only a few minutes walk from the station. The station is a three-minute drive from the M54, on the way to Wolverhampton, and easier to get to than Shrewsbury, for those coming in from Wales. It was a natural stopping point to encourage as Wrexham & Shropshire's Parkway station. The station served a large army camp and airfield and as this was running down, it was possible to reserve some exclusive parking space next to the station, for WSMR passengers.

***Left:** It seemed sensible to take the advertising to a place where the message could be received with interest. It was calculated that if you lived on the edge of Shrewsbury, you would be very much better off driving to Cosford to join a train there, than into the centre of Shrewsbury and paying to park. Similarly, the queue to enter/exit the paid-for car park at Telford took ages. If you lived outside Telford, it made sense to park at Cosford and get the train there. This campaign was quite expensive to run, but it made a lot of sense. It was successful, as the number of cars park in the freebie car park at Cosford steadily rose, beyond the ten mark, and beyond fifteen each day. Feedback though was less complimentary about the journey time.*

***Right:** The RAF Museum at Cosford was the companion to the RAF Museum at Hendon. WSMR thought that as some 300k visitors were generated to this fairly remote spot, that a railway station within easy stroll would present an excellent opportunity for big co-operation. It is a splendid museum, that has a very good Cold War section, but apparently the free car park (at the time) allowed the management to be uninterested in rail. Everyone was expected to arrive by car, and public transport was ignored. Perhaps flying isn't very green, and that's why?*

Much effort was expended in leafleting the area, and in promoting Cosford on petrol pumps in the local area. It took about three months for traffic to grow, but eventually the market responded to the effort and the number of cars parked passed ten, and was regularly reaching fifteen every day. As far as the RAF Museum was concerned, they were uninterested in people arriving by train, and when approached they didn't even show a rail option for reaching the museum. Eventually they reluctantly agreed to carry information on the train option, but it was hard work getting them to agree to joint promotions of the Cosford site in their main museum at Hendon. With free parking at Cosford, and the M54 minutes away, they were dangerously complacent, and Wrexham & Shropshire just had to keep on plugging away in the hope that there would be a change of heart - there wasn't. To make matters worse, the timetable was not convenient. It was an opportunity that was wasted.

Addressing the Leisure Market

When Gordon Rushton attended the first board meeting after joining, with Richard Harper's permission he suggested that the walk-on fare was too high for leisure sales, and that £24 return was likely to be more realistic, whilst remaining beyond the 'average rate'. He was politely informed that careful consideration had been given

modern railways reader

Try the WSMR for £1!

Welcome to Wrexham & Shropshire...the new main line service from London Marylebone to Shropshire and North Wales

History was made on 28 April last year, when trains operated by the new Wrexham & Shropshire Railway commenced running between London's Marylebone station, Banbury, Telford, Shrewsbury and Wrexham in North Wales.

Many readers may remember the expresses on the Great Western Railway's North Main Line, which were curtailed in March 1967, upon West Coast main line electrification. Wrexham & Shropshire seeks to restore the ethos of these services, at least in part.

The company operates quality Inter-City style carriages which all afford generous seating layouts and excellent visibility.

First Class customers enjoy a complimentary two course meal at their seats, seven days a week. The company uses locally sourced food and beverages where possible. (Standard class customers may also purchase full meals.)

Reader offer

As a limited introductory offer, Wrexham & Shropshire is offering al *Modern Railways* readers a chance to ride the new service for just £1, adult or child standard class return.

This offer is valid only on the northbound Wrexham & Shropshire 06.45 train, any weekday (M-F) until 27 February 2009, returning the same day. Complete the coupon (photocopies accepted) and send to the address shown with a self-addressed, stamped envelope. Only one coupon per household. Visa / Visadebit / Mastercard / Maestro payment only, no cheques or cash.

Advance postal bookings only, allow 10 days for tickets. Last date for receipt of coupons: 17 February 2009. For full details of terms and conditions see www.wrexhamandshropshire.co.uk/£1, also for timetables, destination details, and touring suggestions. £1 seats availability is limited. Outwards 06.45 (or 08.00 from Banbury) returning on the 15.23 or 17.23 from Wrexham or intermediately. Issued subject to the National Conditions of Carriage.

Fill in this form and post to: Wrexham & Shropshire Promotions, The Pump House, Shrewsbury, SY1 2DP

Mr/Mrs/Ms

Name (as it appears on your credit card)

Full

Please make any alterations to coupon he

Daytime phone/mobile:

Destination station:

No of persons travelling (max 2):

Day and date in February you wish to travel:

Return time of train:

Card number:

Expiry date: Issue date/issue no:

Security code:

Email:

I do/donot agree to allow my contact details to be used to receive further information from Wrexham and Shropshire Railway.

Modern Railways FEBRUARY 2009 www.modern-railways.com 11

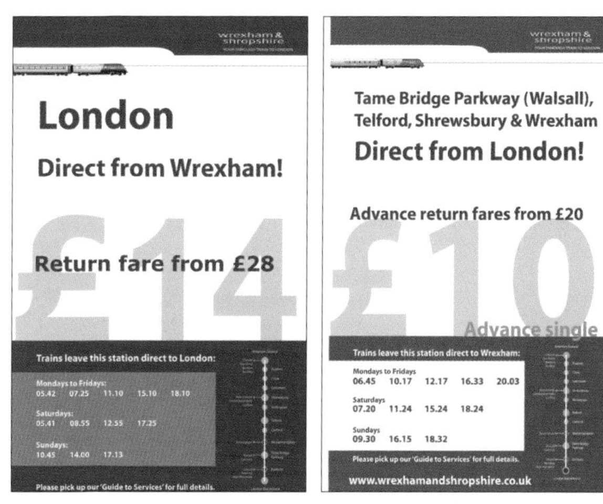

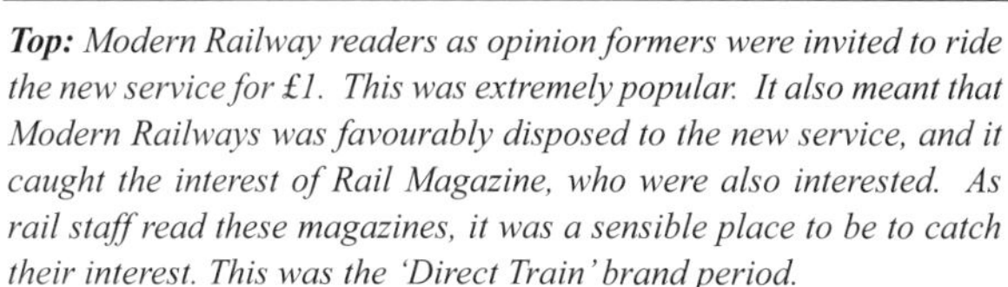

Top: *Modern Railway readers as opinion formers were invited to ride the new service for £1. This was extremely popular. It also meant that Modern Railways was favourably disposed to the new service, and it caught the interest of Rail Magazine, who were also interested. As rail staff read these magazines, it was a sensible place to be to catch their interest. This was the 'Direct Train' brand period.*

Top Right: *The two posters are early (left) and later (right) examples of station posters that gave the headline fare and train times. These posters were unfailingly displayed, as they diverted inquiries away from booking staff. In the places where Wrexham & Shropshire was greeted with some hostility, posters were of great worth. The website address appeared on the later example, as it was soon apparent that the efficient and friendly site was a key means of booking, with 25% or more of bookings being made that way.*

Right: The newsad for the successful Summer Saver promotion differed from the brochure a little, by having the brash yellow lettering needed to stand out in the newspapers.

to fares levels and the Great Men were of the opinion that the levels set were competitive and appropriate for the operation that had begun running . The suggestion was made that getting on with the selling would be more advantageous than revisiting decisions already made. Unfortunately the leisure traffic did not grow, until the introduction of the Summer Saver shown above. Days Out, Santa Specials, and January Sales all followed in their time. Traffic rose steeply in response. But was it enough?

Promotions were intended to offer journey purpose to fill the less busy trains - this was a joke, as none of the trains were busy, except on perhaps Friday nights. In that time since the old GWR and BR(W) had ceased through

The promotions were not shockingly original. London is a natural market for rail companies, and most bang the drum for it energetically. The Santa Special was novel for a main line company - it was hard work, but kids liked it. The rest of the promotions were humdrum, but vital to the interest in trying to boost custom. All was carried out with great speed and almost zero resources. The flow of traffic was not as good as one would have hoped at these prices; it was significant that competition was strong and WSMR had its hands tied behind its back.

service, people had lost the wish to travel to London by train. It was extremely hard work to try to put that back. All were enthusiastic face to face, when promoting in say the Shropshire towns, but it did not mature to solid leisure sector travel in the quantities that the population figures may have led one to suppose when assessing the market.

There were competitions, posters, leaflets; all were backed with radio campaigns and supported in the newspapers. Massive leafleting went on in the communities with great zeal. The poor results were puzzling, as the team expected better, and previous experience was that such activity, never failed. We even had people going round door-to-door with leaflets through the letterbox - that always worked - not here! Of course experience is also clear that with a new service one needs to work hard for six-months before an appreciable demand is visible, unless there are extremely interesting prices, or something much better than the competition.

The rather disturbing conclusion that was beginning to dawn upon those slogging away to sell the Wrexham & Shropshire product was that the journey time difference was just too much to bridge, or there was something else that added to that, which was less obvious and not so visible. The unrewarded effort was rather disappointing.

Right: *David J. Lloyd, 67015 was named on 16th May 2008 in the station that Mr Lloyd knew so well, Ruabon. The locomotive occupied the Oswestry bay platform, in order to be out of the way for other traffic to pass. This was a 'rare' bit of track for a locomotive to occupy. Since the withdrawal of the connecting service, it sees little use, alas. This was the venue where the locomotive was accompanied by the London Routemaster Ruby, that was afterwards recruited as a sales tool.*

Left: *This was the important moment of the naming of 67014 in the bay platform at Wellington Station. It was appropriate to bring Wellington into the limelight. The station had services at one time to Stafford, Market Drayton and Ironbridge, and seems rather forlorn. On 15th July 2008 the station was a buzz of excitement. It was not possible to name the locomotive in the town of Telford, with its new station, as both tracks there are busy, and there would have been no time for ceremony. Shifnall Primary School were proud - and well they might be.*

Naming the locomotives

In recent years locomotive naming has been popular for public relations purposes, but the WSMR team felt there were too many inappropriate examples. So it was resolved to turn the locomotive namings into community-based events. A 'name the train' competition was announced in March 2008, open to primary schools across Shropshire and Wrexham. Children from Key Stage 2 were set the task of suggesting appropriate names for three of the locomotives, and providing reasons for their suggestion. For the winners, the pupil making the suggestion was joined by their class for the naming ceremony, and the class was given a complimentary trip to London.

For the fourth locomotive a different approach was taken, and it is difficult to imagine a closer link to the community. It's first important to understand the very unusual recent history of Gobowen station. Back in the 1980s British Rail closed the station ticket office on the basis it didn't sell enough tickets. David Lloyd, at the time a geography lecturer at nearby Moreton Hall School, decided that running a station ticket office would make an excellent project for his pupils. He approached BR to obtain permission and the necessary equipment, and began selling tickets on a daily basis to passengers at the station, and also meeting the travel needs of local businesses, with students involved in all aspects, from actually selling tickets

***Right:** Fortunately W&S had an managing director who was able to appear everywhere, as fixer, with screwdriver in hand, as strategist at board meetings, or here as ambassador when naming locomotives. Professor Quentin Leiper, Past President of the Institution of Civil Engineers, presents Andy Hamilton, with an engraved glass bust of Thomas Telford (first President of the Institution of Civil Engineers) during the ceremony to name 67014 after the famous engineer. Tuesday 15th July 2008, Wellington station.*

Geoff Plumb

***Left:** Tuesday 15th July was one of those brilliant , cloudless days of summer that everyone loves. Photographer Geoff Plumb chose a high vantage point to record the energetic waves offered by Shifnal Primary School. Everyone from the school had been looking forward to the day, as the fact that they had won a naming competition made it exciting - and it was a rare event. Wellington had never seen anything like it. This was rather rare track for 67014.*

to book-keeping. The project flourished into a community business and is still going strong today. Meanwhile David retired from the school and became a local councillor and champion of the railway between Shrewsbury and Chester. David was the first person to phone John Nelson on the day Wrexham & Shropshire made its proposals public in 2006, was hugely supportive, and excited by the prospect of through trains to London after such a long time without them. The whole team were all saddened when David passed away, after a long illness, before the first train ran. So it seemed only right to name 67015 *David J Lloyd*. The nameplate was unveiled by David's widow and his daughter at Gobowen station on 16th May 2008, as part of a community rail event at the station celebrating his life.

The other locomotives had more obvious names, chosen by schools.

Alfred Edward Housman was born in Bromsgrove in 1859. Considered one of the foremost classical scholars of his age, he is remembered most for his evocative poetry contemplating young lives lost through war, and the changes wrought to life in the English countryside. His most famous cycle of 63 poems, published as 'A Shropshire Lad' in 1896, remains closely associated with the county to this day. So it was not difficult to select *A Shropshire*

Right: *There was a call for 'all hands' when on 3rd July 2008 67012 was named* A Shropshire Lad *at Shrewsbury station by two children of Clee Hill School who had won a competition to name the locomotive. Wrexham & Shropshire Managing Director, Andy Hamilton addresses the class of Clee Hill School that attended the ceremony. This naming created a great deal of interest by providing a platform for local publicity in the Wrexham and Shropshire heartlands. Normally 'PR' people look after this, but not in such a small outfit. That was why 'all hands' were needed.*

Left: *This was the moment just after the unveiling ceremony in the middle of Shrewsbury Station. The bustle of trains coming and going was all around the children from Clee Hill School. It was an appropriate choice of name, as of course Housmann's poems had to be something of a natural choice for their reading after this! The kids very much enjoyed their celebrity status, and they had the pleasure of a trip to London on Wrexham & Shropshire to come.*
The choice of dark grey as a background on the light-grey locomotive sides made the whole locomotive look very smart.

Lad from the list of locomotive names suggested by the schoolchildren. It was appropriate that the suggestion came from Clee Hill County Primary School, as Clee figures in the opening words of the first Shropshire Lad poem. Locomotive 67012 was named with due ceremony in Platform 6 at Shrewsbury station on 3rd July 2008.

Born in Dumfriesshire in 1757, Thomas Telford was the pre-eminent civil engineer of his generation. Famed for his construction of bridges, canals and roads much of his work has links to Shropshire, resulting from his appointment in 1787 as Surveyor of Public Works for the county. The most spectacular structure was the Pontcysyllte Aqueduct, completed in 1805. Rising 38 metres above the River Dee below it is over 300 metres long and consists of 19 cast iron troughs sitting on stone piers. The use of cast iron in this way was a new method of construction, made all the more notable by the size of the aqueduct, which remains the longest and highest in Britain.

In 1818 Telford was one of the founders of the Institution of Civil Engineers, becoming its first President, and he was later elected Fellow of the Royal Society. Many of his achievements in Shropshire and the surrounding area survive today, and his legacy has been marked more recently in naming the new town of Telford.

Right: *On 9th July 2008, David Jones from Froncysyllte County Primary School pulled the curtain string to reveal the new name for locomotive 67013. He is seen here with some of his classmates in the background. The naming took place in the Wrexham & Shropshire depot sidings, conveniently located adjacent to the station at Wrexham. It was an appropriate choice of name, suggested by the children, and endorsed by the County Borough. This was a PR success.*

Left: *Lads from Froncysyllte school were pleased to be conducted into the cab of 67013 and to be shown around. The concentrated looks on their faces tells a tale. If the truth be told, the railway plays only a minor part in these kids' lives today. This was appreciated by the WSMR Team, who set out on this path of calling attention to their service inside the community. This was a positive way to do this, as well as providing an entertainment that the children will remember for a long while. The whole class also got a day out in London, courtesy Wrexham & Shropshire.*

The successful competition entry received from Froncycysllte County Primary, in the shadow of Telford's aqueduct, suggested 'Dyfrbont Pontcycysllte'. At the time of the competition, the County Borough of Wrexham was seeking World Heritage status for the aqueduct, and so this was a very appropriate choice linking to both Telford and the Wrexham area. The naming ceremony for locomotive 67013 took place in Wrexham & Shropshire's sidings at Wrexham General station on 9th July 2008. It has been reported that the locomotive carries its name in Welsh on one side and English on the other – this is not the case. World Heritage status for the aqueduct was confirmed in 2009.

The suggestion for the final naming came from Shifnal Primary. It was that of the famous engineer himself, and so locomotive 67014 was named 'Thomas Telford' on 15th July 2008. Unfortunately there is no suitable location for a naming ceremony at Telford Central station without affecting the normal passage of trains, and so the locomotive was named at Wellington station where there is a bay platform that is very rarely used. So the naming was done there.

Linking with the local community

Wrexham & Shropshire made a big effort to get involved with the local community, whether through attending local

Left: *Of course it is great fun to dress up and have a day out. In this case it had a serious purpose. The idea of a Marylebone Travel Fair was successful as a way of attracting attention to all the services from the terminal. Wrexham & Shropshire was popular as it added to the range of destinations and was well supported, especially by the Chester-Shrewsbury Rail Partnership, led by Shiela Dee with unflagging energy. Here they are on their way to the Fair, in the buffet car, suitably dressed in costume and brimming with good will. The Fairs were well attended and captured attention for the market at the London end in a cost-effective way.*

events or drawing other organisations into joint marketing initiatives. Marylebone Travel Fairs created opportunities for attractions throughout Shropshire and North East Wales directly to promote to the London market, and offered plenty of opportunities for daft costumes that were well appreciated and attracted interest. The Marylebone Travel Fair also called attention to Marylebone as a London terminal station. It was perhaps the only station in London where such an extensive event could be mounted.

Innovations

Wrexham & Shropshire was not expecting to set up retail offices, and retail sales from third-party conventional ticket offices required a rate of 9% commission to be paid. For Internet sales by a third-party, the commission rate was 7% although this reduced to 5% in 2008. This is how it was calculated to make commercial sense for the company to invest in its own Internet retailing platform (see Page 112) with commission rates expected to be as low as 2%. It was possible to simplify the operation as the Wrexham & Shropshire service offer was for few trains to a small number of destinations. The website would only sell Wrexham & Shropshire tickets, escaping the complication of the full range of interavailable tickets, valid on all operators' services, to the complete range of over 2,000 National Rail stations. This partial retailing was possible within the industry's ticketing agreements, with which Wrexham & Shropshire was required to comply, subject to suitable disclaimers on the website. The strategy worked well. Within six months of starting service, close to 50% of Wrexham & Shropshire's ticket sales were on-line, a proportion most train operators could only aspire to given the attractive, low, commission rates incurred.

There were more benefits from the Wrexham & Shropshire on-line booking system. Every single ticket type was available via print-at-home barcode, at a time when other operators were just beginning to experiment with this convenient technology. Few railway companies in the world could boast such a high percentage of their tickets issued in such a modern, cost effective and consumer friendly way.

This was not all. Wrexham & Shropshire sold thousands of tickets through local hotels. They were sold as an ancillary sale, much like car hire and airport parking is sold by travel agents. Far from using high tech wizardry, hotels bought books of paper tickets and wrote them out by hand. Few rail companies have put effort in to packaging rail as an ancillary sale successfully, yet the market showed an appetite for this.

Wrexham & Shropshire was also the first British railway company to experiment with social media. Few people saw the point of Wrexham & Shropshire's Facebook page when it was started. However it quickly became a good way to interact with most frequent passengers. At times like weekends, when the timetable could be changeable, this was a blessing. The page still existed after the end of the service to be full of "we miss you" posts – so much so that after the closure many staff found this overwhelming and asked people to stop as it proved upsetting.

Still the triple whammy of low yield fares, stations that

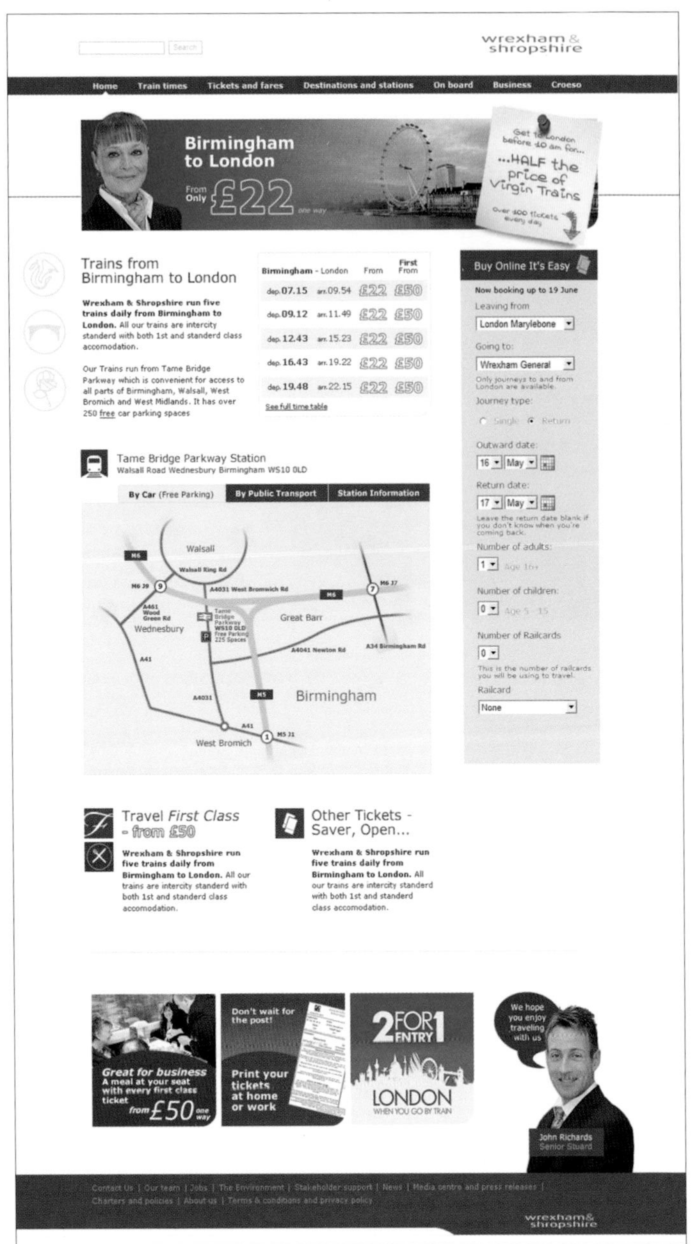

***Left:** Concentrating all upon Wrexham & Shropshire made for a much better sales offer, and more effective access to the tickets. Any message was a Wrexham & Shropshire message, and Assertis managed to combine a high level of technology with a smart and accessible means of delivery. Looking at other Train Operating Company websites of the period, one is less wondering of why it was that such a high level of sales came this way. It was all the more reassuring that dependence on third-party retailing was lessened by effective web retailing.*

ignored the service, and information systems which made them invisible, left the sales team with its work cut out. To help get around these problems, excellent relationships were built with short break companies, who put many weekend trippers aboard the trains. Arrangements like this worked well for both sides and brought in much needed revenue.

Unwelcome Enquiries

The National Rail Enquiries Service (NRES), available to all Internet users and the most popular way to find the times of the trains was one area of huge frustration. When spoken to, the people at ATOC who ran it were so polite and helpful. Nothing was too much trouble - they would ensure that all worked smoothly. Alas they were not masters in their own house - it was the software was. Time and time again the system, when interrogated for a Shrewsbury or Wrexham to London journey, would include Wrexham & Shropshire for some inquiries and not others. It was expected by most on the line from Shrewsbury to Chester that reaching London meant a change. However when the system advised catching a train to Wolverhampton and change, sometimes the train to Wolverhampton was the Wrexham & Shropshire service to London direct! Consumer research demonstrated that many passengers preferred to avoid connections, even if it made their journey longer, and the NRES system was confounding the wish of passengers to pay cheaper Wrexham & Shropshire fares for that longer, direct journey.

It was not understood by the WSMR team why a standard inquiry from London to Shrewsbury failed to show all the Wrexham & Shropshire through services - and neither could the people at ATOC, who at first offered the most charming of blandishments, promising to make changes immediately in order to sort matters out. The promised solutions were reported to the WSMR Board, who received the news with satisfaction, Later questions arose when John Nelson ran a trial of the system. He was peeved to find that the problem had not gone away, despite assurances received. The WSMR sales team was so busy doing other things that the investigation time needed to produce a detailed analysis was not made available until this new discovery.

The apparently erratic delivery of information was eventually understood when a 'teccie' explained that the priority for a through journey was not accorded any high value. The reason for this was that through journeys were almost without exception faster, therefore they needed no priority, as they would be subject to logical nomination as the most rapid transit. 'Almost' in this case excluded Wrexham & Shropshire, where you would leave earlier, but arrive by direct train later. Thus the system just assumed that the inquirer would rather change trains and

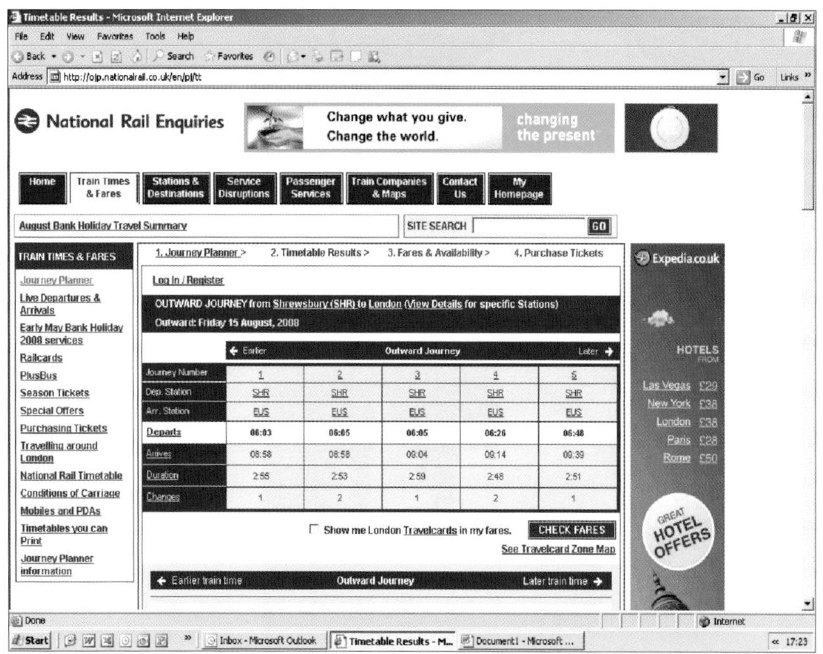

***Left:** The screen display to a simple inquiry for trains from Shrewsbury to London was inconsistent. For many queries the Wrexham & Shropshire direct services were not shown such as the 0625 ex Shrewsbury, that is omitted here, only Euston is shown. This also led to the passenger not being offered the option of a cheap fare. When the inquiry was progressed to the "Check Fares" option, the cheapest fare of £43.50 for an advance single was the only option - this was almost twice the price of the Wrexham & Shropshire Advance Single at £24 which only had availability on the 0625 departure. Later upgrades of the National Rail Enquiries algorithm were altered to insert a button to include direct trains. There was a future option promised to right matters - but that meant altering the system to place a higher 'value' on direct journeys. The reason these anomalies arose was the system's inbuilt assumption that the passenger wanted the 'fastest' journey. Yet there were examples elsewhere that could not show slower, direct services, like on the London-Midland franchise, and on some southern services, but the system managed these. WSMR thought it discriminatory.*

delivered nominated services in those terms. So there were in consequence some illogical and ill-advised journey suggestions, even involving changing off direct Wrexham & Shropshire services, meaning long intermediate waits for the slimmest of end-to-end time advantages. WSMR were, they said, an exception.The only way that Wrexham & Shropshire services could be assured of unfailing nomination was if the customer opted to choose the 'direct services only' button. This was unfailing, but it was not a highlighted choice, it involved a complex explanation to nominate it. To make it 'automatic' meant major alterations in a national system for this one operation.

It was pointed out to no avail that the London, Northampton and Birmingham service was similar, with London Midland offering poorer transit times than Virgin, but much cheaper fares, but WSMR were on a 'loser', and thus were obliged to withdraw politely, and put up with it. So finding that the most popular timetable inquiry system in the land failed to champion the service was a severe blow. National Rail Enquiries favoured the status quo.

Wrexham & Shropshire also had a nominated telephone sales inquiry bureau, and suspicions grew that the service needed to sell the service and its advantages was not being provided. Although a British bureau with staff in UK, they could not place the Wrexham & Shropshire service at the top of their list, as the volume of calls could not justify this. Neither could WSMR justify running its own bureau - this was too costly. Thus it was necessary to compromise is this area, and accept service below the optimum.

There were stations featured in tales coming back from the public where they had been told that either they could not book for Wrexham & Shropshire, or that the service did not exist. Both Shrewsbury and Marylebone were so accused. Visits to the management of both places brought effusive assurances that they were keen to sell WSMR. Yet the complaints did not stop. There was only one thing to do, and that was to try a 'mystery shopper', where someone visits with real money and makes a purchase - the reports were true. The people responsible were 'spoken to' and this revealed the need for better training courses and more product experience. More 'staff educationals' were run and the problem went away; this was all part of the everyday life of 'start-up'.

The story of Tame Bridge

This station was accepted as a challenge by the marketing and sales team. Inspection on-site revealed a busy commuter station, that evidently had the morning rush, but then settled down to slumber until the return of people in the evening. The extensive car park filled up by about 08.30, and from that time on, there were only a handful of spaces. Even though, as a manned station, it was mercifully free of the smashed bits of safety glass that indicated car theft, a full car park wasn't likely to be too useful for the services at nine, or half-past twelve. Interestingly, nearby were large housing estates, like Friar Park, and the Delves. The main road outside offers an excellent bus service, and the M6 Junction 9 is nearby. All-told Tame Bridge Parkway had all the apparent attributes of a potential major success. Yet, looked at more carefully, there were flaws in any boundless expectation. Other

Left: *Tame Bridge Parkway passengers joining the 09.06 train to Wrexham on 28th October 2008. Almost no one got off the train, indeed there were almost no passengers travelling to and from Tame Bridge to London. - which was a problem. Those joining northbound were part of the ORCATS revenue share. Any travelling to or from London were more likely to hold a WSMR exclusive ticket. It proved to be impossible to generate enthusiasm for travel to and from London in Tame Bridge and the surrounding area. The traffic seen joining here may have looked healthy, but it did little to assist the bottom line.*

Parkways seem to have nearer and simpler connections with their adjacent motorways. However, major road routes nearby ought, WSMR thought, to confer potential.

The community leaflet at Tame Bridge attempted to be 'all things'. It was trying to get across the existence of the direct service to London. Other information followed, trying to promote the service. The local populace remained unmoved. The response here was negligible, and that was a shock. If there had been time, focus groups could have been used to find out why A later attempt was made on this community, but as will be explained later, it was no more successful in creating profitable earnings.

Gordon Rushton, and John Nelson were driven carefully round the area by Richard Harper, and all had been impressed by the close-packed housing, generally prosperous air of the surrounding area, a sure potential of a thriving source of business for Wrexham & Shropshire's train service, just down the road. All that was needed was surely to tell everyone about the service, and a stream of gold would issue forth on to the trains. Richard Worrall was sure that he could supply the resources to leaflet every dwelling, so it was agreed to set that up. First it

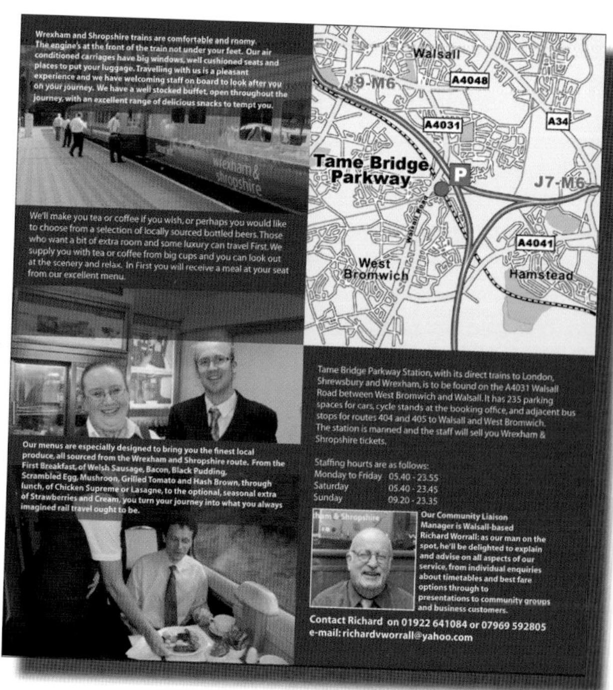

was essential to mount a charm offensive upon the station. Gordon Rushton visited the station staff and made sure they had sufficient information and publicity about the services. The station was administered by London Midland and the staff were helpful and welcoming. The frequent service of trains had only one or two people joining or alighting from Tame Bridge Parkway during the day, which was the reason why the staff had time to listen and to be helpful. They were duly set up with information, and they embarked upon some educational visits. They accepted posters, timetables, leaflets in a display, and welcomed tutelage in selling the Wrexham & Shropshire products.

Trains from Tame Bridge to London left as follows:

Tame Bridge to London (Marylebone)			
Dep:	**06.44**	**09.02**	**13.02**
Arr:	**08.57**	**11.23**	**15.23**

Tame Bridge was a 2hrs 20 mins transit to London, and there was only really one 'comfortable' train. The suburban service run by London Midland was loosely every 20 minutes, and took 20 minutes to get into New Street. In 2008, the 09.45 Virgin Trains Pendolino was in Euston at 11.23. Later the 09.30 Pendolino was in at 10.54, and there was service every twenty minutes. Wrexham & Shropshire had an uphill struggle to compete.

Richard Worrall marshalled his cohorts. The leaflet for house-to-house- drops on all those vast estates was duly prepared, and then the assault began. We were proud of such a major sales drive, and looked forward to the surge of business - but nothing happened. By autumn 2008 Wrexham & Shropshire was only managing to generate 9 return journeys per day between Tame Bridge and London, despite all that sales activity. In contrast 90 journeys daily were generated from Shrewsbury.

Assessing progress

There was a warning note, that soon became apparent. In areas of the Midlands, unlike the London and South East area, people were not in the habit of using the train. The idea of travelling 175 miles by rail needed to be sold as something quite special. The re-arrival of through services to London was too late to capitalise on what had gone before - that was now forgotten. The WSMR team were not selling 'a better alternative' they were selling a slow trip to London, and that is more difficult.

The business community was vital to the interest. It is inevitable that the Wrexham & Shropshire service should seek the business market to achieve the growth in income that it sought. On the face of it, using the train to access London was hardly an unknown concept in this market. There wasn't time to spend analysing all the different competitive flows that may cancel sales effort for Wrexham & Shropshire. Hindsight does this best - and so far little of this had been acquired. Thus the initial effort was put into bringing the existence of the service, and its various unique sales points to the notice of the main potential market. At that time, the two places that seemed to offer the best return for effort expended were Telford and Shrewsbury.

Business events were held, well attended by the local grandees and the business community. Telford was a particularly sparkling example They all listened patiently; most were welcoming, and agreed to have a trial of the service. Many offered to sign up for the Business Travel Service. This all looked very good; all were generally pleased about through services to London. The advantages of working on the train (despite the extended transit times) was carefully explained. There was interest in the refurbished carriages, with comfortable seats, food on board, charging points for computers, and Wi-Fi for e-mails and Internet. It was a very real prospect that one could spend some concentrated working hours on the train with the laptop. Many people would respond to a quiet environment, well fed and undisturbed, getting on with business. Some extra journey minutes were 'not a problem'. A Pendolino journey was devalued by the disturbances of change of train, and the overcrowding that prevailed. Also there was no charging points or free Wi-Fi in standard class. The follow up to the seminars by Chris Rowlands in the Business Travel Service was to generate personal visits to sample the service, and a respectable number of organisations were added to the client list. Chris became kept busy, booking space on (any TOC's) trains, and continuing to sell as many tickets as possible on Wrexham & Shropshire.

Snags came from people that reported back, and the verdict hit Wrexham & Shropshire hard, as it comprised two unassailable problems. The return service choice in the evenings was too meagre, and the journey time was too prolonged. On the former, there was a thought to sell an 'open' return, so that the holder could come back via Euston and Wolverhampton - but it was very expensive. On the latter the locomotive speed restriction for Class 67s between London Marylebone and Aynho Junction kept transit speeds to 60mph. Whether this was from physical constraint or not did not count. It was up to WSMR to raise the limit - if they could not, then the risks were their own. Although beyond Aynho, through Banbury, it was a 90mph railway; around Birmingham, junction speed restrictions were highly restrictive. The need for high productivity

Left: *One of the events to gain the attention of the business community was to attend the Telford Business Breakfast. Invited organisations could address the assembled guests who met to hear information about the latest developments in their area. Telford was of particular importance as there were large organisations based in the town who had personnel that travelled to London regularly by train. Pitching to them was a vital opportunity. WSMR Commercial Manager Richard Harper shows the timetable to delegates in Telford on Wednesday 8th October 2008. On the right is Andrew Mason, the Telford Business Partnership Chairman.* **TBP**

on the train, with an undisturbed working environment was the only card left to play. The Wi-Fi, charging points and new coach environment was not 'yet' available - and wasn't going to be. Those that play down the failure to deliver the refurbished coaches with recharging points miss the fact that a dead laptop, or mobile phone with no charge-point leads to no productivity. One just doesn't travel that way again. So potential W&S customers, did not complain, they just didn't use Wrexham & Shropshire, though they appreciated the goodwill, and the customer care, and said so warmly. No one realised that this could happen: trial, congratulations, excellent feedback, then - no customers. This had an unfortunate effect on the revenue performance, and it affected all market segments.

Budget and Actual Revenue Performance: £k					
	2008			2009	
Period	***Pd 11***	***Pd 12***	***Pd 13***	***Pd 1***	***Pd 2***
Budget	***728***	***728***	***566***	***316***	***351***
Actual	***318***	***298***	***199***	***303***	***335***

It was agreed that the 2008 Budget was undeliverable and thus the 2009 budget was adjusted accordingly. By the end of 2008 there was an accumulated loss of -£6.4m, which became -£10.9m in 2009.

Identity Problems

The question of the match between the corporate identity and the brand values that had been created for the service, and what was being produced on the ground were hampering the strength of the Wrexham & Shropshire financial performance. When out on the 'road' selling, there was much warm and positive response for the concept of the new service. Most of the general public was interested, and enthused by the descriptions they were given. The prospect of through services was greeted with pleasure. Generating trial was encouragingly easy, but the loadings did not indicate the expected results. Never for a moment did the sales team question the brand and its values that had been set for them, and neither did the Board - perhaps that was a mistake. Hindsight shows that nice on-board service, but in rather tatty coaches, would not compensate for such an extended transit time, despite cheerful exhortations to use the train. People got on at Shrewsbury, and got off at Wolverhampton - few took WSMR forward. Wrexham & Shropshire took just under three hours, whereas by Virgin Pendolino it would take one-and-three-quarter hours (though a wait was indicated for the hourly service).

It requires superb niceness and particularly lovely service to sit for an extra hour when you could be at the destination more quickly. People who went on the WSMR service were beginning to feed this back. The start-up income was slow in its increase, and lagged behind the budget figures There were exhortations to work harder to try to overcome this slowdown in the growth, yet the Board still resisted the call to simplify and moderate fares still further, insisting that the new coaches were 'near'. Trial trips continued to be generated by sales. Disappointingly, regular business was not forthcoming.

Matters for WSMR became worse when in the December 2008 timetable, Virgin put on a 20 minute

Right: *Business people at work on the comfortable Wrexham & Shropshire train. Yet you can see the faded grandeur of the second-hand West Coast rolling stock - few were fooled. Fortunately Virgin had done quite a good job, except that there was trim missing in awkward places, and there was no way of recharging that computer on the long journey. Unfortunately refurbishing the existing stock was not entertained, as everyone 'said' the new would be along soon. It took over two years, in which the tatty cars became tattier. This was more like Bulgarian State Railways - not good.*

Left: *The refurbished cars were entering service by 30th July 2010 - but this was unfortunately too late. Yet here at last was the computer plugs for recharging, the Wi-Fi that was awaited, the refurbished standard of service that had been promised when the service started - 'within a few weeks' - but in fact that became 27 long months. The effects of not having the new rolling stock was played down by management and staff, but that was largely because making a fuss about it would achieve little but demoralisation, and would cause rifts in the structure. However, it was more serious an omission than was supposed.*

frequency service from Birmingham New Street to London, and London Midland began hourly service along the Trent Valley Stations, through Tamworth and Lichfield. In the first case the overcrowding on Pendolino Birmingham - London services to London promptly vanished - and the journey became fast and comfortable. In the second case, the tributary stream of people that found their way to Wrexham & Shropshire from Telford and Cosford and potentially from Tame Bridge, had much better choice elsewhere, and the figures showed this.

There was nothing that could be done until journey times were reduced on Wrexham & Shropshire, and the new coaches arrived, except to make as much noise as possible and sell hard. Calling at Wolverhampton was still not an option apparently. There was a base clientele of people, who liked the service, had a bit more time to spare and really appreciated the direct trains. However, it soon became clear that there were not enough to allow a five-train service to run at a profit. This fact was borne in upon the management when the struggle to generate traffic from Tame Bridge with publicity, newspaper advertising and radio campaigns brought back extremely poor results. It did not seem that the large number of people who lived in the area could be stimulated to use the Wrexham & Shropshire service at all. That was not good.

4 of the WSMR Posters

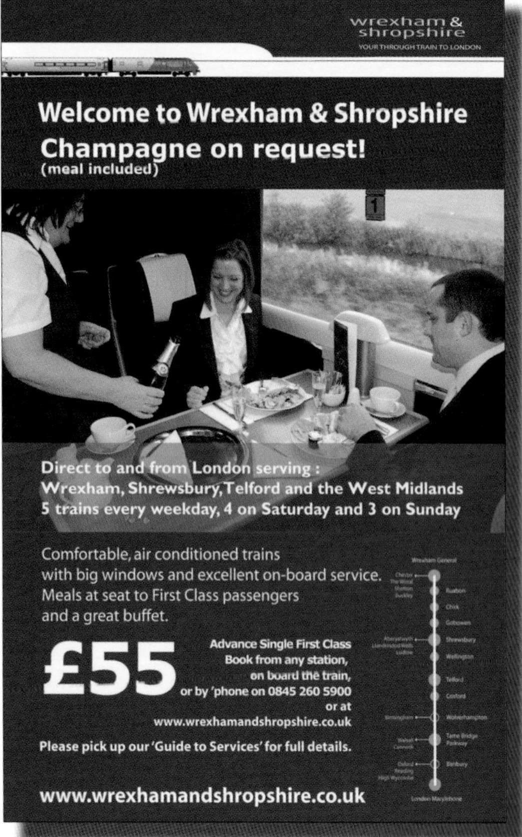

67010 is double-heading with 67021 and 67012 is dead on the rear of the train as 1Z95 passes King's Sutton in the dying rays of the sun at 20:05 on Saturday 23rd May 2009. This was a returning football special from Wembley Stadium to Shrewsbury for Shrewsbury Town fans and at 8 cars was the longest train operated by W&S. Driver Paul Belton waves, while Ops Manager Mark Edlington enjoys the ride in the secondman's seat. **Geoff Plumb**

Going the extra mile

The increasingly business-focused approach of BR in the 1980 saw another round of scrapping, as the widespread introduction of modern, hi-speed, multiple-unit trains, running at frequent, clock-face intervals increased capacity and led to many of these 1950s built carriages being withdrawn. The reduction in locomotive hauled trains, and the concentration on core businesses was coupled with trouble on football specials. The business was abandoned; the excursions were scaled right down, and leisure travellers were left to the flexibility of their own transport.

After privatisation the special trains leisure business passed to specialist operators and the concept of relief or special trains to meet demand peaks was strictly controlled by what could be provided from maintenance spares or from running extra trips with existing assets. Yet with a background of rising traffic congestion and increased fuel costs for the motorist, the attraction of rail for leisure purposes remains. On occasions, Wrexham & Shropshire concluded there was a commercial case for bucking the trend – something the company enjoyed – in order to respond to the opportunity for more passengers to fill its trains.

A great opportunity to show what could be done emerged in May 2009. Shrewsbury Town FC reached the final of the League Two playoffs at Wembley Stadium on 23rd May that year. They faced Gillingham, with the winner promoted to League One. In the days leading up to the match, the town went football crazy, and it was clear there was a huge demand for tickets, and therefore travel to the match. With Wrexham & Shropshire's route in to London passing through Wembley Stadium station, the company was well placed to capitalise. Yet Shrewsbury Town's appearance was only confirmed by their semi-final win over Bury less than two weeks before the final, meaning detailed planning of trains had to wait. On the day, normal timetabled train services from Wrexham to London had additional stops at Wembley Stadium, extra carriages were added to the busiest trains, and three special trains were run from Shrewsbury, one of which was an 8 coach Class 168 borrowed from Chiltern Railways. Over 2,000 football fans, plus families and friends of the players, used Wrexham & Shropshire on the day to get to the game. Sadly Shrewsbury Town's footballers lost out to a last minute Gillingham goal, and would have to wait until 2012 to secure promotion to League One.

Andrew Griffith's splendid picture of the special train for the Three Peaks Challenge special, that ran to Snowdon, Scafell Pike and Ben Nevis. Mr Griffiths placed the picture in the calendar competition, which is why it is available to publish here. The train is crossing the 1894 Rannoch Viaduct, and will then enter the lonely Rannoch Station at 141.2 miles from Glasgow. **Andrew Griffiths**

Early in 2010, Andy Hamilton was approached by the charity Railway Children, asking if Wrexham & Shropshire would be interested in running the "Three Peaks Challenge". This special train takes fundraisers by rail each year in June to climb Snowdon, Scafell Pike and Ben Nevis in 48 hours. Andy sought permission to investigate further, and called Steve Roast.

> *'He asked me if I thought we could do it. My reply was anything's possible, it's a case of arranging it.'*

Andy discussed the possibility further, and came back to Steve and asked him to project manage it. 'I took it away, looking at which companies and depots could help – since Wrexham & Shropshire was not a national operator.' As Steve said, anything's possible and being for charity everyone in the industry is helpful.

> *'The key thing was crewing the train, and I had good knowledge of who could help. But I was a bit stuck north of Preston, so that was a real worry. My friend Ian Kapur at GB Railfreight had helped with the timings but with four months to go we still didn't know how we were getting from Glasgow to Fort William and back'.*

Luckily for Steve, GB Railfreight were about to pull a rabbit from the hat.

> *They said "hang fire" and a couple of weeks later called me back to say they had won the contract for the Alcan freight traffic from Fort William – so could crew the train throughout Scotland.'*

From a railway operations point of view the trip passed off smoothly, although behind the scenes there were some minor issues. Those taking part in the walking of course didn't see the work going on to keep the train running. After depositing them at Bangor, for example, the train ran to Holyhead for water, and whilst they were scaling Scafell the train left Ravenglass and went to Barrow-in-Furness in order to fuel the Class 67 locomotive.

Like many of these affairs the work that went into the Three Peaks Challenge was outwith any reasonable commercial return. Apparently the Board claimed they hadn't been consulted and were somewhat displeased, yet it has the curious effect of really pleasing railway people, and creating much favourable publicity, which was a good idea. And it was fun!

wrexham & shropshire

Summer Promotion 2008

Aims and Assumptions

1. Our objective is to generate awareness and trial within the B, C1, C2, family market, during the school summer hols.
2. The market is Leisure, families: Wrexham – Tame Bridge inclusive to London; London to Tame Bridge -Wrexham - the whole line.
3. We seek to take advantage of the rise in fuel prices, to persuade people to take a train trip in an area where not only is rail user low, but it is further depressed by there having been no through service to London for many years.
4. Thus our tag line ought to seek inclusion of something like: **'Take the Family to London for less than the cost of a tank of petrol'**
5. The product is: a) to London and b) from London.
6. This to be done by single group fare, adjusted to yield at (or near) standard fare levels.
7. The promotion will have a hard job offering an ROI on its own, but is justified by Paras 1 & 3.
8. One reason why we may temper our media spend is the fact that 25% of sales are being contributed by sales from our Website.
9. In acknowledgement of Paras 7 & 8, media spend will be restricted to £25k (subject to discussion with Brandpoint).
10. Estimates are that the promotion will yield £30k income likelihood – however it is wise to note that we do not know, as this is all new to the market and we are on the edge of a period of restricted consumer spending.
11. We will offer ONE fare throughout most of the route. It is not considered to be successful or practical to offer the different Saver fares or Family Railcard fares as a promotion for two reasons:
    - The promotional message is occluded as the Advanced Single, or Standard Saver Single has to be bulked, which changes price with volume, obscuring the main sales message. We get more income for a clear sales message.
    - If we base price on Family Railcard, the above arguments still apply, plus we need to sell that first, in an area where rail is not a well known and popular transport mode. This therefore blunts the promotional message.
12. The **Days Out** promotion, offers a destination led message based all on standard fares – thus we shall have a comparison of both promotions.

Fare and use

1. Available any day, any train but with reservation advice, from Monday 14th July – Fri 5th September.
2. Only available at W&S stations.
3. Standard Class only – Saver single rules – (you could stay for more than one day).
4. Web ticketing method will be by standard booking arrangements.
5. The price will be £69 for 2 adults and 2 children. The price for Tame Bridge will be £59.
6. Extra children or adults will be charged at the Saver fare.
7. Tickets will be 'walk on'.

Promotion

1. By newspaper ¼ page ads - £18k
2. By radio ads where this is effective - £10k
3. By leaflet and poster in all areas - £2k
4. Feature on the Web : a display strip leads to a dedicated page

W&S Summer Promotion June 2008 1

5. The response on the newspaper adverts and on the radio ads will be to:

www: wrexhamandshropshire.co.uk/summer
and at any Wrexham and Shropshire
staffed station or on the train

6. The basic offer of the advert will be :

£69

for 2 adults & 2 children
Travelling together - to or from London
ANY W&S STATION*
ANY W&S TRAIN*
****VALID ON WREXHAM AND SHROPSHIRE SERVICES ONLY***
Reservation in advance is strongly recommended

TICKETS AVAILABLE AT
www: wrexhamandshrophsire.co.uk/summer
and at any Wrexham and Shropshire staffed station
(WREXHAM, GOBOWEN, SHREWSBURY, WELLINGTON, TELFORD)
or on the train

7. Production of leaflets and posters will be put in hand.
8. The appearance of the newsads and the web page must be similar, so there is clear continuity of promotion.
9. All needs to be in place for advertising beginning w/c 7th July

Add ons

1. We may add a hook about staying over in London – the tickets are valid more than for a day.
2. There may be value in adding that we can offer London Travelcards on the day, on the train.
3. The 2 for1 promotion applies to this – ought there to be mention to add value.
4. We ought to have available on train a 'Travel Pack' with tube map, destination leaflets and a small pack with puzzles/games for kids?

DESIGN SUMMARY

1. 99mm X 210mm, 2 page flyer, 90 gsm?, bold design for 1/3 A4 literature rack
2. Do we have to have 2 editions, one Qy 10k - all stations excluding Tame Bridge at £69, the other from TBP at £59, or could we manage to combine them without destroying the price impact?
3. Tag line on the front: something like
   'Take the Family to London for less than the cost of a tank of petrol'
4. Basic information is as follows:
   - Price Message - £69 for 2 adults and 2 children travelling together to or from London in Standard Class
   - Extra adults or extra children may only accompany the ticket holder by booking from the standard range of fares available.
   - Any W&S calling point, on any W&S train – W&S Services only
   - Available any day from Monday 14th July until Friday 5th September
   - Reservation are strongly recommended, but you may purchase tickets from manned W&S calling points or on the day of issue, on the train.
   - Valid for return travel up to a month from date of issue
5. On the back:
   - Enjoy a day out in London and See the Sights. London Marylebone is ideally situated for a visit

Wrexham & Shropshire Days Out

If you would like a day out this summer, then Wrexham & Shropshire services can take you by train direct.

You can use our services to travel to London and enjoy all that the Capital can offer. The London Zoo, Regents' Park and Madame Tussauds are all within walking distance of the London terminus at Marylebone

The station has excellent connections, with the Bakerloo Line right there, and Baker Street Underground Station just down the road. The two of these give access to many of the major tourist sites in London.

Plus outside the door the Nos 2 and 205 buses take your direct to a number of destinations.

Offer valid from Monday 14th July until Friday 5th September only.

Available on any Wrexham & Shropshire train, between Tame Bridge Parkway and London Marylebone only, on any day.

Reservation in advance is strongly recommended.

DAYS OUT

Bakerloo Line stations from Marylebone

OXFORD CIRCUS
The station is at the corner of Oxford and Regent Street, right at the centre of the shopping district of London. Just down Regent Street is Hamleys, absolutely full of toys, nearby is Liberty, a fabulous department store and the streets are lined with interesting and exciting shops.

PICCADILLY CIRCUS
You emerge from the Tube into another world. The famous statue of Eros Statue by Gilbert surmounts the fountain in the middle of the Circus. Roads lead off to Chinatown, to Leicester Square, down Piccadilly to the Royal Academy and Green Park, and down Lower Regent Street to St James's Park.

CHARING CROSS
Here is the delight of Trafalgar Square, ringed by impressive buildings, the National Gallery and St Martins in the Field, Admiralty Arch and its opening to the Mall. Walk down the splendid Whitehall to the Cenotaph and Horse Guards from here, or you may choose to stroll up the Mall through St James Park towards Buckingham Palace.

EMBANKMENT
Adjacent is the Thames in all its glory, with the London Eye across the water and the Charing Cross Pier nearby, for boats to Greenwich or Kew. Turn right and you can stroll to see Big Ben and the Houses of Parliament, turn left for the City.

WATERLOO
The Royal Festival Hall and the National Theatre are a short walk away from this, the largest of London's major railway stations. Plus you can stroll along the South Bank of the Thames as far as the London Eye and Big Ben and the Palace of Westminster.

The plan for a summer promotion is above, with the design summary. There were two prices, £59 from Tame Bridge and £69 from Wrexham - Telford. Above left is the leaflet front and above right the inside. After a little more co-ordination and refinement, the promotion went out. It had been created in about a week, and it was successful. There was so little time to plan and promote traffic, everything had to be dealt with at lightning speed.

Chiltern 165/0 Turbo No. 165 015 is working the 09:52 Birmingham Snow Hill to Marylebone train and is just about to pass WSMR DVT No. 82301 at the head of 1J81, the 10:17 from Marylebone to Wrexham with 67013 Dyfrbont Pontsycyllte *on the rear, just north of Piddington at 11:09 on Wednesday 19th November 2008.* **Geoff Plumb**

Chapter 8
A New Direction

A New Direction

Behind the scenes, early 2009 was a turbulent time. There had been a number of adverse factors during 2008: delays to the rolling stock refurbishment and poor the economic outlook, revenue results had been disappointing. Losses were greater than had been budgeted, and whilst 2009 started well, achievement of budgeted results already looked challenging.

Throughout 2008, financial performance had not met expectations. Despite vigorous efforts at increasing traffic whilst maintaining the revenue yield, income had hovered around £300,000 per month, with the annual figure reaching £2.6m for what was not a complete year of operations. Passenger numbers were around 19,000 per month meaning a typical passenger paid £16 per journey. Given the mix of long and short distance travel made using Wrexham & Shropshire's trains, this yield was in line with expectations. Alas the problem was that insufficient people were travelling to raise this figure to that needed to match expectations.

Losses, already greater than expected, were now projected to continue during 2009, and so the Board were concerned that the availability of funds might not be forthcoming to allow the business to continue operations. Reassurance was given swiftly by confirmation from DB that the money would be made available for continued operations right through until the end of the year. However it was clear that to the Board and to management that it was important to demonstrate an improvement to the prospects of the company in 2009 by reducing operating costs.

After a long involvement with Wrexham & Shropshire throughout the period seeking approval, and having led the mobilisation of the customer services and commercial teams, Richard Harper returned to sister company Chiltern Railways in early 2009. Gordon Rushton stood down, citing advancing years and an eighty hour week. Thomas Ableman joined the team as Marketing Director to bring his skills to bear in that area of the business.

A New Broom

Thomas was free of the original obligations to the brand image and values. His mission was extremely clear - if preventive action is not taken quickly, then the company will cease to trade. This wasn't from a lack of activity, from a failure of competence. The actions taken until 2009 reflected the agreed views of Board and managers about what should be done - however, as it clearly wasn't working, Thomas was given the freedom to get on and do something radical that would work.

The working relationship with Andy Hamilton offered the scope and relationship to change matters and for the two of them to implement those changes very quickly. Thomas had available the freedom to do what he thought was right, and soon found himself also working the expected 80 hour weeks. Using the thinking time of walking to and fro from the station he spent the first two weeks researching, and preparing a report with his proposals for amendment and improvement. As an outsider, it was easier to spotlight radical action without having to appease existing relationships and sensitivities. It was clear that the product offer was fundamentally misaligned with both the price, and the business plan. This was because the journey time and on-board quality did not meet the expectation generated by brand and price; that was dangerous, and acted as a brake on demand.

Thomas Ableman believed that there was a product mis-match, between what the customer was promised, and what could be delivered. The refurbished coaches were not delivered until 2010, almost two years after service began - so he had a point! **Geoff Plumb**

Thomas Ableman thought that what had been intended to be launched wasn't what was actually launched. His view was that the plan needed to be re-conformed to deliver high volume, low value business. This pointed to leisure as the key market segment, and he repositioned the offer to attract leisure users. To do that a flat fare approach was the vital factor. The plan therefore changed the emphasis and organised a rates drop, with marketing action in the leisure segment to grow the volume.

There were other significant influences on the current state of affairs:

- Other open access operators like Hull and Grand Central had always served as comparators. Hull has been a steady profit generator, and Grand Central certainly moved a great deal of volume. Yet those services served large urban centres, whereas W&S was reliant on a more dispersed market that was not delivering the volume.
- The original business case depended on an ability to increase people's propensity to travel. It had not so far proved possible to achieve this in the measures anticipated. The market share from both Telford and Shrewsbury was indeed high, but the overall market for rail had not grown enough.
- On the other hand, West Midlands to London is the most competitive transport market in UK, with many high frequency rail and coach options as well as car options. Wrexham & Shropshire had been unable to gain access to this market at key points such as Wolverhampton and Birmingham, and the market reaction at Tame Bridge was not forthcoming. It seemed that a low frequency service from a location nobody had heard of was not a strong prospect. The Wrexham & Shropshire product was not attractive enough
- The massive size of the West Midlands domiciled area meant that getting a return on the marketing spend necessary to penetrate it would mean that it was never going to be possible to get a return.
- Profit for Wrexham & Shropshire depended on offering a journey time sufficiently competitive with others. Otherwise there was a risk that the available market would be too small to sustain the operation.
- Business people may be persuaded to accept extended

Wolverhampton was a scene of tragedy for Wrexham & Shropshire, as it was unable to secure a pickup stop here for traffic to London, and had instead to rely upon Tame Bridge Parkway, where enthusiasm for a direct service to London was is extremely short supply. Here, Driver Martin Beddows carefully starts the train away from its 'set down only ' stop. **Geoff Plumb**

journey times with the offer of a comfortable working environment - but only up to a point. Chiltern showed a 20 minute differential was acceptable, if the environment was less crowded, and perhaps there was a favourable price difference. However, the Wrexham & Shropshire time difference compared with Virgin's service to Euston was just under one hour longer - that was too much to be competitive within the business sector.

There were other important features of the business

- The first-to-standard customer ratio on Wrexham & Shropshire was higher than most other train operators. This meant that there was an extremely strong niche of First users. Although this was remarkable, and a tribute to the management and staff's efforts, alas it was not a large enough market segment upon which to build a profitable business.
- The original product was predicated on the delivery of the newly refurbished Mk3 carriages that alas were running months late. Mature reflection indicated that the refurbished coaches were relatively unimportant Had they been there for 'service startup' it may have made some difference - but this was not an overriding factor.

Wrexham & Shropshire's extended journey time was the principal weak point. Thus all plans for the vitalisation of Wrexham & Shropshire would have an unassailable weakness unless they could tackle this point. All was not lost however, as lateral thinking meant that if the market was made wider - and a stop at Wolverhampton would have achieved this - then cheaper fares, with better service, but at reduced journey time, would have 'bought time', until the Evergreen Project decreased the journey times into Marylebone.[1]

To gain approval to call at Wolverhampton needed a strong stakeholder approval from opinion formers within the general public. As part of the Ableman plan, a key was to 'talk to people who talk to people' – word of

1 The Chiltern Mainline service that utilised the Wrexham & Shropshire assets is successful because it is able to grow its own market share from competitors, as well as generating growth within the growing market for rail. It can do this because it has better price offers and the journey time comparison is within the vital 20 minutes of difference. The market sees it as a cheaper and more comfortable product, and so it generates patronage.

***Above:** In October 2008 an inbound Arriva Trains Wales service from Aberystwyth pauses at Wolverhampton, on its way to Birmingham New Street. Soon the services will be extended to Birmingham International. Arriva wished them to go as far as London Marylebone. The Rail Regulator refused the application.*

***Right:** Thomas Ableman believed that a bolder style would play better with the market areas most likely to be attracted to the service, Accordingly the new style appeared in the May 2008 timetable leaflet, from a new advertising agency. It kept the logo but the presentation around it was quite different.*

mouth through opinion formers, especially including MPs, who became key advocates for curbing 'Moderation of Competition' and allowing Wrexham & Shropshire trains to pick up and set down at Wolverhampton.

The Plan in action

Thomas Ableman sought and found considerable engagement with elected representatives. All the MPs were met personally, following after an introductory letter. Although it never proved to be possible to lay aside the MoC concerns, as they were enshrined in legislation. However, it was pointed out that the MoC conditions would be removed at the end of the Virgin franchise term in 2012. The exercise was helpful, as it secured much support from sitting MPs.

Peak fares were abolished and the tariff was simplified, so that passengers turning up to travel on the day would benefit from a flat rate return fare valid on any train with no restriction. The standard class price from Telford and Shrewsbury was £40 return, and this headline fare was used extensively to market the proposals. In comparison with competitors throughout the country, this was an astonishing price for a 150 mile journey, especially when passengers could reach London before 0900 at this price. So whilst Wrexham & Shropshire's advance purchase tickets continued to offer low prices, the abolition of peak fares shifted the emphasis further towards affordable prices on rail. It offered great flexibility, and the pay on the day nature of the offer removed irritating yield management techniques which required early booking well in advance, combined restrictions with on travel times. This acted sufficiently against UK rail industry trends to cause a strong, supportive consumer reaction.

The media response was considerable. As always, local radio and newspapers covered the story in detail, but it was the national media coverage that really raised the profile of Wrexham & Shropshire. Andy Hamilton was live on Channel 4's 12 o'clock news, BBC Radio 4's Today Programme and BBC 5 Live's 'Wake up to money'. The Times, Guardian and Sunday Express reached a further national audience. Such exposure naturally left its mark.

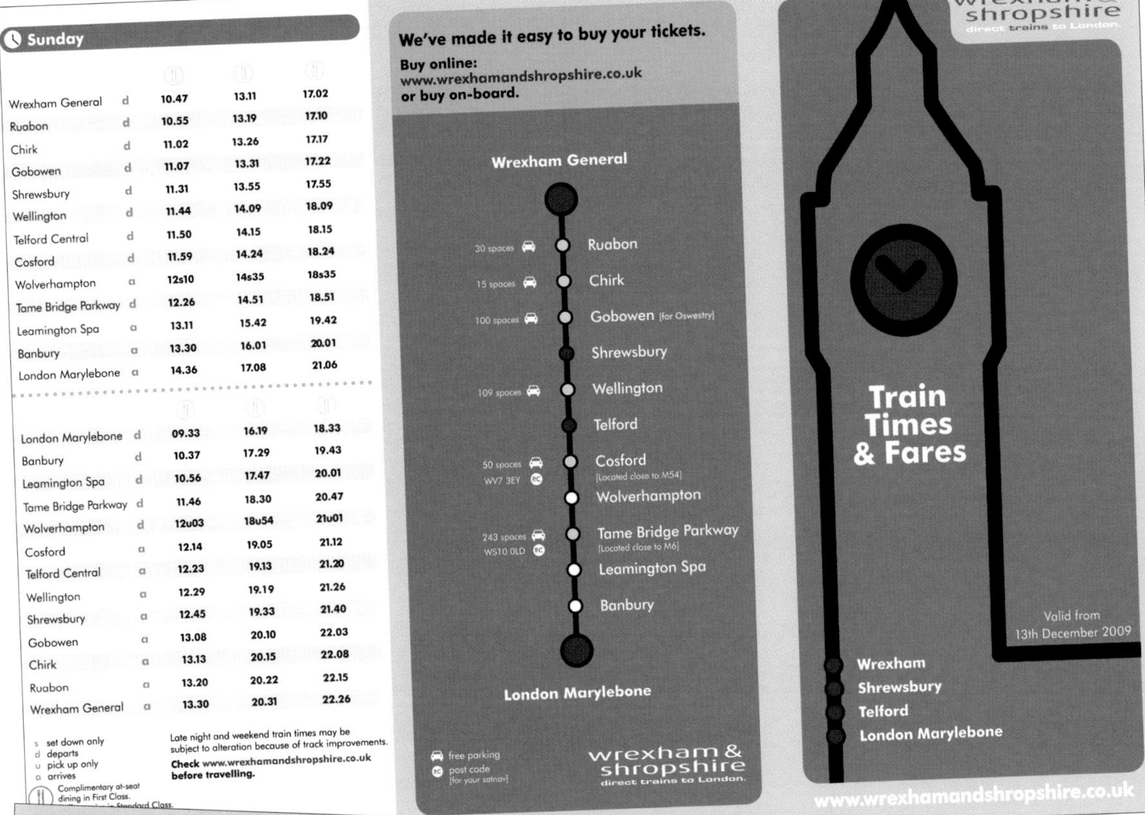

Sunday

Wrexham General	d	10.47	13.11	17.02
Ruabon	d	10.55	13.19	17.10
Chirk	d	11.02	13.26	17.17
Gobowen	d	11.07	13.31	17.22
Shrewsbury	d	11.31	13.55	17.55
Wellington	d	11.44	14.09	18.09
Telford Central	d	11.50	14.15	18.15
Cosford	d	11.59	14.24	18.24
Wolverhampton	a	12s10	14s35	18s35
Tame Bridge Parkway	d	12.26	14.51	18.51
Leamington Spa	a	13.11	15.42	19.42
Banbury	a	13.30	16.01	20.01
London Marylebone	a	14.36	17.08	21.06

London Marylebone	d	09.33	16.19	18.33
Banbury	d	10.37	17.29	19.43
Leamington Spa	d	10.56	17.47	20.01
Tame Bridge Parkway	d	11.46	18.30	20.47
Wolverhampton	d	12u03	18u54	21u01
Cosford	a	12.14	19.05	21.12
Telford Central	a	12.23	19.13	21.20
Wellington	a	12.29	19.19	21.26
Shrewsbury	a	12.45	19.33	21.40
Gobowen	a	13.08	20.10	22.03
Chirk	a	13.13	20.15	22.08
Ruabon	a	13.20	20.22	22.15
Wrexham General	a	13.30	20.31	22.26

s set down only
d departs
u pick up only
a arrives
Complimentary at-seat dining in First Class.

Late night and weekend train times may be subject to alteration because of track improvements.
Check www.wrexhamandshropshire.co.uk before travelling.

We've made it easy to buy your tickets.

Buy online:
www.wrexhamandshropshire.co.uk
or buy on-board.

wrexham & shropshire
direct trains to London.

wrexham & shropshire
direct trains to London.

Train Times & Fares

Valid from 13th December 2009

Wrexham
Shrewsbury
Telford
London Marylebone

www.wrexhamandshropshire.co.uk

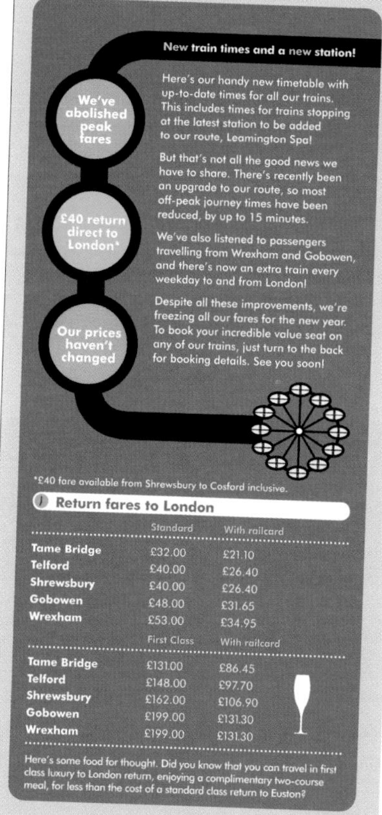

New train times and a new station!

We've abolished peak fares

£40 return direct to London*

Our prices haven't changed

Here's our handy new timetable with up-to-date times for all our trains. This includes times for trains stopping at the latest station to be added to our route, Leamington Spa!

But that's not all the good news we have to share. There's recently been an upgrade to our route, so most off-peak journey times have been reduced, by up to 15 minutes.

We've also listened to passengers travelling from Wrexham and Gobowen, and there's now an extra train every weekday to and from London!

Despite all these improvements, we're freezing all our fares for the new year. To book your incredible value seat on any of our trains, just turn to the back for booking details. See you soon!

*£40 fare available from Shrewsbury to Cosford inclusive.

Return fares to London

	Standard	With railcard
Tame Bridge	£32.00	£21.10
Telford	£40.00	£26.40
Shrewsbury	£40.00	£26.40
Gobowen	£48.00	£31.65
Wrexham	£53.00	£34.95
	First Class	**With railcard**
Tame Bridge	£131.00	£86.45
Telford	£148.00	£97.70
Shrewsbury	£162.00	£106.90
Gobowen	£199.00	£131.30
Wrexham	£199.00	£131.30

Here's some food for thought. Did you know that you can travel in first class luxury to London return, enjoying a complimentary two-course meal, for less than the cost of a standard class return to Euston?

Monday to Friday

Wrexham General	d	05.10	07.23	11.27	15.25
Ruabon	d	-	07.31	-	-
Chirk	d	-	07.38	11.39	15.38
Gobowen	d	05.25	07.43	11.44	15.43
Shrewsbury	d	05.52	08.07	12.07	16.07
Wellington	d	-	08.21	12.21	16.21
Telford Central	d	06.09	08.27	12.27	16.27
Cosford	d	06.17	08.36	12.36	16.36
Wolverhampton	a	-	-	12s47	16s47
Tame Bridge Parkway	d	06.41	09.02	13.02	17.02
Leamington Spa	a	07.29	09.45	13.45	17.45
Banbury	a	07.47	10.04	14.04	18.04
London Marylebone	a	08.57	11.15	15.15	19.15

London Marylebone	d	07.33	11.20	16.30	18.33
Banbury	d	08.37	12.30	17.33	19.37
Leamington Spa	d	08.55	12.48	17.50	19.55
Tame Bridge Parkway	d	09.42	-	18.40	20.40
Wolverhampton	d	09u59	-	18u58	21u04
Cosford	a	10.10	14.10	19.06	21.15
Telford Central	a	10.18	14.18	19.14	21.23
Wellington	a	-	-	19.20	21.29
Shrewsbury	a	10.40	14.36	19.34	21.46
Gobowen	a	11.02	14.58	20.02	22.16
Chirk	a	-	-	20.07	22.21
Ruabon	a	-	-	20.14	22.28
Wrexham General	a	11.19	15.16	20.23	22.36

s set down only
d departs
u pick up only
a arrives

Complimentary at-seat dining in First Class.
Buffet service in Standard Class.

Saturday

Wrexham General	d	07.23	11.23	14.18	17.23
Ruabon	d	07.31	11.31	14.26	17.31
Chirk	d	07.38	11.38	14.32	17.38
Gobowen	d	07.43	11.43	14.37	17.43
Shrewsbury	d	08.07	12.07	15.07	18.07
Wellington	d	08.21	12.21	15.21	18.21
Telford Central	d	08.27	12.27	15.27	18.27
Cosford	d	08.36	12.36	15.36	18.36
Wolverhampton	a	08s47	12s47	15s47	18s49
Tame Bridge Parkway	d	09.01	13.01	16.01	19.02
Leamington Spa	a	09.49	13.49	16.49	19.46
Banbury	a	10.07	14.07	17.07	20.05
London Marylebone	a	11.15	15.15	18.15	21.15

London Marylebone	d	08.14	12.24	17.24	19.24
Banbury	d	09.30	13.37	18.37	20.37
Leamington Spa	d	09.49	13.55	18.55	20.55
Tame Bridge Parkway	d	10.44	14.41	19.43	21.40
Wolverhampton	d	10u59	14u55	20u00	22u00
Cosford	a	11.10	15.06	20.11	22.11
Telford Central	a	11.18	15.14	20.19	22.19
Wellington	a	11.24	15.20	20.26	22.25
Shrewsbury	a	11.40	15.34	20.40	22.39
Gobowen	a	12.04	16.01	21.04	23.04
Chirk	a	12.09	16.06	21.09	23.09
Ruabon	a	12.16	16.13	21.16	23.16
Wrexham General	a	12.26	16.23	21.26	23.25

s set down only
d departs
u pick up only
a arrives

Late night and weekend train times may be subject to alteration because of track improvements.
Check www.wrexhamandshropshire.co.uk before travelling.
*£10 single advance. Subject to availability.

The new web Home Page

WREXHAM TO OUTER SPACE. £10*

Enjoy a trip to The Science Museum.
DIRECT trains from Wrexham to London from £10 single*.

www.wrexhamandshropshire.co.uk *Subject to availability. *£10 single advance fare.

wrexham & shropshire direct trains to London.

***Left:** Internet trading via the Wrexham & Shropshire website was a key segment of the income generation. The organisation did not run any sales outlets, as it was entirely dependent on station facility owners at all of its stops. The vital Home Page was overhauled to match the new style.*

***Above:** Bold rendering of simple ideas in a way that catches the eye, and is memorable was the idea of the new advertising. A range of 'faces' was created for use in the advertising, to ensure that Wrexham & Shropshire took on a more homely style - more in keeping with the target audience.*

Many staff questioned the wisdom of charging a £40 flat fare against the previous £180 peak time ticket. In truth peak time business travellers were often travelling on Wrexham & Shropshire's competitors, taking advantage of their heavily discounted book-ahead tickets. Very few were buying Wrexham & Shropshire's peak fares anyway, but with an attractive flexible price there was a real opportunity to secure more business, more often. Whilst in most railway environments flat low fares don't make commercial sense, Wrexham & Shropshire was in a very different position. There was no point promoting fares nobody buys, and a good PR opportunity was created by abolishing the peak fares, as well as a boost for volume.

Wrexham & Shropshire's business plan forecast that a through service would attract business travellers and that naturally they would likely take up the First offer. Unfortunately just after introduction of the service the disturbance of the financial crisis meant that much of the business travel market was simply banned from using any first class product, on the basic assumption that it was always going to be more expensive than standard. At first this was made worse as Wrexham & Shropshire was unable to access London Marylebone during peak business times, when stringent restrictions were generally eased to ensure key business meetings could be met.

The business communities of Telford, Shropshire and Wrexham are very close knit. There was barely a business community event that the company didn't attend, and the team continued with lunches and sponsored business breakfasts. From these events, Wrexham & Shropshire became an integral part of the local business communities. The number of business travel account holders continued to increase and reached the targets that had been set. To encourage the business user to use Wrexham & Shropshire, thousands of free trial tickets were given away at these events. There is no doubt that customer satisfaction was extremely high, and many people began using the service whenever their schedule allowed. However, quite often their schedule didn't allow. Over time, respectable occupancy levels were achieved in First on key business trains. Yet it was still impossible to reach the original Business Plan forecasts for this segment, and of course they were playing the system to buy much lower fares than had been anticipated, thus lowering the yield.

The slower journey times forced Wrexham & Shropshire to be more dependent on lower yield leisure travel than was wished for. The market was a difficult one as between Shrewsbury and London, there was already a very good value buy-on-the-day off-peak ticket, valid via existing services through Wolverhampton and Birmingham, costing a little more than £40 return. These tickets were popular, and booking offices along the route, at stations sponsored by London Midland tended to favour the 'any train' option for London passengers, and did not offer the 'direct' option via Wrexham & Shropshire. Whilst the London Midland, Arriva Trains and Virgin tickets required passengers to change en-route at Wolverhampton or Birmingham, it was also available outside of peak periods on a wide variety of trains. The matter was compounded as even with an attractive £40 return for a direct service,, some passengers used Wrexham & Shropshire as far as Wolverhampton, and then changed to travel via Virgin to Euston to take advantage of the shorter journey time. This was not helped when Arriva Trains Wales services were extended to run through to Birmingham International

Above: *Marylebone Travel Fair on 13th May 2010 - selling hard, this was the W&S stand with a poster saying how good it is on board.*
Below: *Selling in the Ironbridge Gorge, in the car park by the River Severn. A place of extremely high footfall during events - worthwhile spot.*

Above: *Marylebone Travel Fair on 13th May 2010 - Shiela Dee, ardent supporter, and advocate for the Chester-Shrewsbury Line - tireless selling.*
Below: *Thomas Ableman and on-train staff, proudly pose with Emma Gascoigne for a press photo alongside the new train.* **All Photos WSMR**

Huge amounts of effort went into selling the service to the public. Here the sales team have set up in a shopping mall in Telford, a principal heartland that responded to invitations to travel. The objective was to go out into the public forum and drum up trade. It certainly worked. **WSMR**

in December 2008, thus northbound travellers could avoid the seat scramble at Birmingham New Street for destinations beyond Wolverhampton. Had the Wrexham & Shropshire service been able to offer competitive journey times, then the matter would have been radically different.

Competing services

For most of Wrexham & Shropshire's existence it was directly threatened by competing rail operators. From December 2008, Virgin Trains had extended two of its extremely popular, hourly, Super-Voyager services from Euston to Chester, onwards to Wrexham, therefore launching a daily service from Wrexham General to London Euston in the morning, returning in the evening. This offered an attractive journey time of under 2 hours 40 minutes. Even though it only operated once a day as a round trip from Wrexham, its journey time trounced Wrexham & Shropshire's best of 3 hours 45 minutes. The possibility of Virgin running more of these services in competition was restricted by the hourly Arriva Trains Wales trains already occupying much of the line capacity of the singled track between Wrexham and Chester.

In early 2009 however, Virgin announced an intention to operate several services throughout the day, linking stations throughout Shropshire and North East Wales with London Euston via the West Midlands, all offering a journey time advantage over Wrexham & Shropshire. Although Virgin claimed the proposed services would add to the overall rail service on offer to the public, it was clear from Wrexham & Shropshire's perspective that the proposal was like to wreck any prospects they had hoped for. It was claimed that Virgin was unfairly exercising its MoC advantages by seeking to offer additional services that countered an initiative by a competitor, and that this really was not a .level playing field.

Owen Paterson (MP for North Shropshire) arranged a cross-party meeting with Lord Adonis (then transport minister) to comment on these fears, that a competitor was taking unfair action. The proposal coincided with national media coverage for Wrexham & Shropshire's abolition of peak fares campaign, and the opportunity was taken to fight for the future of the company on the national stage.

The Times summed up the situation cleverly with an article on 7th April 2009 headed:

Wrexham & Shropshire entertained fears that Virgin could use the flexibility of their Super-Voyager trains to introduce a new service that they announced. On the other hand there was some disquiet within Virgin Trains that an open access operator was chipping away at the arrangements that they had made at considerable financial risk. There was an uneasy standoff, but in fact Virgin had little to fear in the end.

'Virgin didn't want these passengers, but now a rival is offering cheap fares, it's war'.

The article made unfavourable comparisons, explaining that whilst Wrexham & Shropshire received no public subsidy it was charging £53 for a Wrexham-London return and yet despite £35 million annual subsidy a similar Virgin Trains ticket would cost £201. The range of fares on offer were of course much more complex, and Virgin offered highly competitive advance purchase fares from Wrexham, but the comment demonstrated exactly the complex and passenger-unfriendly pricing approach that Wrexham & Shropshire was seeking to break through.

Owen Paterson MP asked the Rail Regulator to investigate what he believed was an attempt by Virgin to force a smaller operator out of business which ran counter to an organisation that had built a reputation as a customer-friendly operator, offering choice and good service against entrenched monopolistic organisations. Virgin retrenched, announcing on the 8th April that it was withdrawing its plans. Modified plans re-emerged post Wrexham & Shropshire, as part of the 2012 West Coast Franchise bid by Virgin - so perhaps the proposal was not quite as predatory as it was claimed.

There were proposals put forward by Arriva Trains Wales to run services from Aberystwyth to London Marylebone. The trains would have competed directly for traffic from the main markets of Wrexham & Shropshire., were more considered. The ATW proposal was welcomed by the mid Wales communities as restoring a service lost when Inter-City withdrew through services in 1991. Wrexham & Shropshire had also seen the potential of Aberystwyth as the origin of perhaps one of its services in future. However it was felt that such a proposal could only succeed if the Aberystwyth service also served Shropshire and so had a greater opportunity to earn revenues. This was what the ATW service proposed, and therefore possessed the same characteristics as the Virgin proposal, threatening to remove traffic from W&S. A formal application to the ORR to operate the services was made in the second half of 2009, and Wrexham & Shropshire made its case against. It was felt the proposal could only be financially viable on the basis of abstracted revenues, from Wrexham & Shropshire and from Leamington Spa on Chiltern Railways' network. In early 2010 ORR refused the proposal.

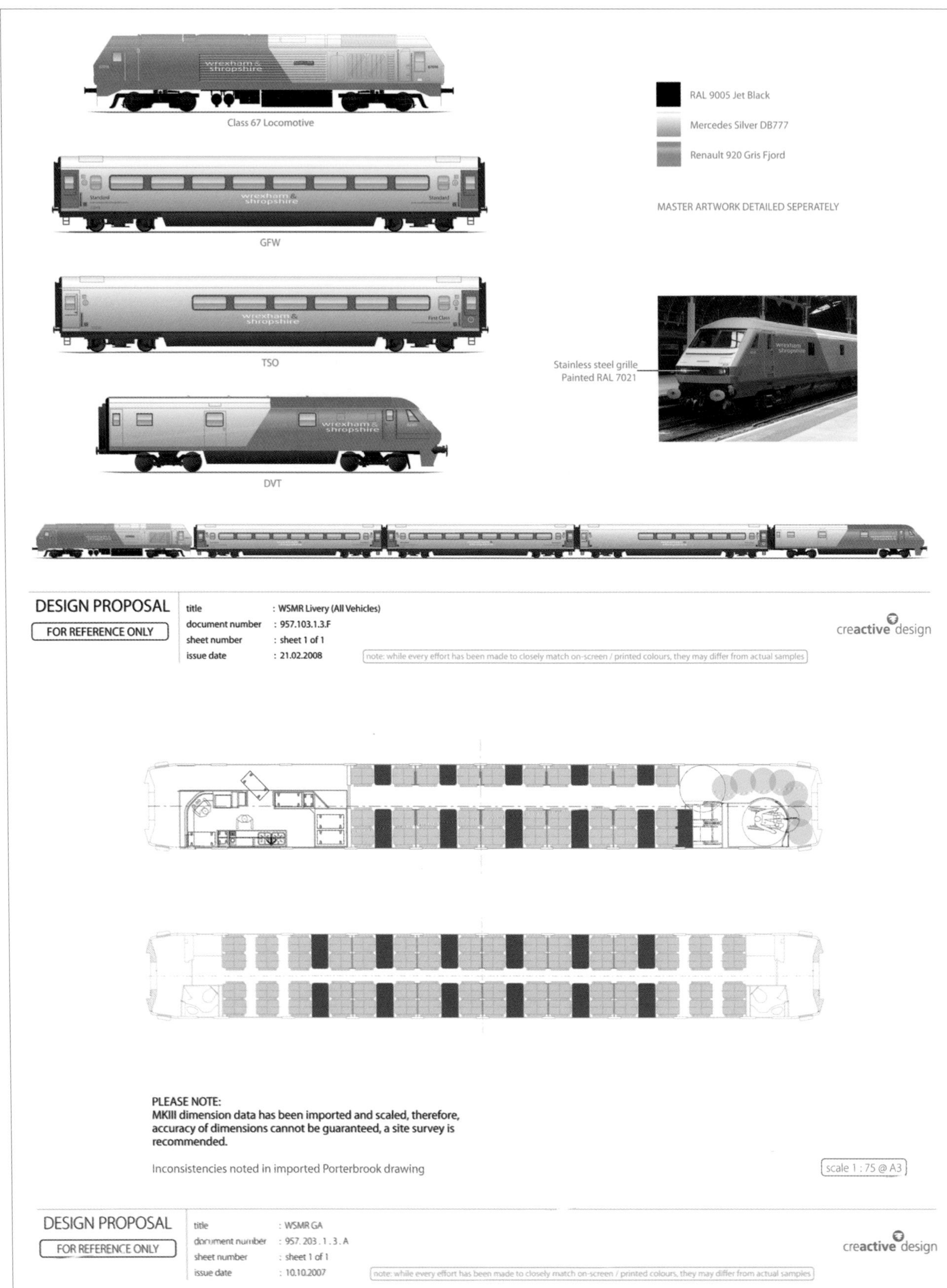
Class 67 Locomotive
GFW
TSO
DVT
RAL 9005 Jet Black
Mercedes Silver DB777
Renault 920 Gris Fjord
MASTER ARTWORK DETAILED SEPERATELY
Stainless steel grille
Painted RAL 7021
DESIGN PROPOSAL
FOR REFERENCE ONLY
title : WSMR Livery (All Vehicles)
document number : 957.103.1.3.F
sheet number : sheet 1 of 1
issue date : 21.02.2008
note: while every effort has been made to closely match on-screen / printed colours, they may differ from actual samples
creactive design
PLEASE NOTE:
MKIII dimension data has been imported and scaled, therefore, accuracy of dimensions cannot be guaranteed, a site survey is recommended.
Inconsistencies noted in imported Porterbrook drawing
scale 1 : 75 @ A3
DESIGN PROPOSAL
FOR REFERENCE ONLY
title : WSMR GA
document number : 957. 203 . 1 . 3 . A
sheet number : sheet 1 of 1
issue date : 10.10.2007
note: while every effort has been made to closely match on-screen / printed colours, they may differ from actual samples
creactive design

Chapter 9 New Trains

Train design

As recorded in earlier chapters, there was a great emphasis placed on the superior design and comfort of the travelling environment. A lot of time and effort went into designing and specifying the decor of the carriages and defining brand images to match. British Rail Mk3 vehicles were chosen, partly because they were available - though with some difficulty - and partly because they were superior to the more easily found, older, cheaper, and more corrosion prone British Rail Mk2 carriages. Of course, there were Mk3 cars currently in service as part of the excellent and popular Inter-City 125 trains, still offered by many of the major train operating companies. The Mk3 cars have air suspension, disc brakes and air conditioning. The ride and noise levels are markedly superior to the Mk2 cars, thus the choice was an easy one to make.

The final examples of the Mk3 type were placed in service in the late 1980s. Although not operational, they had recently been cascaded from main line service, and met all modern standards. The available Mk3s needed a mid-life overhaul. Thus arrangements were made in August 2007 to purchase and upgrade 12 vehicles for Wrexham & Shropshire service. The time-window was frighteningly narrow, as service was due to start in April 2008.

Designing the refurbishment

The specification, for 130 standard class seats and 30 first class seats per train, set the design requirement for the refurbishment of the 12 coaches. A single standard class Mk3 coach can be configured to provide between 64 and 84 seats, depending on the proportion of tables to seats. There were many complaints that seats and windows in standard class never matched, and that this was not appreciated by the passengers. Thus it was decided to provide as many tables as practicable, thus as can be seen from the drawing opposite, 12 tables were incorporated, synchronised with windows, offering 48 seats, and 16 in rows at either end of the coach, making 64 seats per carriage. This was acceptable as the specification for two standard class coaches, and gave them heightened appeal.

The first class coach presented a greater challenge. British Rail built two different types of Mk3 first class vehicles: first class coaches which had typically 42 seats, and galley coaches with 24 first class seats, a kitchen and buffet counter. The first of these had no facility to serve food, and the galley coach had too few seats to meet the specification – and furthermore with a kitchen designed to serve 100 meals into the coaches of an Inter-City train they were over-specified. The solution decided upon was to take four, first class galley coaches, to strip out the old kitchen, to fit a larger seating area with 30 seats, and to fit a new, smaller kitchen – which was designed to be capable of serving up to 45 passengers to allow for future growth.

At this stage, the brand development work was translated into detailed design, livery, and materials specifications for the trains. This was important, given that the biggest single example of a train company's branding is the train itself. The team at Cre'active worked very closely with all concerned to turn the brand and specification into a refurbishment specification for the trains. Alternative configurations for each vehicle, options for refurbished seats and new seats, different colours, fabrics and materials for everything from carpets to partitions to handrails were examined. There are many factors to consider in addition to the specification, such as the DfT's rail vehicle accessibility regulations (RVAR) which demand, for example, doors

This is a rendering, computer generated, and used as part of the design process to demonstrate the concept of refurbishment of a Mk3 carriage. At the time, it was expected that the seat backs would have a metallic insert, and a larger headrest would be made. In the event, both features were dropped and the table design changed. The use of text on a black bulkhead was retained, and the overall feel of the finished coaches was remarkably similar to this. **WSMR**

have be a different colour tone from the bodyside of the train, and vestibule carpets must be a different tone from the saloon carpet, for the visually imparied.

Train refurbishment

ORR's approval was received in autumn 2007, so with the start scheduled for April 2008, there was but little time to find a contractor able to fit the new interiors, and perform the overhaul in time. The new owners, DB Regio UK, decided upon the engineering company Axiom, which was part of the group of companies owned by EWS which had also been bought by DB ; the contract for a six-month refurbishment of 16 coaches was let.

The seats

A good deal of effort was put into seat comfort, with the design company Cre'active, and the seat suppliers. The Wrexham & Shropshire team knew that modern trains were built with seats that were overly hard and uncomfortable. This can result from either a desire to maximise seating capacity, or from the use of harder cushion foam, which more easily meets fire safety standards. Cre'active design assessments of options, initially focused on newly developed designs for seats for

The computer design was show an understated interior, without being too sombre - thus the maroon line along the overhead racks. It was felt that too many interiors were needlessly bright, and disturbing to the eye. The accent with the seats was that they be firm, but comfortable. **WSMR**

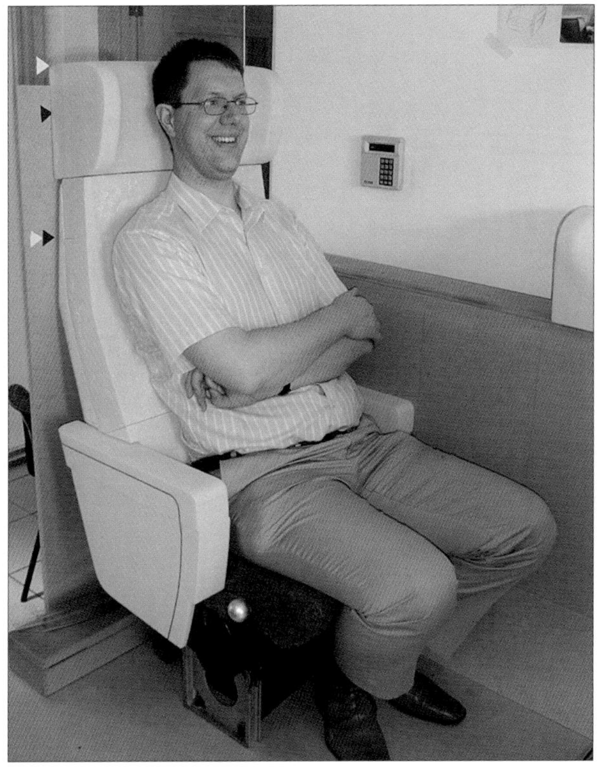

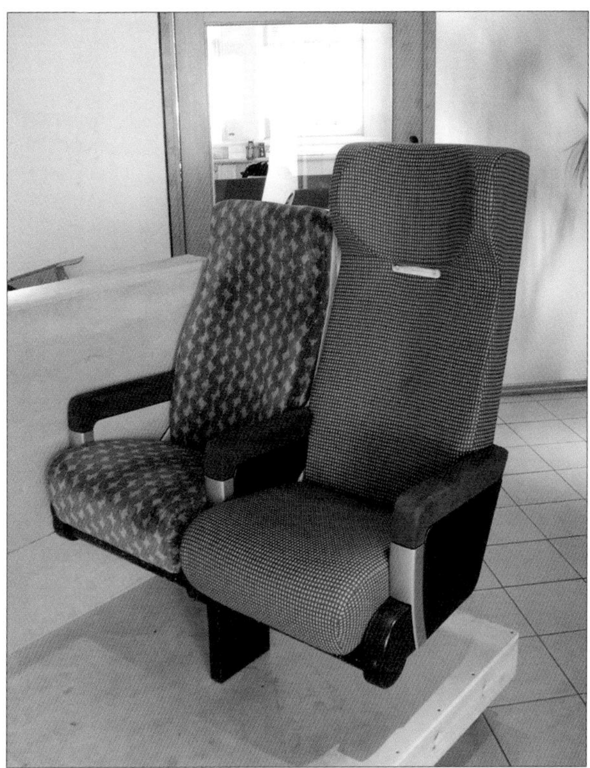

Seats got a lot of attention, and neither of the types shown were actually installed. Mr Harper (left) was in demand, as he is very tall. Careful work was done to seek the best within the limits available. The First seat (right) was eventually a re-covered existing seat - that was best. Standard seats were designed new. The finished articles can be seen in the pictures that follow of the refurbished trains. **WSMR**

both First and Standard class. As the investigation work progressed, it became clear that it was difficult to find a standard class seat that met the desired comfort levels, and a new one was designed. In First it became clear that the best and most economic option was the retention of the existing IC70 seats, which showed high levels of comfort, compared with any new design. Their only downside was the a fixed armrest which makes accessibility more difficult at table bays, and the lack of a significant headrest. Designs were produced to enhance the seat, introducing a larger headrest, but this was dropped in favour of a simple re-covering of the existing seat. A product of British Rail's extensive research programme in the late 1960s and early 1970s, the IC70 seat has stood the test of time, was welcomed by Wrexham & Shropshire passengers, and continues to receive favourable comment from passengers in service with Chiltern Railways Mainline service.

Managing the refurbishment

Axiom had expanded their freight wagon engineering business into the passenger sector and were just completing refurbishment of Mk 3 coaches for Grand Central to operate between London and Sunderland. They gave a good account of the problems they had faced with that project, the completion of which was around one year late, and they explained the lessons they had learned. In fact no other company had offered to complete the refurbishment of Wrexham & Shropshire's fleet in time for the April 2008 launch. As a small contract, for just 16 vehicles; there was some comfort, that due to the reduced timescale the service could at least start with hired in vehicles, thus in the interim, Cargo D cars were hired as short-term cover, in anticipation of the timely introduction of the refurbished cars after startup. There was not much choice about where to place this contract, as the larger organisations in the market, and the only other bidder for the refurbishment of the 16 vehicles were unable to begin work until early summer 2008.

There was confidence in Managing Director Andy Hamilton's background in engineering and experience in previously leading a train refurbishment projects for Chiltern Railways . He was invaluable to Wrexham & Shropshire,

> *'It was a six-month programme, but in late 2007 we realised the coaches weren't going to be finished so we hired some in from Cargo-D. We thought we might need this interim fleet for about 2-3 months.'*

It was disappointing, but not fatal to the project to

The loo had special attention to make it clean and sanitary, one of the innovations - unique to Wrexham & Shropshire - was the fitment of a Dyson Air-Blade hand dryer. Everyone liked this! **WSMR**

This is the galley area, marked out in the end of the first class coach, ready for the studding to be fitted, and this will be followed by the equipment itself. It is a restricted space so planning was vital. **WSMR**

To make quite sure that everything could be got to fit in the restricted space, it was carefully arranged in 'mock-up' form, so that when the time came, it would all slot in. This was time consuming and expensive, but necessary from long experience! **WSMR**

Nikki Roberts checks tickets in the newly designed splendour of First. The carefully re-covered chairs are now in service - but still with the fixed armrests that they had in their previous life. The care of the design has come across in the restful ambience of the inside. This is one of the better Mk3 interior refurbishments, and it is a pity that the late delivery meant it was so short lived in the purpose for which it was designed. **WSMR**

The Galley in action, as Pat Burke serves Liane Tobin with one of the model trains that appeared of a Wrexham & Shropshire Class 67 locomotive. Behind Pat is the interior of the Galley, also well able to serve meals to the First passengers, and more besides. **WSMR**

Despite all the really difficult struggles to get the new trains, when they arrived, they most definitely gave satisfaction. It was such a pity, given all the effort to offer the public such a splendid travelling environment that such delays occurred. Here is Managing Director Andy Hamilton, beaming with pleasure at his new trains, in Marylebone Station - ready to go on 30th September 2009. **WSMR**

have to do this, but alas, that was not the end of the matter - just the beginning. An additional complication arose that the vital Driving Van Trailers (DVTs) were six months late, and were not to be delivered until autumn 2008. These vehicles only required mechanical overhaul, bodywork remedial attention, painting, and the installation of the AAR multiple working equipment. Their loss had unfortunate repercussions. The trains had to be operated with two locomotives, as there was neither capability within Marylebone operations, nor within the turnround schedule, for the Class 67 locos to run round their trains.

Worse was to come, as the coaches estimated six-month overhaul and refurbishment programme timescale was extended to nearly two years Early on, problems came to light in the programme that led to design specification changes. These were made towards the end of 2007, with the intention of making things easier for Axiom. The kitchen module was removed from the Axiom scope, and DB Regio UK let a separate contract for this, but this created more problems rather than were solved. Andy Hamilton says:

'The kitchen team said "tell us where to come up to in the internal space" but then when the people designing the saloon came along they'd designed right up to that limit, and hadn't thought about having to put an internal door pocket.'

The view was that problems like this, emerging during the implementation of the project, surely would not cause a two-year delay on 16 cars. Andy Hamilton recalls that:

'It appeared that the procurement department was only one person, so everything was being funnelled through one individual. Thus there were problems in placing orders, and supply was not timely when parts were needed. This led to a distressed timeline that affected progress.'

Delivery within the 2-3 months timsecale that had been expected in January 2008, turned into delays that dragged on right through 2008 and for most of 2009. Wrexham & Shropshire could enjoy no benefits from the improved accommodation, and all the 'hype' and advertising of them was wasted, and did nothing at all for the credibility of the

One of the features of original Inter-City Mk3 carriages was the coincidence in all classes of seats, tables and windows. The travelling public really enjoy this. All TOCs, except Wrexham & Shropshire crammed seats in to their Mk3s, resulting in few seat/table/window combinations. The airy comfort that resulted was impressive, and the approval rating was high, and the plug-in points at all seats was liked. **WSMR**

service - that began to look rather amateur. In autumn 2008, in the absence of the DVTs, EWS had provided the second locomotive for each train set, at zero hire cost. However, Wrexham & Shropshire still had to bear additional track access charges and the additional fuel costs associated with this 'top and tail' operation. Yet it was the hire of the Cargo-D coaches that was the greatest unexpected expense. The complete fleet of refurbished silver trains were expected to cost Wrexham & Shropshire £35k per month to hire from DB Regio UK. This was a sum reflecting the cost of acquiring and refurbishing the vehicles with the investment sum recouped over an expected 10 year refurbishment life span. The hire of coaches from Cargo-D was costing Wrexham & Shropshire twice this amount, principally because they were sourced on short term hire rates, as each time they were only expected to be required for a couple of months, from the renewed expectations offered by the refurbishers.

'It would have cost us much less from the start if we'd known we needed a two year deal' says Andy.

It appears that Axiom were not well enough equipped to undertake the work required to refurbish the Mk 3 coaches,. Apparently this was understood by neither the senior people in Axiom nor in Wrexham & Shropshire at the time the contract was agreed. Andy Hamilton makes the comment that:

'With hindsight Wrexham & Shropshire should have done more "due diligence" on the reasons why the Grand Central refurbishment was so late, so as to understand better the strength of the promise for speedy overhaul of the DVTs and 16 coaches.'

Launching the new trains

The gloom and the concerns of the grievous delay were quickly laid aside when the newly refurbished carriages arrived. Andy Hamilton remarked on how proud he was of the final result.

'Pete Wilkinson's design brief was turned into a fabulous train. We were only refurbishing a small number of vehicles, but we introduced some important innovative things which should have been done on Mk 3s many years ago. The new interiors were truly splendid'

Nicola Ingham hands out the photoshoot salad -again! The space was pleasant and airy, and restful to the eyes. The quality was ahead of many competing first class interiors , and the seats were indeed comfortable to sit in for extended periods. Note the daring little strip of maroon on the luggage rack fronts - just to give emphasis in the general swirl of greys and whites. It all looked very good. **WSMR**

Tuesday 19th January 2010 was a very proud day for Wrexham & Shropshire. Invited guests sampled the refurbished coaches, before Michael Palin cut a ribbon at London (Marylebone) to launch the fleet. Mr Palin added:

> *'What I like about the Wrexham & Shropshire railway is that it embodies a lot of the things that the railways have lost in a bid for speed and volume – customer care, courtesy, a good meal, and the ability to look after the people for whom the railway is for.'*

North Shropshire MP Owen Paterson and Montgomery MP Lembit Opik added to the praise for Wrexham & Shropshire.

The 'new' carriages

Evidence collected over 30 years in the UK rail sector does suggest that improved quality rolling stock delivers extra revenue, but the impact is variable – somewhere between nothing and 4%. Crucially the benefit is really dependent on the scale of improvement. So evidence from across the industry is not particularly helpful in understanding the potential revenue impact of late carriages in Wrexham & Shropshire's case. By looking at the graphs on page 160, we can seek that there doesn't appear to have been strong revenue growth in late 2009 and early 2010 when the new trains were entering service, so this might suggest that the benefit of the trains in revenue terms was limited to no more than 2% of revenue[1]. So is it true to say that the company missed out on less than £200,000 in lost revenue in the first two years?

To understand this it's important to compare the benefits to passengers from the refurbished trains when compared with the hired stock:

- A nicer environment, with new fabrics and surfaces throughout. Curtains were provided at windows in both classes, and there was improved lighting
- Space for wheelchairs and a fully accessible toilet
- Power sockets and WiFi internet throughout the

1. It is interesting that 'experts' say that the 'new' rolling stock is only worth up to 4% on revenue - for if that is so, then the reciprocal is true, and passengers will travel in any old 'tat'. No one believes this? The Cargo-D Mk3 carriages did not have the fitments and the new environment promised faithfully in the advertising. Customers noticed! Thomas Ableman thought the mismatch so important that he changed the Board's policy radically - he was right to.

The new carriages looked very well in the open. Here on Saturday 12th December 2009 67010 arrives at the head of 1P03, the 11:23 train from Wrexham. The train is running now with four coaches, strengthened for the start of the new timetable from the following day, from when open stops at Banbury and Leamington Spa can be made. **Geoff Plumb**

train

So whilst the train felt 'new' and 'nice', the refurbished trains didn't offer significant benefits over the Cargo-D Mk 3s in terms of noise levels, seat pitch, room for luggage or catering offer. The Cargo-D vehicles provided the core features of the Mark 3 coach in terms of comfort, air conditioning and space on board. Only the power sockets and Wi-Fi offered something new to benefit every potential passenger. So is the opinion expressed in Chapter 8 supported by the facts when it comes to revenue impact. - this bears more thought? (See note1)

Yet the impact of the new trains was not just about revenue. During the two years spent waiting for their arrival, the company hired coaches at short term rates, incurring additional costs. The arrival of the coaches kept being put back, and often seemed only a few months away, so the opportunity to negotiate a longer term deal with Cargo-D was lost. Wrexham & Shropshire wasn't paying for the refurbished coaches before they entered service – those costs were borne by parent DB Regio UK which suffered a loss in earnings. Yet the extra expense associated with short term hire still cost Wrexham & Shropshire almost £500,000 over the first two years. The real financial impact of delays to the refurbished trains was also accompanied by the need for management effort to be constantly devoted to the problems needing resolution to secure the delivery of the trains. This is much more difficult to quantify, yet nevertheless there is an associated opportunity cost.

Overall it is estimated that perhaps £750,000 was lost by Wrexham & Shropshire in those first two years due to the delays in the train refurbishment, with most of that relating to additional costs, not lost revenue. This is a significant sum, yet it accounts for less than 6% of the losses made by the company. So the delays to the refurbished trains had a financial impact, but what is not known, is how much was lost by the 'polite' notice of customers that they were travelling in 'old' coaches, and not bright shiny ones. Few said anything, but then little effort was made to make the Cargo-D coaches more acceptable, as the refurbished coaches were always 'coming soon'.

David Gee flags away an immaculate new train with a smile of pride **WSMR**

Chapter 10 Analysis

Signs of trouble

The first signs that all was not well with Wrexham & Shropshire came within a year, and culminated in a service reduction. The nature of the service offer coupled with the market response meant there were busy trains at the weekend, whereas loadings on weekdays exhibited greater variability. Afternoon trains from Shropshire southbound, particularly the 1810 from Wrexham, and morning trains northbound from London were struggling to generate traffic even when attractively low advance fares were offered. There was pressure on to reduce costs by making timetable reductions, to overcome the resultant shortfalls in revenue.

Given the variability of loadings on weekday trains, options to reduce the service to four or even three trains per day on weekdays were analysed towards the end of 2008. It was established that the maximum reduction of costs with the minimum loss of income would be achieved by withdrawing the 1810 service from Wrexham and the 1017 service from London on weekdays. It was desirable to make the changes at the earliest opportunity, and so at the end of January 2009 the Board decided to reduce the service from 9th March.

An unfortunate consequence of the change was that in addition to the services removed from the timetable altogether, it was necessary to terminate the 1217 from London at Shrewsbury and to start the 1523 from Wrexham, so that these two trains could be operated with the same train set. Thus for the remainder of 2009, Wrexham lost two of its five weekday trains, and there was a further undesirable consequence. Staff were required to book on duty in Wrexham, but then to travel to Shrewsbury to work their train forward at 1607. Similarly, staff arriving at Shrewsbury at 1539 needed to return home to Wrexham depot. To facilitate this, a surplus minibus was purchased from Chiltern Railways to convey the staff by road to and from Shrewsbury. There was the compensation that the vehicle was adorned with the company's branding, and acted as effective mobile advertising along the A5 and A483 each afternoon.

Drastic action needed

The service reduction in 2009 was, with hindsight, an unfortunate indicator of the company's long term financial vulnerability. A year of concerted efforts to win traffic followed, which brought success, yet despite this in 2010 the company was still well behind its income targets. It was distressing that although volume was steadily increased, the yield lagged such that profitability was eluded.

Earnings and Journeys for travel between Wrexham/Shropshire and London

	Revenue	Journeys	Yield/ Jrney
2008 (part year)	£2.06m	73,400	£28
2008 (full yr equiv)	£3.05m	101,800	£30
2009	£3.44m	181,800	£19
Year/year growth	13%	79%	-37%

Source : Wrexham & Shropshire

The core of the company's financial performance revolved around the demand for travel to and from London, which throughout Wrexham & Shropshire's existence was responsible for around 70% of the company's revenue.

There was substantial growth in passenger journeys to and from London from launch in 2008 to mid-2010.

The railway manages its affairs through a cycle of 13 annual four week periods. From a start in 2008 of 8,000 journeys to and from London each period, the changes in strategy meant that by the middle of 2010 Wrexham & Shropshire was carrying over 15,000 passengers every four weeks. This near doubling of passengers meant around 750 journeys were being made to and from London each day. Significant growth in travel occurred in 2009, but by 2010 the rate of growth had slowed, as seen in Graph A.

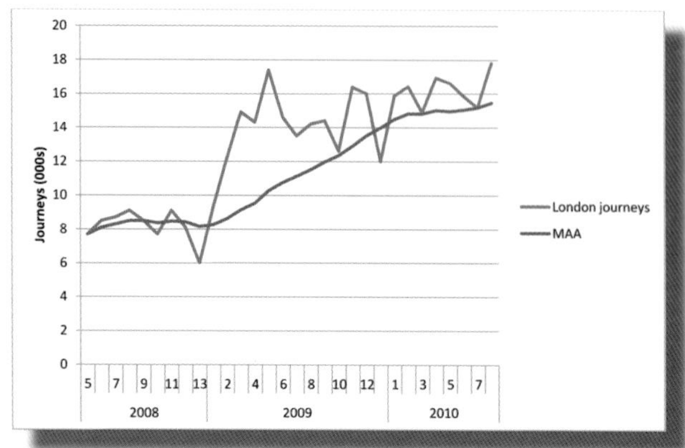

Graph A: London Journeys

The trouble was that the new growth in passenger numbers had been partly achieved by reducing the price. Economists promote the concept of price elasticity of demand, whereby a reduction in price will stimulate an increase in demand, or alternatively an increase in price will diminish demand. The effectiveness of any such exercise depends on how 'elastic' the market is, and Wrexham & Shropshire had hoped that its market was very elastic – such that the price reductions in 2009 would stimulate a much better than 'par' response, and that the result would grow income with no increase of cost, and therefore lead to a profitable operation.

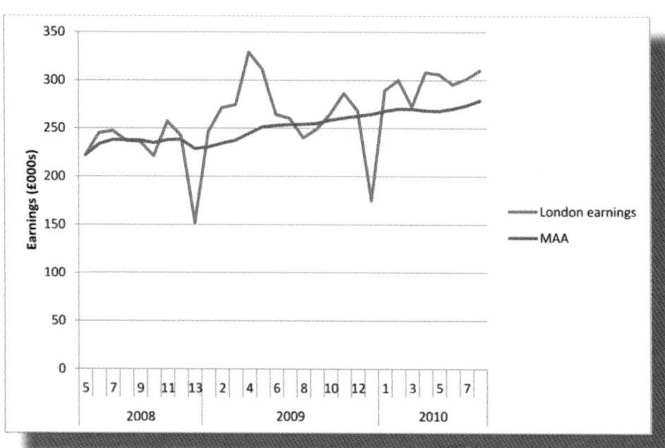

Graph B: London Earnings

This graph of earnings, Graph B, adjacent, shows that in the event, revenue earned from London travel only increased from £225,000 per period in 2008 to £300,000 per period in 2010, and the near doubling of passenger journeys, shown in Graph A, therefore had only modest benefits for the company's bottom line. The average earned from each London journey, the yield, is shown in the final graph, Graph C, demonstrating how the changes had seen this reduce from around £28 per journey initially to around £18 in 2010.

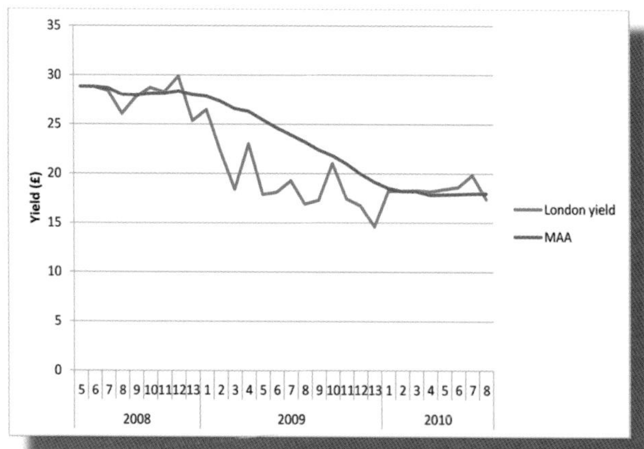

Graph C: London Yield (Income / Journeys)

It is well understood that for a new transport service, the third year of operations should see the market approaching maturity, unless there have been significant other factors changing in the meantime. The recession had clearly been an external factor affecting this, as had improvements to the Virgin Trains services in December 2008 – although these had been offset largely by improvements to the Wrexham & Shropshire timetable at the same time. These factors are difficult to quantify precisely, however Wrexham & Shropshire was still earning less than £5m per annum in passenger revenue by 2010 when the original forecasts indicated revenue above £8m per annum. It's difficult to argue the gap is entirely due to the recession and competition from competing route – there are more fundamental factors at work. Furthermore, the impact this revenue shortfall was having on the overall financial performance of the company is only too clear from the figures:

Financial Performance			
£m	2008	2009	2010
Passenger Revenue	2.6	4.0	4.4
Other Income	0.3	0.4	1.1*
Costs	-9.3	-8.9	-8.4
Profit/Loss	-6.4	-4.5	-2.9

*** Note – includes Leamington/Banbury-London passengers carried for Chiltern**

With the fall in yield causing the growth in passenger revenue to level off in 2010, it was clear that the many factors preventing Wrexham & Shropshire from realising its profit targets were in danger of blocking the service ever reaching its full potential, and that this was likely to become terminal.

The general financial situation for rail had been affected by the collapse of Northern Rock in 2007, the American sub-prime mortgage scandal, and the crisis in banking. This crisis swept through Britain's financial establishment, yet although in previous downturns, rail passenger numbers followed the economy into the doldrums, this time the situation was different. Although strong passenger growth pre-recession was halted, it was only temporary. In 2009-10, growth in general on rail increased. This increased demand, seen in the table below, impacted on all UK TOCs as a trend, and Wrexham & Shropshire should have benefited from it too. Yet the financial performance indicated that 'other' factors had a worsening effect that negated the increase from general trend, and the Company failed to achieve profitability.

UK Rail Passenger Journeys		
Year	Passengers Bn	Annual Growth
2006-7	1.15	
2007-8	1.22	6%
2008-9	1.27	4%
2009-10	1.26	-1%
2010-11	1.36	8%

Source : National Rail Statistics, Office of Rail Regulation

The UK rail passenger journeys show 17% growth in passenger volume in just four years, right through the recession: there was a sharp rise in fuel prices that significantly increased the cost of motoring;, alterations were made in tax arrangements that made company cars less attractive; a reduction of access to cars for young people arose through increasing insurance premiums; there was a decline in domestic, low cost airline services, and there was an increase in rail's market share within the London catchment from the increased availability of Oyster ticketing.

All these factors should have stimulated rail demand on Wrexham & Shropshire further; that they did not leads to the conclusion that the underlying demand trend was heavily offset by the 'other' factors. In support of this assertion was the fall in yield per passenger journey. Businesses re-evaluated their travel choices and traded from first to standard class, to save money. All passengers searched for and moved to cheaper off-peak services. So Wrexham & Shropshire was launched at a time of sharp decline in yields. Pete Wilkinson is clear that the recession had a huge influence.

'The markets we were serving – people running small businesses, innovators and start-ups – their business was London. With the recession, their access to finance went, their confidence went, and they had to find other ways to get their ideas to market'.

Forecasting the demand

The application made to ORR to launch the service included some interesting benchmarking to support the forecasts of demand. This analysis is worth reviewing, given that the overall market, in terms of journeys made by rail between Wrexham, Shropshire and London, did not respond as expected and grow significantly during the life of Wrexham & Shropshire. Journeys by rail were assessed on a per capita basis:

In order to understand the performance of these areas, further analysis was carried out showing similar statistics for a range of other locations across the UK. Care was taken to select locations situated between two and four hours from London, with a comparable direct rail service in terms of trains per day to that proposed by Wrexham & Shropshire. Large cities were avoided and similar provincial towns and counties were selected. The results were very compelling as the tables overleaf show.

The places – large and small – across the UK, all demonstrated a journey per capita markedly greater than those calculated for the Wrexham & Shropshire catchment. It was acknowledged that there was considerable variability, and care was necessary in interpreting the analysis, as there are often local factors that can distort such high level statistics. However, it is difficult to argue

Shrewsbury (population 71k) kicked rather at its severance from London through trains. Yet, when one was put back, with the introduction of Wrexham and Shropshire, somehow the traffic never came up to the expectation for such a town and its populated 'county' hinterland. Perhaps the reasons are not so difficult to find, and the search begins with the simplest explanations.

Population and Rail Travel
Wrexham & Shropshire catchment area

	2001 Census Population	2005/6 Rail Jnys to/from London	Journeys per Capita
Wrexham	128,476	16,040	0.12
Shropshire	283,173	85,347	0.30
Telford & Wrekin	158,325	54,769	0.35
Tame Bridge catchment	252,400	20,652	0.08

Source : Wrexham & Shropshire, from 2001 Census and rail industry LENNON data

Population and Rail Travel
Other UK catchment areas

	2001 Census Population	2005/6 Rail Jnys to/from London	Journeys per Capita
North Staffordshire	597,078	432,569	0.72
South/East Staffordshire	209,666	145,704	0.69
Herefordshire	174,871	95,427	0.55
Lancaster	133,914	112,418	0.84
East Devon	125,520	91,540	0.73
Worcestershire	542,107	1,309,126	2.41
Hambleton	84,111	59,059	0.70

Source : Wrexham & Shropshire, from 2001 Census and rail industry LENNON data

with the hypothesis that the Wrexham & Shropshire catchment population was travelling to and from London at a rate well below what would be expected. It may be that with an hourly service to London an hour's drive away at Stafford, with a 1hr 20 mins transit time, people were driving across to Stafford. For Wrexham one can drive to Crewe in about 45 minutes, for a more than hourly service to London with a transit time of 1hr 42 mins. At Telford the choices are even better: 35 mins to drive to Stafford, 30 mins to drive to Wolverhampton, or take the train to Wolverhampton for an hourly service, or stay on to Birmingham International for even more frequency to London. At Tame Bridge the offer was four trains per

Stafford station on 14th September 2005 with the 13.36 train to Euston running in on time. The passengers can expect to be in London in 1hr 20 minutes, and there are trains from here every hour from early morning. It's a very good service. In 2001, with loco hauled services the frequency was the same, but the journey time was 20 minutes longer. Drive time from Shrewsbury is 1 hour.

hour to Birmingham New Street, and then two (increasing to three) trains an hour from there to Euston. Looking back, these customer choices represented somewhat of a challenge for Wrexham & Shropshire.

The analyses here are of course in danger of being 'wise after the event'. The indicators for the WSMR service looked promising to the promoters. Part of the success of Hull Trains was that it stimulated a rail travel market that had been depressed by the lack of through services, and it was expected that a similar outcome was possible for Wrexham & Shropshire. Whilst there were clearly several factors affecting the market response, including unattractive journey times and the recession, it is still the case that the total market for rail travel to London from the Wrexham & Shropshire catchment simply did not grow overall in the way that had been forecast, and this is surprising.

DfT short term approval

There was always potential synergy between Chiltern Railways and Wrexham & Shropshire. An uninformed observer may have thought that an unsubsidised service bringing advantage to one funded by the taxpayer might have been welcomed. Yet this did not appear to be so. Several attempts were made at mutual co-operation, but it appeared that the reaction from DfT was not very supportive. The first try came during 2009, when Chiltern was in need of more capacity, as the latest order for rolling stock was running late. Wrexham & Shropshire had the capacity to cover by providing additional services to London from both Leamington Spa and Banbury - restoring links between Shropshire and Leamington in the process. Short term approval was secured from both Department for Transport and ORR for Wrexham & Shropshire to carry these passengers, starting in December 2009.

A second round of cuts

Midway through 2010, it was becoming clear that the reduction in service to four trains per day, and other changes made to the fares structure, had only gone so far to stem the losses made by Wrexham & Shropshire, and that more action was required. Andy Hamilton issued a 'use it or lose it' plea in local media in August 2010, although it is difficult to know how seriously this was taken locally. There had been several similar messages from Wrexham & Shropshire in the past, usually linked to announcements of proposals for competitor services. Some had also suggested that with the backing of DB, such announcements were just a publicity stunt and the plug would never be pulled.

The company examined the potential for further cost savings, through a reduction in weekday services from four to three per day. The predominance of leisure travel on Wrexham & Shropshire meant that whilst peak trains were profitable, off peak trains on weekdays continued to perform poorly, with increased travel at weekends. However, it was found that the proposed reduction would only produce a profitable outcome if staff numbers were also reduced, unless it was possible to redeploy them.

The second co-operative measure came at the time the reduction in the Wrexham service to three trains per day was being contemplated, Chiltern Railways was now facing a shortfall in capacity as a result of volume growth, and the loss of train availability due to additional maintenance and modifications being carried out. Building in some relief from Wrexham & Shropshire's assessment of the impact of running three trains per weekday was found to be attractive overall. From the December 2010 timetable, a Wrexham & Shropshire train and crew was therefore allocated to operate Chiltern's 05.46 Birmingham-London and 16.33 London-Birmingham services. The crew lodged overnight in Birmingham, ending the long-running practice of Wrexham & Shropshire crews lodging overnight in London.

A last throw of the dice

By 2010 Wrexham & Shropshire had lost £13 million over the three years since startup. Every opportunity for significant revenue growth had been tried to coax profit from the operation without success. By late 2010 it was becoming difficult to see any bright future for the business. Although the 'Moderation of Competition' protection for Virgin Trains would end in April 2012, the forecast of around £0.5m per annum income would not bridge the gap. The long term future of fully open stops at Leamington and Banbury was also under threat, along with the financial boost they had brought to the company. The deal agreed with Chiltern Railways and signed off by DfT and ORR was temporary, and DfT made it clear it could not continue beyond May 2011, leading to an annual reduction of £0.5m.

One final opportunity had emerged when overall owner. Deutsche Bahn had acquired Arriva Group in 2010. Thus one of Wrexham & Shropshire's competitors Arriva Trains Wales (ATW) had become part of the same owning group. DB asked for a review of the options for Wrexham & Shropshire, to include improving the financial results by examining opportunities for synergy with ATW as well as the option of closure of the service.

During autumn 2010, joint work was carried out to establish the potential scale of benefit from combining some ATW and Wrexham & Shropshire services. Focus fell on the ATW Birmingham-Shrewsbury Chester-Holyhead services, which Wrexham & Shropshire shadowed for a large part of their route. Serious consideration was given to running Wrexham & Shropshire services from Marylebone to serve Birmingham, provide local services from the West Midlands into Shropshire and to explore running to Chester or even Holyhead. The potential financial benefits from the train mileage savings were established. As nobody had ever attempted to combine open access and franchised services, the implications for DfT, Welsh Assembly Government, and ORR were unclear. It did not appear that DfT had any enthusiasm for such a combination, despite extra choice, extra flexibility, and savings in costs to the taxpayer, so the idea looked unlikely to succeed.

The final financial analysis and evaluation was prepared towards the end of 2010. The paper diplomatically explained that:

> *"the decision on the future of W&S needs to balance the forecast financial position with other non-financial risks and opportunities".*

In the end, the financial benefits of synergy with ATW were not great enough make this an attractive alternative. It was concluded that the ATW synergy option did:

> *"not offer... financial benefits over the alternatives and brings with it a number of risks linked principally to approvals".*

The final decision

The table opposite shows the long term business analysis which was presented to the WSMR Board in 2010. This outlines the financial analysis of Wrexham & Shropshire remaining as a stand-alone business.

1. The operation was still expected to make losses in future years. The forecast was no profit until 2014.

2. The revenue forecast reflected the losses expected as a result of reducing the service to three trains, which of course was itself a mitigating factor against traffic growth.

3. The income improvements were predicated on:
   +£0.9m over three-years, from improved journey

W&S Base Plan - 3 train service					
Passenger Revenue Build-up	***2010 forecast***	***2011***	***2012***	***2013***	***2014***
Starting revenue		*4.4*	*4.8*	*6.3*	*7.4*
Service reduced to 3 trains		*-0.4*			
Exogenous growth and fares		*0.5*	*0.8*	*0.7*	*0.6*
Evergreen 3 journey times		*0.3*	*0.4*	*0.2*	
Wolverhampton			*0.3*	*0.2*	*0.2*
Passenger Revenue Forecast	*4.4*	*4.8*	*6.3*	*7.4*	*8.2*
Other Income					
Catering		*0.3*	*0.4*	*0.4*	*0.4*
Chiltern Leamington/Banbury capacity		*0.7*	*0.3*		
Other		*0.1*	*0.2*	*0.2*	*0.2*
Other Income Forecast	*1.1*	*1.1*	*0.9*	*0.6*	*0.6*
Cost Forecast	*-8.4*	*-7.4*	*-7.7*	*-8.3*	*-8.5*
Profit	*-2.9*	*-1.5*	*-0.5*	*-0.3*	*0.3*

times brought about by Chiltern's Evergreen 3 project +£0.7m over three-years from picking up passengers in Wolverhampton, anticipating the removal of MoC in 2012, the end of Virgin Trains' franchise.

4. The cost forecast expected that £1 million reduction would occur in 2011, principally as a result of the reduction in service to three trains each way, per weekday.

5. The figures also included assumptions of annual revenue uplifts driven by the resumption of economic growth which now look optimistic given the performance of UK economy in the years since 2010.

Despite the improvements forecast in income, the operation was still expected to make losses between 2011 and 2013 totalling £2.3m before breaking even,

As Christmas 2010 approached the difficult decision was taken at Board level to close Wrexham & Shropshire as soon as was practical, and to redistribute the assets to the Birmingham (Moor Street) Chiltern Railways Mainline project, that had a better basis by far for achieving a profitable operation. Staff would be redeployed where possible.

Summary : the significant factors

1. Transit times were so sub-standard from Wrexham and points en-route that the market was not large enough at the yields that could be gained, to achieve profitable operation. This was not obvious at the start.

2. Moderation of Competition rules prevented access to any effective pick-up point in the West Midlands. This too was not obvious from the start.. Even if the problems of the transit time had been solved, this point could still have stymied the operation.

3. Despite award winning on-board service, and the most excellent catering service, these advantages were not enough to win market share that was needed vitally. Even the refurbished coaches for the service were not delivered on time.

4. Service frequency cutback to three trains daily, made worse an already difficult sell on frequency of service.

5. Wrexham & Shropshire was not able to offer sufficient differential in price to win market share at an income price that could be afforded. Competitors with better service frequency, and superior transit times could match the prices.

Transit times comparisons - Wrexham & Shropshire, Virgin Trains, and others 2009 EWD

	VT	VT	W&S	VT	W&S	VT	W&S	VT	W&S	VT
Wrexham	07.00		07.23		11.23		14.18		17.23	
Ruabon			07.31		11.31		14.26		17.31	
Chirk			07.38		11.38		14.32		17.38	
Gobowen			07.43		11.43		14.37		17.43	
Shrewsbury			08.07		12.07		15.07		18.07	
Stafford		08.36								
Wellington			08.21		12.21		15.21		18.21	
Telford			08.27		12.27		15.27		18.27	
Cosford			08.36		12.36		15.36		18.36	
Wolverhampton			08s47	08.45	12s47	12.45	15s47	15.45	18s49	18.45
Tame Bridge			09.01		13.01		16.01		19.02	
Leamington Spa			09.49		13.49		16.49		19.46	
Banbury			10.07		14.07		17.07		20.05	
Marylebone			11.15		15.15		18.15		21.15	
Euston	09.38	09.56		10.34		14.34		17.34		20.34
Transit time	2h 38m	1h 20m	3h 52m	1h 49m	3h 52m	1h 49m	3h 57m	1h 49m	3h 52m	1h 49m

	W&S	VT	VT	W&S	VT	W&S	VT	VT	VT	W&S
Euston		08.07	08.23		11.23		16.43	18.10*	18.23	
Marylebone	07.33			11.20		16.30				18.33
Banbury	08.37			12.30		17.33				19.37
Leamington Spa	08.55			12.48		17.50				19.55
Tame Bridge	09.42			-		18.40				20.40
Wolverhampton	09u59		10.11	-	13.11	18u58	*18b43*		20.12	21u04
Cosford	10.10			14.10		19.06				21.15
Telford	10.18			14.18		19.14				21.23
Wellington	-			-		19.20				21.29
Stafford		09.22								
Shrewsbury	10.40			14.36	*14w15*	19.34	*19b19*		*21w15*	21.46
Gobowen	11.02			14.58		20.02				22.16
Chirk	-			-		20.07				22.21
Ruabon	-			-		20.14				22.28
Wrexham	11.19			15.16		20.23		20.38		22.36
Transit time	3h 46m	1h 15m	1h 48m	3h 56m	1h 48m	3h 53m	2h 00m	2h 28m	1h 49m	4h 03m
Shrewsbury Transit direct	W&S			3h 16m		3h 04m				3h 13m
Shrewsbury Transit + change	VT/LM or ATW				2h 52m		2h 36m		2h 43m	

Notes: s - set down only u - pick up only w - change at Wolverhampton b - change at Birmingham (New Street)

* *It is worth noting that the 19.10 London (Euston) to Chester had connection for Wrexham, arr: 21.37 - 2h 27m transit*

Dyfrbont Pontcysyllte leads the 10:47 from Wrexham to Marylebone on Sunday 31st January 2010. The diverted train is shown on the West Coast Main Line between Blisworth and Roade. Would matters have been different, one wonders, if it could have gone (from Shrewsbury) into Euston at 110mph as London Midland now does from Birmingham? Perhaps with a DfT with partiality and not antipathy to Open Access it could? **Geoff Plumb**

Transit times and consequences

The information that is set out in the table is intended to make it easier to see 'what time would I have arrived if I had set off at: x?'. The simple facts are that leaving Wrexham, via Chester on the early morning direct train, by Super-Voyager, the transit time to London is 2h 38m, but by Wrexham & Shropshire it is just short of four hours.

For the Shrewsbury passenger, a drive across to Stafford secures a 1h 20m transit to London, but by Wrexham & Shropshire this is 3h 08m, more than twice as long. The Chester and Stafford options persist throughout the day at hourly intervals.

Note too that the comparison between Shrewsbury direct trains on Wrexham & Shropshire, and the Virgin Wolverhampton, or Birmingham services give better transits with changing of up to half-an-hour, even with the change interval (the comparisons here are made with the 'from London' journeys) but that even if Wrexham & Shropshire could have picked up at Wolverhampton, with the tortuous route, and the lower maximum speeds available, Marylebone to Wolverhampton carries a forty-minute extra time penalty.

These transit shortfalls by Wrexham & Shropshire do not mean they will carry no traffic, but it narrows the range of appeal. The discounted fare market will be interested - the less time-constrained will travel. Those who prefer direct services will welcome calls at Ruabon, Chirk, Gobowen, etc. Alas, the massive population area of the West Midlands will recognise the freedom of a twenty-minute interval from Birmingham, with a London transit time of about 1h 22m, which is probably why the response from Tame Bridge was so feeble.

The organisation prided itself on the quality if its First product, so heavily discounted against Virgin, and better in delivery by far - except in one respect. With transit times so unfavourably compared, and unable to compete in the West Midlands area with its massive population, it is hardly surprising that loadings were diminished. The premium market is speed aware. Wrexham, Shrewsbury and Telford, (all quite small markets) and the West Midlands (the large market) were effectively suppressed by such extended transit times. Even Chiltern Mainline, the service that has employed the assets of the closed Wrexham & Shropshire service is taking time to build, despite heavily discounted fare (VT £48, Ch £15, £12 LM - cheapest , standard, 'walk-on'). Mainline is around 20 minutes slower than VT, Birmingham-London. The transit time and service frequency narrowed the market to unsustainable levels for Wrexham and Shropshire. At heavily discounted fares, the volume base rose, but then the effect of that on profitability was unsustainable.

It may be easy after the event to make these observations. At the time of planning of the service transit time comparisons were much more favourable to the Wrexham & Shropshire plan. The VT Birmingham and Wolverhampton service was hourly for some of the day, and was 110mph loco-hauled trains. The Chester service did not exist, and that from Stafford was less frequent.

Geoff Plumb

Chapter 11 Closure with Regret

Closure, with regret

In the first week of January 2011, Adrian Shooter assembled a small team of managers, including Andy Hamilton, Thomas Ableman and Richard Harper, in order to determine the most appropriate way to implement the Board's decision to close Wrexham & Shropshire. There was a great deal to consider. Should a swift announcement be made? How long should trains continue to run? What were the legal requirements? How should the staff be told?

It was quickly realised that there were a large number of things to be prepared, including formal letters to staff, stakeholders and suppliers, press notices, and internal communications within all the railway companies to operations and retail staff. A programme was prepared, which covered three weeks of preparations. During this time it was vital that everyone involved remained discreet – the last thing anyone wanted was for staff to find out informally.

If something as drastic as closing a railway company, and particularly one so well respected in its local community has to be done, then it is important to do it right. The only appropriate way to inform the staff before they heard it from elsewhere, and to do so face-to-face. Once the staff were informed, a swift public announcement of the news would be necessary, with Adrian Shooter available to talk to the media. It was felt that once the announcement had been made, trains should cease running as soon as practical afterwards. Subsequently, some commentators were angry at the short notice given to intending passengers, particularly those who had booked tickets in advance for travel weeks ahead, but to ask staff under threat of redundancy to work, when their work puts them in constant contact with the public, felt neither fair nor moral.

A key issue concerned arrangements for those passengers who had booked tickets in the weeks after the proposed closure. In order to avoid generation of rumours, Wrexham & Shropshire's own website was still selling tickets the day before the closure announcement, and the company's retail system was allowing the booking of advance tickets and reservations by other ticket retailers. Whilst refunds would be available – Wrexham & Shropshire was not insolvent – it was felt that the offer of an alternative rail service would be welcomed by those who were to be disappointed. After discussions, agreement was reached with the operators of all the alternative rail services – principally Arriva Trains Wales, London Midland and Virgin Trains – to accept pre-booked Wrexham & Shropshire tickets after closure. This positive response from competitors demonstrates yet again the ability of the whole railway to work as a team when presented with a big challenge.

Adrian Shooter, Andy Hamilton and Thomas Ableman broke the sad news to the staff at Wrexham General on the evening of Tuesday 25th January 2011. Staff were well aware the company had struggled to meet its financial targets. They had been kept well informed by the management team, and of course the earlier service reductions had demonstrated the tough times faced by the company.

The announcement of closure was nevertheless a huge shock to everyone, and not only was the company ceasing operations, but it was going to happen in just three days' time. On the morning of 26th January, a coordinated communications plan was enacted which was designed

W&S 67014 "Thomas Telford" is providing the power on the rear of the Chiltern LHCS with DVT 82302 leading a six coach set. This is the 06:53 from Banbury to Marylebone during the stop at Princes Risborough, from where it proceeded nonstop to London (Marylebone). The train was running on time and departed at 07:30. Monday 10th January 2011. Not long before the rolling stock resources will make their way to Chiltern permanently.

Geoff Plumb

to inform passengers, stakeholders and other railway company staff as quickly as possible. Press releases were issued and phone calls made to MPs, councillors and other key contacts. The previous night, letters were posted to everyone with an interest in Wrexham & Shropshire. Adrian Shooter's announcement stated that 'regrettably, we have concluded that the potential for further changes to the company's operations, including synergy with Arriva Trains Wales, will not improve the financial position sufficiently. The shareholders have invested in excess of £13 million in launching the business and funding its losses, and have now concluded that there is no reasonable prospect that Wrexham & Shropshire can become profitable, or offer a return on this investment'. The last train would run on Friday 28th January 2011.

Very soon, reaction to the news of closure began. Richard Harper spent the day of the announcement travelling to several of the stations to make sure station staff were aware, putting up posters announcing Wrexham & Shropshire's closure and removing publicity material.

On the penultimate day of running, Thursday 27th January 2011, 67001 is in charge of 1P03, the 07.23 from Wrexham to London (Marylebone), carrying the "84L WSMR" headboard. It has just emerged from Ardley Tunnel and is heading for Bicester at 10:14 on. Time is running out for Wrexham & Shropshire.

Geoff Plumb

In weather conditions as miserable as the circumstances, 67013 Dyfrbont Pontcysyllte *and 67012* Shropshire Lad *approach Princes Risborough station at 08.39 on Wednesday 26th January 2011. This was the first train to run after the staff of the railway had been informed that operations were to finish. This was a sad day for the railway and its staff, they have done a wonderful job which has been appreciated by thousands of people.The specially made headboard is on the pilot locomotive.*

Geoff Plumb

"I spent most of the morning in the car, listening to Jim Hawkins on BBC Radio Shropshire. Listeners were phoning in and texting the show with a mixture of shock and sadness, concern for the staff and sanguine reflections that had more people from the area supported the service, maybe it wouldn't be facing closure. I remember Jim being speechless when one listener texted that they 'hadn't been to that awful metropolis in fifteen years, and had no intention of going any time soon'".

Jim wondered if there was a tendency for Shropshire folk to be insular, which naturally results from the county's contrast with city life. That's certainly a view sometimes held by those outside the county – Nick Pigott's editorial in the next edition of The Railway Magazine was blunt:

'Wrexham & Shropshire Railway has had to call it a day in the face of poor passenger loadings. It was a wonderful little operator and those who were too apathetic to use it have only themselves to blame'.

Thomas Ableman got the blame from some of the staff

A staff car was added on the 13.28 train from Wrexham on 28th January 2011, and the return working, the last Wrexham & Shropshire train, the 18.33 from London (Marylebone) to Wrexham. Here on that day are the rather sad scenes as staff and their families travel up to London to wish goodbye to the service.

Geoff Plumb

A staff car was added on the 13.28 train from Wrexham on 28th January 2011, and the return working, the last Wrexham & Shropshire train, the 18.33 from London (Marylebone) to Wrexham. Here on that day are the rather sad scenes as staff and their families travel up to London to wish goodbye to the service.

Geoff Plumb

for dropping the fares and then not raising them quickly enough again when the volume went up. In fact that was not quite true. The objective was to try to generate more volume, and with it more income; the volume went up and so the revenue went up. It was a careful calculation and a risk to get this right - and Thomas did. However, it was not enough as it seems that the market was not big enough to cover the costs; the service was unprofitable and therefore vulnerable. By this late stage, even if MoC had permitted the Wolverhampton stop instead of at Tame Bridge (Parkway), the income advantage was calculated to be an additional £500k, and that was not enough to bridge the gap between cost and income. The game was up; this service could not and would not be profitable without general growth in the market for rail and/or more of the difference in transit time being recovered - and that was impossible, was how the story of the time went..

The indifference of the Shropshire market to their much coveted through service meant that expected loadings failed to appear. Perhaps these people wanted the security of the service without the obligations of using it, or perhaps WSMR just got it wrong. It was not surprising that a careful, sanguine examination of the whole Wrexham & Shropshire operation concluded that if the resources were transferred to a Birmingham (Moor Street) - London (Marylebone) express service, then they could perform far better. Indeed the potential for growth on this route would deliver profit. That was the logical conclusion reached and that is what happened. It was sad, but inevitable. The Wrexham to Birmingham part of the operation was effectively ditched. There was now no longer any need for a separate WSMR, and so the trains went to Chiltern to assist with the Mainline product. The staff were determined to go out with a bang, but there is no doubt the final three days were a challenge. Emotions ran high as everyone worked their last trains to London, and their final Wrexham & Shropshire train to their home depot in Wrexham. Everybody did their best to support each other.

Ahead of the final day, an extra coach was added to one of the train sets, making five coaches in all. This was rostered to work the last train in each direction – 1P23 the 1328 Wrexham to Marylebone and 1J83 the 1833 Marylebone to Wrexham – with the extra coach reserved for staff. Most of the team made that last round trip, in uniform, a demonstration if any were needed of the commitment and affection they felt for WSMR. There was a lot of anger later – people naturally care more about a job when they think they're part of a good thing.

Tony Stickells was at the controls of 67013 for the final up service on 28th January. 'Tell them we're coming' on arrival at Marylebone was the instruction, and Tony was joined by Peter Ward who made sure of a cacophony on the horns. The Internet forums afterwards suggested they were reported for excessive use of the horn. Not true – Mark Edlington says 'the truth is I told them they didn't sound the horn enough.' Diane Davidson had secured a wreath in Wrexham & Shropshire colours, to which Mark added an inscription of 'A Local Train of Thought' by

At London Marylebone there was a wreath and much emotion. Well there might be, as this enterprise was set up so near as could be to a railway run by its employees, for the pleasure and convenience of its users.
There was a poem attached to the wreath, and that is recorded below.

Geoff Plumb

Siegfried Sassoon. The wreath was left on the bufferstops at Marylebone by Paul Belton.

And so the last Wrexham & Shropshire service departed Marylebone with 67013 powering on the rear. It arrived at Wrexham General just after 2200, and brought to a close this chapter in the history of rail services between London, Shropshire and North East Wales.

There were frequent messages of goodwill and farewell over the last three days, including some nice gestures such as messages on the information screens. At Shrewsbury, there was a banner which read 'Salopians eat your heart out, you've lost the jewel in the crown'.

A Local Train of Thought, Siegfried Sassoon (1940)
Alone, in silence, at a certain time of night,
Listening, and looking up from what I'm trying to write,
I hear a local train along the Valley. And "There
Goes the one-fifty", think I to myself; aware
That somehow its habitual travelling comforts me,
Making my world seem safer, homelier, sure to be
The same to-morrow; and the same, one hopes, next year.
"There's peacetime in that train." One hears it disappear
With needless warning whistle and rail-resounding wheels.
"That train's quite like an old familiar friend," one feels.

On Saturday morning, 29th January, the two train sets berthed overnight in Wrexham were returned to Wembley depot. To minimise staff and planning requirements, they were combined into a single 13 vehicle train. This operation didn't pass without some difficulty as the brake pipes didn't stretch from DVT to DVT – luckily a pair of extension pipes were found in one of the loco cabs.

Local and national media responded rapidly to the mournful news. Coverage in the local media was extensive, and its tone is perhaps summed up by this report from 27th January 2011 on the Shropshire Star website:

> *'The Wrexham, Shropshire, and Marylebone Railway had a hard working, committed, management team who provided Shropshire with its only direct rail link to London. Which lost £2.8 million last year. Staff were very friendly and helpful. The service was as good as could be found on any train anywhere in the world. It topped virtually every customer satisfaction survey. And still lost £2.8 million last year. Management played their part in our local community, getting involved in many events and supporting projects. It didn't prevent last year's £2.8 million loss.*
>
> *Tomorrow the service stops, after almost three years. What did they have to do to make it succeed? It deserved to succeed. Everything was done to help it succeed. The fares were, as train fares go, cheap. There were many people, this newspaper among them, who campaigned for the return of Shropshire's direct rail link to London. But as a commercial venture it naturally had to be just that – commercial. The hard truth of the matter is that not enough Salopians were using it to make it viable.*

When the last Up train arrived at Marylebone, there was little to laugh about, but a great deal of comradeship. Those involved with running the train were invited to sign the headboard. This neat artefact will move graciously into history, to be much prized by future generations.

Geoff Plumb

Fine words and entreaties are no substitute for bums on train seats. This is the second time a revived direct rail link has come, run for a few years, and then gone. We are sorry to see the loss of the latest service, and the loss of 55 jobs into the bargain.

Thank you to the WSMR for giving it a go.'

Sadly, doing a first class job still wasn't enough. The reaction wasn't all positive as, and RMT General Secretary (the late) Bob Crow said :

"The closure of the Wrexham and Shropshire service is an act of corporate vandalism and is a bitter blow to the UK rail industry. It is a scandal that a giant company like Deutsche Bahn can play fast and loose with our rail services in this way and then cut run when they decide the profit margins aren't fat enough for their liking.

"The UK Government should now step in and nationalise the route to protect both the jobs and the popular Wrexham & Shropshire services and there should be a full inquiry into how this operation, set up with Welsh government and taxpayer support, has been ground into the dust by Deutsche Bahn. Public ownership would protect that public investment rather than allowing the private rail asset strippers to walk away from the wreckage."

This would have been fair criticism had the company produced a profit margin. In fact it looked to the employees like an uninformed statement by someone trying to gain advantage with ignorant partisan points. The worst part of that was that it was said by a union boss - who should have been offering some sympathy, and might actually have tried to understand what was happening, instead of aggressively mouthing nonsense. People shook their heads sadly and made a mental note to have nothing to do with RMT.

An online campaign was launched to rescue the service, with an petition to Westminster raising over 6,000 signatures by 3rd February. Shrewsbury MP Daniel Kawczynski ensured the petitioners were heard in Parliament, but there were no organisations coming forward with funding to rescue the business – which is not unexpected given the commercial reasons for the company's demise.

Adrian Shooter's willingness to front up to press and media received much positive comment given the circumstances, and any concerns he may have had about the strategic reasons for it he sensibly kept to himself. . He didn't like the closure any more than the staff. He didn't hide behind a corporate communications team, cleared his diary and made time available for the many challenging media enquiries. You and Yours on BBC Radio 4 from 1st February 2011 was just one of those:

There was a photographer with the presence of mind amongst all the sadness of the gathering to get people together for a group photograph, before the train set off back to Wrexham, and at the same time, Wrexham & Shropshire departed into the history books. It was over.

Geoff Plumb

'We receive so many complaints about poor customer service here on You and Yours, it's quite something to hear customers enthusing about a company and its products and services. it's even more of a surprise when the praise is directed at a rail service. Yet that's exactly what happened when we spoke to passengers taking one of the last trains on the Wrexham & Shropshire Railway. The company, which operated from north Wales to London, boasts a customer satisfaction rating of 99 per cent and we heard from passengers who were prepared to have slightly longer journeys and pay somewhat higher fares just to travel on a service which felt personal.

Unfortunately Wrexham & Shropshire went out of business last week leaving cynics wondering whether that high level of customer service and its unprofitability might be connected.

A question for Wrexham & Shropshire's boss Adrian Shooter. Many a business leader faced with such bad news, would have hidden behind a written statement but he rearranged his diary to come live on You and Yours to explain publicly what went wrong.

What he told us was an interesting insight into rail privatisation and the subsequent benefits of competition. As part of the Virgin Trains franchise, Shooter's trains were not allowed to stop at Wolverhampton. Had they been able to do so, who knows, they might have allowed Wrexham and Shropshire to turn a profit. Two years and £13 million later, the service has been forced to close.

Those who have already bought tickets can use them on Arriva Trains Wales, London Midland, Virgin and Chiltern. Is it too much to hope travellers might receive an equally warm welcome to the one they'd been hoping for when they booked?'

The 28th January 2011 was the end for the WSMR service between London and Wrexham, but it didn't signal the end for the trains or the staff. The following Monday, 31st January, WSMR staff and trains were required to work the 0546 Birmingham Moor Street to Marylebone service, and in conjunction with the balancing 16.30 departure from Marylebone was expected to continue at least until the end of the timetable period in May 2011. Over the next few weeks, the WSMR staff continued to provide excellent service on the Chiltern route, as the team began to find jobs elsewhere. Adrian Shooter and the management team were determined to retain as many of the staff as possible, within the Arriva Group or the railway more widely. Chiltern Railways was able to provide jobs for some, as it was recruiting staff in advance of the launch of Mainline in September 2011. Former staff also found work across the UK at Cross Country, Arriva Trains Wales, First Great Western, DRS and Tyne & Wear Metro.

Mark Edlington remembers the shutdown only to well

as he expresses in his own words:

"I remember Andy telling me on the afternoon of the closure announcement. I'd suspected, but it's always hard hearing something like that. I was pleased he'd not told me before, it's very hard to keep those things secret even though it must have been hard for him. It had been a risk for a long time, but it felt like were just about going to survive. There's still a lot of anger because people care about a good thing. No-one cares if it's crap. The fact that a year later they all still feel angry shows you it was a thing of value. That night Adrian was coming on the train, and the train was delayed. When he finally arrived and told everyone the company was going to be closed down, everyone was shocked, and doubly so when he said it was going to happen at the end of the week. Andy told me they had considered closing it that night, and I'm really pleased they didn't because the staff deserved more.

All too soon our last day of operation arrived, with some excellent support from the ASLEF & RMT trade union representatives we had persuaded as many of the staff as possible to travel together (and in uniform) on the last Up service from Wrexham General to Marylebone and return, we intended to maintain our professionalism right to the very end! Managing Director Andy Hamilton had arranged for these last trains to be specially strengthened by adding an additional MkIII vehicle to the formation.

When I arrived at the offices at Wrexham General everyone was making preparations for our final run to London, I said that I thought we should have a wreath, Diane Davidson answered that she had already arranged one as she knew it was customary when a railway closed down, I tried to think of a suitable epitaph to write on the accompanying card and settled for Siegfried Sassoon's poem 'Local train of thought' as it felt that during our all too short existence as a railway company that we had indeed become quite like an 'old familiar friend' to the good people of Shropshire and Clwyd. Under this I added 'Goodbye Wrexham & Shropshire, God bless old friend'.

As the departure time approached I reluctantly made my way over the footbridge to platform 3 to join the 13:28 departure with driver Tony Stickells who would be driving the company's final trains, Tony told me that the drivers wanted me to drive the final empty stock movement into the Up Bay sidings at Wrexham on our return later that evening, this small gesture of kindness was too much for me and I was grateful that Kath Chelton was there to provide a shoulder to cry on.

I spent the Up journey in the train talking to colleagues and friends, railway photographer Geoff Plumb who had recorded the company's birth and operations was appropriately able to join us to record the last rites; he had become a firm friend of the company and often provided us with copies of his photographs of our trains in action.

On reaching Marylebone Driver Peter Ward who had joined Tony Stickells in the leading cab of 67013 sounded a melancholy series of blasts on the horn as we entered platform 3 for the last time.

Barricades had been set up for the attendant railway photographers and Tony Stickells and Peter Ward were joined at the front of the train by fellow drivers, Peter Griffin, Ivan Marriott and Paul Belton.

Paul Belton then dropped down into the 'four foot' to retrieve his headboard and to place the wreath on the stop blocks, the photographers missed this small but poignant moment and had to ask him to repeat it which after a moment's hesitation he duly did.

I saw our Chairman Adrian Shooter on the platform, he is not the kind of man you normally hug but this was not a normal situation and I knew W&S was very close to his heart and that he had done much to bring the company into being as well as doing all that he possibly could to prevent its closure. I gave him a big hug and looked him in the eye saying 'W&S may not have been the most successful railway company in the world, but it was the best railway company'.

All of the company's employees who had travelled on the train then gathered for some group photos, this became a particularly bittersweet moment with some of the photographer's admonishments for us to smile or wave more being met with derision.

On our return run to Wrexham General I again initially travelled in our reserved staff coach but after Adrian Shooter and Andy Hamilton had alighted at Banbury (the latter after making a short speech) I joined driver Tony Stickells in the DVT.

Everywhere we stopped we encountered touching acts of kindness, good wishes on an electronic departure board or an announcement over the PA helped us

The neat and tidy bay platforms at Wrexham (General), renewed to act as the northern base for Wrexham & Shropshire now lie unuused again, waiting for trains that will never come. Perhaps it was nice while it lasted. Perhaps 'the system' might be a little more sympathetic to innovators and entrepreneurs, or the Brits are in for an increasingly tough time as a nation in the future. **Mark Edlington**

on our way, as we entered Shropshire these gestures grew in size and feeling; at Shrewsbury we received 'three cheers' and a banner proclaimed 'Salopians eat your hearts out, you have lost the jewel in your crown'.

On reaching Gobowen which was my home station I noticed Brandon my next-store neighbour amid the throng of passengers and well-wishers on the platform; he often took his young son Ethan to Gobowen station to watch the trains go by and had come to see the final train. I had promised him a cab ride some day, and it was a case of now or never! I opened the cab door and when he held out his hand to shake mine, I pulled him up into the cab and told him to sit in the second man's seat, after all, a promise is a promise!

At Wrexham General we ran into platform 3 as usual, all of our staff, now increased in numbers by those who had worked our services earlier in the day and therefore being unable to join us for the final trip, stood on the platform as I prepared to make the shunt moment over Croes Newydd level crossing and then back into Up siding No.1, I asked Chiltern Driver Instructor Steve Roast to accompany me as by now my head was spinning and this was no time to make a mistake and blot our good operational record! The signal cleared and as 67013 started to move the staff stood close alongside the train at the edge of the platform and started to applaud their company, this was a very emotional moment and I'm surprised I managed to drive the train at all!

After changing ends we made the final movement into the bay platform and secured the train and then it really was all over; there was still the small matter of getting the two sets of rolling stock safely back to Wembley Depot the following morning but by now, nothing really seemed to matter anymore.

Wrexham & Shropshire had ended."

67014 **Thomas Telford** *looms out of the mist approaching Launton with the 11:20 Marylebone to Wrexham train, Tuesday 16th November 2010.* **Geoff Plumb**

Chapter 12 What Lessons can be Learnt?

An uncomfortable tale

In 2013 'the railway' was carrying more passengers than it had done since *The Great Age of Steam* - about which those who were never immersed in its filth will generally gush emotionally. Some claim that the railway privatisation was conducted incorrectly - but twenty years on this cannot have been so far wrong if the traffic is flowing so well and the system is managing to absorb it - the roads are not.

In 2014 large sections of the network are gaining the investment they need, and the system is returning a growing 'passenger miles' figures to justify that investment. However, the public perception still seems to be the one belonging to British Rail. Despite many television programmes bordering on the reasonable, just below the veneer of civilisation is the persistent criticism of the railways, even in the face of facts to the contrary.

If there are any lessons to be learned from this they must be about how those who work in the industry have adapted in the face of continued inconsistency. There are vitriolic complaints about the complexity of rail fares, yet airlines fares complications are not included. *Disgusted of Tunbridge Wells* becomes enervated about late running, yet accepts being stationary on the M25 despite the massive amounts of tax that goes into the exchequer from the motorist. Also inconsistent is the lady from Stevenage who enjoys a subsidised season ticket, and who makes a row about not being able to get a seat. This could be cured by fully reserved trains, but that would probably be accompanied by ugly scenes on the platforms - yet the same strictures do not apply on the tube; and if you really want a seat, most line frequencies offer this if you arrive early for the train. No one seems to question why there is a massive daily migration to offices far from home, in a world of communications connectivity, with Skype and the Internet. Passenger volume continues to rise in the face of the alleged discontent, and a major requirement to head off worse problems, with the increased capacity from HS2 is also condemned. The cost of HS2 is equivalent to three nuclear power stations, and we want to build four of those. So what's the problem?

There appears to be a perverse pleasure from some to argue down HS2 from within the industry - handing opponents a valuable weapon. The surge of current investment is tribute enough to the arguments in favour of rail, and HS2 is on offer 'as well'. Perhaps the railway pundits are steadily sawing off the tree branch on which they are sat. Current investment exceeds the Modernisation Plan, and is happening on a rising market not on a falling one - thus it is likely to succeed. The silence in support from all those who stand to benefit, all those who have complained for years about misguided government policy, is deafening.

The problem - and the lesson to be learned - is that no one speaks clearly, consistently, loudly and accurately in favour of the rail industry. It is the heritage rail industry, of Thomas the Tank engine, that has the positive voice, that knows how to talk money out of the public for their projects, that has active supporters within the legislature, and promotes, guards, and succours itself. The professionals, during all the setbacks of the last sixty years, have failed to maintain charismatic and articulate spokespersons in enough quantity to argue down detractors.

Until they do, then the best that any of us can hope for is to throw ourselves upon the mercy of the civil servants - an uncertain and uncomfortable serfdom.

How privatisation fared during twenty years

Not a single world railway privatisation subsequently adopted the British method, and UK privatisation seems to have reverted to state control in all but name, with competition much reduced. Rescue arrived from a direction that none of the wise ladies and gentlemen who advocated the, at first unreliable, untenable, and ill-thought through system foresaw. It wasn't a record to be proud of.

The method chosen for competition carried within itself the seeds of its own destruction that were sown and grew to take twenty years to stabilise.

- The menace of the legacy of the maintenance and renewals underspend was not clearly understood. The panic that followed the Hatfield GNER accident (see later), when deficiencies were discovered, brought it all into sharp focus.
- The jostling franchises carried a dangerous risk element. If they lost money, then they had to be bailed out, one way or another, by the government (even if re-let on more favourable terms to the franchisee)[1]. If they made money then it exposed the government to criticism for allowing capitalist fat cats to profit from state assets.
- There was no way of escaping the visibility of increased costs: of redeeming the maintenance of renewals underspend, and the PSO. Thus it was bound to appear as though the privatised railway was more expensive than British Rail. (And in fact this might indeed be the case, but more by the disappearance of BR's old ability to employ smoke and mirrors to conceal the true position.)

What pleasure it was for some to see the biter bit in this way. The correction was more complication from civil servants for franchise agreements, and a tighter grip on prescribing service patterns, frequencies, and rolling stock provision: all to try to control risk. Yet this offered no solution to the basic problems, as the fragmentation of the rail industry, that all the railwaymen recommended against, added complication and extra costs. The resulting reduction of operators reduced competition, and the infrastructure went back to the state with Network Rail.

There were some early franchises that performed well, applied innovation, and improved the service frequency and quality in a way that BR previously had seldom been able to do. These were the success stories of privatisation, but such improvements suddenly had to keep pace with the surge of traffic that arrived to change the game radically.

1 The weakness of the franchising system was illustrated with the ECML, relet after the GNER pull-out. In 2007 National Express took over but matters did not go well. Renegotiation was refused by DfT, who played hardball. NEx handed back the franchise, and the state had to run it (very well in fact) Alas the refranchising process went badly and the reputation of DfT suffered, leaving the privatisation process greatly criticised. Detractors loved it.

Potentially lucrative Inter-City services had been let at competitive rates, but with unanticipated rapid growth in volume; some ran service on hitherto underinvested main lines that delivered strong profit. Under BR such profit would have flowed to the Exchequer, after subtle cross-subsidy adjustment by British Rail. Now, these windfall profits went to the shareholders. This left poor performing services paid for by the taxpayers, and accusations that the good profit performers offered cream for the fat cats. Service betterment was often ignored.

As has already been noted, for many years under British Rail, there had been an 'establishment' policy of underinvestment in the railway and its infrastructure. At Hatfield on 17th October 2000, a northbound GNER Leeds service, running at 115mph, experienced a catastrophic failure of the left-hand running rail at Hatfield The train left the rails; four people died and seventy were injured in the subsequent pile-up. Though this sad outcome could have been treated as a miracle, based on the splendid integrity of the BR Mk4 carriage, and though the tragic loss of life was on a par with a serious road crash - a daily occurrence - the media feeding frenzy went on for days. Yet the almost prurient devotion of the media to a railway disaster concealed matters of grave concern that were attempted by the uninformed to be placed at the doors of the 'fat cat' franchise stakeholders. The informed knew of the years of infrastructure underinvestment in renewals and maintenance. This news was overlooked.

Within the Rail Industry, people who knew about the track and infrastructure deficit were attached to a vertically integrated organisation[2]. Those who admired the ingenious sub-prime mortgage culture (that was in 2000 considered clever) would not rate such burdensome safeguards. The entitlement to a 'return', upon which franchisees depended, encouraged the running of more trains as a matter of urgent necessity. On West Coast this led to the rebuilding of the railway, on East Coast it meant deferring renewals to accommodate the operators' upward-spiralling demand to run more trains: at Hatfield the need for the replacement rails was apparently known beforehand. Railtrack's sober investigation on the *'if it's like this on East Coast, what is it like across the system?'* question brought the true nature of the deficit of maintenance and renewals into sharp focus. Many speed restrictions were suddenly imposed and massive delays ensued; Railtrack was eventually cast as the *'Titanic'* in this tragedy. However, the legacy has been a massively increased maintenance and renewals programme, and

2 Underinvestment in infrastructure and track is no newer than the nuisance of potholes in the road. A vertically integrated railway can more easily cope, as the engineer is there to moderate excess. Place the engineer in a separate organisation with a commercial mission to stakeholders and not to the 'railway' and the matter changes radically.

The East Coast franchise in 2013 is in public hands after a few mishaps concerning the levels of payment that GNER and NEx were obliged to make for running the service. So 'the State' took it over and it is generally agreed that it was run excellently. Thus there are questions as to why it must be refranchised at all? There was the most dreadful brou-ha-ha in 2012 over the franchising process for the West Coast Main Line, but the government came back for more; the ECML will be returned to the private sector in 2015. Here a London to Leeds service passes Adwick on 6th June 2013.

when all was made safe, a continuous programme of improvements and acknowledgement that a useful railway is always an 'expensive' railway[3], and that to justify this the numbers should be on the rise - and they are. It was a redressed balance for British Rail's claimed excellent unit performance, which was perhaps much due to the steady rise of the unfortunate infrastructure deficit. It also had another result, Railtrack became ailing. The delays and cost-overruns of the West Coast route modernisation precipitated its demise and replacement with state owned Network Rail. The Potters Bar accident in 2001 exposed weakness in the interface between Network Rail and maintainer (private contractor) - the solution was to return maintenance 'in house' and back under quasi-state control. Privatisation had now been nationalised.

Volume increases have been sustained; this highlighted another problem. The BR integrated managements were used to managing risk, from safety to financial. For the private sector this is 'meat and drink'. Perhaps it had escaped the politicians that developed risk management skills were needed to handle transport enterprises. Civil servants, have skill, and competence, but risk management is not high on the list (consider defence spending). To counter the threat the palliative was complexity. They DfT increased their control over the investment plans as well as controlling the franchises, their capacity, timetables, and rolling stock plans. Having one organisation managing strategy and tactics should be avoided. WSMR it seems though tiny was an unnecessary, uncontrolled complication.

With good intention the SRA stifled competition when they incorporated smaller commuter providers like Thames Trains, Gatwick Express and WAGN within larger franchises. If passenger numbers continue to rise the problems of the peak will never go away. The rise in complaints may force attempts at 're-nationalisation', whatever that means. It is likely that this will solve no problems - only more strategic investment will do that.

In 2004 Professor Stephen Glaister published a paper entitled: 'British Rail Privatisation - Competition Destroyed

3. The point being that to run a high speed, intensive service the track and infrastructure has to be in tip-top condition, and after Hatfield there were accusations that this was not so. Much more money was needed to bring the track up to a satisfactory condition, and these sums are now being spent.

In the 1980s the French were investing heavily in new high speed railways, whereas during the whole decade, investment in British railways stayed at around £600m per year until the end of the decade. The view is of Thalys trains, the consortium operator running 300kmh high speed service between Paris, Brussels, Cologne and Amsterdam. The picture is taken at the Gare du Nord in Paris in November 2003. On the right is a PBA type tri-current unit of 1996 bound for Amsterdam, on the left is a PBKA quadri-current unit of 1997 bound for Cologne. They are now doing it better than we are. HS2 is not a luxury; it is a necessity.

by Politics'. Privatisation was political dogma; in fact British Rail had been headed very much in the right direction. Privatisation at that time, it was claimed, had neither made the railways fitter, nor better than what went before. More recent experience suggests that only some of this is true. Privatisation was not responsible alone for the increases in volume, but it has helped.

In the first ten years of the century, volume growth was 37%. In 2010 demand for rail travel rose by 6.9%, driven by the 15% rise in petrol prices and supported by the more general features of a changed tax regime for company cars, and the rise in insurance premiums for the young: making cars less available to them than to their forebears. Such growth, to a high of 1.32bn journeys, takes the number of passengers carried to that before the WW1. The growth continues into 2014 and endorses concern over maintaining the capacity to cope. The ability to cater for the demand is inhibited by the number of trains that can be run, their length and speed. This is the supporting argument for HS2. The public see trains not full, when they are told the railway is at capacity. No one explains that the motorways are 'full', yet the cars upon them often contain only one person. Upgrading the West Coast Main Line was bruising in terms of the constraints the work imposed on the running railway, the overspend and overtime, and the fact that the speed targets were not met. Everything still runs at 200kmh and not 225kmh - so no one is recommending this way of increasing capacity. Indeed it is considered cheaper and more effective to construct a new high speed line (HS2) where 400kmh may be possible. This is the view looking twenty years ahead, and many have a problem in grasping the undeniable benefits of such a course of action in stimulating local economies and outperforming other modes of transport by many orders of magnitude, yet still maintaining a 'green' pedigree.

There is a 'Bring Back British Rail' movement supported by the 'incognoscente'. Yet the railway has almost been renationalised. and the impossibility of satisfying the demand for travel in the conurbations will remain the source of expressed dissatisfaction. Yet with the surge of

Heathrow Connect is the slow train to the Airport. It runs from a nook in London (Paddington) Station, calling at all points to Airport Junction, including Southall. It takes longer to reach Heathrow, but is cheaper than Heathrow Express. It is a pity that the connecting lines across the north of London have not yet been electrified, as a direct service to St Pancras could have been developed, and the Olympics could have been connected directly with Heathrow Airport. However, instead, Heathrow Express is likely to benefit from connectivity with Crossrial and with HS2, if it comes this way. The picture of 5 car unit 360-204 was taken at Southall in May 2011. Built by Siemens in 2005, 5 units operate, 4 for Connect, 1 for Express.

volume, it is likely that the financial improvement will take people by surprise. The civil servants have understood this already, which is why investment has risen, electrification is taking place, capacity constraints are being eased, and there is activity to provide HS2 - 'as well! '

Open access was meant to stimulate competition and to offer lower prices, and where open access services compete indeed this happens. If there is a serious wish to introduce price competition, instead of the current quasi-State run enterprise, then the current barriers to entry for open access operators must ease. Apparently the ORR thinks that the existing charging regime does not cover the full costs that open access services impose on the infrastructure, and abstraction takes place. One hopes that the open access provision at the risk of the operator, with no contribution from the State, will not continue to be seen as a liability rather than an asset.. Abstraction is meant to take place: it's called competition.

Open Access operations: Their progress

Heathrow Express

Heathrow Express could perhaps have been built to other than Paddington. Right now this is not as convenient a station as St Pancras would be. In fact Heathrow Express could have found its way to St Pancras or Euston - the rail routes exist, but would have needed additional electrification to achieve it; although along relatively short lengths of track. It could have been an 'as well option' which would have been likely had the line been in Germany - instead it was kept as a 'simple' operation. A deciding factor must have been the problem that to make any speed, large sums in expenditure would have been needed, as the route is tortuous and would have been problematic at St Pancras, which is now six stations in one.

Perhaps the planners were being subtle and playing a waiting game. Sure enough, Crossrail, after many years in the wings, came to centre stage. By feeding into that, the Airport Express service will reach far into a major market

In July 2009 First Hull Trains, Alstom Adelante unit 180-113 has arrived in London (Kings Cross) with a service from Hull. These trains have a poor record for reliability, yet to grow Hull Trains needed five cars, and there had been problems through the loss of one of their three Bombardier Pioneer units. A deal was done to take on these 'difficult' trains, and sure enough major reliability problems arrived promptly. The expedient of recruiting the engineers who attended them on Great Western rescued the situation and the benefits then flowed from what is a rapid and comfortable train.

area and still offer a twenty minute transit from Paddington to the Airport.

Currently the service carries 16k passengers per day on its 150 services: around 5m passengers per year. When connected into Crossrail this number will increase. Any third runway will be better served by rail, as road access to Heathrow is difficult because of expensive, limited parking, and a high level of road congestion on the M4 and airport approach roads.

As Heathrow continues to develop it becomes clear that an extension, west to Slough could be practical to build. There were also plans for HS2 to call at the airport. The prospect is good for this open access service just as long as Heathrow prospers. If London Mayor Boris Johnson gets his Thames Estuary Airport then matters will change. However, Heathrow Express, combined with Crossrail could make Heathrow such an attractive airport to access that developing it further is the obvious action. This is yet to be seen.

Hull Trains

Although the open access service to Hull was perhaps less difficult to bring off in 2000, its arrival on the prosperous East Coast scene did not go unchallenged. Hull Trains managed to exploit a gap in the market as there was only one through service from Hull to London run by GNER. Moderation of Competition rules were not breached by the proposed through service from Hull to London (Kings Cross), but here was direct competition between one mainline rail operator and another. The promoters had chosen to operate under the auspices of GB Railways to run the Hull Trains operation. They had been granted a four-year track access agreement by the ORR, as the second open access passenger franchise; the first truly independent operation after the Heathrow Express. The SRA changed its policy to prohibit TOC assets being hired out, and so the new operation was obliged to acquire its own fleet of Class 170 DMUs to run the service. This was successful but their 100 mph top speed made pathing difficult, thus the interim arrangement was replaced by 4 Class 222 Pioneer, 125 mph units in 2005. New services to use the Class 170s were rejected by ORR and the units

Grand Central have a diesel fleet of IC 125 and Adelante units. They run services between Kings Cross and Bradford (Interchange) via Doncaster, Wakefield and Halifax, and Kings Cross and Sunderland via York, and Hartlepool. In November 2011, Grand Central was sold to Arriva, now itself owned by Deutsche Bahn. Four daily services are offered to Sunderland, and three to Bradford. Up to 2012, unlike Hull Trains, Grand Central has not run profitably, though this has now changed.

went to Scotrail. In June 2002 a ten-year access agreement was gained and the service increased to four trains, five in 2005 and seven in 2007. Hull needed to expand and improve their service to be profitable. However GNER mounted a judicial review over the ORR decision to allow Hull Trains an additional path over the East Coast Route in 2006. The ORR's decision was upheld by the court, and the new services ran.

GB Railways sold the £22m business to First Group, to become First Hull Trains. In 2008 Hull Trains experienced rolling stock problems with the Class 180 units acquired to replace the Pioneers. This led to service unreliabilities that set them back. In 2014 these problems have been overcome, and notwithstanding the reduction of traffic from Hull during the recession, profitability has returned.

Grand Central

After much hammering on the door that began way back in 1998, Grand Central were eventually allowed to offer services from London (Kings Cross) to Sunderland and Bradford in 2007 and 2009 respectively, after the favourable decision of the courts against GNER objections. The operation only gradually gained ground, with three services per day to Bradford, and in 2009 four to Sunderland, all beset with rolling stock reliability problems. The access rights now stretch to 2016.

The difficulties in obtaining rolling stock, running it reliably, operating enough services to span the market, and filling the seats at affordable prices that offer sufficient return, represent a major barrier to entry for open access operators. Grand Central runs in the teeth of competition from the other operators. The two GC service groups accrued a loss of £40m, but open access is a 'long game'. There is a strong belief in the future of the service, bearing in mind that like Hull Trains it is 'uncomplicated'. The quality of service was been good enough to warrant a Passenger Focus satisfaction rating of 95%. The £18.9m operation with 125 staff, was bought by operator Arriva in November 2011. Arriva had been acquired by DB in 2010. Now within such a well resourced ownership framework, continued operation and expansion seems assured as it emerges into profitable operation.

New track was being put into position at Princes Risborough, restoring the through line as the 07:27 Wrexham to Marylebone, passes through the station non-stop behind 67012 A Shropshire Lad *on Thursday 9th December 2010. The service ceased on 28th January 2011 and then the assets were deployed to offer the Chiltern Mainline service from Birmingham Snow Hill to London Marylebone. The irony of it is that on the Mainline service the assets now compete far more seriously than they did from Wrexham, and there is no Moderation of Competition available for protection. The Mainline service will steadily improve to abstract more traffic from West Coast than Wrexham & Shropshire ever could - but there is little comfort in that!* **Geoff Plumb**

Both open access operators have found their way into large groups. Perhaps this is no accident as the implications of the provision in the 1993 Act were that the minnows would grow to join the main shoal of services. The current political atmosphere however, does not seem conducive to any more attempts. Will this change?

Wrexham & Shropshire

WSMR's business model drew from Hull Trains experience but in retrospect the differences were:

- Hull Trains uses the ECML infrastructure, running at ECML speeds. There are therefore excellent journey times.
- The operation started early and established its rights to paths over a period of growth.
- Growth arose form easy-to-see marketing reasons. This encouraged tenacity, and that was rewarded by more growth from enhanced service.
- Hull trains was restricted in the calls that it could make, but the restrictions did not exclude it from whole markets, and the company was still able to expand.
- Its success insulates it from detractors; operating under First Group offers strength.
- Though attempts at expansion have been thwarted, electrification to Hull is being planned; the enterprise is operating profitably and is most persistent as a feature.

There is no doubt Wrexham & Shropshire was very unlucky with the timing of its introduction. The recession of 2009 really started in late 2007, and whilst the full extent of the economic downturn wasn't clear, the company had already mobilised in early 2008. In 2009 the effect of the Virgin hi-frequency services began to bite. To have justified a pause in the expensive WSMR business mobilisation would have been questionable, given that it was already underway. The promoters hung on.

The thought at the time of inception was that WSMR would do well. The promoters considered that this was a proposal to generate enough traffic from North East Wales and Shropshire, and that with a top-up from Wolverhampton, and stops at Banbury, a potentially profitable operation was possible. Research suggested that the promise of traffic was potentially greater than when the Hull Trains operation was being planned, but this may not have been in enough depth. It was considered that the extended journey times could be improved, and their effect countered by exceptional quality of service, together with a simple, and reasonable fares offer.

It became clear that:

- Exceptional quality of service cannot bridge a journey time difference of an hour, and low service frequency, unless the general demand for travel is much larger.
- Complex routing is undesirable, as it opens the service to delays and slack timings in an effort to promote reliable running.
- The effects of developing services from Stafford and Chester to London, unclear at the time of planning, became a strong attraction to custom in the area, particularly after the December 2008 Virgin high-frequency timetable improvements.
- The Railways Act 1993 offered a level of expectation to promoters not redeemed by government
- Virgin and the ORR had agreed 'special terms' for protection, that added to the MoC provisions. These precluded WSMR carrying passengers to and from Wolverhampton and London.
- Apparently the provisions were in the Track Access Agreement, but were not stated by Network Rail until into the WSMR mobilisation period.

More sensible would have been open access into Euston, but MoC and 100mph pathing halted that. Neither party in Government seemed interested in doing much to help. Weakened by the Wolverhampton restriction; unable to gain the transit times demanded, and a paying load, Wrexham & Shropshire closed.

The fall of Wrexham & Shropshire was to everyone's disadvantage - certainly to that of competition, outlined in the 1992 White Paper. The operation was run at the risk of DB Regio, the German not the British taxpayer. Protection for the Virgin franchise was offered from any West Midlands Virgin calling point to any London station in acknowledgement of Virgin's large capital risk in pursuit of its side of the West Coast rebuilding. The WCML infrastructure overhaul was neither finished to time, nor budget, nor advertised level of performance. Thus Virgin, placed at risk by this failure, ran service for a time on a management contract. To claim that WSMR services were primarily abstractive in any serious way, given their journey time and destination set was strange. The British taxpayer was now funding Virgin in proper acknowledgement of their contribution - but to constrain WSMR's freedom at Wolverhampton was unfortunate and hampered its continued existence. The boon of the Marylebone through service against the abstraction at Wolverhampton seemed fair exchange to WSMR. It seems that the 'agreement' was rigidly interpreted and an unbending stance maintained.

It is said that Wrexham & Shropshire would still have gone ahead had the intention to apply restrictive access at Wolverhampton been understood beforehand, as there were hopes that this could be changed. Although the restriction applied until 2012 DB Regio could have supported the service until then. DB Regio was not disheartened by losses on Grand Central, but it became clear that WSMR prospects for profit were too far into the future, despite pending Evergreen 3 transit time reductions south of Aynho Junction. It is clear that WSMR closed because the assets could be better used elsewhere, and in addition, many staff have found alternative employment.

Perhaps the irony of the situation was that the assets redeployed abstract more traffic from West Coast than they ever could on Wrexham & Shropshire. Rules have unintended consequences. A further irony was the further agonising of Shropshire MPs over being left without a through service to London. Though innovative attempts by Virgin to do so were rejected until recently. Perhaps one is left with the simple observation that English transport strategy and planning is peculiar.

Rule of thumb on service quality							
1	**2**	**3**	**4**	**5**	**6**	**7**	**8**
slow 1	***fast 2***	***slow 1***	***fast 2***	***slow 1***	***fast 2***	***slow 1***	***fast 2***
expensive 1	***cheap 2***	***cheap 2***	***expensive 1***	***cheap 2***	***expensive 1***	***expensive 1***	***cheap 2***
infrequent 1	***frequent 2***	***frequent 2***	***infequent 1***	***infrequent 1***	***frequent 2***	***frequent 2***	***infrequent 1***
3	***6***	***5***	***4***	***4***	***5***	***4***	***5***
0	***4***	***1***	***0***	***0***	***2***	***0***	***1***
3	***10***	***6***	***4***	***4***	***7***	***4***	***6***
fast & frequent = bonus of 2 ; cheap & frequent = bonus of 1; fast & cheap = bonus of 1							
Wrexham & Shropshire: slow, cheap, infrequent = 4							

67015 **David J. Lloyd** *approaches Princes Risborough station with 1P03, the 07:23 train from Wrexham to Marylebone, running on time at 10:32 on the morning of Monday 4th January 2010*

Geoff Plumb

Chapter 13 The people

Wrexham & Shropshire did not conform to normal practice. This was entirely down to the people who worked for it. They were quite special, rather determined, and very loyal. This is a brief sketch of some of them, with some revealing insights in the pink pages that follow.

Diane Davidson: joined the Wrexham & Shropshire mobilisation team in 2007, to lead the on-board service delivery. Diane is in the pub trade, owning establishments in the area, as well as having a railway catering background. She arranged the food from a Wrexham base. She was polite and firm about standards; they were to be strictly adhered to. She devised, set out, sourced and managed the First Dining menu and the fare in the buffets - and very good it was.

Charlotte Price: obtained a Fine Art Degree at Hull University before joining Hull Trains. She was Safety Quality & Environment Manager for Wrexham and Shropshire, joining the company before train services started and carried out a wide variety of risk assessments, producing most of the company standards. Charlotte's positive attitude to life means that she is realistic about what is achievable with the resources that are available and always seeks to get the best out of people and play to their strengths. Although the staff didn't always enjoy Charlotte's mass random drugs and alcohol screening sessions, when everyone who booked on for duty during a certain period of time would be required to take a drugs and alcohol test. They all knew it was fair and reasonable and fortunately they always passed!

Andy Deacon: Andy's early career in finance was in the retail sector at Laura Ashley, followed by a spell at a social housing charity. He joined Wrexham & Shropshire in October 2008 as its Finance Manager, with full responsibility for this – in true Wrexham & Shropshire fashion he was the only member of staff involved in financial matters. Andy brought great enthusiasm to the task and was keen to understand the railway from the inside out, providing great support to the rest of the management team. It was no surprise that he was in demand for bigger things, and moved within the Group in 2009 to support tendering, subsequently taking the position of Finance Director, DB Tyne & Wear.

John-James Davidson: Having started as a Graduate Trainee with National Express Group, John joined Wrexham & Shropshire from Chiltern Railways where he'd worked as Duty Station Manager London Marylebone and Business Relationship Manager. John left Wrexham & Shropshire to help DB's successful bid for Tyne & Wear Metro. After that he became part of the team which launched Chiltern's new intercity Mainline service between Birmingham and London. John left Chiltern in 2013.

Joanna Seabright: Jo worked for a Massey Ferguson dealership in Church Stoke in Powys before joining Wrexham & Shropshire. Jo was employed by Wrexham and Shropshire as Marketing Executive. Jo was heavily involved in promoting Wrexham & Shropshire at outside events, these included the prestigious Shrewsbury Flower Show, giving talks at local Women's Institute meetings. Following the closure of Wrexham & Shropshire in January 2011 Jo has transferred to Chiltern Railways where she is employed as the Marketing Manager responsible for the Chiltern Mainline Services which operate between Birmingham and London Marylebone.

Chris Rowlands: Before joining WSMR Chris was working in the Arriva Trains Wales booking office at Shrewsbury Station. With WSMR Chris held the position of Business Travel Manager and was based at the Pump House at Coton Hill in Shrewsbury. After Wrexham & Shropshire's closure Chris initially set up a new café at Gobowen station in partnership with Severn-Dee Travel. More recently Chris has moved to the North East to join her other half (Neill Kenderdine) she is currently working in revenue protection, with Tyne & Wear Metro.

Liane Tobin: Liane joined Wrexham & Shropshire in early 2008 as PA to the Managing Director Andy Hamilton. Liane could turn her hand to almost anything, which was just perfect for a small Open Access railway company like Wrexham & Shropshire. Liane is an extremely hard working, bright, resourceful, and conscientious addition to any team. No matter how much work was loaded onto her, it was always completed accurately, and within the required timescales. Liane was great fun to work with, and you often knew that she was there before you saw her, as her laughter could be heard a long way off! Since the closure she has since moved into the Health, Safety, Quality & Environment Team as HSQE Performance Manager based at Banbury.

The Drivers

Les Baines: Les worked for British Gas before joining the railways. Les was employed by ATW at Chester prior to joining WSMR. He often helped WSMR out and often came to work when he was meant to be on leave. Without his flexibility we would certainly have cancelled trains on some occasions. Les was famous for his singing at WSMR parties especially the Verve's 'The drugs don't work'. When WSMR closed Les transferred to Arriva Trains Wales Holyhead depot, he has since moved to their Chester depot.

Photo: Geoff Plumb

Martin Beddows: Martin had worked as coppersmith building ships in Birkenhead, he had also repaired Russian trawlers in the Shetland Islands. He then joined the railways at Chester as a guard, and after spending time instructing, he qualified as a driver. He was employed by Arriva Trains Wales prior to joining WSMR he acted as Deputy Operations Manager and a driver instructor. He was also Chairman of the ASLEF branch at Chester. Martin joined Direct Rail Services when WSMR closed and is based at Crewe; he drives both Class 1 (passenger) and freight services between Daventry and Carlisle.

Photo: Stephen Vidal

Paul Belton: Hailing from Sussex, Paul had previously worked in the South East at both Brighton and Clapham Junction Yard as a TOC employed signaller controlling maintenance depots and yard movements. Paul joined Chiltern Railways as a Trainee Driver in the early 2000s and was based at Marylebone initially before moving to Tyseley (Birmingham). Paul's wide railway experience was a real asset to WSMR and he was often proactive in identifying problems and then resolving them on his own initiative. Paul is currently driving trains for First Great Western and is based at their depot at Bristol Temple Meads station.

Martin Crammond: Martin was a former Central Trains Driver who had left the railway industry but wished to return to train driving. He was the only member of train crew who left WSMR before the company closed in January 2011, to work for London Midland at their Worcester Depot.

Andy Cz (Tadeusz Czerniaiewicz): A former British Rail Driver, Andy was working for Freightliner at Crewe prior to joining WSMR. Andy was unique in that he possesses a commercial helicopter pilot's licence, and often pilots an Agusta twin engined helicopter; he is certainly the only Driver that has been known to complain that he had had to buy a new rotor blade at the weekend after a bird strike. Andy was the ASLEF Drivers Health & Safety Representative throughout the company's operation. When WSMR closed Andy joined DRS at Crewe, he is currently driving trains for ATW at Chester.

Neil Farm: Neil had originally joined British Rail as a railman in Fifeshire. He left the rail industry to pursue a career in mechanical engineering mainly working on trucks. He had spent some time volunteering as a Driver on the Boness & Kinneil Railway in West Lothian before applying for a trainee drivers position with Chiltern Railways at Aylesbury in 2002. Neil once remained at work even though he had just completed an eleven hour driving turn. Without this there is virtually no way that two London bound services from Wrexham General (the 05:10 & 07:43) would have left the following morning. Neil has a very dry sense of humour and famously stated that at times there was too much 'chit chat' on WSMR. His was also known to request a 'wee Kitkat with a cup of tea' from the buffet car! After WSMR closed Neil initially worked for Chiltern Railways at Birmingham Moor Street; he has since left the rail industry and is currently building his own working boats in Inverkeithing almost in the shadow of the Forth Rail Bridge.

Photo: Stephen Vidal

Martin Graves: Another former British Rail Driver Martin or 'Digger' as he Is universally known was based at Chester with Arriva Trains Wales prior to joining WSMR. In his younger days Martin had been a decent sportsman and had even faced some of the legendary West Indian fast bowlers from the 1980s in the nets. Martin is currently driving for Direct Rail Services at Crewe.

Peter Griffin: Having previously worked for Cross Country as a Catering Steward, Peter was employed by EWS as a Driver at Toton before joining WSMR. As such he was the only Driver with knowledge of the Class 67 diesel locomotives.

Peter was another Driver who would come to work when there was no one else available, he certainly saved several trains from cancellation. Peter is currently working as a Driver for Direct Rail Services.

Michael Hayhurst: Mike had spent most of his career working in the banking industry in the Middle East. He was working for Southern immediately prior to joining WSMR. The start of the recession in 2008 meant it was difficult to sell his home in the south of England, as a result Mike ended up lodging near to the world famous Pontcysyllte Aqueduct, Mike spent ages trying to get the correct pronunciation, but try as he might there was always a local who would suggest yet another version! When WSMR closed Mike moved to Chiltern Railways Depot at Stourbridge, he has since retired from the rail industry.

Damien McNamara: Damien previously worked for Arriva Trains Wales at Chester before joining WSMR. His catch phrase was 'its got to be done', an expression which was often heard when we were trying to persuade him to cover a long turn of duty when he was spare or meant to be Rest Day off. Damien was very straight forward and would always say very succinctly when he felt that things were not as they should be! Damien is currently working as a Driver at Chiltern Railways Birmingham Depot.

Photo: Stephen Vidal

Tony Stickells: Tony had previously worked as a Driver in the South East although immediately prior to working for WSMR he was employed by Arriva Trains Wales at Crewe Depot. As Tony lived in Wrexham he was delighted when someone decided to start a new railway company right on his doorstep! Tony's driving was to a very high standard, if you went out with him for a drive or to carry out one of his assessments it was almost like being with a human computer! Tony would know to the absolute second which power notch to be in and where to shut off in order to exactly comply with all permanent and temporary speed restrictions. Tony had also previously worked as a Driver Standards Manager and this experience was often invaluable to WSMR, Tony assisted in the production of assessment material and even undertook some of the initial Driver route assessments as he was fully competent on the ATW sections of route WSMR were to use. Tony worked very hard to look after everyone especially in the aftermath of the WSMR closure. He and his wife Debbie opened their home to anyone who was connected to WSMR. When WSMR closed Tony moved to Chiltern Railways Birmingham Depot, he has since moved to Arriva Trains Wales Depot at Chester.

Peter Ward: Peter started on the Southern Region of British Railways in the early 1970s. He then emigrated to Australia where he spent the next 30 years. Peter initially drove suburban trains in eastern Australia, after doing this for a while he then gained employment with the Hammersley Iron Co, in Western Australia one of the largest ore producers in the country; Hammersley's ore trains often weighed in excess of 30,000 tons! During his time in Western Australia Peter was able to drive and fire the former Great Western 4-6-0 Castle Class steam locomotive *Pendennis Castle* No.4079 which was then owned by Hammersley Iron. *Pendennis Castle* has also returned to the UK and is now based at the Great Western Society's Didcot Railway Centre in Oxfordshire where Peter has had the opportunity to again make her acquaintance. Peter acted as a very able Drivers Union Representative for ASLEF he was always very professional in his dealings with management and did all he could to look after his members interests. Peter now works at Chiltern Railways Banbury Depot in Oxfordshire.

Photo: Geoff Plumb

Ivan Marriott: worked for Thameslink driving electric trains across London between Brighton and Bedford prior to joining WSMR. At his WSMR interview Ivan told us that 'if management are wrong I'll tell them'. I later discovered that this statement was completely true! Many years before this Ivan had been involved in a serious car crash (an argument between an MG and a tree) which had resulted in him having to spend many months recuperating in hospital, Ivan was only too happy to roll up his trouser legs and show you the scars whether you wanted to see them or not! Ivan was also renowned for his singing, Ivan was probably the only one who believed that he actually could sing, but he certainly raised all of our spirits on more than one occasion, and you always knew that he was there! Ivan was the early turn spare driver on the morning after the WSMR closure was announced; he famously showed his rear to a CCTV security camera in the booking on point in way of protest! After initially joining Chiltern Railways following the WSMR closure, Ivan now works for ATW at Chester.

Steve Roast: Originally a BR Driver, Steve is a very experienced and professional railwayman, he had worked as an Operations Manager for EWS before joining Chiltern Railways as a driver at Marylebone in 2005. Steve initially came to WSMR's attention as he knew the Class 67 locomotives from his days with EWS. This led to him being seconded to WSMR as a driver instructor training the Chiltern Railways Banbury Drivers on the Class 67s and Mk3 coaches and later the Class 82/3 Driving Van Trailers when these became available after refurbishment. Steve learnt the WSMR route on a piecemeal basis eventually signing as far as Shrewsbury, he also learnt the West Coast Mainline, originally for the purpose of making rolling stock movements to Wolverton Works and later on locomotives transfers at Crewe IETD. This route knowledge later proved to be invaluable when he and Banbury Driver Steve (Kitkat) Read helped to drive our services when they were diverted via the WMCL during Evergreen3 engineering works on the Chiltern route at the weekends in 2010. If W&S had been Thunderbirds, Steve would have acted as our 'London Agent', it was a real bonus having someone at the southern end of the route who was prepared to tackle almost any job however big or small. If our driver on the 'return lodge' (initially the 06:45 from Marylebone to Wrexham General) was unavailable for any reason Steve could be relied on to drop everything and drive this service for us.

The Train Managers

Photo: Mark Edlington

Neill Kenderdine: Neill started working for British Rail at Birmingham New Street in the 1970s, he then had the opportunity to become a 'Second Man' in the Train Drivers line of promotion but instead decided to move to Mid Wales to work as a Gate Keeper on the former Cambrian route between Shrewsbury and Aberystwyth. Over the years he gained promotion firstly to a Guard's position and eventually into senior management roles with ATW. Immediately prior to joining WSMR, Neill was driving trucks around Europe for his brother-in-law who had broken his leg! He joined the WSMR management team in advance of the other Train Managers in the role of Train Manager Team Leader to assist with starting the company. He successfully trained the Train Manager team in a way that reflected the very high standards he sets himself. Neill is quite a comedian and could impersonate almost all of the WSMR employees; he regularly did slots during WSMR parties. Following the WSMR closure, staff were given the opportunity to take the aptitude test for train driving. Neill took and passed the test and is currently driving for Tyne & Wear Metro being based at their South Gosforth depot in Newcastle-Upon-Tyne.

Richard Rayworth: Richard worked as a Guard/Conductor for ATW at Chester prior to joining WSMR, he was also an RMT union representative. On joining WSMR

Richard again represented the Train Managers who were members of the RMT union. Richard is a quiet individual who performs his duties in a very professional manner, this is reflected in the way he carries out his duties on-board the train and also when completing paper work, writing reports and handling cash.

Toward the end of WSMR Operations Richard undertook the duties of Train Manager Team Leader, again proving to be a considerable asset to the business. Richard initially transferred to Chiltern Railways Depot at Birmingham Moor Street following the closure of WSMR; he has since moved to Arriva Trains Wales depot at Chester. Since returning to ATW, Richard has been involved in the training of Train Managers on DVTs and Mk3 coaches used to operate the Welsh Assembly Government sponsored trains which operate between Holyhead and Cardiff and has recently been promoted to Conductor Instructor.

Photo: Stephen Vidal

Will Flanaghan: Originally hailing from Rhodesia, Will had worked in sales in South Africa before moving to the UK. Will initially worked in the UK as a Taxi Driver, this was followed by a stint with London Underground Ltd, as Platform Staff. He was working for Southern as a Guard/Conductor prior to joining WSMR. Will was always ready to help out any of his colleagues who needed assistance. He also sought to look after our customers too even buying blankets on one occasion to keep them warm when we were experiencing problems with the air conditioning being too cold on some of our Mk3 coaches. Will is currently working for Chiltern Railways and is based at their Stourbridge Junction depot.

Michele Holbrook/Pendleton Originally from Manchester, Michele worked in financial services as a mortgage advisor prior to joining WSMR. As she lived on the North Wales Coast (near Rhyl) Michele had one of the longest journeys to work and was right on the 45 minute maximum journey time limit imposed on their train crew by WSMR. Michele covered the Operations Assistants role at Wrexham whenever Kath Chelton was on holiday. Michele left the rail industry following the closure of WSMR.

Gaynor Mathews: Gaynor was working as a caterer at weddings and other similar functions prior to joining WSMR. She had applied for a position with the WSMR catering team but her potential had being spotted and when two of the existing Train Manager candidates dropped out due to the delay in obtaining permission to launch the service she was asked to consider stepping up to the Train Manager role which she did with complete success. Gaynor's positive and friendly approach worked well with WSMR customers as she was quite unflappable, even when her train became divided at Birmingham New Street station. Her background in catering meant that she was used to working under pressure and she could handle any problem that was thrown at her including difficult customers.

Niki Roberts: Niki had previously been employed as an air stewardess but immediately prior to joining WSMR she was working at the Lord Moreton Pub and Restaurant near Chirk so that she could be closer to her home town of Oswestry. Niki was a model Train Manager and displayed excellent customer services skills, her public address announcements were also outstanding. After WSMR closed Niki initially transferred to Chiltern Railways train crew depot Stourbridge Junction but has since moved to Shrewsbury where she now works for Arriva Trains Wales.

Photo: Geoff Plumb

Jane Meredith: Prior to joining WSMR Jane had recently graduated from Reading University; her father Steve is a Conductor with Arriva Train Wales at Chester so railways were in her blood. It was alleged in fun that Jane had a habit of dropping various bits of railway equipment onto the track and she was teased that the ballast between Wrexham and London Marylebone was littered with carriage keys not to mention parts of 'chip 'n pin' machines! Jane made a totally heartfelt if rather tearful announcement on her last working on the day that WSMR closed that totally summed up how we were all feeling at the time. After the closure of WSMR Jane initially joined Chiltern Railways at Birmingham Moor Street but has since moved to Arriva Trains Wales depot at Shrewsbury.

Robin Smith: Having started his career as a fire fighter Rob had spent most of his career as a policeman, during this time he had been both a police driving and firearms instructor. Being an ex-policeman Rob had no problems

Photo: Stephen Vidal

dealings with those who sought to avoid paying their fares or committing other minor infractions on our services. Rob was certainly a joker in the pack and could often be found gently winding up some of the more formidable members of the catering team; having stirred up a veritable hornets nest Rob would know exactly when to retreat in order to avoid serious retribution and could often be observed returning to the Train Managers office snickering to himself in a way that reminded you of Muttley, Dick Dastardly's loyal canine sidekick in the Wacky Races! Rob is currently driving taxis at Wrexham General Station; he is also a volunteer Guard on the Llangollen Steam Railway in Denbighshire.

Photo: Mark Edlington

Steve Owen: Immediately before joining WSMR Steve was working as a bus driver in Wrexham, his earlier employment had included being a Metropolitan Police Officer in London in Kentish Town and later working in or owning a hair dressers in Pembrokeshire. Shortly after the start of WSMR services Steve discovered that he had a serious illness which prevented him from working for approximately 12 months. Treatment was a success and much to the delight of all of the WSMR staff, Steve was eventually able to return to work following a period of retraining with Neill Kendcrdine, this was much to Steve's credit and really showed the strength of his character. When WSMR closed Steve moved to Chiltern Railways with his two daughters Amy and Lori who were also employed by WSMR within the catering team. Steve is currently based at Birmingham Moor Street.

Photo: Mark Edlington

Steve Holt: Steve worked as a qualified electrician prior to joining WSMR; he has an interest in railways and had gained experience working as a volunteer on the East Lancashire railway. This experience proved to be an advantage to WSMR as Steve was willing to roll up his sleeves and couple locomotives onto trains when needed. For Steve working for WSMR had the added benefit that it led to romance and ultimately marriage! His future wife Ffion was a nurse working at the Maelor Hospital in Wrexham and happened to be lodging with Steve's fellow Train Manager, Gaynor Mathews. Gaynor introduced them to each other and they married in 2010, they are now proud parents to Evan. Steve transferred to Chiltern Railways train crew depot at Birmingham Moor Street following the closure of WSMR. Steve is hoping to have the opportunity to pursue a career as a Train Driver in the near future.

Chris Turner: Chris was working for a company that repaired billiard tables prior to joining WSMR. Chris appeared in print in an early newspaper article about WSMR; the reporter recorded that a little old lady on one of Chris's trains had forgotten her purse and had no money, Chris used his mobile to speak to the lady's daughter and made arrangements for her to meet the train at Banbury with the required fare. The reporter remarked that "he couldn't believe that everything was going so right" Following the closure of WSMR Chris wanted to change roles and he is a qualified Depot Driver with East Midlands Trains based at Derby.

Alan Riley: Alan worked for many years as a geography & history teacher at Wellington before joining WSMR. Alan had an interest in railways and when dispatching his train from stations with the DVT leading he would often look out from the Train Managers office window in a forward facing direction looking for all the world like the Driver of a 1930s streamlined steam locomotive! When WSMR closed Alan transferred to Chiltern Railways train crew depot at Stourbridge Junction.

Photo: Mark Edlington

David Shrewsbury Gee: David was working as a chauffeur prior to working for WSMR; he had previously been a member of the Manchester Ship Canal Police Force. David was, and is always willing to help out his fellow/former colleagues when they need help, for example driving them from A to B when they have car trouble and he has recently appeared as Santa in Wrexham to help out Richard Rayworth when the booked Santa was not available due to sickness. David left the railway industry following the closure of WSMR and currently is running a catering outlet at the Fauxdegla shooting ground, near Wrexham.

Kath Chelton (Operations Assistant): Considerable care was taken in selecting the Operations Assistant as getting train crew to do

what you want is no easy sinecure. Persuading humans to do things they would sometimes rather not be doing takes considerable skill and different tactics need to be employed for each individual, this ranged from begging, cajoling, pleading bargaining, threatening or just asking nicely! Kath, (whose nickname was Secret Squirrel) quickly turned out to be the glue that held the operations team together at Wrexham General Station; she was often accompanied by her faithful rescue dog known as 'Fat Dog'. Kath's made sure that all of our train crew diagrams were covered so that no services were cancelled. She also kept notice cases up to date and dealt with annual and ad-hoc leave, cash handling, uniform orders, office supplies, lost property as well as the hundred and one other things that are needed to keep a train crew depot functioning effectively.

The Stewards

Photo: Stephen Vidal

Andre Brown: Had run her own café in Wrexham town centre prior to working for WSMR. Andre originally worked on board as a steward but later ran the WSMR café at Wrexham General Station where amongst her many other tasks she prepared sandwiches which were sold on board the trains. Andre also often provided excellent sandwiches and snacks for the management and other staff based at Wrexham General which was much appreciated by all. Andre has a dry sense of humour and calls everyone 'Sweety' and her nickname on WSMR was 'Coo-ee' as this was her universal greeting to anyone entering the café!

Fiona Jones: Fiona worked for Sharp in Wrexham where she met her husband the lovely Gary (they were Wrexham & Shropshire's only married couple). Affectionately known as 'Scotch', Fiona has a heart of gold and will do anything for anyone; she is always smiling and very outgoing. Since the W&S closure, Fiona has worked at the Asda Wrexham Superstore.

Gary Jones: Gary wasn't part of the original catering team joining after the company had already become established; he had previously worked for Pizza Express in Wrexham. A team player, he is very capable, reliable and completely unflappable. He currently works at the Asda Wrexham Superstore as a delivery driver

Rhys Evans: Rhys joined Wrexham & Shropshire as a steward later in the company's existence. He has always had an interest in railways and regularly volunteers at the Llangollen Railway in Denbighshire. Rhys is currently working at Chester providing at seat catering for Arriva Trains Wales.

Pat Burke: From leaving school in 2000 to 2008 Pat worked for the Inland Revenue in Wrexham. He was on the first return lodge (Marylebone to Wrexham) with Driver Peter Ward, Train Manager Neill Kenderdine and Senior Steward Alom Ali. Pat was one of two Stewards who were trained up as acting Train Managers in 2010, this was part of a trial programme which was intended to provide additional flexibility for the company and career progression for the employees. Pat was also the Rail Maritime & Transport (RMT) union representative for the Stewards and Senior Stewards. After Wrexham & Shropshire closed Pat spent three months between June to September 2011 with Arriva Trains Wales based at Shrewsbury providing at seat catering. Pat then obtained a Train Manager's position with Cross Country, initially at Leicester; he is currently based at Manchester Piccadilly.

Paul Halliwell: Paul was interested in railway from an early age and he considered joining WSMR to be his 'dream job'. Paul had previously worked for WH Smith on Chester Station; this was followed by a move to Wrexham firstly as a Sales Manager for TJ Hughes, and immediately before joining WSMR as a Section Leader at Wilkinsons. Paul was seconded to Chiltern Railways to provide advice on how they could improve their at seat catering offer to their customers. He was the second of two Stewards who were trained up as acting Train Managers in 2010; they are another of WSMR's success stories as they have both deservedly obtained Train Managers positions with other train operating companies; Paul is currently employed by Arriva Trains Wales at their Chester Depot.

Jemma Ali: Jemma had a zero hours contact with W&S before going to university. Jemma now works at Rhosnesni High School in Wrexham.

Photo: Geoff Plumb

Lowri Owen: Lowri worked part time for Primark and had a Saturday job with WH Smith prior to joining WSMR. Lowri was the third member of the Owen dynasty to join WSMR, she is currently employed by Chiltern Railways as a Train Dispatcher at Leamington Spa.

Pippa Smaje: Pippa was not an original member of the WSMR team; she had previously worked at a petrol station near the Gledrid Roundabout close to the village of Weston Rhyn. Pippa was always a cheerful and hard working member of the WSMR on board team. Since the WSMR closure, Pippa has worked for Origin Analytical in Welshpool as a lab technician testing rock samples.

Richard Oldfield: Joined the catering team once Wrexham & Shorpshire had started, Richard formerly worked for FWB Products Ltd before joining Wrexham & Shropshire. Richard worked on-board and also in the café at Wrexham General Station. Richard is currently working at the Maelor Hospital in Wrexham in the catering department.

Lee Lewis: Not an original member of the W&S team, Lee worked at Asda in Wrexham before joining W&S. He was affectionately known as 'Lee Man Lee'. Lee is an accomplished guitarist and currently plays in his band called 'The Kalm'. Lee currently works at the Carden Park Country Hotel, Golf Resort & Spa in Cheshire as a greenkeeper on the golf course.

Daran Hughes: Not an original member of the W&S team, Daran was another member of Asda staff who's quality infiltrated the WSMR team. Daran was affectionately known as 'Daran Chuckle' the third Chuckle brother….. Daran Initially worked on-board before working in the Café at Wrexham General Station.

Photo: Stephen Vidal

Rob Davies (S): Had run a pub restaurant and worked at Manchester Airport café, had also preformed as a Drag Queen in Blackpool. Rob's catch phrase was 'I'm a feeder', and he was always ready to enhance dishes with extra cheese and double portions of desert; trying to say 'no' was like telling the tide not to come in! Rob is currently working for Arriva at Shrewsbury providing at seat catering

Helen Guy (S): Prior to joining WSMR Helen worked as a cook in a care home. Even though she was once involved in a car accident she still managed to come to work, reporting for duty only ten minutes late. Helen always liked to cut her sandwiches straight down the middle not corner to corner! She always coped well under pressure. Helen went to works in a Spar shop part time, and as a teaching assistant at Castell Alun/Alyn school

Nicky Ingam (S): Prior to joining WSMR Nicky worked as the Assistant Bar Manager at Measgwyn Hall in Wrexham where she was also a *commis chef* for 7years. She was always professional and hard working. Since Wrexham & Shropshire's demise, Nicky has been mostly working as a chef, and also breakfast supervisor at the Holiday Inn at Chester. Her most recent job however has seen her move to Excelsior Technologies in Deeside where she is working as a printer.

Photo: Stephen Vidal

Peter Holt (S): Prior to W&S Pete had his own stone chip company repairing damaged cars. Pete was one of WSMR's jokers (famous for his one-liners) he was also a big Michael Buble fan. Pete's nicknames included Pistol Pete and the Silver Fox. Pete was jokingly reputed to throw in the tea towel if too many 1st Class passengers were seen boarding the train! Peter is currently working as a driver delivering car parts.

Photo: Stephen Vidal

Alom Ali (S): Before joining W&S Alom worked in the Rowan Food Factory on the Wrexham Industrial Estate. He loved KFC and the pint of Hobgoblin on the lodge turn. Alom looked out for his colleagues, for example helping Train Manager Jane Meredith when she had trouble with drunken rugby fans at Telford when he wasn't on duty. After W&S Alom worked for Chiltern Railways for a while but is now working in security.

Caroline Quiney (S): Ran the Golden Lion pub in Coed Poeth with her husband David. Caroline was known to always greet passengers with a cheery 'Hello!' Caroline was reliable and hard working she never complained. Caroline is currently a Supervisor in the National Trust restaurant at Erddig House near Wrexham. Caroline was nicknamed 'Maggie' after revealing that she considered the late Prime Minister Mrs Thatcher to be an inspirational figure.

Gabbi Stephens (S): Worked for Asda prior to joining Wrexham & Shropshire. Known for the good presentation of her meals, speaking Italian and making wigs!

Nicknamed 'Sarge' by Train Manager Robin Smith. Gabbi has now realised her ambition by becoming an air stewardess with Monarch Airlines and is currently based at East Midlands Airport.

Photo: Stephen Vidal

Lynn Williams (later S, first steward to be promoted to Senior Steward). Before joining Wrexham & Shropshire Lynn was the restaurant manager at the National Trust property Erddig House near Wrexham. Andy Hamilton said he knew Lynn was working the train because he could see smoke coming out of the RFM/GFW window. Nothing was too much trouble, she was a team player. Lynn was famed for her extra crispy bacon and caramelised toast but of course Lynn was laid back and a very good professional. After the passing of Wrexham and Shropshire Lynn worked for Cross Country, Chiltern Railways and Arriva Trains Wales providing at seat catering. She has now found a position closer to home at Gobowen Station were she is employed as a booking office clerk working for Severn Dee Travel.

Photo: Stephen Vidal

Vanessa Roberts (S): Vanessa's previous jobs before WSMR included working in a Butchers in Wrexham and latterly as a beautician in morgue. Vanessa's catch phases included 'Oh no' & 'Not on my train' she was nicknamed Mr Punch. Vanessa always got on with it and worked hard, she had a contagious laugh and a Yorkshire sense of humour. She is now working in private health care and is involved with the rehabilitation of people with spinal injuries.

Dot Crimes (S): Dot previously worked at Asda in Wrexham before joining WSMR.. She started as one of the original Senior Stewards but later ran the Catering Stores as Catering and Stores Supervisor, where she was affectionately known as 'Director of Trains'. She is now running the former W&S café, now known as the 'Dot to Dot' Café at Wrexham General Station.

Mark Collins (S): Worked at Cross Country as a Retail Service Manager in the on-board shop. Mark as one of the original Stewards then ran the catering stores at Wrexham prior to Dot Crimes being appointed as Stores Supervisor. Mark then rejoined the on-board team as a steward. Mark has since set up his own companies and has specialised in coach tours, training staff for the airline industry and employee training and development

Stephen Vidal (S): Steve is from Llanfairfechan near Bangor in North Wales. He is well travelled and multilingual. He once called the Operations Manager's bluff by serving him a white wine spritzer, which he foolishly requested one as a joke once too often! Being on duty the Operations Manager sadly wasn't able to drink it. Steve was known for being very creative with his cooking techniques. He was never shy to make his feelings known, for example at a WSMR staff meeting at Wrexham Football Clubs premises, he asked MD Andy Hamilton if he was 'real' (an unfair suggestion that Andy didn't visit Wrexham General often enough!) Steve was the only Senior Steward who could make public address announcements in perfect Welsh as well as English. Thus whilst the train was in Wales, beautifully modulated and accurate announcements in Cymraeg were often forthcoming. Steve left WSMR to join South Eastern Trains (High Speed) as an On Board Manager based at Ramsgate.

Photo: Geoff Plumb

Ruth Jones (S): Ruth worked at a Yale's café/bar in Wrexham town centre before joining W&S. Ruth started as a Senior Steward before becoming a Marketing Executive based at the Pump House Offices in Shrewsbury. She is a nice, genuine person the salt of the earth always professional. Ruth took maternity leave to start a family, she had only just returned to work when the announcement to close the company was made.

Amy Owen (S): Amy started as a steward but was quickly promoted to a Senior Steward position. Amy was nicknamed 'tiny tears' by her colleagues. When WSMR closed Amy moved to Chiltern Railways in a Marketing Role, based initially at Bicester North, and latterly at Birmingham Moor Street. Amy has passed her driver's aptitude test and is going for training.

Mike Jones is a 'proper' railwayman, having started at the bottom, and worked his way up. Indeed during schoolday forays he was seen working signalboxes and heard making station announcements at his home station of Hitchin. Mike's career took him through operations hotspots, in the thick of it, right up to being a freight National Business Manager. He then offered his expertise to Racal Telecoms, and set up renowned consultancy First Class Partnerships with John Nelson. Mike was on the front line of franchising, and very nearly gained Great Western. As a consolation he and his colleagues launched the successful Hull Trains - and WSMR.

Early in my railway career the 4-year Chartered Institute of Transport course considered the relationship between infrastructure and operating costs in detail. What struck me then was that a structure where the operator paid an access fee, similar to a road fund licence, to use the network would produce a business model that removed the endless arguments of the day about how the fixed costs of the network should be allocated to given services. My final CIT examination thesis exampled separated infrastructure and operations, with Inter City Limited as an operating company. Later I received feedback that what I had written was interesting but irrelevant, and that I was therefore lucky to pass the exam!

This was far from my mind while engaged in the hard-nosed task of running the railway at locations such as the London Docks, Liverpool Street, and Leeds, but as sector management emerged I was appointed in 1982 as National Business Manager for Railfreight responsible for its Chemicals and Minerals Division. It had been BR policy that apart from coal and steel traffic customers would be expected to invest in their own rolling stock and this had been a largely successful policy in that it encouraged greater use of the assets once they had been acquired. But by this time customers were agitating to go further and run their own trains by providing the haulage as well as the wagons, and this was about to happen with the introduction of privately owned locomotives hauling aggregate traffic from the Mendips.

BR had an archaic system for calculating train haulage costs in that the locomotive used had to be accounted for on the basis of its replacement cost even if there was no plan to make this investment. The result was that financial returns that a road haulier would regard as profitable were loss making as far as railway accountants and Government officials were concerned.

Much of railway senior management and the civil servants in the Ministry of Transport had grown up in the Beeching era and many regarded the job as only half done – there was an endless search for the profitable core which the 1982 Serpell report revealed wasn't there, apart from a very basic core network, if rail customers had to bear the whole cost of providing the infrastructure without regard to wider social benefit.

It wasn't until 1994 that the Royal Commission on Transport and the Environment identified the penalty in terms of harmful emissions and other costs associated with promoting greater road use and reducing the role of the railway. I always felt I hadn't joined the railway to close it and recognised that the financial conventions adopted for a nationalised industry were causing management behaviour that concluded this was often the right thing to do. I became an active campaigner for change and if other industries could be privatised and gain greater access to investment then why not apply this to the railway?

Once the 1993 Railways Act was passed I wanted to support the principles it embraced and Resurgence Railways was formed with the support of the then accounting firm Touche Ross (now Deloitte's) and a bid was prepared for the Great Western franchise. We won but for a last minute debacle when the London based venture capital company could not obtain authority from the credit committed of its Swiss owning group to provide the necessary guarantees. As a response to this setback I concluded that there was another channel available to operate private sector services using the right to network open access contained in the legislation.

The original regulatory stance was that the new franchises would be protected from competition for a limited period of time while the businesses were established. There were three phases to this process

Peterborough Station on 17th September 2003, as Hull Trains 170 206 roars through the station at full speed, on its way north. Of course in a competitive model, this unit would probably have stopped to exchange passengers at this busy place, thus improving east-west connections. Yet Moderation of Competition prevented such a stop, indeed the service was deeply resented by GNER.

known as the Moderation of Competition or in industry jargon MoC1 to MoC3. The initial regime made the provision of new open access services very difficult. Any flows which accounted for more than 2% of the revenue earned by the franchise were protected. This brought its own nonsense when intermediate stops such as at Crewe were prohibited when new services were started between Manchester Airport and Euston in 1998. This was when the North Western franchise was operated by Great Western Holdings and once this organisation was taken over by First Group the service was withdrawn.

MoC2 moved the threshold to 20% of franchise revenue which allowed the opportunity to create Hull Trains as the East Coast (GNER) revenue from the Humber conurbation was far below that figure. The original idea was to serve Sheffield as well by running trains that divided at Retford but as the Midland Main Line franchise owner was able to show that the Sheffield to London flow accounted for more than 20% of its revenue this was barred by the Regulator. This was in fact as sleight of hand as the Sheffield revenue was much less but within the rules it was possible to say that the franchise did not require protection on some flows where competition was unlikely so that it could inflate the protected element to cross the 20% threshold.

Much later in a discussion with John Swift QC who was the initial Rail Regulator the view was offered that what had happened was as a mistake driven by the insecurity Government officials had about the prospects for a successful privatisation of the train operating company franchises. This was probably an undesirable necessity as from my own experience of early franchise bidding there were virtually no takers from the established financial community.

To deliver the Hull Trains proposition I had formed Renaissance Trains with John Nelson joining me as a partner and operations between Kings Cross and Hull started in September 2000. It was a modest affair with 3 weekday return services using Class 170 units hired from Anglia Railways. With the understanding of the economic characteristics of the Hull Trains business there was a motivation to look for further new service opportunities. As a result the Wrexham and Shropshire proposition came increasingly into focus. The stations concerned had no direct London services and the population served suggested that the success could be repeated.

During this period the Department for Transport and the Strategic Rail Authority had become hostile to the concept of open access, believing that whatever the service it would abstract revenue from the franchised operators, and as a result either reduce the potential for premium payments, or add to the requirement for financial support. The Hull Trains experience had of course completely debunked this argument, as Grand Central was also to do later, but there were obstacles that the DfT could put in the way of the legitimate regulatory process, and this certainly happened.

Meetings were held to test the options for pathing of the Wrexham services, initially with Class 170 DMUs, but later with Class 67 locomotives and Mk3 coaches. This did not present any operational difficulty in terms of the point to point timings, but there was substantial cost penalty with the overall annual cost of running the service rising to £8.7 million, in the order of £2 million more than the Class 170 option. The Mark 3 coaches that had been acquired to operate with the locomotives were run down, but a plan was put in hand to refurbish these to high standards. The design elements were orchestrated by Peter Wilkinson who by this time had joined Renaissance Trains because of his undoubted commercial skills, and enthusiasm for promoting new services. Peter was later to be appointed as the DfT Franchising Director, and developed policy that reflected a greater recognition of the role that open access services can play, particularly in the economic stimulation of poorer UK cities.

As a new applicant for track access rights, the timings have to fit in with what is on the graph already. There was no capacity, and so the conclusion was reached that the trains would have to run on the slower Grand Junction diversionary route to Coventry. This was achievable because there were far fewer freight trains running to Bescot yard than in the past so it was possible to find paths that also presented an opportunity to serve Tame Bridge Parkway station.

The track access agreement is a complex document and it was very fortunate that in negotiating this agreement I had the support of Mary Bonar, a leading industry expert in the field. By this time Mary had become part of the Renaissance Trains team and her advice on track access issues was essential. What Mary and I sought to do was to commit NR to a year by year reduction in the point to point timings by a combination of optimising the timetable, raising track speed and reducing signalling headways. In fact they were already investing to achieve this output but there was no joined up thinking in converting this work to faster timings, and it wasn't possible to persuade NR to reflect this in the track access contract obligations.

The traffic figures for week one were not in line expectations, and this continued. There is a remarkable consistency about rail revenue on a week-by-week comparison, and once the service started, income settled at a run-rate of around £4 million per annum. The budget had been £5.7 million. There now followed a herculean effort by the commercial team which is described elsewhere by Gordon Rushton, who answered a call to arms at very short notice.

The make-up of the business plan used well established principles based on likely per capita trips to London in a mature market environment, with an assessment of the timescale required for attracting users who had not considered rail, and a claw-back of existing journeys by reduced rail heading and journeys that involved changing trains. Assumptions were also made about additional revenue that would accrue as a result of economic growth. The forecast was 'stress tested' against what was known to have happened after the introduction of services by Hull Trains. The WSMR revenue forecast was dominated by receipts from Shrewsbury and Telford which together made up 60% of revenue. North of Shrewsbury there was an expectation that only 15% of income would be earned at start-up but this was expected to grow as new travel patterns were established.

In initial trading revenue was a third less than expected, but the surprise was that demand from stations served north of Shrewsbury was considerably above that predicted but this statistic could not overcome the weakness of the expected core flows based on the per capita model. Nevertheless there was confidence that annual revenue would increase in the way that had been seen at Hull Trains which had reached £18 million by 2007 after the start-up in 2000, with receipts growing by an average of 27% annually.

There was though a big difference in the product – with typical journey times of a shade over 2hrs 35mins the London-Hull timings were faster than other options. With a typical journey time 3hrs 25mins between London and Shrewsbury there were many journey opportunities involving a change of train that were considerably quicker and it was the same story at Wrexham and Telford.

The conclusion was that a breakeven would be reached before 2013 and that this could be brought within a much closer timeframe by speeding up the

On 6th June 2013 the First Hull Trains 11.25 from Doncaster to Hull awaits departure, formed by Class 180 118. This open access service, operated by First has access rights from the ORR until December 2016. The fact that these rights were granted means that Hull Trains, and the other ECML open access operator, Grand Central, fall inside the MoC criteria. The question now is whether such arrangements will extend to other operations.

WSMR services as the infrastructure was improved and of course removing the monopoly rights held by Virgin Trains at Wolverhampton. This was not a MoC restriction, as revenue was far below the 20% benchmark, but caused by a contractual commitment that had been given to Virgin Trains as part of the negotiations to acquire the Pendolino fleet. It was due to expire in 2012 and informal regulatory advice was given that it would not be continued.

External factors resulted in the business taking an unexpected hit when the banking crisis occurred in 2008, and national economic output plummeted by 6%. The economy had not recovered by 2011 when the decision was taken by Deutsche Bahn that the prospects to earn a financial return remained too far into the future. As well as the journey time constraint, the business had to cope with a number of market characteristics that only became evident once services started. For many years British Rail had promoted rail -heading as the product solution to population centres that were not served by through services. Quite clearly driving to Stafford or Wolverhampton to catch a fast London service to Euston saved a lot of time, and people could not be persuaded forsake this. For a variety of reasons the population centres that the line served demonstrated a low propensity for rail travel, which is difficult to explain given the relative wealth in the area served, which far exceeds the per capita income in the Hull conurbation.

It was and remains relevant that Wrexham is a town in Wales, and as such Government devolution has meant that public officials have a requirement to travel to Cardiff rather than London. This is a factor recognised by the Welsh Government promotion of a rail service between Cardiff and destinations in North Wales. On the positive side it was found that Wrexham attracted travel from a wider hinterland than had been expected which accounted for the higher traffic figures at this originating point.

Since the cessation of services stakeholders in Shropshire have continued to call for the area to have through trains to London. I suspect this will only become a reality when electrification is extended beyond Wolverhampton which will allow timings to be improved and operating costs reduced.

John Nelson

John Nelson is a railway 'heavyweight' having risen through the industry to become the head of Network South East. He and colleagues had founded First Class Partnerships, a successful railway consultancy, and together with Mike Jones, and others they began Renaissance Trains, an organisation created to examine, evaluate and set up open access services. The successful Hull Trains sprang from this, and Wrexham & Shropshire was one of a number of other proposals that offered themselves as sustainable opportunities. Given a fair wind, Wrexham & Shropshire would have been successful. John describes what happened with stark reality.

The success of the case as far as Hull Trains was concerned re-enforced my view that Open Access was now a key, if still relatively minor element, in the liberalised railway. The success of the Hull operation had already caused Mike Jones and me to consider the development of further open access opportunities, and the verdict in this case appeared to be grist to the mill.

Mike and I had always viewed open access as complementing rather than competing head on with franchised operations; essentially plugging obvious gaps in the network, and had first talked about operating a service between Nottingham and Glasgow around the year 2000, but didn't progress things much beyond the bright idea stage. We did some initial desk research, and concluded that the business case probably required a degree of public funding to make it work, so we put it on the back-burner. However, we held some initial discussions with senior people in Virgin Trains who were running the West Coast and Cross country franchises, that included services between the North West of England and Glasgow. At a meeting with Chris Green, who was then the Chief Executive of Virgin Trains but someone whom I had known for several years in various roles, he told me of the major stakeholder problems he had with communities in his area of responsibility, and as a result of a chance remark he made, I decided to undertake a feasibility study on a train service from Shrewsbury to London using the Marylebone route operated by Chiltern Railways. At the time I was a Non Executive Director of Laing Rail, owners of that franchise.

I did a great deal of work on validating the business potential, and also drafted a provisional timetable for the purposes of testing the business case. The prospects looked quite good such that there was clearly mileage in progressing the idea to the next stage. Mike and I decided that we needed some help to develop all of the ideas we were then contemplating, and asked Peter Wilkinson to join us. Although Pete was the Managing Director of First Class Partnerships, we felt his negotiating and commercial skills would benefit our open access business, and this is precisely what followed..

Meanwhile I approached Adrian Shooter, Chairman of Laing Rail, to ascertain the level of interest that existed there in getting involved with Open Access. Laing had already made a decision to opt out of the current round of franchises, due to the high risk of failure associated with the expense of bidding, and I judged that they might be receptive to open access. Adrian undertook to discuss this in principle with John Laing plc and also made some useful suggestions as to how the service might operate. These included the idea of routing the trains via Wolverhampton and Walsall, providing the latter with a through service to London for the first time. Subsequently we abandoned what had seemed like a good idea at the time because the alternative route via Sutton Park was considered by Network Rail to be too unreliable. Eventually our plans settled on a proposition to run five trains a day each way, from the North East Wales town of Wrexham, calling at Shrewsbury, Telford, and Wolverhampton, en-route to Marylebone.

By now Renaissance Trains comprised Mike, Peter and myself, each with a third of the shares, but in early 2005 we decided that we should invite a fourth person to join the group, someone who had a legal background and a good knowledge of railway industry procedures and processes. Pete and I both knew Mary Bonar, a partner at the law firm Nabarro Nathanson, and I asked her if she would be interested to join us in return for a 5% stake. She was approaching the end of her partnership with Nabarros, and decided that getting involved with this type of project fitted well with her desire to pursue a portfolio career. After her contribution proved to

It was a pity that an organisation with such graceful, modern trains such as these should in the British context display all the manoeuvring finesse of a supertanker. Warning didn't seem to be an option, so in moving from Laing to DB WSMR got none of the wheeling-dealing necessary to help the new service to succeed. There was stolid support that in the end was withdrawn; this hardly helped to make a cutting edge of competition in rail!

be more time consuming than we originally thought, her share was increased to 10% and each of ours was reduced to 30%.

The division of duties between us was that I concentrated on developing the revenue case and dealing with stakeholders whilst Mike took the lead with Network Rail supported by Mary, whose principal focus was on legal aspects, especially the submission we would need to make to the Regulator. Pete would concentrate initially on rolling stock leasing issues and negotiating the basis of a shareholders' agreement with Laing, again with Mary supporting from a legal point of view.

I helped sell the idea to Laing Rail at Board level and a Memorandum of Understanding was signed in February 2006 followed by a public announcement to stakeholders and news media throughout the areas to be served. The public reaction was very positive and on the back of this we moved to the next stage which was a serious negotiation with Network Rail to secure a track access agreement. I made the initial presentation to the Network Rail Directors in Birmingham and also took the lead in discussions that we opened up with the Welsh Assembly Government in Cardiff, which we hoped to persuade fund facilities in Wrexham necessary for trains to be berthed there overnight. Without such a facility the business case was better to run more frequent services only as far as Shrewsbury.

Between February and November 2006 action occurred on many fronts and at the end of the period we were in a position to make a formal application to the Office of Rail Regulation (ORR) to support our Track Access Agreement with Network Rail. I played the biggest part for Renaissance in developing our submission to ORR and in talking to the Welsh Assembly and other key stakeholders, whilst Mike Jones with Mary Bonar conducted the detailed negotiations with Network Rail. We managed to secure substantial stakeholder support for our proposals and the Welsh Government went so far as to provide a million pounds to fund infrastructure at Wrexham that would enable the company to operate from there. This money went to Network Rail as the Welsh Government did not have the statutory powers to fund a private train company, although they did provide additional funding towards the selection and recruitment of staff in Wrexham, something they were allowed to finance.

Whilst we were finalising the arrangements for the company's start up, we were advised by John Laing plc, who had recently been acquired by a private equity company, that a decision had been made to divest all its rail interests, which included WSMR and the Chiltern franchise. John Laing consulted us over the arrangements for selling WSMR and I was deputed to represent Renaissance Trains in the negotiations with short listed bidders. The four selected were Arriva (a UK based listed company), Transdev (a French transport utility part owned by RATP, the operators of the Paris metro), Ned Rail the Dutch State Railways, (an existing player in the UK as the Joint Venture partner of Serco in operating the MerseyRail Electrics and Northern Rail franchises), and DB Regio (a subsidiary of the German State Railways).

The only bidder that we knew from the start would be a problem for Renaissance was Arriva. This was because we had approached them after the formation of the company to see if they would like to be a shareholder. Their initial interest in the idea quickly turned hostile as they thought WSMR would detract from the business prospects of the Welsh rail franchise which they held. We thought this was a miscalculation on their part but there was no shifting their opposition, and we told John Laing that we would oppose a sale of WSMR to Arriva.

This left us with three foreign state railways to consider. Each had its own merits and demerits but we were fairly agnostic. Of the three we felt that the Germans had deep pockets to invest in the business, although we were very nervous about their management methods, which we thought might be centralising and slow moving. We were to be proved right on all these essential points.

John Laing informed us that DB Regio was the preferred bidder. Mary reminded us that the shareholders agreement we had with Laing required us to give our permission for the sale of the shares. Pete then informed John Laing that there would be a price to pay for the German acquisition. After a great deal of toing and froing, Peter and I met with the Chief Executive of John Laing plc and told him that the price to pay for DB acquiring WSMR was the acquisition by John Laing of a quantity of shares. The price was as calculated by the business plan to which we were working, as an equivalent value which John Laing would have to pay Renaissance, if they were to acquire all Renaissance Shares in the business in the fifth year of trading, something we had accepted as a "call option" in the original shareholders agreement.

John Laing was not entirely happy to find itself in this position, then neither were we. We had embarked on the venture with a private sector partner with a proven track record of innovation, and we tended not to view the three state-owned bidders quite as highly in the open access stakes. Nevertheless, with the need to close the deal with the Germans before Christmas, Laing had little option but to agree to the terms and the deal was done. The shareholders agreement was amended to provide us with a "put option" enabling us to sell a proportion of our shares to John Laing at a time of our choosing. In the event we exercised the option in the early summer of 2008.

Of course the Germans were keen to acquire the shares instead and offered us the same price. However, since this would have given them majority control of the company we thought the price should be higher and said so. DB chose not to acquire the shares but within a matter of weeks approached Peter to see if we would be willing to sell all of our shares to them. We agreed on the basis that the price would be pro rata to the shares we had already sold but the Germans argued for a discounted price and, believing this to be too low, we turned it down. As it turned out this was a big mistake because for a number of reasons WSMR (or Wrexham & Shropshire as it was known to the travelling public) proved to be a commercial failure.

A newly liveried Wrexham & Shropshire train at Marylebone station

The principal reason for this was the failure of the management to obtain the journey times on which the revenue projections were based. Their optimism that everything would be alright on the night was in stark contrast to the reality of Network Rail's inept approach to timetable planning, which favoured the franchised operators and was probably illegal. Secondly the management failed to secure the rolling stock on which the business case was also based. Instead of bright, beautifully refurbished coaches, old ones were substituted, which provided for an unattractive appearance that was not ideal for gaining new customers. Finally, a clause in the Track Access agreement of West Coast Trains (a franchise run by Virgin) prevented us from conveying passengers between Wolverhampton and London. Whilst this was bound to be overturned in time, ORR said it was legally unable to allow us to compete. Although we substituted this with a stop at nearby Tame Bridge Parkway, it never developed in the way we expected.

Services began operating in April 2008 and within months it was apparent that the money needed to bank roll operations would be more than the £2 million stated within the shareholders agreement and which DB was obliged to provide. The agreement did not provide for any of the Renaissance shareholders to provide funding and we very quickly got into a difficult area with the Germans who, although continuing to fund losses, said that they would only do so if we gave up our shares for nil value. In return they proposed an arrangement whereby we would be rewarded on the basis of consulting fees and a future profit share. Because we had lost confidence in the management to deliver the business plan, and because it was apparent that the money to fund activity could only come from DB, we agreed to their proposal. We did so as early as August 2008, and entered negotiations with Adrian Shooter, very quickly reaching agreement to the principal terms of an agreement but the bureaucracy we had identified in the acquisition of John Laing soon became apparent.

Over Christmas 2008 I exchanged e-mails and phone calls with Adrian's Finance Director, Tony Allen, and we reached an agreement which Adrian Shooter endorsed having received the blessing of his masters in Germany. We wrote a letter to Adrian in February 2009 which encompassed everything that had been agreed. Adrian told me on more than one occasion that the Germans would promise to keep the business going until December 2009 at the earliest. However, we then entered yet another period in which we heard nothing. We were not entirely surprised therefore when we were told by Adrian that the Germans had changed their minds again and that they were considering withdrawing all funding from the business, something that could happen any day. All bets were off.

We considered the possibility that this was brinkmanship negotiation but were much more inclined to the view that we were dealing with a state bureaucracy that was simply not in control of its own decision-making. Our principal concern for many months had been to avoid the company becoming insolvent and there now seemed a possibility that this inept handling by DB could inadvertently lead to such a situation. Meanwhile we were aware that DB had written to the ORR when it acquired Laing Rail committing to support WSMR for its first year of operation. Given that the anniversary date of that commitment was approaching and that we had said all along that we were not prepared to fund the business we decided to resign as directors of the company.

The saga rumbled on without resolution for several more months and eventually in September 2009, having discussed the position again many times with Adrian, we concluded that the best interests of the staff, the passengers and of ourselves would be to agree to yet another proposal from the Germans. This transferred all the assets and liabilities of WSMR to DB Regio UK. A special meeting of shareholders was held at Marylebone at which this was agreed, and the main Board of DB in Germany endorsed it on 21st September. A public announcement was made to that effect on 24th. We couldn't complain at this outcome. We may have missed an opportunity to sell our remaining shares to the Germans in early 2008 but since then they had funded the business pretty much to the tune of £10 million so it was not unreasonable for them to ask us to give up our interest in the business. If they subsequently made money out of the ongoing operation it would be good luck to them.

Wrexham & Shropshire was voted by its passengers the most popular railway service in the country with a customer satisfaction rating of 97%, the highest ever recorded for any train company. So our efforts had not been entirely unsuccessful after all. Indeed with the probability that finances would improve in future years it was disappointing that DB did not see the value in retaining a brand that could claim such high approval. Viewed as a marketing tool across the range of DB's global activities to claim, operating such a valued service should have been worth a great deal when demonstrating capability in delivering franchise operations. Sadly I dont think any of this entered their heads and it was ironic that, having closed WSMR down, DB subsequently acquired another open access company (Grand Central) which was losing far more money. The logic of these decisions was never clear to me.

Adrian Shooter joined British Railways in 1970 as an engineer. He rose quickly to become the Area Maintenance Engineer at Bletchley, with the technical end of the railway to run. He ran Heaton Depot in Newcastle at the difficult time of the introduction to the East Coast of the Inter-City 125 trains. He had several higher profile posts, including Area Manager St Pancras, Managing Director Red Star Parcels, Director Parcels and was appointed as the Manager of the Chiltern Lines. His team's was the only successful management bid into privatisation, as Chiltern Railways had been transformed under his leadership. He only relinquished his post to enter honourable retirement in 2011, from what was openly stated as the best run TOC in Britain.

Having been MD of Chiltern Railways since 1994, I had been approached many times by individuals and Local Authorities in Telford and Shrewsbury to see if Chiltern would consider extending its services to those places. My response was always that it was impracticable because the direct route from Snow Hill to Wolverhampton had (very shortsightedly) been closed in the 1970's. Matters were made much worse as it was now not even possible to re-open it because the Midland Metro had been built on the trackbed. As a former board member, and for a time as Chairman of the Midland Metro Concession Co, I can confidently say that the Metro was a solution looking for a problem, and never should have been built, certainly not in isolation like it was.

Another bar to extending the Chiltern service was that it seemed unfeasible that the revenue density per coach that we had achieved south of Birmingham could be equalled on an extended northern route. The concept of a sustainable revenue density per coach was key to the ability of Chiltern to invest and grow. The success of the concept was demonstrated by the length of time which it had been thus. It was one thing to steadily augment and increase the service which we had introduced between Marylebone and Birmingham, it was quite another to expect the additional coaches that we would have to acquire ever to offer the promise to earn as much on a northern route as they could on the southern. Thus when John Nelson approached me in 2006 with a proposition that we should participate in a new open access company to link Marylebone to Shropshire, my instinct was to decline politely. You should think carefully before disregarding your instincts.

Apart from doubting whether the revenue density was achievable (in part because of very low level of the regulated fares north of Wolverhampton), I had a very good working knowledge of the complicated rail network in the West Midlands, and this was something which none of John's team had. With the complex nature of the Network and an intensive service on many lines reducing available paths to a minimum, I calculated that it would be very difficult, if not impossible, to get fast enough journey times from Leamington to Wolverhampton unless the main Stour Valley line was chosen. Unfortunately this line was used more heavily than any other. Thus even if Network Rail were very helpful, no matter how little chance there was for this eventuality, the insuperable problem was going to be the transit time for the journey.

The key question of competitive transit times had dogged Chiltern's competing Birmingham to London services from the start. It was true that Chiltern was serving the western population area that the more direct services were not, but the biggest potential business came from Birmingham City Centre itself. The penalty for failing to match journey times had to be lower prices, and perhaps better service. However, service as an attractive feature was almost marginal when it stood against transit time - higher speed services have always commanded a premium. Thus we already knew very well how important the fastest transit time was, and the Evergreen 3 proposal, on lines we controlled directly, was aimed at raising speeds radically to achieve just that. Whilst Wrexham & Shropshire would eventually benefit from that, a tortuous route via the Grand Junction Lines would do nothing at all for the service's popularity - it was a risk.

It seemed logical to ask Richard Harper and Andy Hamilton, both fresh from franchise bidding work, to look carefully at the proposition, and to make a recommendation for me to take to the Laing Rail Board.

At Millbrook , just south of Bedford, on 31st July 2004, unit 170 110 gathers pace on the Up Fast towards London. These trains would have been ideal for the start up of the Wrexham & Shropshire service. The circumstantial evidence alleges that the DfT put a spoke in the wheel of the plans to transfer trains to WSMR, and that the final result of this, taken with the other problems encountered, went a fair way to making sure that the project would not succeed. Until the East Coast franchising debacle, such allegations of interference were considered fanciful - not any more?

John Nelson and his Renaissance team had done a very thorough analysis of the potential ridership and hence revenue for the proposed service. It was persuasive in that it demonstrated very low present propensities for people to travel to London in the Wrexham & Shropshire market area, in comparison with other places at similar distance. They considered that the market for the service was rather larger than it looked without careful analysis. In addition to that, I formed the view that Renaissance Trains would probably go ahead with their plan anyway, whether Chiltern were on board or not. One thing we absolutely did not want was another operator coming into Marylebone without our having any control over their timetable. We had spent a great deal of time and effort in planning and implementing the precise capacity required into and out of Marylebone. The tracks were and still are very heavily used and it was very important to Chiltern Railways to optimise its timetable to maximise its commercial benefit. The entry of another operator had the potential to disrupt that, and to disrupt our carefully laid forward plans.

As a result of these two factors, I decided to recommend to the Laing Rail Board that we should enter into a 50:50 Joint Venture with John and his fellow Renaissance Trains shareholders. Thus the Wrexham & Shropshire project was inaugurated as a deliberate risk, but one, given the determinations made, one worth taking.

An important and very attractive part of the plan was to use Class 170 DMU's (which are almost identical to Chiltern's Class 168 units). A provisional agreement was reached with Porterbrook to take on lease a small number of ex-Midland Mainline vehicles, which would have been entirely suitable. After a time,Porterbrook told us that they had suddenly become unavailable for reasons that did not make sense. They were very embarrassed about this. It was obvious to me, and the likelihood became even clearer later, that someone in the DfT had had a brutal conversation in a dark alley with Porterbrook, and made it clear that such a deal was not with DfT approval - a rather ominous circumstance for organisations so dependent on government departments for a comfortable future existence. Such action, if it were proven, would be a disgraceful abuse of power by a

At High Wycombe Station on 30th July 2001 a Class 168 Clubman pauses on its way north. Few remember now exactly how low the Chiltern service had fallen before Adrian Shooter and his team revived it with new equipment, new services, new tracks, an overhauled service ethos, and most of all, loads of innovation and enterprise. The steady progress of Chiltern continued after privatisation, and whilst Wrexham & Shropshire was welcomed as a 'supplement' there was little Chiltern could do in the face of the odds stacked against it. Sad event though the closure was, it gave a fillip to Chiltern Mainline - the fast Birmingham Moor street to London service, that now uses ex-WSMR locomotives and coaches.

government department, as it would have been acting 'ultra vires', outside its powers. We were extremely annoyed by the circumstantial evidence that the DfT had interfered in perfectly legal and vital commercial arrangements between two private sector companies. With hindsight, this would have been a good time to call the whole project off. Yet the whole rather murky and uncertain business was a warning that this enterprise was not enjoying a game on a level playing field, and that so far the provisions for Open Access were neither open, nor did they offer much access.

In fact, an ingenious solution to the loss of the Class 170 DMUs was found which involved operating EWS Class 67 Diesel locomotives with refurbished Mk III coaches and ex-West Coast Driving Van Trailers to provide push-pull capacity. Whilst all this worked very well, eventually, and the coaches were liked by passengers, the amount of management time and aggravation that resulted from the failure to gain Class 170s was immense. The maintenance opportunity for these units to be dealt with alongside the similar Chiltern Class 168 units, the ease with which drivers from Chiltern could have operated Class 170 WSMR trains and vice-versa, would have made training and operations so much easier. However the whole scenario was made worse because dealing with EWS commercially was an absolute nightmare.

I will not detail all the problems of the start-up here because they have been set out elsewhere in this book. Suffice it to say that in my opinion, Wrexham & Shropshire might well have survived the problems it encountered, and could still have been still operating now, if the Class 170s DMU had been available as they had been promised. For all that, the course of action had been decided upon, and come prejudice, obstruction and plain perfidy, it was resolved to give the whole venture our best shot.

The loss of the Sales Manager and the failure to acquire the specified push-pull equipment made for a rather shaky start. However, it soon became clear that the quality of on-board service was well in excess of anything else in Britain. The returns from the critics were extremely good - everyone enjoyed the service. However, that Achilles heel of long transit times dogged

The seemingly simple matter of getting the train coaches refurbished and upgraded eluded Wrexham & Shropshire. Thus the stop-gap measure of hiring in second hand Mk3s in old BR blue and grey livery was required for an extended period. If the customer was not discouraged by the long journey time to London, then they just may have been impressed by the new interior - but this was not delivered until September 2009. By that time it had become fairly clear that this service did not have a future. Beautiful interior - far too late for WSMR. **Geoff Plumb**

the service, as it was not even able to meet the operating criteria to which the Laing Board had been agreeable. To make matters worse, there was a prohibition in the picking up of business from Wolverhampton, regardless of the different time and stopping pattern of competing, protected services. This was an interesting reflection upon politicians and the DfT, who were paying out money for the Inter-City service to operate, yet refusing calling points to operators accepting all risk at entirely their own expense. As the alternative calling point of Tame Bridge failed to attract traffic, it became increasingly clear that the Business Plan was not achievable, and that the service would be loss-making, whilst the rolling assets could be so much better employed with profit elsewhere.

It was with great sadness that I had no alternative but to tell the Board in December 2010, that I recommended that we should close the Company. I went to see all the 55 staff at the appointed time, and told them the very bad news. It was a shock but not a great surprise to them as we had been honest with them all along as to how Wrexham & Shropshire was doing, but this did not stop it from being a very sad day.

I undertook to the assembled company that we would do whatever we possibly could to find them alternative jobs. I am very pleased that we had fantastic support from many other TOCs, so the majority were able to go to other jobs within the industry.

It is immensely rewarding to have been involved in Wrexham & Shropshire, because it was one of the few enterprises that I have been privileged to be associated with that at all levels, everyone, hand-on-heart, really tried hard to make the enterprise work. The measure of this was how the staff went more than the extra mile to delight passengers, and this was demonstrated when Wrexham & Shropshire set new, high standards of Customer Service.

In conclusion, I am very sorry that the risk did not succeed - it deserved to - but it makes me feel proud that we were able to show how a small Train Operating Company could really do things in a different, and often outstandingly better way.

Andy Hamilton

Andy Hamilton joined British Rail from school in 1986 and was sponsored through an Engineering Degree. He spent a year at Bletchley as Warranty Engineer for the new Class 321 fleet and in 1993 became number 2 to the Aylesbury Depot Engineer. Andy became known for his 'people led' style and in 2005 he moved to the Laing Rail team to assist with the bidding of the London Overground Concession. After, Andy was asked to explore the WSMR proposal, and was offered by Adrian the chance to be involved in either the London Overground business, or to lead the Wrexham & Shropshire development – it took about 2 seconds to make the decision.

My first memory involves a meeting with Adrian Shooter and Mark Beckett (Laing Rail Business Development Director), and following the meeting Adrian asked me to work with Richard Harper to establish if we agreed with John Nelson and Mike Jones's analysis of the opportunity..

The early phase of the work was to establish the reality of the operation and to say whether we believed the revenue prospects. We did, and following this work and a presentation to the Laing Rail Board, we were given the green light to start developing the concept for submission to the ORR for approval to operate. A key element was to develop the timetable with Network Rail, to secure their support for the bid to the ORR. At the time the NR timetable team were developing the West Coast Main Line (WCML) timetable upgrade for December 2008, which meant that they did not want the distraction of trying to find 5 paths a day for what was no more than a possible service, and then having to align with pre and post WCML implementation. I quickly learnt the Mark Laney style of excel spreadsheet timetabling, and spent many hours trying to find good paths that were available. It has become convention that Network Rail will not adjust other operators paths without their permission, even when allowed to do so under the Network Code and respective Track Access agreements, and therefore we constantly struggled to approach other operators directly to get movement of their services – usually by only a minute or two – but we were always met with a negative or hostile response. Despite the issues with the NR team as a whole Simon Pilkington, in charge of the WCML development, would often roll his eyes at Mark Laney and my suggestions, but he would always do his best find solutions with us within the scope he was allowed. It seemed evident that the DfT were bringing their influence to bear through the Dec 08 timetable development in trying to thwart our progress – this time was at the height of the very public battle with Grand Central, to seek to block their proposals on the East Coast Mainline, and it was rumoured that DfT wished to block both open access services.

A key part of timetable development was establishing what rolling stock was to be used. All the early work was established on the basis of using Class 170 DMUs as was the case with Hull Trains – the Class 170 is almost identical to the Class 168s that Chiltern were familiar with, and were therefore ideal for the operation. However it was alleged that DfT influenced the process as Porterbrook suddenly told us that they could not entertain leasing the Class 170s to us. Thus Class 67s and Mk3 coaches became a prospect. Mark Laney had already mentioned this idea both Adrian and I had told him not to be daft! However with the prospect of Class170s extinguished and even the possibility of the Class 158s dismissed on the basis of a similar block from 'on high' – it was necessary to find an alternative that we could control. At the time a reasonable number of Mk3 coaches were sat idle following replacement on WCML by Pendolinos. Mark Laney arranged a run with the EWS company train to demonstrate what was possible – and I clearly recall boarding the train at Paddington (it was not cleared into Marylebone at this stage) for a trip down the Chiltern route, to demonstrate the concept and timings. A subsequent trip was made all the way to Wrexham General, and these runs reminded us all how good an environment the Mk3 could provide, despite its age.

Following all this activity it was of immense frustration that NR in the end decided that they could not fully support our application to the ORR for paths, hiding behind the timing of the timetable development process for Dec 08 as an excuse – again you wonder how much

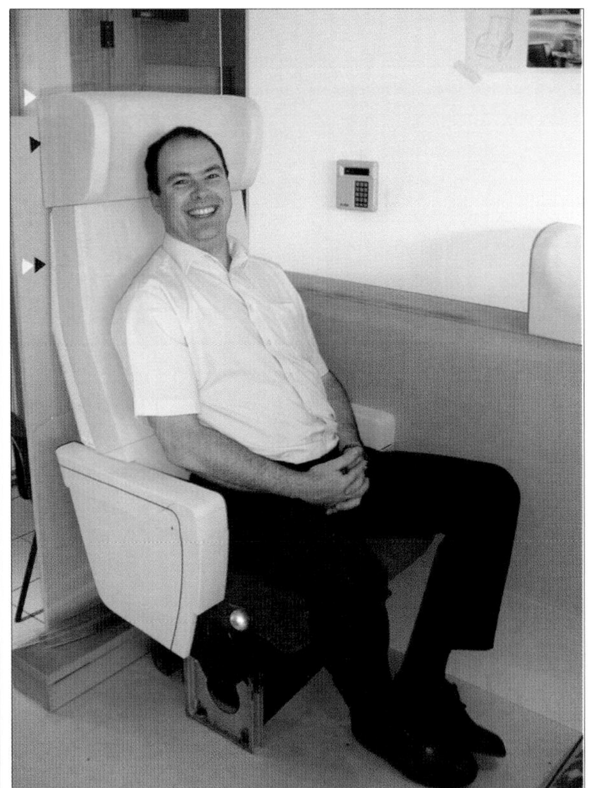

Choosing the right seats - a deeply important process, as today so many appeared to be a tiny bit of foam on some plywood - not ours!

influence DfT was having.

We were aware of the need to be prepared and to minimise the time between eventual permission being granted and the start of operation, and so we conducted the recruitment process for the teams whilst ORR were deliberating the application. The success we experienced in the terms of passenger experience was in large part due to the success of this process and getting the right people from the start. My mantra was very much that we could teach people about railways – you cannot always teach people to deal well with people!

Having acquired the Mk3 coaches and DVTs we set about finding a suitable party to refurbish them. I consider this process to be the biggest error of judgement that we made. At the time Grand Central had delayed their service introduction due to the refurbishment of their rolling stock taking far longer than planned with the work being undertaken by Axiom (part of the DB Group) at Marcroft. We allowed ourselves to be convinced that Axiom had learnt the lessons of the Grand Central contract, and that our proposals were much simpler due to not involving the conversion of loco hauled coaches to HSTs, and so on that basis we agreed to a programme with Axiom that would be ready to go when we got approval to operate. It rapidly became apparent that Axiom had neither the technical, commercial or project management acumen to undertake the project. With the help of the Chiltern Engineering team we ended up carrying them every step of the way, and whilst we ended up with the product that we wanted, it was 2 years too late and the damage had been done!

There were therefore problems 'floating around' with the launch because of the non-delivery of our rolling stock from Axiom. Rather than wait we managed to source alternative Mk3s from Cargo D to enable us to start the service. They were a company that had acquired a small fleet and had repainted them in BR InterCity blue and grey, to operate on charter services. These vehicles paired with some of the DB Regio fleet that I had managed to procure, and they too were repainted in the same BR Inter City to provide a consistent image. Yet there was no hiding that most of these vehicles had been in store for at least 2 years and were in need of refurbishment even before that. In the absence of the DVTs we also had to resort to using Top and Tail Class 67s which created a number of issues – I recall receiving a letter of authority to operate our chosen formation (a letter I did not believe I needed!) from a bureaucrat in the NR Black tower on the Saturday before we started service on the Monday! None the less we had a fleet of trains available and arranged ready for the launch date.

Or at least we thought we did. The coaches that we had hired from Cargo-D had been in use on Hull Trains due to one of their sets being unavailable on a long term basis. That was due to end several weeks prior to our launch, but as ever their release got delayed and it was not until the Friday afternoon of the launch weekend that Hull Trains confirmed that they had released the vehicles and that we were able to take them on hire. We had to arrange a transit move from Bounds Green to Crewe – the move finally taking place on the Sunday afternoon/evening. I recall standing in the sidings at Crewe when they finally appeared on the main line just after midnight. We then spent a frantic 4 hours shunting them all into the correct formations, cleaning them and applying Wrexham & Shropshire logos on the side ready for the first set to leave for Wrexham at about 0430. That Sunday afternoon I started work at Crewe on the coaching stock at about 1700. At 04.30 I left Crewe on the first set heading towards Wrexham, had a wash and changed into my uniform on the way, then started the vast number of media interviews at Wrexham at around 05.45. I travelled to London on the 07.23 ex Wrexham

General, again undertaking media activities as well as taking the time to meet our passengers. I finally got home around 24hrs after I had started on the Sunday evening, exhausted, but immensely proud of what the team had achieved!

Elsewhere in this book you will read about the things the team did to make that first day and few months work. This set the tone for the way we would run our railway – the passenger would always come first in everything we did – even when that meant doing extraordinary things, and this led to our fantastic achievement in earning 99% customer satisfaction in the National Passenger Survey of all rail passengers – a figure announced within 2 or 3 days of the decision to close the company!

The memories that stand out for me during our operation are all around people going that extra mile – on some occasions including the Chiltern team, where they interfaced with us; our attitude rubbed off on some of them - this usually occurred when the service was under pressure. Late running trains displacing crews and stock, usually due to disruption in the West Midlands was often a problem. On one occasion I recall there being no prospect of the crew for the prime evening train from London being in London in time to operate the service. With the help of the Chiltern Control we found a Chiltern driver available to drive, and a guard to allow us to operate, and Adrian and myself climbed on as the buffet stewards for the first leg of the journey to Banbury where the crew were able to join us. On another occasion when the incoming WSMR train was very late, I recall Paul Belton (an ex Chiltern Driver) commandeering an idle Chiltern 168 set at Marylebone, and quickly getting all permissions in place for using it to form a Wrexham & Shropshire service, thus allowing the passengers to transfer to the Wrexham & Shropshire set which was terminated and turned round at Banbury.

If getting it right meant donning PPE and going 'out there' to sort matters out first hand, then Andy was up for it. It had quite an effect!

I remember the day I was sat in a meeting with Adrian Shooter and senior members of the Network Rail LNW team at the Chiltern Control room in Banbury. As we sat there, I heard a WSMR train come to a stand shortly after pulling away from Banbury platform, and not move for a couple of minutes. The Chiltern Control Manager popped his head through the door to say that the Driver was reporting that he could not release the brakes, so on with the orange coat and out to help the driver. I was very pleased that my knowledge of the Mk3s did not fail me, and we found the fault within 2 or 3 minutes, a strange fault – an air pipe had pulled out of its fitting on a coach and was allowing the brake pipe to vent via the passenger communication system. After isolating the system on that coach we found Chiltern guard on board who travelled in the affected coach with a radio to contact the driver if required and off the train went to London!

On numerous occasions little unseen tasks would just happen without query or question, when in most train companies – including Chiltern - the initiative or willingness to take that extra step would just not happen. Why this was I think depended on two main reasons: firstly the team genuinely knew that their future employment depended on the company being successful, and secondly we managed to instil in them a sense that they were empowered to make it right for the passenger – no matter what the situation – and that their actions would be backed. I would not allow the health and safety brigade, or anyone else, to prevent intelligent and well briefed individuals stepping outside their normal brief or scope to make things happen for the good of our passengers. At times this led to conflict with other companies staff and health and safety representatives over the silliest niff-naff and trivia that may have been unusual, but was perfectly safe and reasonable, usually in circumstances where they did not understand the context of the decisions we took or the mitigation we put in place. I firmly believe that the paralysis created by over-bearing adherence to poorly thought out process, masquerading as 'Rules', rather than a properly risk managed operation and business, is one of the major weaknesses of our industry, leading to baffling decisions that passengers cannot understand. I am determined that wherever I am involved in the industry going forward that legacy of Wrexham & Shropshire will live on in that respect! There were some quirky little victories from which I drew personal satisfaction, like in managing to obtain permission to operate passenger trains via the West Coast Main Line and via Neasden curve, when we were unable to get access to the Chiltern route from the West Midlands. This was another example of where there was excess head shaking, as we were sombrely told that it could not be done...... of course it could!

In this respect specific people warrant a mention. Liane Tobin was superb throughout; very few other MD's PAs would have the wherewithal, the drive or determination to undertake some of the tasks that Liane took on. On a Monday she could be managing the office at Shrewsbury, but nip out during the day to be at the station when our trains went through, particularly if one was running late or we knew that a passenger required assistance at the station; on Tuesday could be marshalling a photo shoot and press statement with a local MP; on Wednesday manning the buffet on the early train to London due to late staff sickness, or because we knew we were carrying a big party; on Thursday checking a freshly refurbished set of coaches at Wembley depot before they went into traffic, and on Friday probably back in the office to catch up with post! Then on Saturday she would probably be out managing a football special that we were running to Wembley. Liane was a huge asset to me individually and to the wider company, but she was not alone – Charlotte Price, our Quality, Safety and Environment Manager was much the same, having previously been a Train Manager on Hull Trains, so she knew the score. Richard Sturgess, our allocated Technical Engineer within the Chiltern Engineering team did a similarly above and beyond job in keeping the Mk3s running with the assistance of the Wembley Depot Team, as well as other individuals on the fringes, particularly within the Chiltern team, who really stepped up for us.

The toughest thing I have ever had to do in my professional career was to tell 50 committed people that they had lost their livelihood, their community, and their friends, despite all the fantastic things that they had done, and through no fault of their own. 'Friends' may not even be strong enough – they had become a family, who supported each other through professional and personal strife. Yet despite the initial anger and bewilderment, I will never forget the dignity of that last week of operation, nor the accolades that we received from passengers – many of whom came and travelled with us in that last week to show their support and appreciation for what we had done for them and their communities. So I am left reflecting proudly on what my team achieved, hopefully in part due to my leadership, but with the regret of letting them and the communities that we served down.

I understand the reasons for the decision, and could not argue with the logic that DB Regio could earn more money from the rolling stock on the London to Birmingham route. However I also believe that within 2 years from when we closed we would have been turning a profit, and Shropshire and North Wales would have had a high quality and enduring direct service to London with all the socioeconomic benefits that would have brought. So we are left with the what ifs – what if Class 170s had been available – but then the service quality would possibly not have achieved the same levels. What if Axiom had delivered the refurbished rolling stock on time, what if Chiltern had the funds to refurbish their own coaches rather than needing the W&S ones, what if we had been able to serve Wolverhampton, and what if we had been able to have the timetable that could have been achieved with better joined-up industry thinking and some support from government?

There are many more what ifs, but we should not have needed to fight for the paths we achieved in the way that we did – there must be a better way of allocating appropriate capacity, and don't blame the rules. The flexibility exists but if for whatever reason, someone refuses to apply it, then the effectice management of the timetabling will not deliver the results. Wrexham & Shropshire should not have needed to fight for the operating restrictions on the Class 67 & Mk3 formations to be revised. Sensible engineering and operating analysis should not be paralysed by what appeared even then as bureaucratic nonsense and paranoia about cost and risk.

Today with the Evergreen improvements on the Chiltern route, coupled with the revised standard hour timetable (designed in part to facilitate Wrexham & Shropshire success!) a journey time to Shrewsbury of 2 hours 30 minutes would have been possible. Oh dear!

Richard Harper

Richard Harper joined the railway in 2001 after an initial career in public transport planning. After spells in business development at Chiltern and franchise bidding with parent company Laing, Richard joined the Wrexham & Shropshire team to secure regulatory approval, and then to get the show on the road at start up. After nine months in the front line, he returned to Chiltern in 2009 to join the effort to deliver the Evergreen 3 infrastructure project, and has since led the train planning arm of Chiltern Railways. Richard had the sad job of returning as one of those given the task of closing the operation down.

It's easy to deal almost exclusively in acronym and cliché when you've worked on the railway for a while, and only to see the output measure in figures. The industry is inevitably process driven and so reputation for performance is only as good as the next train failure. So can you deliver the Passenger Service Requirement as laid down, and also maintain the Public Performance Measure? Yet experience brings home the important lesson every day that running the railway is all about being proactive, not reactive. Success in running a railway depends on the effective management of a team of people; PSRs and PPMs are a measure of the outcome.

The Wrexham & Shropshire operation was unusual in that we were able to recruit a team from scratch. This is almost unheard of and it conferred upon us a difficult selection process which delivered an advantage. Train companies often inherit staff who have experienced several different organisations, who have run the same train service over many years. There have been major changes within the Industry, brought on by privatisation and the franchises which emerged, yet often it is the same people that continue to do the same job. We were able to inspire fresh team to deliver better results for a new company that could employ a different ethos. So Wrexham & Shropshire was fortunate in being able to build a complete team from scratch, and it was that team that had the resilience and fortitude to create something new, and to battle against insuperable odds.

We really had to build up a fully functioning Open Access Train Operating Company in a remarkably short period of time - it was an educational experience. The recruitment of the train managers was particularly memorable for me. We advertised for 13 positions in the local press, and we were stunned to receive over 200 applications. It was a real challenge, and it took a lot of time and effort to sift these down to around 25 for the next stage. We designed an assessment centre, with support from Chiltern, and put the potential candidates through a full day of testing, interviews and group exercises, which were carried out at the North East Wales Institute of Higher Education (NEWI) campus near Wrexham General station. We sold it to them as an essentially 'local' exercise, 'Wrexham' & Shropshire. The staff at NEWI – which is now part of Glyndwr University – gave us a great deal of support, made us really welcome, and we were able to use their meeting facilities regularly during the active phase of recruitment and training. The candidates hardly enjoy everything we threw at them, and there were plenty of expletives when it came to the literacy and numeracy tests. However, people sharp with money and resilient in the face of difficulty is what we sought. The group exercise was challenging, but thought provoking when we created small groups of candidates and asked them to discuss problems that Wrexham & Shropshire might face, and what their solutions to those problems might be. Characters began to emerge; the innovative and able stood out, and at the end of the day we knew we had found a group of talented and practical individuals who would give Wrexham & Shropshire the customer service focus we wanted. We needed thirteen train managers and it was hard to narrow the candidates choices to the number required. The process achieved the right result; we had equipped the new service with a calibre of staff unrivalled in any TOC elsewhere. Better still, we were able to repeat the main elements of the selection choice for the team of stewards we needed. As these people would have the direct customer interface, particularly in the area of catering - something at which we were determined to excel - a careful selection process was key, and we had those not selected for train managers to draw from.

The whole of this extended process of staff choice was a valuable one, and in retrospect, when difficult times

Coventry Station - 15th July 2008, entering from the north, headed for Leamington. Although Richard was not directly responsible for the operating function, it was both the context and environment that shaped his commercial management task. Fifty years after Beeching, the repercussions of the decisions made at that time still haunt the railways. There is not enough rail capacity, at the speeds expected, between Wolverhampton and Coventry. The foolish conversion of the former GWR Line to tramway stripped any affordable solution to this problem and blighted Wrexham & Shropshire. True, there were other factors, but improving the Wolverhampton to Leamington running times would have worked wonders. **Geoff Plumb**

came, it was those carefully selected, inventive, and loyal people whose determination carried the service through.

The timetable for any railway service is the core part of the product, around which other elements of the service offer are built. The timetable generates journey opportunities; these attract custom, and therefore income. The aspirations we had for our timetable were not going to meet those of the electric service to Euston, but then as has been described elsewhere, people were forced to change at Wolverhampton for that, and over the years, the connecting times had become slack as focus was turned elsewhere. Thus provided we were able to secure paths along normal lines, although Wrexham & Shropshire would not match Virgin's journey times, we believed that the service quality we intended to offer would bridge the 'gap' for us.

There were unpleasant shocks to come. My own role was not to negotiate the timetable, but it was to plan the optimum advantage that could be taken of it. The timetable anticipated by the promoters and stakeholders was diluted in incremental steps. As optimism lagged at each step downwards, determination increased to give it a go, make it work, and prove detractors wrong. The first disappointment was a firm refusal by Network Rail to allocate any regular and commercially useful paths via the direct Stour Valley route. This was a blow which had as its solution diversion via the Grand Junction Line, which added up to 30 minutes to the journey time. No one said we couldn't ever have the times we wanted, Network Rail, governed by guidelines intended to ensure fairness, applied the Network Code. We would have to wait our turn behind established franchised operators. The ORR would only offer a track access agreement subject to practical negotiations for train paths with Network Rail - and these could not meet our aspirations. Things got worse. The Didcot and Chester Line through Banbury was geared for 90mph running, 20mph below the Coventry to Birmingham section. After Banbury on the Chiltern Line to Marylebone, some of this was 90mph, and most was in the process of being raised to 100mph under Evergreen 3. Unfortunately Network Rail placed a locomotive speed limit on our Class 67s

This was the image that those who battled away at start-up saw of the service on offer. To generate the immense effort needed to drive this service through to full production, any other sort of vision would have been unthinkable. Yet for the most part, this image was well away from reality. I never saw this product - it simply was not there during Richard's time. All the people were doing a heroic job, but looking back, it was rather like making water flow uphill. Ultimately this vision was delivered, and ultimately the sheer innovation and cheek of the service would have succeeded - but that was not to be . The braking force against success was applied slowly and relentlessly, making the job harder and harder. This was a pity. **WSMR**

of 60mph. The damage to the timetable aspirations was serious, but the bad news had come in 'dribs and drabs'. The decision was taken to battle through, anticipating steady and regular journey time improvements whilst we started the business up with superb standards of service in compensation. Unfortunately, the competing operation was on a more rapid and sustained product improvement curve, and Wrexham & Shropshire had yet one more body-blow to suffer.

The decision to apply the rules of Moderation of Competition (MoC) to prevent Wrexham & Shropshire from picking up southbound passengers from Wolverhampton led to an unrecoverable income gap of about £500k per year. It was clear from careful questioning that MoC would be applied to any attempt to offer service to London stations, let alone Marylebone, so variations were 'out'. Alas the alternative calling point in the West Midlands, Tame Bridge (Parkway) was a commercial failure, despite best efforts. We began here with hope and fortitude, but the restrictions on market access, the rule imposed, plus the extended journey times hampered our commercial efforts.

Railway catering has been a regular topic of conversation for generations, with the curled up British Rail sandwich as a staple music hall gag. Catering on trains has eroded steadily in recent years with few 'real' meals being served. Even the much-vaunted GNER service was significantly downgraded in the changeover of the franchise to East Coast, and the meals service on the Anglia, Norwich service has also disappeared, making sure that the subject remains high on the agenda for passenger groups, and the media.. Of course railway catering has a profile that requires high staffing levels, exemplary logistics, and the challenge of quality control. It is subject to unpredictable changes in demand that generates potentially high wastage levels, and with the radical reduction of journey times, full-meals service is less in demand on board. Railway companies have always had difficulty in valuing catering, and of how much the ticket income is supported by the quality of the catering offer. The outcome has tended to be to avoid full-meals service like the plague. We took a contrary view, developing an integrated, low-wastage, 'easy to provide' offer that was innovative and economical in operation. It was outstanding enough to capture the imagination of the media and the Wrexham

This is the passenger load from the morning arrival of the 05.41 train from Wrexham on 26th June 2008, at 09.54, two-minutes early, in London (Marylebone), four-hours after leaving Wrexham, with 67017 David Lloyd *in charge. This was some two months after the start of the service, and hearts sank at such a loading performance. Bear in mind that the last revenue-earning stop was Tame Bridge at 07.28, and that the 07.45 Virgin train was in London (Euston) at 09.34 with four stops. The 08.36 from Stafford arrived in Euston at 09.56; with a departure time of 06.25 from Shrewsbury by Wrexham & Shropshire, and only a half-hour drive to Stafford from Shrewsbury, this may be why the WSMR loading is so meagre.*

& Shropshire name acquired excellent brand values from it. Quality was maintained in first and standard, and sales from the buffet counter exceeded the costs of supply for both classes, typically making a margin of 50%. The surplus didn't cover all of the staff costs, but the staff were integral to the overall service offer. Several commentators suggested that the quality on-board was a reason for the demise of Wrexham & Shropshire, that the company was haemorrhaging money on a level of on-train staff and catering that was unsustainable. The truth is that the modest financial gains that may have resulted from abandoning the on-board offer would never have saved the company, and having such an outstanding level of on-board service quality sustained the operation by its brand reinforcement and generated wonderful publicity.

That choice of excellent staff paid off time and time again. When the ancient catering equipment let us down, there was always an innovative response. The cash float was used to buy something to make do from the shops at Marylebone; wonders were worked with a toaster and kettle. On those dreaded times when a train failed, the on-board crew accompanied the passengers on the alternative service, if necessary conducting them across Birmingham, to ensure no-one got lost and that connections were made.

It was disturbing to see the budget results always falling short of the aspirations, despite intense activity. We drove it to within £25k of the target per period, but that target was set to rise steeply before we got there. I developed an effective yield control mechanism, but its subtle workings indicated that although we could exchange yield for volume, the 'sweet spot' could not produce the profit levels we needed. Indeed journey times were falling, on-board service was improving and the horizon for MoC was approaching. Wrexham & Shropshire was not unusual as a service that failed to meet its budget aspirations on time, but the circumstances that negated all effort were somewhat cruel, unnecessary, and malign in a privatised rail industry where competition was 'moderated' in the strangest of ways. Wrexham & Shropshire will be remembered for its superb, loyal and high-achieving staff. It was they who piloted the service through. They were a privilege to work with.

Mark Edlington

Mark Edlington is one of those irrepressible people in the Rail Industry who have 'trains' written through as in seaside rock. He started on the railway in 1987 in Aylesbury as a guard, and worked his way to the front of the train, driving. It was obvious that Mark was also a capable manager, and so he rose to be asked to handle the setting up of the operations for Wrexham & Shropshire under Managing Director Andy Hamilton. It was a complex and difficult job, and Wrexham & Shropshire pursued its chequered career with immaculate operating procedures. It was a sad, additional experience for Mark to preside over closedown - all part of the experience!

I can remember hearing about this new proposed operation when I was a driver standards manager. I didn't think any more of it, when one day Andy Hamilton turned up out of the blue, and was asking how he could get a train from Marylebone to Wrexham. So we got some Quail maps out. Andy kept coming back; it got more serious and a team formed, and to my surprise, I was on it.

We did a lot of recruitment fairly early in 2007. There was that period when we weren't sure what was going to happen but we maintained a list and kept contact with them. That was a very interesting process. One of the things I had to do was a presentation to the Wrexham & Shropshire Board about how the company was going to start operationally. They were very starchy and they were like 'yes, you say that, but will it?' I remember Mike Jones saying they wanted everyone to wear safety shoes because they'd had problems on Hull Trains with stewards wearing inappropriate footwear, and the other thing he suggested was straw boaters. Can you imagine our lot in straw boaters? Crossing Chirk Viaduct we'd have 'I'm sorry I've lost my straw boater'. I can assure you that's what would have happened. I remained calm.

We had a some trouble with getting enough drivers and train managers in the timescale. Even though we got approval from the Regulator in September 2007, we still didn't know when we could start, and having recruited early we had quite a lot of change because people had dropped out or changed their minds.

I ordered some IVRS radios for the drivers – big chunky yellow handsets. I daringly ordered 20 so we would have some spares. One day I turned up at Tramway (Banbury offices) and it was the week after Charlotte, Diane and Neill had started.. The office atmosphere was quite strange – you know when you go in a room and you can tell something's up? After a while I said 'what's up with you lot?' and they said 'oh well it's our mobile phones. Look at the size of them!' They'd been told their phones were arriving on this day, so when the box arrived they just opened it.

It was a big ask to get ready for 28th April. Nearly all the drivers were going to loco work for the first time and RPD came up with the great idea of training trains. Our Operations Administrator, Kath Chelton started close to the launch date – she was excellent, and part of a group of women who really ran the company. I was so busy I'd hardly seen her in the two weeks since she started. I heard a driver say 'we're the drivers and you'll do as we say' and she replied 'I've worked in mental health for 20 years, and I think I can handle you lot', so I knew if she could stand up for herself like that she'd be alright.

Network Rail wouldn't take the performance figures of the EWS company train and apply them to our trains. They said 'you'll have to do your own braking tests'. Tony Stickells and I did some braking tests between Chester and Crewe – it was probably the Friday night (before the launch). We didn't have the ability to analyse the download from the on-board computer, so Andy e-mailed it to Nick Edwards at EWS, who was on the Royal Train at the time, and overnight he analysed the data. On the Saturday on the staff special I got a phonecall at Wellington – I was in the cab, but I thought I'd better take the call. It was Nick who said the data's fine, the train can outperform a Class 168 at any point, and so he e-mailed the data back to us and Network Rail.

The time before the start of service passed like a blur. But we must have done all the right things, because everything was in position and ready to go in time. Then at the vital moment, the first train on the Monday morning hadn't even got out of sight of the station

This is the administrative office on Wrexham General Station on 18th March 2008, and the service is going to open next month! This was running things a bit close - but then running things close was what this service was about. Before the trains began to roll out of Wrexham we were in there, conducting all the frantic business of getting together an operation with a fleet of locomotives and carriages to run a service to London. This was not an experience I have ever had before - and it isn't one I expect to have again - but it was terrific! **Mark Edlington**

before it stopped. Paul Belton was the driver, he got it going again, but at Wellington it shut down again. The controller was faulty, but I was determined it was going to get to London, and it did!. The whole of that first day – I wondered if it would ever end - started at 05.00 and finished at 01.00 the next morning. I worked 100 hours in the first week. That first day was like an open day at Wrexham General in BR days. Four extra 67s appeared due to the problems we were having. A Class 37 brought something over from Crewe and towed away 67025, which had failed at Wellington earlier. There were twelve Class 67s at Wrexham plus the Class 37. I remember phoning Network Rail control in Manchester on the first day, because I needed authority for a train to leave Wrexham with one loco, with an extra one to be attached on the back at Shrewsbury, and they said 'nothing to do with us mate' and I said 'yes it is' and they said 'Wales and Borders, we don't touch Wrexham' and then a little voice in the background was saying 'yes it is us'. After the first week I remember thinking 'if its going to be like this I don't know if I can carry on'. The phone rang never-endingly.

There were some problems - especially at the London end . Everyone in Chiltern used to say 'no'. In response we mischievously created a piece of paper which had a diagram that said 'here's us explaining what we want to do' then 'here's you saying "no"'. Then 'over here is us going to Adrian and then here's you saying "yes"'. So we'd say you can just say yes now, or we'll follow this "flowchart".

I got into a system for about 10-12 weeks: in the week I stayed in the Ramada, and early on I stayed at the weekend. I went out with the drivers when they were shunting and going to Crewe, and we gradually got matters into a workable system. Later I travelled on the trains as much as anyone from Banbury to Wrexham in the morning, and back in the evening. The catering was stunning – the whole ambience of it – and also the quality of the Mark 3, and how we eventually refurbished them. One journey I remember particularly, it was Amy Owen and Rob Davies, who would always try to feed everyone. They spent the whole journey coming through 'KitKats?'...'No' and then right at the end Gaynor Matthews (TM) came along – I'm sure she was set up –

EWS Class 67 67029 on D Day minus-two at Wrexham, in the refurbished bay platforms that are now the northern 'operating base'. The scene has been made tidy and ready for operations. The train is of three Mk3 coaches hired in from Cargo D, and the missing DVT vehicles are compensated for by another Class 67 on the buffer stops. The work has now basically been done. We didn't know that 67025 on the front of the first train had hidden inside it a controller fault that would give us such trouble. **Mark Edlington**

and said 'I've brought you a KitKat'. They were almost unstoppable. It took a while for that team to gel and for everyone to get used to everyone else's little ways, but once they did it formed into a very strong unit. Turnover was nothing like I've seen elsewhere. One of the great things about catering on train is you can use it to solve so many problems. When the train was delayed prior to departure from Wrexham, Di's team would go out and take everyone cake and tea – what an amazing thing that is. At Wolverhampton, the Virgin staff were very aggressive but once the staff had started slipping them the odd bacon butty they lost their ability to be angry with us. The experience of good food on a train is stunning.

Neill Kenderdine did a superb job with the Train Managers. Alan Newman was talking to someone else recently and I overheard him say 'I was on a train the other day and it was an ex-Wrexham Train Manager. They're 20 years ahead of anything Chiltern's got'. He doesn't give out praise where it's not called for. There was never a big plan to put all the people through a system to make them 'nice', but the company was a masterclass in how to treat people well, and what you reap is what you sow. We were really lucky that lots of good people applied to work for us.

Crewe ETD sometimes took longer than expected. You'd phone and say you were coming to pick up a Class 67, and making sure it was not blocked in, and you'd get there and they'd say 'Oh, I've just shunted 75 Class 92s in front of it'. Once, I can't remember why, but I was bothered about breakfast, and this shunt went on through the night, and I walked back into the Ramada at one-minute to seven, just in time for breakfast - the next morning! I had my breakfast and went to bed. Not the right way round really!

I took Tony Parkins with Ian Jack of the Guardian who wrote a lovely article. He rode in the train but then got a cab ride at the north end, but one thing that completely proved we were who and what we said we were, was when we rolled in to Chirk station where Charlotte Price was dead-heading the flowers. And I was saying '...and there's our safety manager!' Where else in the world would that have happened?

This was the first run in normal WSMR service of a train including a DVT, after the trial run to Marylebone from Crewe the previous day. Once the DVTs were in operation, and we had our own fleet of dedicated locomotives then matters improved greatly. This is 1P03, the 08:55 Wrexham to Marylebone train, with 67015 David J. Lloyd *leading the train towards London. The location is just south of Haddenham on Saturday 11the October.*
Geof Plumb

One day on the train I caught north in the morning, there was a Cross Country in front which always used to delay it. This train was cancelled, so we requested to run via Leamington, Coventry and Birmingham International - but Network Rail wouldn't let us. Andy phoned our control and the DCM was Dave George, and he said 'get us routed via Coventry' and we'll prove to them that we can keep to time. The train came in and the next thing we were confronted by this very distressed Eastern European guy in a bad way. The train manager brought him and he explained that he should have got on the CrossCountry to International for his flight, I've missed my flight'. So Andy got on the phone and arranged for us to stop additionally at International, but as the guy didn't speak good English he couldn't understand, and said 'it's not possible'. I remember us stopping at International, and I remember this Virgin supervisor coming up and snarling, and when the door opened shouting 'stand clear', and Andy saying to the Eastern European chap 'just ignore her' as he jumped off, his flight saved.

We let staff travel with us on their passes even though we never had the reciprocal facilities on other services. We looked after everyone and treated them really well; the rest of the industry should be ashamed of themselves. One day we had four senior managers in First who all consumed a bit too much alcohol; it was an unrefurbished set. Then a bit later there was some crashing noises from the front of the train, and Neill Kenderdine went to investigate. He came to me and said 'there's something wrong, will you come and have a look'. So I went to the front gangway and I could hear this 'thump, thump', but we looked at the gangway and the coupler and everything was fine. Mark Collins had earlier collected the disabled ramp from the store cupboard which at one time was a staff toilet, and one of these First Class railway gents had come and thought 'a toilet' even though it said 'Private'. He had gone in, and shut the door even though there was no door handle and no lights. Eventually we let him out and he launched into Neill 'how dare you lock me in a toilet' and of course Neill responded 'It's not a toilet! It's a cupboard! It says Private, so what are you doing in my cupboard?'.

The WSMR experience was certainly one that can be branded as utterly unforgettable.

Gordon Rushton has known John Nelson since training days in the 1960s. They worked together in the 1970s, but he left to pursue a career in shipping, tourist railways, and video. Upon hearing about Wrexham & Shropshire he was most interested in the operation, but the opportunity came when the newly appointed Sales Manager left. Gordon was asked to enter the fray right on startup. There was little time for carefully thinking and long-term plans. The service had begun and action was required at once. Gordon plunged straight into the onerous task of selling the service, and immediately realised that whilst it was exhilarating, it was a tough number.

Anyone who takes a job has to embrace the culture that surrounds it. However, walking into the middle of the muddle of getting things going is quite an experience. It was clear that as there were many problems to be solved all sensible suggestions would be considered. My welcome was never in doubt; straight away I was greeted, informed of the bits that needed attention, and the skills they were looking for to do that work - and I had joined the team. I was certainly up for this. My only concern was that I may not be able to deliver with the energy and vigour of someone younger, and so for the start, I laid down guidelines to follow to make sure that as much of the activity was cerebral rather than physical. Mind you, there was no avoiding an 80 hour week. It was necessary to do this in order the get through the tasks. But by far the most important time devoted to making this service work was thinking. It was the problem consigned to the brain upon sleeping, the mulling over of choices in front of the television - notebook and pencil at the ready, that promoted the intense activity on the computer to turn emerging ideas into practical action - that's why it was 80 hours a week.

A long career in marketing and sales, and rugged customer handling experience offered lots of innovations, but these were really pleasurable icings on the cake compared with the real task of plugging the product wherever and whenever possible. There is always an uneasy compromise between product price, quality, and volume - and Wrexham Shropshire was no different. It was difficult not to have been present at the formative stages, as there was great pressure to accept the current status quo, despite anomalies, and just to get on with the selling effort. Yet even from the start of my effort, it was clear that price and volume were deeply affected by quality - most importantly journey time. The question was 'how much,' as this had a great bearing on where to sell and to whom. This judgement had to be right or effort and resources would be wasted, yet there were some areas of 'hopeless case' that innovation and effort had a great deal of difficulty in addressing. Of course it was the culmination of these that caused the eventual demise of the service, but trying to deal with them even at an early stage was difficult.

- Getting people to patronise the 06.45 departure from Marylebone to Wrexham was a steep struggle uphill - splendid breakfast or no.
- The steadily increasing Virgin service frequency from Birmingham to London made competitive selling really difficult.
- The stringent application of Moderation of Competition legislation, and the unwitting decision to make a call in the unresponsive market area of Tame Bridge made life very difficult, and we were despairing.
- The discovery of the effect of Stafford on travel habits from Shrewsbury, post the boost of Virgin's Pendolino service introduction, was an unpleasant surprise.

I could see from the face of my new colleague Richard Harper just how needed was an extra pair of hands on the pump. The water in the deep end may have certain amount of distortion - but no one argues about how wet it will be - in I went! The three old Mk3 carriages, topped and tailed by two Class 67 locomotives was a mild surprise at Banbury, but I was assured that this was but a temporary measure. The 08.00 train from Banbury was almost devoid of passengers, and there was nothing there to announce the service, no leaflets, no posters, and even the train describer did not show the name Wrexham & Shropshire. This was a rather muted beginning, and one to 'get on to' straight away. It was a revelation that intermediate stations like Shrewsbury, Telford and Banbury, and even the London terminus Marylebone, seemed unaware of and indeed unwilling to sell the new service - the staff had not received invitations to travel. This had to be put right. Indeed the formidable

The genteel and unhurried atmosphere of Marylebone Station was not the place to expect services to the West Midlands and Shropshire. Everyone knows you go to Euston for that. The feeble transport connections to Marylebone, together with its rather isolated position made it a difficult sell, especially early in the morning. And unless a station repaint was contemplated, Wrexham & Shropshire branding, as unstartling as it was, became lost in the background. Shifting entrenched opinion was almost impossible for someone coming in after startup. Spot the WSMR branding!

Chiltern Railways selling machine seemed to believe that this service was not only merely a remote connection with them, but perhaps some sort of competition. There appeared to be a whispering campaign at the London end that took an age to dispel, and needed the 'big guns' himself to eradicate the prejudice finally. In fact, like Hull Trains, there was no selling in London before the service started. It all felt for a while like having opened a hamburger stall next to McDonalds, yet our hamburgers, though delicious, came in plain, second-hand wrappers, at nearly the same price, but delivered much more slowly.

The note to promoters of open access services in the future is to make quite sure - however it is that you do it - that the introduction phase is adequately resourced, and that 'startup' is accompanied with enough trumpets and drums to startle the market into more than just trial of the new service. To have to do all of this afterwards doesn't mean the service will fail; the market you are in and your performance will decide that. What it means is that the enterprise will lose more money to begin with, almost no matter what. However, the losses will be less and growth will be more in the initial phase, and the staff will be heartened if a wave of custom follows an introduction with a really major fuss. We didn't do that.

There seemed to be a notion, firmly set within the promoters of this new service, that they had discovered a sure-fire formula, that if applied from their careful researches beforehand, would be certain to offer a growing business that would come to profit within the terms of the business plan. To be sure, such plans have to be flexible, but they are a hostage to the fortune of ever-changing events. As an 'innocent' the mismatch between what the promoters were saying, and what was being delivered was not obvious to start with. The absence of new carriages affected market credibility from the beginning even though the 'bottom line effect' was continually forsworn: what nonsense. There was no welcome for the idea that the £48 advance purchase return was set too high, and that a temporary fare of £28 (£14 e/w) should be set initially. The reaction was that much care had been taken with the business plan, and that what was needed was to 'get out there and make that work before dropping prices'. This is a difficult obstacle to overcome. Firefighters are unwelcome at the

Few can muster such an iconic image to sell with. Ruby the Routemaster was such a draw, that few passed her by without a second glance. She is shown here set up in the market square at Wrexham. The destination was already sold before anyone said anything . Better still was the attitude of councils and shopping mall administrators.. Most, if they couldn't be convinced that the presence of the bus itself was a public draw, were sympathetic to the promotion of London rail services from their town and offered welcome. Compact and intensive product selling like this really generated trial of the service - the question was, would the trial generate regular custom at the prices being asked? That was much more difficult.

scene of the blaze, if they wish before starting to engage the Chief in a discussion about the better performance of alternative hose nozzles. I had been invited to turn the handle of 'the sales machine', and was expected to do this. Indeed, this was urgent and necessary. Alas, whilst doing so matters did not remain constant, and similarly, the performance refused to conform to the business plan that was set for it, regardless of the hours put in.

Energy was needed to get out into the market, to ensure that the product was on offer, and that the public had the maximum opportunity to buy. The mismatch anomaly was laid aside, pending solution by others. The body of the book explains how many were the problems in delivering that solution. When I stepped aside, so that others more able could face the problem, the classic panacea was applied, of lower price for higher volume, yet it too was still unable to raise the income desired - the 'solution' had still not been found and it was now too late. Regardless of any matters of strategy, the tactics were clear whatever refined policy discussions there may be. The common action to all was to go out and sell the product. The various methods of media advertising, radio, newspaper and leaflet were applied, as far as the promotional pocket could stretch. More efficient methods were needed. A friend with a London Routemaster Bus provided a novel solution. This went down extremely well in towns along the route, and we attended regularly in Wrexham, Oswestry and most successfully Telford with business resulting..

It was necessary to pace the ground, visiting all the stations where the train stopped, to overcome the staff hostility to the service, and to make sure that the booking staff had the chance to sample the service, but perhaps most effective of all were the activities of Richard Worrall. Richard's selling effort with his cohorts of temporary staff, recruited in Walsall and surrounding areas, made sure that all households were leafletted at prices we could otherwise not have afforded. In the south, Tony Parkins was pacing the streets, persuading Chiltern booking offices to sell the services, and visiting travel agents and Central London outlets to make sure that they knew about it. The returns were interesting, as they showed how although we thought that the service had been well publicised, the actual level of knowledge at

The catering staff tend to feature in pictures, as one hopes to sell nice things to customers on board. Fiona Jones and Stephen Vidal are shown here at the counter of the buffet car, with its rather individual equipment, that sometimes worked perfectly and other times did not. Despite the unpredictability of the equipment staff always managed to offer service. I do not know of a closed catering section on a train - they would always manage to offer something. With a three car set, such a level of offer did get through to all the passengers travelling. This was the level of service that one would hope to encounter on rail. It wasn't the quality of offer that was the problem, access to markets and journey time were the weak areas.

the point of sale was extremely low. And the 'system' was not helping. The National Rail Enquiries people offered the most charming platitudes - but in truth, for most of the time they were talking apples, and we apricots. Settlement was elusive, and vital help from that quarter never came. The saviour was the wonderful web site. It couldn't span the whole market, there were swathes of business that were missed, but the sales energy put into the website gave a wonderful, healthy return.

Wrexham & Shropshire was a child of the Internet age, and depended on computers for the growth it achieved. Whilst 'Sales' were generating interest in the service, Richard Harper was behind the scenes, manipulating the computer system to manage the yield. This was a vital part of the operation - and the one sure argument for carefully placed reduced fares to stimulate travel, without diluting the revenue from potentially more lucrative markets. In 2008, shoe leather was no longer enough. The one serious disappointment in pure sales performance was our total inability to generate any worthwhile response from Tame Bridge and the surrounding area. My goodness how we tried - but voices of appeal there vanished as into an anechoic chamber. Some success in this area may have provided the impulse needed to bridge the gap in performance to sustain the risk that the service would 'come good'. Alas the response was flat, and remained so.

One things is however perfectly clear. It was the staff that made this service unprecedented. From top to bottom, the quality of service from the staff was quite beyond compare. They really worked hard to try to make Wrexham & Shropshire successful. This wasn't just the catering staff, though their unfailing politeness, their willingness to soldier on under extreme adverse conditions, was exemplary, it was the operating staff as well Helpful and co-operative drivers, with bright ideas, loyal and skilled Train Managers, who looked after customers and brought home the revenue; all of their performances were remarkable. It didn't end there; from the Managing Director, through to the Chairman and the Board, all were willing to roll up their sleeves and appear on the train, or at a sales venue, ready to help. This service deserved to succeed. That in the end it did not, just goes to show that you cannot win them all!

Thomas Ableman

Thomas Ableman was quite different to those that had gone before in Wrexham & Shropshire. He was an example of one of the industry's bright young men. He came to the job full of fresh energy, and considered his strategy most carefully, determined to think and act logically, quite outside the influence of what had gone before. He came to Wrexham & Shropshire from National Express, and upon the demise of WSMR he set about Chiltern Railways. The experience was telling, as playing such energies on the ailing service eventually went on to show that even when stolidity was supplemented by innovation, the assets would best be employed elsewhere.

Two things struck me immediately on arrival at Wrexham & Shropshire. The first was the extraordinary commitment and dedication of everyone in the company to making it work. The second was that they were selling a product that did not match what people wished to buy.

The key customer "buying points" for travel are journey time and price, with most purchase decisions driven largely by a balance between these two competing demands. Wrexham & Shropshire was selling a service that was slow and expensive. For customers willing to book in advance, it was often both slower and more expensive than its main competitors.

The problem was that it viewed its key selling points as being a direct train service, and the on-board cooking. Unfortunately, these are secondary considerations for the majority of passengers, with journey time and price being the key drivers of decision making.

I subsequently realised that part of the problem was a disparity between the business that had been planned, and the business that actually existed. They had ended up with the pricing structure and cost base of a premium intercity style service, but slow trains and infrequent journeys. The marketing was designed around a business audience, with peak pricing to match, but business travellers were never going to spend that much money on a train service that took so long.

My brief on arrival was very simple. Increase revenue and do it quickly!

I spent the first month meeting a lot of people and asking a lot of questions. I then wrote a strategy paper to the Board which proposed a series of fundamental changes. The key points were moving the core of the proposition from directness to value, and changing the focus from business to leisure.

This meant redesigning the fares structure, branding and our marketing activity. I also suggested reducing the cost of catering, but this was a step too far.

Reducing prices gave us a huge opportunity to get build awareness. Instead of just cutting the fares, I decided to abolish the expensive peak fare (that no-one was buying anyway) and promote this as a move towards 'flat fares'. This took advantage of journalists' ignorance of the multiplicity of train companies to promote ourselves as the first train company to abolish complex peak and off peak pricing in favour of a move towards flat fares. Not realising that we only ran four trains per day, the media gave us massive coverage.

To accompany the pricing structure, we launched a 'buy on board' campaign. Why were we encouraging passengers to go to another operators' booking office, where we lost commission and risked them being sold another operator's ticket? Instead, we pushed hard to get people buying our tickets on our website (already going well, thanks to an elegant and simple booking engine already in place) or on our trains.

Instead of trying to gain market share of the business market, we focused on reasons to travel for the leisure market. We joined the Atoc 2- for -1 scheme and used this extensively as way of highlighting value. Building on the lower fares, we relaunched the branding, so that instead of looking expensive and formal, we were colourful and casual. Our marketing focused on reasons to travel to London, with simple messages around the destination and not the journey.

Peter Holt, Thomas Ableman, and Lee Lewis posing before the newly introduced rolling stock at Marylebone Station. Alas the much heralded refitted Mk3s were delivered too late to make the impact so needed earlier; the service was unfortunately terminated soon afterwards, and the carriages moved to be used on the rapidly growing Chiltern Mainline service between Birmingham (Moor St) and (London Marylebone).

I got the sense that before I joined, the sales team had felt pressured by Board members to divert marketing effort to stations such as Tame Bridge Parkway, Banbury and Cosford that had almost no chance of success. As a result, the budget was dispersed over such a wide area that none of it could have much effect. Moreover, the marketing effort was largely tactical, with the result that the whole was less than the sum of its parts.

Early on, I put together a very clear marketing strategy that limited our focus to some very clearly defined geographic and business segments. I was glad to be allowed to do this. The result was that the budget we had available could be used to its full effect.

When I arrived, most of the marketing was being done by a constellation of people that didn't live on the patch and were not professional marketers.[1] This meant it was not consistent and not always well targeted, so we hired an excellent local marketing executive who had previously worked for the Shropshire Star and Massey tractors! Jo Seabright went on to make a huge contribution to professionalising our marketing and communication.

1 Those who are interested may see the difference between the 'constellation' and the 'professional' marketer's achievements by looking at the facts of the performance rather than relying on the purple prose; it is enlightening. Chapter 10 gives the game away, and suggests that this gift horse repays careful mouth examination.

Part of the problem, I think, was the business had been modelled heavily on Hull Trains. In noting the similarities, not enough attention was paid to the differences. Hull Trains (and later Grand Central) were able to launch in a position where they quickly became the fastest option to London from the main markets served. They were therefore the default market leader, with the incumbent reduced to challenger. They also ran into the same London terminal as the incumbent, and so were able to communicate directly to their competitors' customer base. None of these were true for Wrexham & Shropshire, making the proposition required completely different. Despite this, Wrexham & Shropshire had launched with a high cost base and a flawed focus on the business traveller.

Within two months we had reduced the train service (so reducing the cost base), launched the new pricing structure, replaced the marketing agencies, launched the new branding, implemented the new marketing strategy both in terms of targeting and messaging and were now engaged in fighting Virgin Trains through the pages of almost every national newspaper. Our campaign against Virgin subsequently went onto win the UK PR industry's leading award – normally won by vast international brands!

As the trains grew busier, we never really moved back to the business market. The problem was that the key differentiator for WSMR had been meant to be that we offered direct trains. However, in the only significant business market we served, people already believed they had direct trains. True, they didn't run from Telford station, but the established route to London from Telford was to drive to Stafford and get a non-stop Virgin train taking 1hr 17 mins and running twice an hour. A train service four times a day and taking three hours was never going to compete.

However, the leisure market still wasn't easy. The problem with Shropshire as a market was that the kind of people that chose to live in Shropshire tended to be the kind of people that didn't want to go to London. I remember once, at an event in Shrewsbury town square, trying to sell WSMR travel to a passerby. He said "Oh no, I've done all my travelling in my younger days. I went to Birmingham in 1981 and Bristol in 1984, so that's me done." It's an extreme example, but it did reflect a wider problem for someone selling travel. When friends in London asked why I was making such heavy weather of trying to make this railway profitable, I pointed out that The Archers is set in Shropshire. When, I asked, was the last time you heard a storyline in which someone had a need to visit London?

Having said that, we did have some successes. There is nowhere like an open access operator for enthusiasm. We took advantage of this by running marketing events in shopping centres along the route at weekends. Instead of staffing these with hired promotional staff (as would be the case for most companies), we staffed them with volunteer guards, drivers and catering stewards. None were paid for their time, but came because they wanted to see the service succeed.

On one memorable day, Shrewsbury Town football club got into the play-offs at Wembley. We ran the equivalent of our entire week's loadings to London in a two hour window! It was an amazing team effort. I was due to be in Oxford that day, having a much belated graduation. I missed it to take part in the Wembley specials. I don't think I even mentioned to anyone where I was meant to be. That was the incredible thing about WSMR: you didn't mind making sacrifices, because everyone was pulling together to try to make it work.

The combination of more appropriate marketing, cheaper fares and a lot of effort was successful – but not successful enough. I was solely at Wrexham & Shropshire for just nine months. In September 2009, Adrian asked me to apply for the Commercial Director's role at Chiltern. It was an invitation that came with a strong hint that I had no choice but to obey, despite my protestations that I was enjoying the task at Wrexham & Shropshire. In that nine month period we increased passenger numbers by 90% and revenue by 30% - despite a 20% reduction in service to Shropshire and a 40% reduction in service to Wrexham.

I remember writing endless business plans, and we always sold the story that stops at Wolverhampton would save it. I'm not sure that's true. The fundamental problem for WSMR was the market it served was too small and didn't want to go to London, except for a minority of business travellers who had much better alternatives. We built up a loyal following of regulars who adored the service, and we continued to pour new leisure travellers into the pot. However, a leisure traveller from Shropshire to London is the kind of person who might not go again for a decade. You can't build a business on that.

I was very fortunate (and grateful) to be given a huge amount of freedom to make the necessary changes. I have never worked anywhere with the ability to make things happen and get things done so quickly. It was a privilege to work somewhere with such energy and enthusiasm, and I very much doubt I'll have such an experience again. The staff were awe-inspiring, and there is no doubt that it was their passionate devotion to their passengers that made the company loved by its regulars.

In many ways, the thing that made Wrexham & Shropshire great was also the thing that killed it. There was so much energy and enthusiasm and desire to make it work that the wrong product was launched as opposed to launching nothing or waiting until the right one became possible. However, that energy and excitement also gave me the most memorable nine months of my career to date.

Tony Allen

Tony Allen was the thirty-third accountant that Adrian Shooter interviewed when he was setting up Chiltern Railways in 1994. Tony was chosen because, as well as having all the technical skills that one would expect of a Finance Director, he had a passion for analysing sales figures and offering sage recommendations for action therefrom. This was to be vitally important for the growth of the business that was about to be created. He had previously worked for South African Breweries, and the makers of the world famous "Corby Trouser Press". It only later emerged that Tony had a deep and abiding interest in railways.

WSMR was set up in April 1998 by Laing Rail and Renaissance Trains and subsequently absorbed within the Deutsche Bahn passenger rail operations. It achieved record levels of customer satisfaction ratings through its excellent customer service and value for money ticketing. A satisfaction level of 96% was achieved immediately prior to its closure in January 2011.

The Business proposition was originally modelled on the successful Hull Trains open access operation, which was very profitable. Wrexham, Shrewsbury and Telford had no direct services to London. However, perhaps a warning sign may have been that their combined population levels were far smaller than Hull and its environs, and the journey time between London and Hull was also much shorter despite the longer distance.

Marylebone station is solely operated and used by Chiltern Railways. The operator of Chiltern franchise was extremely wary of the threat of another operator potentially extracting income from some of Chiltern's key revenue flows. Also Chiltern's PPM (punctuality targets) were challenging, and interaction with an open access operator could potentially have threatened Chiltern's operational flexibility. A decision was taken reluctantly to become involved in the joint venture rather than to see the proposal develop into an independent threat.

All new Business start-ups inevitably incur initial losses. Budgeting for a break even position by end of year two in hindsight was a mistake. It raised misguided expectations from the new owner DB, especially when large losses were incurred with revenue numbers/passenger numbers failing to live up to forecast. The economic environment was also unhelpful. The cost base was far too high, with only 65% of cost being covered by revenue. The oil price remained inflated, and diesel costs consequently were greater than originally anticipated. The services were operated by 6 class 67 locomotives and 20 Mk 3 coaches. The full operating lease cost were far higher than alternatively using one the 100mph Class 170 Turbostars (used by Hull trains). Unfortunately no Turbostars were available to operate the service.

The brutal conclusions reached were that the commercial proposition was flawed. The journey time was far too long and not competitive. Fares were too cheap with an over-dependence on leisure travellers, with too many ineffective giveaway promotions. It's easy to achieve high level of customers satisfaction with so few passengers travelling per train. Only five services in each direction ran per day (latterly reduced to three) with many trains virtually empty, operating largely outside peak travel times. The Regulator allows the National franchise operators to run services which protects them from any open access competition, thus WSMR was unable to call at lucrative stations such as Birmingham and Coventry en route, with the absurd example of being able to set down at Wolverhampton (unpaid) but not allowed to pick up passengers at the station. Competitive operators received preferential treatment on rail paths from Network Rail. They also received subsidy from Central Government, along with cherry picked routes and stopping patterns. The open access operator has no safety net, and therefore is forced to compete without there being a level playing field.

Deutsche Bahn invested over £13 million funding trading losses and the jobs of 55 staff. The business incurred losses of £2.8 million in its final year. Sadly a service that was beloved by its passengers for its very high standards of customer service, financially ran into the "buffers".

WSMR Managing Director Andy Hamilton, with Driver Peter Griffin, shows off the interior of a refurbished First Class Mk. 3 coach at Marylebone station prior to its first run in public service, Wednesday 30th September 2009. **Geoff Plumb**

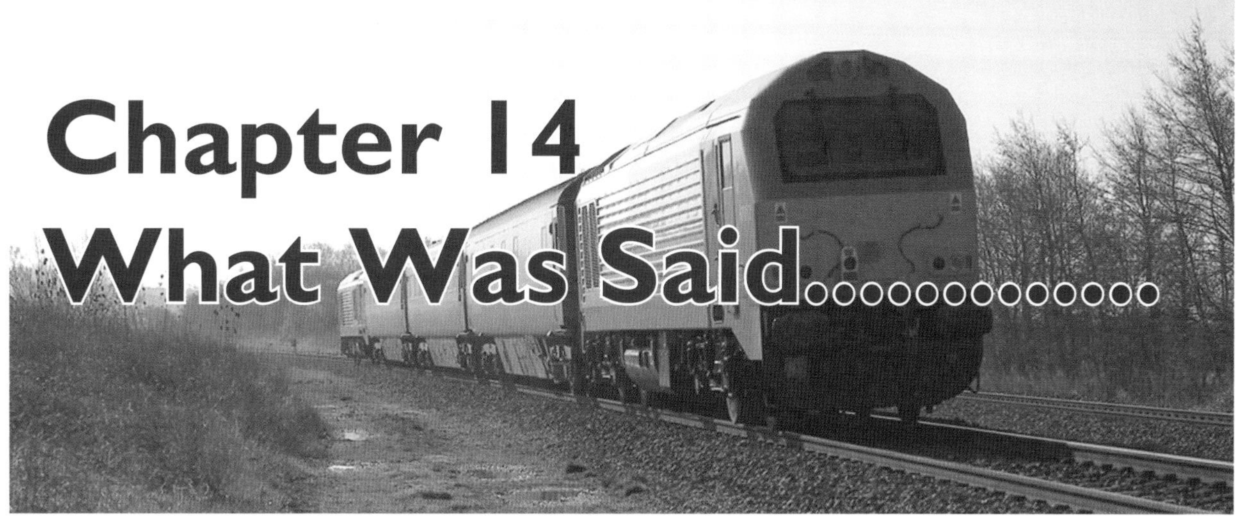

Chapter 14 What Was Said..............

When Wrexham & Shropshire closed, there was a fair bit of comment that invites close inspection. Here's a chance therefore to review what the Daily Mail wrote. The piece was entitled:

You can get off at Wolverhampton but you can't get on: How crazy rules killed Britain's last great railway.

It appeared on 29th January 2011. The text is shown on the left in red, review comment on the right in black.

Close your eyes and imagine yourself on the perfect railway journey of your dreams. It is lunchtime and we are travelling through some of England's loveliest countryside in a commodious carriage where the armchairs are soft and the wide windows offer gorgeous views – in this case over the 'blue remembered hills' of A. E. Housman's Shropshire. There is proper cutlery on the neatly-set table, and at your elbow is a smart, liveried steward offering a menu for the freshly cooked food from the train's kitchen.

Final whistle, the Wrexham & Shropshire service between London and north Wales is no more. Lamb in red wine and rosemary sauce with a decent glass of Chilean Merlot. A fantasy? Well it wasn't until last Friday night when the very last train run by the Wrexham & Shropshire Railway from London Marylebone pulled into Wrexham station at 22.36, bringing to an end not just the services of Britain's best loved railway company, but an era of gracious rail travel extending back almost 150 years.

The elegant offering of the W&S was a world away from the overcrowding, rude staff, dirty toilets, cramped seats, microwaved burgers, plastic cups and lack of information that too often defines the modern railway.

Here was a chance to review and make a critique of an article written on something you know about. It matters, what the press says, and it's important if it falls short. Here is a well informed journalist making a national comment. Of course the article is written in the style of the publication - but how does it actually measure? Perhaps this article was supposed to be 'friendly' - but is it? This response is picky and hard-hitting - but accurate.

Think seriously - are we really travelling through England's 'lovliest countryside' - isn't this pushing it a bit, bearing in mind the delights of Exeter to Newton Abbot, the grandeur of Leeds to Carlisle, the smooth rise of Carnforth to Carlisle, the calm of the Thames Valley? Well, OK, there's some establishing going on - stop being a detail freak. But hang on - here's A E Housman, who wrote his 'blue remembered hills' before ever visiting Shropshire, and it took rather a long time (from 1896 until the Great War) for the collection to become popular. Is this a bit of 'pseudery' here, or is it masterful allusion to Wrexham & Shropshire having to stay longer before doing more?

Is the proper cutlery not there on Virgin I wonder, or is the smart steward absent - probably because most are ladies? Not quite fresh food - but nearly - it's true. But did the 'era' that closed stretch back 150 years? It's a bit pushed and it is hardly the real story. I am not sure it was Britain's best loved railway company, though it was top in its offer of customer service - but with serious limitations. If these factors has been so deeply significant - why did it close?

I've had a few tiddles on the train in my time and I wouldn't strike the railways down as a generalisation for having malodorous toilets. I may have a go at many pubs,

Even though it took more than four hours to trundle from London along secondary lines to its destination in North Wales, it inspired a fanatical band of followers who loved it because it seemed to encapsulate a lost golden age.

Here were spacious carriages with generous legroom and seats that lined up with the window. The staff were welcoming and kept passengers informed of delays.

The fares were cheap. It was possible to hop on the train without a ticket and not to be made to feel like a criminal for doing so. In fact, climbing aboard a W&S service was like being made to feel a member of an exclusive club.

It was fitting that the announcement of its demise came on the same day that W&S topped the National Passenger Survey with a 96 per cent approval rating.

So how come a train service defined by the public and critics as the best in the land ended up being shunted into the buffers?

It might be easy to write it off as a casualty of the recession – after all, Wrexham is hardly the commercial powerhouse of Britain and the company had run up losses of £13 million, according to its chairman Adrian Shooter.

But the truth is more wretched. The Wrexham & Shropshire, founded three years ago to bring back mainline services to an area which hadn't had regular London trains since the Sixties, fell foul of the Alice In Wonderland rules that govern Britain's privatised railways in which enterprise is stifled and quality too often goes down the rabbit hole.

When John Major privatised the old British Rail in 1994, he hinted at a romantic vision of a new era of competition, recalling the days when the old LNER and LMS raced each other to the North with ever higher speeds and ever more glamorous trains such as the *Coronation* and the *Coronation Scot.*

That's certainly how most of us hoped it would turn out. Instead, we appear to have been conned.

Our great railway system, where once upon a time hundreds of colourful train companies vied with each other to attract business, has been carved up – with the connivance of successive Governments – by a small number of big corporate players who bid vast sums of money for monopoly franchises and receive lavish guarantees from the taxpayer.

For these big conglomerates, such as Virgin, First Group, Stagecoach and National Express, it's a win-win situation. If they fall short on their business plans, the Government bails them out.

And if they fail completely, as National Express East Coast line from London to Edinburgh did in 2009, they can walk away from the worst of the losses and the taxpayer most motorway service stations, many of the dwindling stock of municipal toilets - but not particularly on trains. Overcrowding is more of a problem - especially at peak times - but so are roads, airports, the streets, buses - why do the railways cop it so? And if they were running empty trains at busy times - wouldn't this be an area for criticism? Yes, I agree with cramped seats - the same as on Ryanair, East Jet, five-up in a car, on buses, especially at that insane period when we all submit to the tyranny of going to the office at the same time. We all allow this foolishness - why isn't he having a go at that? And rude staff - I don't find them especially rude. The passengers are: barging each other, muttering imprecations (as if it is the staffs' fault), passengers being selfish with bags on seats, and shouting down mobile phones. No criticism at all there for the users? In fact I think the modern railway's actually doing quite well - the general public think so too, with volume increasing over the last ten years by up to five percent per year. Isn't this rather better than the Daily Mail, whose sales appear to be in decline? So the railways for all of these accusations are hardly unpopular.

And why 'shunted into the buffers' - funny that? If you shunt into most self-respecting buffers, you bounce back. The rusty tracks or grassy sidings are the ones that generally trains don't come back from. Perhaps I am being too precious - but no I'm not. A person of the immense intelligence of the author of this piece must surely know that Moderation of Competition (whilst irksome) is hardly 'Alice in Wonderland Rules'. The ironic thing is that the introduction of Virgin's Pendolinos on the West Coast Main Line is exactly the enterprise that was hoped for with privatisation - so what is he thinking of? Enterprise has hardly been stifled, and when John Major privatised the railway it wasn't for romance - it was political, and for cash. The romantic vision of the old companies is piffle. They raced each other to the north with elite streamlined trains that each ran about twice per day. After privatisation service frequency to Manchester is every twenty minutes, and York isn't far behind - there's a train from England to Glasgow on the West Coast about every half-hour. It rather leaves the 'our great railway system' image of the past in the shade. And if you're worried about the connivance of successive governments, then remember that it was the lower middle class Tory voters, readers of the Mail that elected Major to do his 'dirty deeds' - so can this writing survive rational inquiry?

The bill the taxpayer is picking up is largely that of deferred maintenance. But this may be a bill worth paying, as the rise in traffic, in frequency, has almost certainly swung away the civil servants from the last gasp of the old 'roads' policy, and into rail. The deal the Department of Transport picks up the bill.

There's no such cushion for aspiring new operators, such as Wrexham & Shropshire, who get no subsidy, can pick up only the crumbs under the Government's so called 'open access' rules by offering services the main firms don't want and are under often ludicrously restrictive conditions.

The W&S trains passed through Coventry and Birmingham but were forbidden to stop there to protect the commercial interests of Virgin, which holds the franchise for most long-distance services on the route.

Under this crazy system, when I travelled on the W&S I was permitted to get off the train at Wolverhampton but not to get back on again, even though it stopped there.

To reach Birmingham I was forced to alight at a bleak Black Country station, Tame Bridge Parkway, where I had a freezing wait for a service into the city.

What kind of competition is that? It's no wonder the railway's managers – and some passengers – eventually gave up the ghost. One of the staff told me: 'Level playing field? It's like Wrexham playing Arsenal and then being told to take their best players off.'

Worth a visit: Travellers on the line could have spent time in Shrewsbury where these Tudor buildings are on the High Street

But before we shed too many tears for the W&S it should be said that, far from being a plucky little David fighting the corporate Goliaths, it, too, became a subsidiary of a giant multinational – German national railway company DB.

Another 'open access' company, Hull Trains, was gobbled up by First Group, which has franchises in Scotland, the Home Counties and the West of England. But both made a brave try.

The real losers are passengers caught in a pincer between soaring fares and ever declining levels of service.

It is a shocking fact that nearly 20 years after privatisation only two stations in Britain – York and Doncaster – offer significant competitive services to London.

These are provided by the last remaining independent 'open access' operator Grand Central. It is hardly surprising that it was voted Britain's second most popular service in last week's Passenger Focus survey.

The firm's Rupert Brennan-Brown said: 'The trouble with the big train companies is that they're only interested in the low-hanging fruit. We can think local, and our trains go to places like Pontefract and Sunderland where the big boys can't be bothered to reach.'

But don't hold your breath. Transport Secretary Philip Hammond has made it clear no new small operators will be allowed to enter the new round of franchise negotiations.

As a sad postscript, the final Wrexham train marked a significant loss of opportunity to dine well on a British train.

has tried to do is to charge enough to curb excessive profits for the private shareholders (but keep them interested), and to pour enough dosh into the Treasury coffers to keep the whole thing going. East Coast is now State run - and it's not doing badly! The net surplus generated by TOCs going to government was around £1.7bn in 2011-12, with the subsidy - the taxpayer bill - falling in real terms from £1.4bn to £81m. Never let the truth stand in the way of a good tub-thump, eh?

The nub of the matter, anti-open access prejudice, plainly isn't going to get out of the 'Janet and John' stage in this article; it looks like just another railway bashing piece from the popular press. The WSMR 'no subsidy' has registered, but the restrictive conditions are hardly 'ludicrous'. This wasn't a laughable lack of efficiency, it was more akin to a deliberate attempt to prevent an open access operator from threatening neatly laid plans. If true that's much more serious, and you may have hoped that a big player like the Mail could have got behind the arguments and delivered some insight, instead of cheap, popular jibes. Sorry if you are disappointed but is it simply lack of skill, or is it malign - don't know?

We've to be less sympathetic to Wrexham & Shropshire as it passed to the giant multinational Deutsche Bahn, the German Railway? Yet Daily Mail is hardly owned by a 'local' newspaper group, and in times past German Railways have been hailed as the acme of train operators. First Hull Trains came about after they had looked for and chosen partners to help them to survive against 'the big boys' on the East Coast. And the passengers are voting with their feet, they are flocking at up to 5% per year to travel on these trains with 'soaring fares and declining levels of service' - the comments made cannot be true?

Is the shocking fact that a major newspaper player, either doesn't know or chooses to ignore that, competition or not, rail passenger user figures are the highest now since the golden years of railways before the Great War - 'caught in a pincer' indeed!. And as for York and Doncaster being the only two stations to offer significant competitive services to London, this is hardly borne out by the facts. Even with Moderation of Competition Birmingham has three operators offering service to London. And it's hardly a monopoly, is it, if customers can choose their cars, the bus, the plane or any other mode that is not rail, to go to London?

Of course Rupert Brennan-Brown said that big TOCs are interested in the lucrative passenger flows - their survival depends upon that. The bits this article fails to spotlight is how something 'not in accordance with the

Big draw: the Iron Bridge in Ironbridge, Shropshire, was in easy reach for visitors who took the train

The first restaurant car ran between Leeds and London in 1879. When BR reached the end of the line, there were 279 such services across the land. With the demise of the W&S just a handful of restaurant cars remain, despite overwhelming evidence that passengers want good food well served.

How nice it would be to summon a steward to bring a glass to toast the brief life of an enterprising little railway and the hope that other minnows will emerge. Sadly, it seems increasingly unlikely.

approved doctrine' was systematically discriminated against, despite no risk to the taxpayer. Something that had the chance of doing some good was throttled, because it didn't 'conform'. We have all lost because of that. The overwhelming evidence (not offered) that train passengers want good food is frippery in comparison. How nice it would be to think that someone intelligent writing for a major daily would be able to get his facts right; to tackle the real scandal instead of a series of oft stated factoids. Other minnows will not emerge; the barriers to entry have been buttressed. This article has done nothing to give hope to anyone. I think we jut got a message from the Titanic about how ice-free the ocean is at this time of year?

Wrexham & Shropshire Mk. 3 trains are 'best in the world' says Palin (and he should know!)

IT WAS A REAL PLEASURE to spend a short time in the company of former Monty Python team member and travel writer Michael Palin at a recent function in London. A genuine and instantly likeable man, he was visiting Marylebone station to formally launch Wrexham & Shropshire's much delayed refurbished coaching stock. Palin has used the service on several occasions to visit friends in Shrewsbury, where he spent a period of his schooling. During the event he was complimentary about the upgraded Mk. 3s telling the assembled media at the photocall that these loco-hauled trains were "the best in the world". When questioned afterwards, he said he was being brutally honest. The Python star's opinion is entirely valid, explaining to your editor that he travels extensively by rail and found the Mk. 3 to be an "absolute delight" to travel aboard.

It is no surprise to find him so informed, having revealed his railway interest and trainspotting background during his first travel documentary, part of the 1980 BBC *Great Railway Journeys of the World* series. In that programme, he travelled from London to Kyle of Lochalsh via a convoluted route, also describing spotting around Sheffield as a kid before returning home, struggling, with a large enamel station sign. It was a big break, leading eventually to *Around The World in 80 Days* and numerous other highly-popular travelogues.

A number of MPs from all parties also attended the launch including Liberal Democrat Lembit Öpik who availed himself of a copy of RAIL EXPRESS and was far too knowledgeable about the rolling stock to be merely well informed... count yourself outed, Lembit! ■

WORKING OF THE YEAR? With Eurostar having disposed of its Class 37 & Class 73 locos, it was left to Eurotunnel MaK locos Nos. 0002 & 0003 (cleared for HS1 running) to drag this failed Class 373 into St Pancras on December 18th. We suspect the company is rather regretting that decision and may look at hiring Class 92s for rescue cover in the future. Ryan Tranmer

Self-confessed railway enthusiast Michael Palin formally launched WSMR's refurbished Mk. 3 rolling stock at Marylebone station on January 19th. He is seen here cutting the ribbon before being caught flicking through the latest issue of 'Camel Spotting Monthly'! He agreed to support our campaign for more 'real' trains and will no doubt be delighted to hear about Chiltern's plans, revealed elsewhere in this issue. Philip Sutton

Settle down for some fun with our 'seen and heard' column.

Send in your letters, cuttings and any other items you think are of interest or amusing.

There's no business like snow business

The recent cold weather led to several nice stories not least of which was on the East Lancs Railway where a free diesel unit shuttle was operated between Bury and Ramsbottom in an effort to get people between work and home after the local bus service was suspended and the roads blocked. The railway even used its resident miniature snowplough-fitted Class 37/4 to clear the line in advance. It seems strange that DB Schenker struggles to fulfil a similar roll in Scotland when this Type 3 cast-off is clearly up to the job!

It was more scary on the Settle & Carlisle line. With the route blanketed in snow, Network Rail imposed a 20mph speed restriction through Rise Hill and Blea Moor tunnels when it discovered massive icicles weighing several tonnes hanging from the ventilation shafts.

It was steam to the rescue in Kent when 'The Cathedrals Express' ran two trips from Victoria to Dover and back on December 21st. On the second run, the train, hauled by 60163 *Tornado*, was used to pick up 100 commuters who had been left stranded, dropping them off at stations en-route. Great copy for the London papers!

Michael Palin liked Wrexham & Shropshire, and was enthusiastic about the Mk3, refitted coaches. Being one of the nicest personalities around, he travelled and broadcast his charm to the good of Wrexham & Shropshire. He was reported on by Rail Express, a particularly thoughtful and popular magazine for 'the interested'. This is their report of the day.

Courtesy Rail Express Magazine

67013 **Dyfrbont Pontcysyllte** *with the 11:27 train from Wrexham to Marylebone, near Haddenham on 22nd December 2009. The first refurbished carriages came into service in September, and Michael Palin's launch of the new trains was in January 2010.* **Geoff Plumb**

Threats, and 'politics'

To add to all the other worries, it seemed that Virgin Trains may be contemplating some action to buttress its future plans for the West Coast Franchise. It was thought that vigorous defensive action was needed to head this threat off, and so this was summarised succinctly by Thomas Ableman, and you may understand from this fascinating paper how the matter was seen and dealt with.

Virgin Campaign

Background

Wrexham & Shropshire commenced operation in April 2008, providing services between Wrexham, Shrewsbury, Telford and London Marylebone.

Wrexham & Shropshire was successful in receiving regulatory approval, as it was designed to provide new connections. None of the locations served had direct services to London, with passengers forced to take a local train to an interchange station and use the West Coast mainline to reach London Euston.

The rights to operate the West Coast franchise had been granted to the Virgin Rail Group in 1996, operating under the brand name Virgin Trains.

Virgin briefly restored a direct train service to Shrewsbury but withdrew it in 2004. Virgin has never operated services to Wrexham.

Virgin proposal

In December 2008, Virgin launched a daily service from Wrexham to London. This service is operated via an existing North Wales coast service that now splits at Chester. This service was widely perceived as a 'spoiler' designed to undermine the Wrexham & Shropshire business plan. In this, it was partially successful. In combination with a significant increase in the frequency of Virgin's service to Chester, the impact of this service was approximately £125k per year, with the result that the December 2008 timetable improvements did not deliver the expected revenue uplift for Wrexham & Shropshire.

In February 2009, Virgin announced their intention to operate a much more intensive service providing direct connections to every location served by Wrexham & Shropshire.

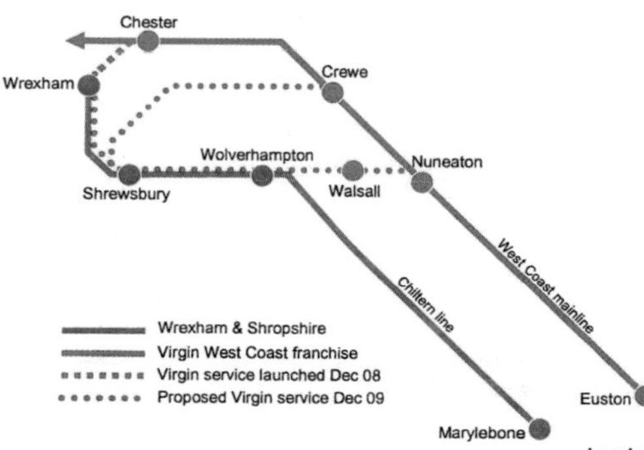

In March 2009, they issued a proposed timetable for the new service. This provided for two trains per day (Monday – Saturday) from London to Shrewsbury via Nuneaton and Wolverhampton. One of these extended to Chester via Wrexham, the other to Crewe. In addition, an extra service to Wrexham via Chester was to be provided. As a result, Wrexham would have a total of three Virgin trains per day to London. On Sundays, the existing train to Wrexham via Chester would be supplemented by a train to Crewe via Nuneaton, Wolverhampton and Shrewsbury.

Potential impact

This scale of service would have had a devastating impact on the Wrexham & Shropshire business plan. Given that there was no reasonable possibility of the Virgin service being profitable, it was clear that this service was intended to put Wrexham & Shropshire out of business. As a result, highly predatory pricing activity could have been expected.

Virgin would also have significant competitive advantages due to the nature of their franchise:

- The trains to be used were specified in the franchise agreement and indirectly paid for using public subsidy
- Virgin would have been able to pick up and set down in the West Midlands
- Virgin's overheads are covered by the rest of the franchise, so the trains would only have had to operate at marginal cost

If the Virgin service had launched, the Wrexham & Shropshire business would have become unviable.

Response

Our response was a two-pronged approach. Our first objective was to prevent an application being made to the Office of Rail Regulation (ORR). Our second objective was to prevent ORR granting regulatory approval.

Objective One:

We identified two potential ways to prevent Virgin making an application to the ORR. The first was to generate political pressure within the Department for Transport (DfT), and specifically from the Rail Minister, Lord Adonis. The second was to generate sufficient media coverage that Virgin risked damage to their brand.

Objective Two:

Key to preventing the ORR granting regulatory approval was to generate large volume of letters to the ORR from local stakeholders and customers. ORR have to take into account the public interest in reaching their decision, therefore we wished to ensure that the volume and nature of letters received made it impossible to reasonably argue that this service could be in the public interest.

In practice, it was not necessary to complete all activity for objective two as Virgin withdrew their proposal through activity in objective one.

Activity

As a result of these objectives, the following activities took place:

Stakeholder lobbying:

The local MPs on our line of route were identified as the best route to achieve both objectives. They would be able to assist mobilise letters to the ORR, but would also enable us to target Lord Adonis.

Initial meetings were held by Thomas Ableman, Marketing Director, with all local MPs. At these meetings, the situation was outlined and the consequences for Wrexham & Shropshire explained.

As a result, the following local MPs agreed to support our case:

- Owen Paterson MP, North Shropshire (Conservative)
- Ian Lucas MP, Wrexham (Labour)
- Daniel Kawczynski MP, Shrewsbury and Atcham (Conservative)
- Lembit Opik MP, Montgomeryshire (Liberal Democrat)
- Philip Dunne MP, Ludlow (Conservative)
- David Wright MP, Telford (Labour)

Of these, Owen Paterson MP and Ian Lucas MP were identified as core supporters.

Only one MP, Mark Pritchard, The Wrekin (Conservative), did not support us, arguing that he was in favour of all train operators and would not take sides.

Owen Paterson MP agreed to request a meeting with Lord Adonis for us to make our case.

This meeting took place on 30th March 2009. It was attended by a delegation including all the MPs that had agreed to support us (with the exception of Daniel Kawczynski who was in Africa on select committee business), Andy Hamilton, Managing Director, and Thomas Ableman, Marketing Director.

At a pre-meeting attended by the MPs, we agreed objectives and a common line for the meeting.

Ian Lucas had an informal preliminary conversation with Lord Adonis in which the Minister made clear that his response would be that he had no locus over decisions made by franchised businesses.

The key objective was to persuade the Minister that, regardless of the statutory position, by virtue of the DfT's dominance of the rail industry, he had the power to prevent this service launching by placing internal pressure on Virgin. It was agreed that we were not seeking a public statement from the Minister, but that we were seeking for him to stop the service launching behind the scenes.

The agreed line was as follows:

- We welcome competition, but it has to be fair competition.
- The presence of the Moderation of Competition clause in Virgin's franchise agreement mean this is not possible
- As a result, competition should not be permitted until 2012 when competition should be fair

As a subsidiary point:

- The trains Virgin intend to use for this service are franchise assets that have been paid for using public subsidy
- These trains should not be used for an open access style service

The MPs were to emphasise that the fact Virgin received taxpayer subsidy meant it must be a political issue the Minister needs to take responsibility for; we were to emphasise that DfT exercises considerable informal power beyond that outlined in the Railways Act. All of us were to emphasise the degree of local support for Wrexham & Shropshire.

The meeting was highly successful with Lord Adonis appearing convinced by our arguments, though offering no formal guarantees.

This meeting received considerable coverage in the local press, and helped build local awareness of the threat to our business.

MPs unite in call over rail service fears

By John Hipwood

Tory, Labour and Liberal Democrat MPs have made a united demand to the Government's public transport minister for a "fair run" for the new direct train service between Shropshire and London.

MPs and bosses of the Wrexham, Shropshire and Marylebone Railway (WSMR) met Lord Adonis in Whitehall yesterday to ask him to intervene and prevent Virgin Trains from operating a rival "spoiler" service.

The MPs told the minister that Wrexham & Shropshire had made an "excellent start" in running its direct service to London.

Rival

But they said they were concerned about a rival Virgin service, which they believed had been proposed to kill off the WSMR.

North Shropshire MP Owen Paterson said: "We had a most constructive meeting. It was striking how all the local MPs agreed. Our position is that we are all in favour of competition.

"However, it would not be right for Virgin to go ahead with a rival operation backed by £162 million of public subsidy while Virgin's franchise contracts exclude Wrexham & Shropshire from competing equally with them.

"Wrexham and Shropshire do not currently have free access to Wolverhampton and Birmingham International stations," said the Conservative MP.

The MPs proposed that the Wrexham & Shropshire service should be given time to bed in. "By 2012, the competition restrictions in Virgin's franchise will have expired, and track upgrades will have improved journey times allowing Wrexham & Shropshire to reach London in just two hours 30 minutes from Shrewsbury.

"We argue that Virgin should not be permitted to operate a spoiler service until these circumstances, allowing fair competition, are in place," said Mr Paterson, who added that he now proposes arranging a meeting with Chris Bolt, chairman of the Office of Rail Regulation.

Also at yesterday's meeting were MPs Philip Dunne (Conservative, Ludlow), David Wright (Labour, Telford), Lembit Opik (Liberal Democrat, Montgomeryshire) and Ian Lucas (Labour, Wrexham) with Wrexham & Shropshire managing director Andy Hamilton and marketing director Thomas Ableman.

WSMR managing director Andy Hamilton, Lembit Opik, Owen Paterson, David Wright and WSMR marketing director Thomas Ableman

National media:

The timing of the Virgin proposal coincided with the launch of our new flat fares strategy. As part of the fares campaign, it was decided to brief Ben Webster of *The Times* about both the fares and the Virgin competition story. Ben Webster agreed to run the story, provided he had exclusivity of the Virgin element.

In order to provide a basis for the currency of the story (given that Virgin announced their proposal in February), Ben Webster requested that we write to the ORR. We worked with Owen Paterson MP on the text of a letter that was sent in his name.

On Tuesday 7 April, *The Times* ran a prominent story combining the letter from Owen Paterson and the fares launch.

THE TIMES Tuesday April 7 2009 19

News

Virgin didn't want these passengers, but now a rival is offering cheap fares, it's war

Ben Webster
Transport Correspondent

The train company that offers Britain's cheapest rail tickets is engaged in a battle with Virgin that threatens to force it out of business.

Wrexham & Shropshire, which runs trains between North Wales, the West Midlands and London, began operating a year ago after spotting a gap in the market for direct services.

Despite receiving no subsidy it charges £53 for a standard class anytime return ticket from Wrexham to London. A similar ticket bought from Virgin costs £201.

Now Virgin plans to run trains in direct competition with W&S despite having previously shown no interest in providing services to the key stations served by W&S.

Virgin, which receives £35 million a year in public subsidy, won the West Coast franchise 12 years ago. It withdrew its direct service to Shrewsbury in 2004, claiming that there was insufficient demand. Now, having observed the success of W&S, Virgin is planning to run trains from London to Shrewsbury and Wrexham.

It intends to apply to the Rail Regulator for permission to operate services that, in some cases, would depart within 45 minutes of a W&S train.

The rail industry is watching closely to see whether the regulator will step in to protect W&S from its larger rival. If it does, more small companies are likely to take on the regional monopolies enjoyed by the big companies.

W&S said that it would be likely to close down if it faced direct competition from Virgin. It believes that Virgin would attract a significant proportion of its passengers by offering cheap "advance" fares restricted to a single train. W&S only just covers its costs because it cannot pick up passengers at Wolverhampton and Birmingham International, where Virgin has exclusive rights under its franchise.

W&S is the only long-distance company to offer cheap flat fares on all its services. It is also the only company that allows passengers to pay on board at the same price. Virgin's cheap fares are available only if tickets are booked up to 12 weeks in advance, and are valid on only one train. Sir Richard Branson's company forces passengers who pay on board to buy the most expensive peak ticket, even if they are travelling off-peak.

Owen Paterson, the Conservative MP for Shropshire North, has asked the Rail Regulator to investigate what he believes is an attempt by Virgin to force a smaller operator out of business. He wrote: "We are very concerned that if Virgin succeeds in using the market dominance entrenched by its franchise to force out the competition, it will then withdraw the direct connections; our constituents will again be forced to use indirect Virgin services without any alternative."

A Virgin spokesman denied that it was trying to force W&S out of business. He said that the Virgin trains, due to start in December, would complement those of W&S. "We think it provides greater choice throughout the day for the people of Shropshire," he said.

Fair fares?

£53
Wrexham and Shropshire

£201
Virgin Trains

Wrexham & Shropshire says it will be forced out of business if the Virgin service goes ahead

Corruption case rail chief is found dead

David Brown

A senior rail executive who was under investigation for allegedly accepting bribes to award contracts was found dead with his wife in an apparent suicide pact.

Anthony Burgess, 45, was arrested as part of a corruption inquiry into claims that he had received gifts including a Porsche and Rolex watches. Mr Burgess was sacked from his £75,000-a-year job by Network Rail last year after an internal investigation into the allegations.

He was found dead beside his wife Marian, 51. They had apparently gassed themselves in a car at their home in Clavering, Essex, in January. Mrs Burgess, a part-time classroom assistant, was not suspected of any wrongdoing. The couple's teenage daughter is being cared for by relatives. A spokesman for the Essex Coroner said that the deaths were not being treated as suspicious. An inquest has been opened and adjourned.

Mr Burgess was corporate offices manager for Network Rail and responsible for overseeing contracts worth millions of pounds to equip, furnish and manage company offices.

A spokesman for Network Rail said: "Following an internal investigation, disciplinary action was taken against Mr Burgess, which resulted in his summary dismissal."

This was followed up the next day by a leading article:

Parallel Lines

Virgin Trains must not be allowed to behave like a predator to quash rivals

Britain's train companies have done much to suck the pleasure out of rail travel. Carriages are often standing-room-only crowded. Catering can be grim, if available at all. Fares for a trip across England can top a return flight to New York.

The calculation of fares is so mysteriously complex — varying on how far in advance tickets are bought; for what hour of travel; on board or online — that they seem to have been decided by a bingo caller barking out numbers at random.

So rail travellers were understandably delighted when Wrexham & Shropshire began to run direct trains between North Wales, the West Midlands and London for a cheap flat fare. Its standard-class anytime return from Wrexham to London costs £53. To buy a similar seat on Virgin, which won the West Coast franchise 12 years ago but withdrew its direct London-to-Shrewsbury service several years ago, costs £201. Virgin now plans to run trains in direct competition with W&S, some within 45 minutes of a W&S train.

The rail regulator should think twice before giving Virgin its blessing. It must clarify if, by doing so, it would genuinely be making life sweeter for travellers by boosting competition, or just giving Virgin a permit to use its muscle to cut fares for as long as it takes to bully W&S into bankruptcy and then to drop its direct services again.

In the meantime, Virgin might consider responding to the challenge from W&S not just by replicating its timetable, but by imitating some of its passenger-friendly innovations, such as offering flat fares, and also the ability to buy a ticket on board at the same price. If this encourages more people to catch a train, everyone will profit. That is the true spirit and reward of competition.

The Guardian, which had previously run two stories sold through the fares campaign, followed this up with a similar leading article:

In praise of... Wrexham and Shropshire trains

Why, all of a sudden, does everyone want to go to Wrexham? Or perhaps they want to leave. Either way, the town is caught between two battling train companies, each offering to carry the citizens of north-east Wales to London. The contest pits rail-borne David against Goliath. The upstart takes the form of Wrexham and Shropshire, which began running a new service to the capital last year via a roundabout route. The giant is played by Virgin Trains, which has recently begun running its own rather faster direct service to London. Wrexham, for all its charms, is not big enough for both. The suspicion is that Virgin has decided to kill off its impudent rival by running a spoiler service - a cause for alarm in the Welsh Marches, which has come to prize its quirky local train company. It runs without a subsidy - unlike Virgin - and is fighting back with cheap fares on sale at any time, and free kippers for breakfast in first class. A peak-time return ticket to London is £53, against £201 on Virgin. Now comes news that its big rival plans to target Shrewsbury too, which is another of the little company's stops, by reintroducing a London service that was cut several years ago. Meanwhile the Welsh firm is banned from picking up any Virgin passengers in Birmingham. The contest mirrors one under way on the east coast, where two small companies are challenging National Express. For now, this is good for travellers. But if Virgin wins, the new trains could stop, and Wrexham would end up back on a rusty siding.

We continued to brief this story aggressively to both local and national media, and gained further prominent coverage in all relevant local newspapers, *The Financial Times*, *The Observer* and *The Birmingham Post* (the local paper to Virgin Trains' head office).

Tiny rail group has Virgin in retreat

News analysis

Old-fashioned W&S has repelled one big competitor but others wait in the sidings, writes Jonathan Guthrie

Virgin 'spoiler service' threat to small rail rival

"We have this fantastic, reliable, old fashioned, friendly service and all this may go, it's tragic"

NEWS 19

Victory of the 'Shropshire thunderbolt'

Its staff are polite, serve afternoon tea and let you buy your ticket on the train – and now they've seen off competition from Virgin

Top left: *Financial Times*
Left: *Observer*
Above: *Birmingham Post*

Virgin Trains announced their decision to withdraw their proposal after *The Times, Guardian* and *Birmingham Post* stories had been published. *The Observer* and *Financial Times* stories had not yet appeared, however the stories had been sold in, so it is likely Virgin were aware that further hostile coverage was imminent.

We had also interested the BBC in the story, and they had agreed to run it on *Today* (the key morning radio current affairs programme) if Virgin made a formal application to ORR. *Today* had previously run a story about us as part of the fares campaign.

<u>Local media:</u>

On Tuesday 7 April, our objections to the Virgin proposal were covered on the front page of the Shropshire Star. On the same day, Thomas Ableman met with Sarah Jane Smith, the Editor of the Shropshire Star (also responsible for 11 weekly papers) to outline our case in detail and request that the Shropshire Star run an openly partisan campaign in our favour against Virgin.

The purpose of this campaign was to stimulate letters to the ORR, and was intended to provide details of who to write to at the ORR and key messages.

This was agreed, and was intended to launch on Tuesday 14 April. In fact, it was not required as Virgin withdrew their proposal on Thursday 9 April, followed by a letter to *The Times* by Sir Richard Branson which cited the hostile media coverage as a reason.

Virgin Trains

Sir, Several claims have been made about Virgin Trains' plans to run a service between Shrewsbury and London (April 7, 8, 10). Wrexham & Shropshire is a "tiddler" but it is owned by the German state railway Deutsche Bahn. Virgin believes that this investment is part of DB's move into the UK rail industry.

The claim that W&S has the cheapest fares in Britain is wrong as Virgin Trains already offers lower fares on services between Wrexham and London, starting from £8. Virgin Trains planned to run faster trains than W&S at different times and to guarantee our service until the end of our franchise. However, we would not want to be accused of being anti-competitive, so we have decided to withdraw the additional services.

In return, I think that the people of Shrewsbury should now receive firm assurances from DB and W&S that they will continue to run this service for years to come.

SIR RICHARD BRANSON
London W6

Customers:

We also sought to make use of the loyalty of our existing customer base to stimulate letters to the ORR. Once the *Times* article went live, we activated a "Sign up to support us" feature on the front page of the website. This included a field for customers to enter their email address and we would contact them to outline how they could support us. The objective was to generate letters to the ORR. This was supported by collecting email addresses onboard (from customers that raised the Virgin issue with us).

To date, this has generated a database of over 200 customers willing to act on our behalf. It has also provided a library of supportive comments we will be using as marketing material (see Appendix attached).

In reality, we have not needed to use these customers to write to ORR on Virgin, though they will be redeployed for future use.

Conclusion

This has proved a highly successful campaign that is delivering all key objectives. It was closely related to the flat fares campaign, therefore also delivered significant commercial benefit as well as eliminating the Virgin threat.

Thomas Ableman
22 April 2009

Threats, and 'politics' - Summary

Wrexham & Shropshire ultimately failed, for reasons that have been well explained. Yet Virgin was strategically wise to guard against even a 'minnow' backed by the mighty strength of Deutsche Bahn. The paper gives a glimpse of how much activity was needed behind the scenes to try to support the enterprise, and how vulnerable rail is to competitive threats. It also shows that wise councils prevailed within Virgin. To be in a 'monopoly' position, backed by Moderation of Competition, however reasonable that was in terms of protecting a giant investment, still allows positioning as a money-grabbing bully-boy in the public eye. The aspirations for serving places like Shrewsbury became clear in the subsequent row about the West Coast Franchise, where Virgin wanted to run through trains from Shewsbury to London via Stafford, using the Oxley Chord.

The elephant in the room with all of this is the application of the Moderation of Competition conditions to Wrexham & Shropshire, as it was this restriction that hampered the service. This apparently tight shut door was said not in fact to be locked, (subsequent comment by senior civil servant after closure) and so it seems that the alternative approach of welcoming the Virgin competition in exchange for removal of the 'no pick-up' restrictions was not explored with the Minister.

Letters

There was a lot of correspondence about the closure of the service, almost all of it complimentary. It came in various different expressions, by e-mail and by personal letter. This one is included as an example as it was both articulate and typical in what it said. However, at this stage letters would achieve little, as the service had gone. It was rather too late for such sentiments.

Mr Adrian Shooter
Chairman
Wrexham and Shropshire
Banbury ICC
Merton Street
Banbury OX16 9RN

27th January 2011

RECEIVED
- 1 FEB 2011
CUSTOMER SERVICES

Dear Mr Shooter,

Closure of Wrexham and Shropshire Railway

I was shocked to hear on the BBC *Today* programme yesterday morning that Wrexham and Shropshire is to close down with immediate effect. For the past two years or so, I have been a weekly customer between Shrewsbury and Banbury/Marylebone.

Travelling with W&S has been an absolute joy in general and a refreshingly different experience than my experiences travelling with all other operators in the past. What was almost always a stressful, anonymous and often unpleasant experience was completely different with yourselves and I actually looked forward to my trips. How sad that it can be no more.

I'm writing to ask you to thank your staff for an excellent service. Although they are undoubtedly devastated from the point of view of losing jobs, I'm sure they are also very sad to see this development in terms of having worked in a personally satisfying environment. Many things about W&S made it clearly distinguishable from every other provider including a fair and sensible ticketing policy (W&S should be congratulated for challenging the status quo which the majority of people detest) and the well-kept, comfortable, spacious and clean carriages. However, above and beyond those things, without doubt the most positive distinguishing feature of W&S is the (genuine) friendliness and dedication of staff to the whole experience for passengers. What a rarity! A quite incredible phenomenon, if I can put it that way, associated with the W&S service was bumping into ordinary people in many different situations who had been on the service and wanted, quite 'evangelically' to talk about what an amazing experience it was and promote it to others! Sadly, I'm afraid I can't think of one instance where this has been the case regarding another rail service provider. The fact that Wrexham and Shropshire topped the customer satisfaction survey ratings recently says it all, I believe.

I'm copying this letter to the Secretary of State for Transport and also to Philip Dunne, MP for the area in which I live, simply to highlight the passing of W&S as a sad loss and another failure of the overall system to support the existence of a public service which was important for many people and the quality of which, in my view, all other providers ought be required to imitate. This service has been a vital link for people, like me, living in rural areas, to be able to travel comfortably, conveniently and directly, either to commute for work (as in my case) or for leisure. The direct connection with London and also (for me) easy link via Banbury to Oxford, was fantastic. The thought of now having to revert to the, frankly, unpleasant, unfriendly and regularly over-crowded Arriva and Virgin services, hectic and stressful changes at Wolverhampton or Birmingham, not to mention the extortionate prices, fills me - and I'm sure many others – with dread. With all of this in mind, I should also note that Wrexham and Shropshire was a reasonable option for older/elderly relatives visiting us from London. This will simply no longer be an option.

Why could this service have not received more support to keep it running? Surely the overall economic advantages of creating the direct link for people in North Wales/Shropshire to London was in itself reason enough? Not to mention the jobs created by the service itself. How sad that the only way for train operators to be able to make their business viable these days is by charging people the earth to be crammed into already packed carriages where, if they are lucky they may get a seat, and where genuinely personal, pleasant service is almost non-existent. Or perhaps it's profit margins that are keeping quality and performance low.

My final hope is that someone might just recognise what a vital and impressive service this was and take it over using the same model.

Once again, thank you, Wrexham and Shropshire, for a great experience and a great example set.

Yours sincerely,

Chris Rayment

CC:
Philip Hammond, MP and Secretary of State for Transport
Philip Dunne, MP

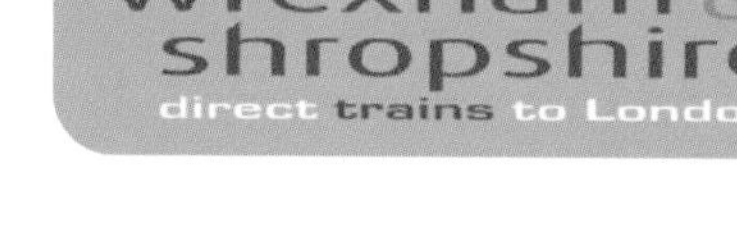

Awards and accolades

Business/group travel promotion

Rewarding custom

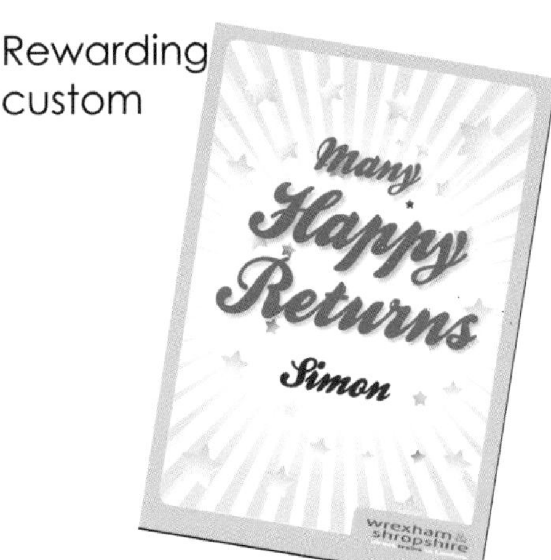

Encouraging trial

WebTis redesign

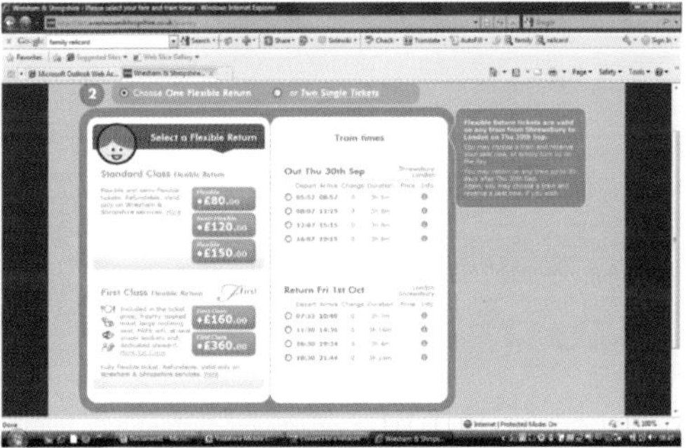

London outbound:

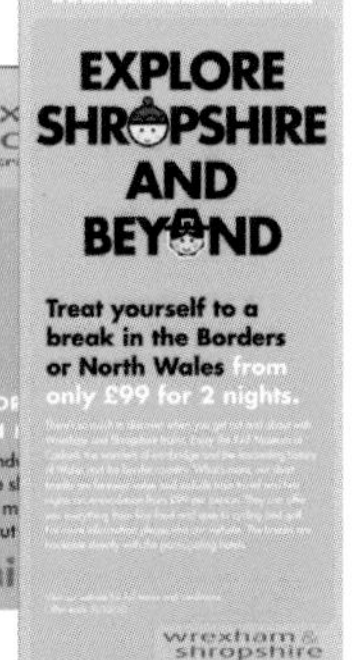

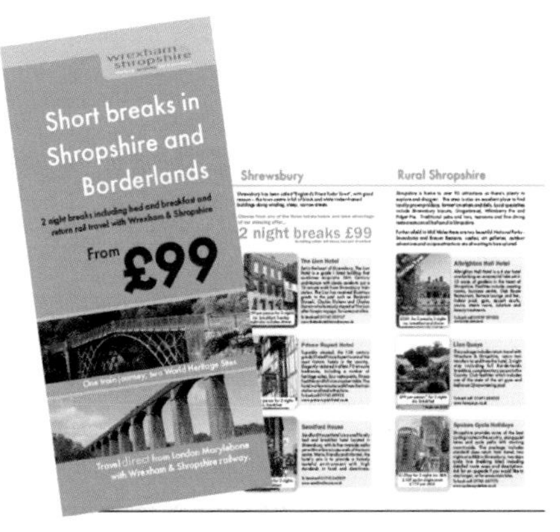

Press ads:

Outdoor:

Filming:

wrexham & shropshire
direct trains to London.

BBC Inside Out

To everyone who helped make the BBC Inside Out programme a success, both on camera and behind the scenes. It was a great success and really showcased our service.

Events:

Shropshire Show

Second Birthday

Ironbridge Festival

Shrewsbury Flower Show 'faces' in the flowers

Shrewsbury Town Centre

Wrexham Station

Events:

wrexham & shropshire
direct trains to London.

Shrewsbury Flower Show

Michael Palin

As a travel journalist I have experienced the best and the worst of rail travel. The Wrexham & Shropshire experience proved truly different from the norm. The service is friendly, unrushed and genuinely concerned with your comfort; do you know of anywhere else on today's railway where you'd hear the words "I'll show you to your seat"?

"In the past I have opted for a long and often grinding slog on the motorway due to the lack of a direct rail route. Instead, using Wrexham & Shropshire, I arrived in Shrewsbury feeling in altogether better shape, having done some work and enjoyed a fine meal, cooked to order on the train. For me, Wrexham & Shropshire is a pioneer, setting an example of high service standards which other lines would do well to follow."

As dusk falls 67010 heads south over Souldern No.1 Viaduct, just south of Aynho Junction, heading the 16:07 from Shrewsbury to Marylebone. 18:11, on Tuesday 13th October 2009. **Geoff Plumb**

Index
Acknowledgements
& Afterword
Gwybodaeth / Information
2
Y Waun Chirk
smile
Smoking is not allowed anywhere on this station

Key
WSMR associated people Railway Companies & co.
Stations

Acknowledgements

People need to be thanked - and the first people that should be thanked are all those who helped with this volume that don't find their name in here. Then it's as many as we can remember - and there are lots of those.

Mark Edlington has a habit of being everywhere. 'Oh you'll have to talk to Mark about that', is a comment heard with great frequency. So thanks are due to his unfailing enthusiasm. In Wrexham & Shropshire everyone was paid, but my goodness, the willingness to act was reminiscent of the best of the volunteering heritage railways. There weren't moaning, unwilling staff, who would have done themselves a favour if they had failed to appear again for work. However, it is fairly clear that all the goodwill, all the willingness to go the 'extra mile' was what made all the difference. It is probably Andy Hamilton's piece as MD that reflects most clearly the debt owed to the Wrexham & Shropshire staff for the effort and sacrifices they made to run a caring railway that was so good that it outstripped every other in passenger performance. One of the contributors tends to suggest that the lack of patrons was what accounted for the excellent service. That must mean that the chap spent too much time indoors, and not enough on the trains. Empty trains tend to make staff 'hide', and makes them dispirited - not this lot. They were exceptional, and well led. Perhaps the fact that so many managed to find employment elsewhere in the Industry is testament to that.

Closure was a sad reward for such effort and devotion. Yet even then, the staff carried on doing an exemplary job until the trains were handed to Chiltern.

Whatever misgivings Adrian Shooter may have had about Wrexham & Shropshire, his guidance and support was the key to giving it a 'best shot'. His attention was vital, and his sympathy in its ending was deeply appreciated. As usual he has been quite frank in his entry in this volume. He is now retired, but it wouldn't have made any difference.

Mike Jones, John Nelson and their confreres like Pete Wilkinson offer the Industry entrepreneurial expertise that it hardly deserves. They beat their heads against the walls of bureaucracy that surround us, and by their sheer persistence, in this instance they prevailed in getting the service operating. All who read the book now know the full story. However, do not think that a failure in this instance will prevent these guys from starting afresh if the circumstances allow. The lessons of this project have been analysed and absorbed. Watch this space!

One should not forget that WSMR would have not been able to perform without the help of the staff of Chiltern Railways. The operating staff, upon whom so much depends, were at first suspicious of WSMR and most reluctant to assist. The word went out that the new railway was 'family' and there was a turnround in attitude. In the end the Chiltern staff had to be restrained from helping Wrexham & Shropshire at the expense of their own operations.

Featured in these pages, but not properly acknowledged were Richard Worrall and Tony Parkins. These were the drivers of the 'constellation' that went out into the community to look for custom, using cottage industry' techniques. They were successful in helping the figures up to the £100k per period mark. Some evidently didn't understand about how their base was created, and were unable to drive up the trade of yield for volume, even in the face of the undoubtedly correct analysis that the profile of the marketing did not reflect the product. The analysis in Chapter 10 shows the sluggish growth of London earnings.

High on the list of acknowledgement has to be Geoff Plumb. Those superb pictures he took are a wonderful record, and the authors have tried very hard to include as many as possible in this volume. As railway photographers ourselves (well - sort of) we really appreciate the time, trouble and real effort that has gone into making superb images. Wrexham & Shropshire is not a railway that passed away unrecorded. The technical quality of Geoff's pictures are deeply appreciated. Those pictures (all carefully acknowledged in the book) are a tribute to someone who really 'got it right'.

Thank you to everyone who contributed to make this record of Wrexham & Shropshire - an excellent try to create a rail service unlike others. This has allowed an accurate record to be created for some to celebrate and for some to learn from.

One must not forget the generosity of the German taxpayer. Like it or not, they faithfully dug deep to allow WSMR to 'have a go'. One may comment that they could have been sharper - but i It's a pity that the party ended, but one should commend the operation on an altogether larger scale running with Grand Central. However, whilst normal persons shift uncomfortably on the cushion of their chairs at the thought of massive losses, if you are determined, and committed to rail, then a continued advance is likely until you win. The logic behind the speculation is impressive, and Britain would do well to learn from it

Afterword

Mr John Nelson and Mr Mike Jones battered away at this project, against the odds, and they managed to get it going with Adrian Shooter's (at first reluctant) help. Pete Wilkinson, Mary Bonar,, Cre'active Design, and a whole host of others fought the WSMR concept through to fruition. Its evolution was a bit like Eric Morecambe's comment. He said,

"I'm playing all the right notes, but not necessarily in the right order".

The score was a difficult one to read. The figures seemed to stack up at first, but then, when they faltered and the enterprise deserved a little help from fate, problems seemed to appear to make life difficult on a regular basis.

The Wrexham & Shropshire story revolves around the interpretation of the 1993 Railway Act. A significant segment of our elected representatives held the view that some competition inside the railway operations of the country might be good for business. The story you have read tells you that the concept of Open Access was meant to encourage the provision of entrepreneurial railway services in areas that had been ignored by Great Men.

Yet Moderation of Competition, was thought a necessary restraining feature for those entrepreneurs who would barge, cherry pick what spoils there were, and carry off the profits. 'They' were right to protect the vulnerable areas, but who could have predicted the sudden, steady 3-5% per year passenger numbers growth that appeared?

The careful, well crafted 'deal' with Virgin for West Coast Pendolino trains, and the West Coast Route Modernisation - an undoubted boon - became the instrument of 'restriction' for a modest proposal to give Wrexham, Shrewsbury and Telford, a quality, through London service that no one else offered. Yet was it within the meaning of the 1993 Act that others, with intentions of supplying good burghers with a service to the capital, should be beset with restrictions that prevented people from joining trains at Wolverhampton, for 'slow' travel to Marylebone?

Let's be rude about Wrexham & Shropshire, before it is canonised as the celestial service that misguided people ruined. The heresy to follow must acknowledge the effect of hindsight, but must also question the intensity of the fog of foresight.

1. There's got to be a question over the strength of Wrexham & Shropshire's implied competition threat to Chiltern. If Laing Rail had told the promoters to 'go away' it's likely that the project would have been still born - Virgin's protection was too strong.
2. The unnoticed DfT protection for Virgin that removed the chance of calling at Wolverhampton and New Street, for whatever reason, slashed income potential and relegated the operation to a Grand Junction Line trundle with a 20 minute time penalty. Shouldn't WSMR have quit at that point? If not there, then when the Class 170s were snatched away?
3. The MoC problem obscured an even greater blow: that DfT were planning an intensive Virgin service from Birmingham to London, and a splendid offer of trains to London from Trent Valley stations by London Midland.
4. Worse still, in the pipeline was a boost to frequency and reduction in journey time from Stafford and Chester to London. No wonder it was difficult for WSMR to find traffic for a 4hr transit from Wrexham to Marylebone! It was therefore unfortunate that research failed to reveal the then current travel habits of Salopians and that Tame Bridge was chosen without revealing before starting that it was likely to be a dead duck? (see tables p. 162)
5. If superior brand values support a direct train to London, then expecting old carriages to stand in for a year is surely like the BR curly sandwich? Despite pleading from within, almost nothing was spent on improving the oldies, nor even was there success in reducing the level of the 'short term' charges. It was an unfortunate assumption that the 'new' carriages were 'coming soon', when plainly they were not.
6. The assumption that the transit time could be reduced later to competitive levels with Virgin, and that any gap left would be bridged by direct trains and superior service quality was flawed. Together with its old carriages, this service had become a dead horse from the start. Flogging Wrexham & Shropshire was glorious, but Tony Allen on Page 229 has a ring of truth.

The problem was that all the blows were incremental, and so increased determination not analytical assessment. WSMR was too slow to survive; the market base was too small without successful West Midlands stops. One must conclude that DB Regio had little choice but to deploy the resources elsewhere. The worst comment is that the screws were gradually and needlessly turned against this service by hidden forces, and a misguided *éminence grise* with malign intent. The signs were there early that this would happen, and WSMR was unable to prevail against covert, foolish, and counter-productive, protectionist prejudice. Irritatingly, not only did an important person concerned speak later, off the record, that MoC was applied too stringently, and WSMR could have been allowed to stop at Wolverhampton, but after closure there was worry by politicians that Shrewsbury and Telford were without direct London services, and must have them soon.

67012 **A Shropshire Lad** *heads the 07.23 Wrexham to Marylebone through Princes Risborough on Tuesday 19th May 2009. In the foreground is the 09.54 from Marylebone to Bicester North.*
Geoff Plumb

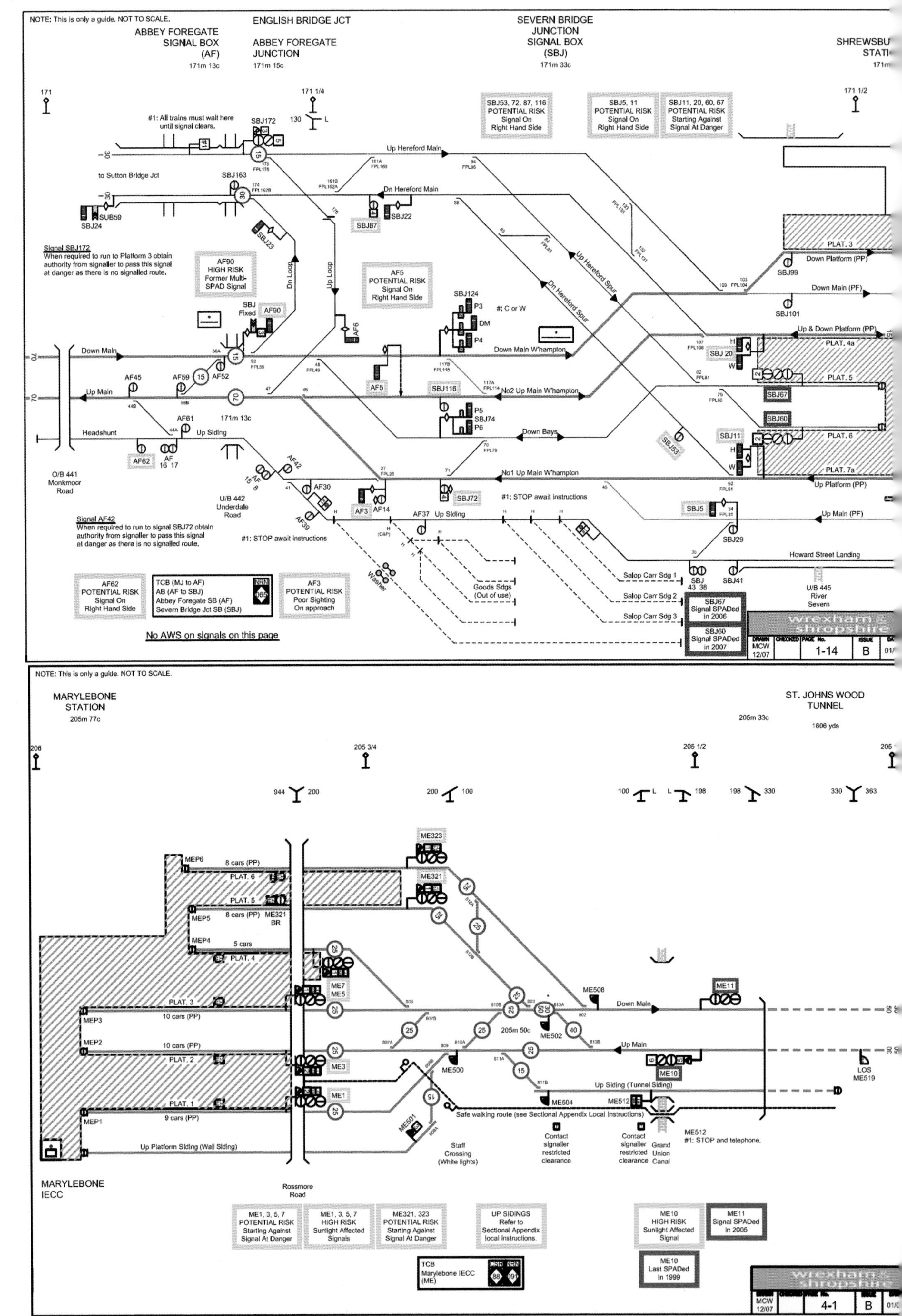

NOTE: This is only a guide. NOT TO SCALE.
ABBEY FOREGATE SIGNAL BOX (AF) 171m 13c
ENGLISH BRIDGE JCT
ABBEY FOREGATE JUNCTION 171m 15c
SEVERN BRIDGE JUNCTION SIGNAL BOX (SBJ) 171m 33c
SHREWSBU STATI 171m
SBJ53, 72, 87, 116 POTENTIAL RISK Signal On Right Hand Side
SBJ5, 11 POTENTIAL RISK Signal On Right Hand Side
SBJ11, 20, 60, 67 POTENTIAL RISK Starting Against Signal At Danger
#1: All trains must wait here until signal clears.
Up Hereford Main
Dn Hereford Main
to Sutton Bridge Jct
Signal SBJ172
When required to run to Platform 3 obtain authority from signaller to pass this signal at danger as there is no signalled route.
AF90 HIGH RISK Former Multi-SPAD Signal
AF5 POTENTIAL RISK Signal On Right Hand Side
Dn Loop
Up Loop
#: C or W
Up Hereford Spur
Dn Hereford Spur
PLAT. 3
Down Platform (PP)
Down Main (PF)
Up & Down Platform (PP)
PLAT. 4a
PLAT. 5
PLAT. 6
PLAT. 7a
Down Main
Up Main
Down Main W'hampton
No2 Up Main W'hampton
Down Bays
No1 Up Main W'hampton
Headshunt
Up Siding
O/B 441 Monkmoor Road
U/B 442 Underdale Road
Signal AF42
When required to run to signal SBJ72 obtain authority from signaller to pass this signal at danger as there is no signalled route.
#1: STOP await instructions
Up Platform (PP)
Up Main (PF)
Howard Street Landing
Goods Sdgs (Out of use)
Salop Carr Sdg 1
Salop Carr Sdg 2
Salop Carr Sdg 3
Washer
U/B 445 River Severn
AF62 POTENTIAL RISK Signal On Right Hand Side
TCB (MJ to AF) AB (AF to SBJ) Abbey Foregate SB (AF) Severn Bridge Jct SB (SBJ)
AF3 POTENTIAL RISK Poor Sighting On approach
No AWS on signals on this page
SBJ67 Signal SPADed in 2006
SBJ60 Signal SPADed in 2007
wrexham & shropshire
MCW 12/07
1-14
B
NOTE: This is only a guide. NOT TO SCALE.
MARYLEBONE STATION 205m 77c
ST. JOHNS WOOD TUNNEL 205m 33c 1606 yds
PLAT. 6
PLAT. 5
PLAT. 4
PLAT. 3
PLAT. 2
PLAT. 1
8 cars (PP)
8 cars (PP)
5 cars
10 cars (PP)
10 cars (PP)
9 cars (PP)
Up Platform Siding (Wall Siding)
Down Main
Up Main
Up Siding (Tunnel Siding)
Safe walking route (see Sectional Appendix Local Instructions)
205m 50c
LOS ME519
Staff Crossing (White lights)
Contact signaller restricted clearance
Contact signaller restricted clearance
Grand Union Canal
ME512 #1: STOP and telephone.
MARYLEBONE IECC
Rossmore Road
ME1, 3, 5, 7 POTENTIAL RISK Starting Against Signal At Danger
ME1, 3, 5, 7 HIGH RISK Sunlight Affected Signals
ME321, 323 POTENTIAL RISK Starting Against Signal At Danger
UP SIDINGS Refer to Sectional Appendix local instructions.
ME10 HIGH RISK Sunlight Affected Signal
ME11 Signal SPADed in 2005
ME10 Last SPADed in 1999
TCB Marylebone IECC (ME)
wrexham & shropshire
MCW 12/07
4-1
B